CULTURAL ANTHROPOLOGY

Recent Titles in
Reference Sources in the Social Sciences

American Military History: A Guide to Reference and Information Sources
Daniel K. Blewett

Education: A Guide to Reference and Information Sources
Nancy Patricia O'Brien

Northern Africa: A Guide to Reference and Information Sources
Paula Youngman Skreslet

Sports, Exercise, and Fitness: A Guide to Reference and Information Sources
Mary Beth Allen

Sociology: A Guide to Reference and Information Sources, Third Edition
Stephen H. Aby, James Nalen, and Lori Fielding

CULTURAL ANTHROPOLOGY

A Guide to Reference and Information Sources

Second Edition

JOANN JACOBY AND JOSEPHINE Z. KIBBEE

Reference Sources in the Social Sciences
Bob Burger, Series Editor

A Member of the Greenwood Publishing Group
Westport, Connecticut • London

Library of Congress Cataloging-in-Publication Data

Jacoby, JoAnn, 1966–
  Cultural anthropology : a guide to reference and information sources / JoAnn Jacoby and Josephine Z. Kibbee.—2nd ed.
      p.   cm.—(Reference sources in the social sciences)
    Rev. ed. of: Cultural anthropology / Josephine Z. Kibbee. 1991.
    Includes bibliographical references and indexes.
    ISBN 978–1–59158–357–8 (alk. paper)
    1. Anthropology—Reference books—Bibliography.   2. Anthropology—Bibliography.   I. Kibbee, Josephine Z., 1950–   II. Kibbee, Josephine Z., 1950– Cultural anthropology.   III. Title.
  Z5111.J33   2007 GN42
  016.301—dc22   2007009010

British Library Cataloguing in Publication Data is available.

Copyright © 2007 by Libraries Unlimited

All rights reserved. No portion of this book may be
reproduced, by any process or technique, without the
express written consent of the publisher.

Library of Congress Catalog Card Number: 2007009010
ISBN-13: 978–1–59158–357–8

First published in 2007

Libraries Unlimited, 88 Post Road West, Westport, CT 06881
A Member of the Greenwood Publishing Group, Inc.
www.lu.com

Printed in the United States of America

The paper used in this book complies with the
Permanent Paper Standard issued by the National
Information Standards Organization (Z39.48–1984).

10 9 8 7 6 5 4 3 2 1

CONTENTS

Acknowledgments vii
Introduction ix
Chapter 1: General and Social Science Sources 1
   Guides to Reference Literature 1
   Indexes, Abstracts, and Databases 2
   Dictionaries and Encyclopedias 3
   Handbooks and Manuals 5
   Internet Gateways 6
Chapter 2: General Anthropology Reference Sources 9
   Ready Reference 9
      Guides to the Reference Literature 9
      Dictionaries, Encyclopedias, and Handbooks 10
      Style and Writing Guides 14
      Biographical Sources 15
      Directories of Individual Anthropologists 18
      Internet Gateways 19
   Bibliographic Tools (Finding Publications) 21
      Literature Surveys and Reviews 22
      Indexes, Abstracts, and Databases 23
      Book and Media Reviews 29
      News and Newsletters 31
      Bibliography of Bibliographies 32
      Periodical Bibliographies and Directories 33
      Published Library Catalogs and Guides 34
Chapter 3: Methods and Practice 41
   Methods 41
   Fieldwork and Ethnography 43
   Ethics 49
   Applied Anthropology 50
   Museum and Cultural Heritage Studies 55
   Visual Anthropology 58
Chapter 4: Subfields of Anthropology 63
   Archaeology 63
   Biological Anthropology 73
   Linguistic Anthroplogy 77
Chapter 5: Research Areas 85
   Agriculture, Food, and Nutrition 85
   Art and Material Culture 89
   Cognitive Anthropology 93
   Economic Anthropology 95
   Education 97
   Environmental Anthropology 99
   Ethnohistory 99

Evolutionary Anthropology 100
History of Anthropology 101
Marriage and Family 104
Medical Anthropology 105
Political and Legal Anthropology 109
Psychological Anthropology 112
Religion 115
Sexuality and Gender Studies 118
Urban, National, and Transnational/Global Anthropology 121
Women 124
Other Topics 127
Chapter 6: Humanities Related Fields 131
General Humanities Sources 131
Ethnomusicology 132
Folklore and Mythology 136
Performance Studies and Dance 144
Chapter 7: Area and Ethnic Studies 147
General Area and Ethnic Studies 147
Human Relation Area Files (HRAF) 150
Africa 154
Asia 160
    East Asia 162
    South Asia 162
    Southeast Asia 163
Australia and the Pacific 165
Europe 170
Middle East, North Africa, and Islam 174
North America and the Arctic 177
    Ethnic Studies 178
    Native Americans 182
Latin America and the Caribbean 188
Chapter 8: Supplemental Resources 197
Journals 197
Publishers 208
Departments and Programs 221
Organizations and Institutes 221
Museum Directories 237
Libraries, Archives, and Special Collections 238
Career Development Resources 246
Grants and Funding 249

Author Index 253
Title Index 261
Subject Index 279

ACKNOWLEDGMENTS

The authors wish to acknowledge the Research and Publication Committee of the University of Illinois at Urbana-Champaign (UIUC) Library, which provided support for the completion of this research. Thanks to the committee's support, we were able to secure the services of Annie Paprocki, whose capable research assistance was essential in getting this project off the ground. Thanks also to Laurie Chipps for her insightful work inputting the index terms, Merinda Hensley who helped with innumerable small tasks along the way, and Megan Gaffney who provided attentive assistance with the bibliographic verification, and our series editor, Bob Burger, who helped pull it all together. Thanks goes out as well to our colleagues in the Education and Social Science Library and Central Reference Services at UIUC for bearing with us during this long process. And finally, to our soul-mates Steve Taylor and Doug Kibbee, thanks for your patience, support, and encouragement. We're done!

INTRODUCTION

Library Research and Anthropology

Much of the allure of anthropology lies in the opportunity to become immersed in another culture, whether with indigenous peoples in an exotic locale or around the corner with the local teenagers. Fieldwork and data gathering remain critical for generating new knowledge and insights into human behavior. But like all research, anthropological inquiry doesn't take place in a vacuum: it builds upon the foundation of those who have gone before. It is this foundation, whose locale is typically the library (real or virtual), rather than the field, that our book explores. We consider it a guide to immersing the students and practitioners of anthropology in the culture of library research.

Anthropology's "literature" can take many forms. Fieldnotes and collections often serve as a primary source of raw data, but, except for archival collections, these are not generally available in libraries. Likewise important, and also difficult to find, is the extensive body of "gray literature"—articles, reports, conference proceedings, working papers, etc., issued by university departments, research institutes, or associations. Periodicals serve a critical function for communicating focused research projects, and last but not least, "ethnographic monographs" (i.e., books) remain the core means of disseminating the results of extensive sociocultural research.

Like its predecessor, this second edition of *Cultural Anthropology: A Guide to Reference and Information Sources* is intended as a tool for finding relevant anthropological literature—online and in print. The Internet has undeniably transformed library research. To begin with, a wealth of good "free" information can be found on the Internet—websites developed by indigenous people give voice to their perspective; portals created by enterprising individuals or associations provide the full text of reports, notes, bibliographies, sound and images, or bring together a useful collection of links to related sites. In the library sphere, the Internet is the platform upon which online library catalogs (that have replaced card catalogs) provide researchers with the ability to search library collections across the world; many journals are accessible online as well as in print format; indexes to periodical literature have been digitized and increasingly provide the full text of an article—and to the sources it cites—and multimedia databases deliver sound, image, and text. Nonetheless, the publishing industry has not languished. In the 15+ years since the first edition of this guide was published, an impressive number of major reference sources have been published. Perhaps the most significant trend is the publication of multivolume encyclopedia sets or handbooks that include among their contributors a marked increase in scholars native to the culture they write about. Increasingly these print volumes have digital counterparts, and libraries have the option of licensing the content of these e-books. As librarians well know, a *Google* search does not uncover and organize the wealth of digital content available only by subscription, nor are quality websites automatically retrieved.

Much relevant information for anthropologists, however, is not available in digital format, but still lies between the covers of books and journals. The result is that a great deal of information still resides in libraries (real and virtual), and we wrote this guide as a roadmap to identifying print and online resources that will direct the student, librarian, or seasoned scholar to the source most likely to provide background information (encyclopedias and handbooks); current scholarship (indexes to articles, theses, conference proceedings); and historical or retrospective scholarship on specific topics or regions (bibliographies of the ethnographic monographs that are the basic product of anthropological research).

Purpose and Scope

The purpose of this book is to facilitate library research by identifying, synthesizing, and organizing the extensive body of print and online resources relevant to anthropology. It is written to assist researchers at all levels in their quest for information relating to sociocultural anthropology—whether the need be for brief, factual information (definitions, addresses), for background or overview, or for doing an extensive literature search.

Like the human species on which it focuses, the discipline of anthropology is remarkable for its diversity. With historical depth, geographic breadth, and a strong interdisciplinary orientation, anthropology can draw from a wealth of materials in its own discipline as well as from related sources in the natural sciences, social sciences, and humanities. Because anthropology holds the potential to intersect with virtually all fields of knowledge, the scope of this book focuses primarily on the subfield of sociocultural anthropology, incorporating cultural and social anthropology (and a host of related areas) but excluding specialized sources relevant to biological anthropology, linguistics, and archaeology.

In North America, anthropology has traditionally been divided into four fields of study: biological (or physical) anthropology, archaeology, anthropological linguistics, and cultural anthropology. Within this framework, cultural anthropology deals with the description and analysis of manifestations of human culture, such as social systems, religious beliefs, material objects. Within the European model, the term *anthropology* is roughly synonymous with physical anthropology, while *ethnology* refers to the studies involving the social-cultural milieu. In the British tradition, the concept of *social anthropology* eschews the notion of culture, placing emphasis instead upon social structure as a conceptual scheme. Despite these theoretical differences, however, the field of anthropology can be seen as having two major divisions: physical and cultural. Because the intellectual content and methodological approaches of these two divisions can differ sharply, our efforts concentrate primarily on cultural anthropology (broadly conceived), though many of the titles are applicable to the field of anthropology as a whole. The major sources related to the other subfields of anthropology are treated briefly in Chapter 4.

Reference sources refers to books and serial publications that are either compilations of factual data, such as dictionaries and encyclopedias, atlases, and ethnographic surveys, or to sources that provide citations to previously published research, such as literature surveys and reviews, indexes and abstracts, and bibliographies. Researchers familiar with their topic often identify scholarship relevant to their work through footnotes in the literature, but for a student new to the field, a more systematic approach involves the use of indexes or bibliographies to identify current and retrospective books and articles on the topic. (Though the distinction between index and bibliography is frequently blurred, here *index* refers to a serial or ongoing publication that primarily identifies and organizes citations to books and/or periodical literature. *Bibliography* refers to an individually published compilation of retrospective citations.) *Guides to reference literature* constitute a particular type of bibliography that identifies indexes and other secondary sources. For the most part, we have interpreted the term *reference* loosely and have included overview texts and surveys that synthesize extant scholarship, particularly in areas where more traditional reference works have not been published. The majority of entries are books and serials, though review articles and individual chapters are occasionally cited. We define *Internet gateways* as portals that identify and organize links to related websites. In many cases the provenance of these portals is difficult to determine. Affiliation, authorship, or date may not be apparent, and because they are often maintained by individuals, they are more transient than commercial publications or websites. Nonetheless, they're useful while they last!

Despite the number of entries, this guide is not comprehensive. Bibliographies on Native American cultures alone number in the thousands, so by necessity we were selective. In cases such as areas studies, the titles included represent core works and broad, historically significant compilations and generally exclude works on individual ethnic groups. With few exceptions, popular treatments are excluded.

Though great effort was made to ensure this guide's timeliness, selection is not restricted to recent titles or to works currently in print. Because the major indexes to periodical literature were not established until relatively recently (1960s to 1970s), retrospective bibliographies are essential for identifying earlier scholarship. Therefore no restriction was set on date of publication or in-print status. Works that are clearly dated or that have been superseded, however, are omitted. Titles published through 2006 have been included, with mention of any forthcoming titles.

Although broad and balanced coverage is ideal, the emphasis is weighed toward North America. In Chapter 8 "Supplemental Resources," for instance, providing a worldwide directory of anthropological organizations, libraries, and publishers would necessitate several extra volumes! The majority of the entries are English-language sources, though selected French, German, and Spanish titles are also included. Titles were generally chosen with an eye toward research in North American libraries, though not all the materials identified in the guide will be widely available. Titles such as *Experta Indonesica* (entry 522) fill important information needs yet may not be found on the shelves of most college libraries.

Their inclusion is predicated on the assumption that resource-sharing among libraries, already facilitated by national bibliographic networks like OCLC (the Online Computer Library Center), will enable researchers to gain access to other library collections. At the very least, including these titles will alert researchers to their existence.

Though designed for users at all levels, many of the entries (e.g., library catalogs) are aimed toward advanced students or anthropologists working outside their area of specialty. And because librarians frequently serve as intermediaries between researchers and library collections, the book is likewise designed to help our colleagues identify useful sources as well as to aid in collection development for anthropology.

Methodology and Organization

In compiling this guide, we relied upon the major guides to reference literature (discussed in Chapter 2) to develop a core list of titles. We updated and expanded the list by consulting book reviews and announcements in library and anthropological literature, and used multiple strategies to identify relevant websites. With few exceptions, we examined every title and endeavored to write an annotation with sufficient descriptive/evaluative information to enable users to decide whether consulting the tile is warranted. In generating the journal titles, we consulted core lists, studies of citation analyses, articles in professional journals, and announcements of new titles. Information on associations and libraries was gathered from the standard reference works such as the *Encyclopedia of Associations*, as well as from announcements in professional literature and the websites of the organizations themselves. The list of publishers (definitely not comprehensive) was compiled by consulting reference sources such as *Literary Market Place*, by examining lists of publishers exhibiting at the Anthropological Association, and by surveying book reviews and announcements in anthropological journals and newsletters.

This book is organized, in principle, to loosely reflect the structure and areas of interest of the field. Beginning with seminal reference works in the social sciences, we then discuss core reference titles for the field of anthropology as whole as well as the subfields of archaeology, biological, and linguistic anthropology. Narrowing the scope to cultural anthropology, we identify research areas such as applied or medical anthropology that have developed distinctive theoretical and methodological orientations, and areas of specialty such as psychological or economic anthropology that have developed a broad literature base and professional identity. Some of these research areas, such as the anthropology of art or religion, reflect the intersection of anthropology with the humanities, and we also address related disciplines such as folklore and ethnomusicology. Studies of distinctive cultures lie at the core of the field, but we were judicious in our selection of titles for the ethnic and area studies chapter due to the extensive output of ethnographic and related literature. We conclude with a directory of resources, such as core anthropological journals, publishers, libraries, and associations that provide ready-reference information.

Entries within each section are organized by type of reference source, with the caveat that categories can be fluid. "Guides to Reference Literature," for example, are a type of bibliography; the terms dictionary, encyclopedia, or handbook may be used interchangeably; "database" can be synonymous with an article index or with full text content; and Internet websites can be all of the above. We were generous in our definition of "information resource," and include for example, introductory or survey texts (within the category of "Literature Surveys and Reviews"). The selection of internet resources provided the greatest challenge, and in the category of "Internet Gateways," we identify representative websites that serve as portals to other relevant websites.

Arrangement within each section is alphabetical by title, because most reference sources are known by their title rather than by author, but in all other respects our citations follow our publisher's recommended format based on the *Chicago Manual of Style*. Though we made every attempt to provide complete and accurate information, in some cases we were unable to find complete bibliographic information, e.g., update frequency of online resources. We hope, however, that the resources we have selected, organized, and described will find their way into the hands of our readers and expedite their "fieldwork" in the library.

Chapter 1

General and Social Science Sources

Considering the breadth of scholarly inquiry within sociocultural anthropology, the number of potentially relevant reference sources in the social sciences and humanities is significant. This chapter identifies selected core general sources in the social sciences. Reference sources for specific related disciplines (e.g., psychology) or formats (e.g., dissertations) are discussed elsewhere in the text.

Guides to Reference Literature

1. **Social Science Reference Sources: A Practical Guide.** Li, Tze-chung. 3rd ed. Westport, CT: Greenwood, 2000. 495p. ISBN 0313304831.

    Given the multidisciplinary character of anthropology, this guide to reference sources in social science disciplines provides a good overview of library resources in related disciplines, including geography, history, political science, psychology, sociology, and area studies. Electronic databases receive good coverage, as do bibliographies and indexes, proceedings, dissertations, statistical sources, and government publications. A core list of social science periodicals is provided.

2. **Social Sciences: A Cross-Disciplinary Guide to Selected Sources.** Herron, Nancy L. 3rd ed. Englewood, CO: Libraries Unlimited, 2002. 494p. ISBN 1563089858; 1563088827pa.

    This book essentially serves as a text that identifies and describes the most important reference sources in the social sciences, both print and electronic. Twelve social science disciplines are represented, and each chapter begins with an essay on the nature of research in that area. Comparative and critical comments on the resources are included, as well as information on how to use them.

Indexes, Abstracts, and Databases

3. **FRANCIS.** Institut de l'Information Scientifique et Technique du Centre National de la Recherche Scientifique (INIST-CNRS) and the Getty Research Institute (GRI). 1984-. Monthly. ISSN 1161-0395. Available on CD-ROM and online by subscription.

Incorporating former *Bulletin Signalétique* subfiles, this international bibliographic database identifies publications from over 4,200 Western European and North American periodicals in the humanities and social sciences, with particularly good coverage of the European literature. Subject headings are provided in French and English, and there are searchable abstracts in French. The online version has coverage back to 1984. For earlier material, consult *Bulletin Signalétique 529: Ethnologie* and *Bulletin Signalétique 525: Préhistoire et Protohistoire* and their predecessors.

4. **International Bibliography of the Social Sciences (IBSS).** London: London School of Economics and Political Science. 1951-. Available online by subscription.

IBSS continues the prestigious *London Bibliography of the Social Sciences* (entry 6) and provides extensive coverage of international publications in more than 60 languages. Over 2,800 current social science journals are indexed, with abstracts in English provided for the majority of articles. Retrospective coverage for journals, some of which are no longer published, dates to 1951. Citations to books and book reviews are also included. Subfiles include the *International Bibliography of Anthropology* (entry 79) as well as sets in economics, political science, and sociology.

5. **International Development Abstracts.** New York: Elsevier. 1982-. Monthly. ISSN 0262-0855. Available in print and online by subscription.

International Development Abstracts is a monthly publication that provides abstracts of articles drawn from over 200 journals in multiple disciplines and languages that relate to development issues. Citations are divided into 40 topics including sections on agriculture and rural development; environment; industrial policy; social policies, health, demography; gender, culture; international relations; and politics. Title and abstract translations are provided for non-English articles. Available online through *Geobase* (entry 203).

6. **London Bibliography of the Social Sciences.** London: Mansell. 1929–1989. ISSN 0076-051X.

This extensive, historically significant bibliography, with coverage from the mid-1600s, was produced under the editorial direction of the London School of Economics, one of the world's leading social science institutions. The focus is on the four core social science subjects of anthropology, economics, politics, and sociology, with coverage of related materials in human geography, gender studies, development, and others. Continued by the *International Bibliography of Social Sciences* (entry 4).

7. **Social Sciences Citation Index.** Philadelphia: Thompson Scientific. 1956-. ISSN 0091-3707. Available online by subscription.

This database indexes the core journal literature from over 1,700 of the world's leading social science journals and provides the ability to view the references these articles cite, as well as to determine where specific articles have been cited. These citation analyses form the basis for establishing the "impact factor" of an article. The online database can provide links to the full text of selected articles, as well as contact information for authors. The print version is cumbersome and was discontinued. Print and online backfiles date to 1956.

8. **Social Sciences Index.** New York: H. W. Wilson. 1975-. ISSN 0094-4920. Available in print, on CD-ROM and online by subscription.

The *Social Sciences Index* has long been a standard index for undergraduates, providing coverage of over 500 English-language periodicals in all areas of the social sciences. The index continues *Social Sciences and Humanities Index* (1966–1974) and *International Index* (1907–1065) and together they provide good retrospective coverage of the core social science literature dating from the early twentieth century to date. It is also available online with abstracts (as *Social Science Abstracts*) and full text (as *Social Science Abstracts Full Text*).

9. **SocINDEX.** Birmingham, AL: EBSCO. 2005-. Available online by subscription.

SocINDEX contains abstracts and selected full text for more than 720 core journals, some dating back to 1898; 3,000 selectively covered journals; and the full text of over 6,000 conference papers. The focus is primarily on sociology, encompassing subdisciplines, such as rural sociology, and closely related areas, such as ethnic studies.

10. **Sociological Abstracts.** San Diego, CA: CSA. 1952-. Monthly. ISSN 0038-0202. Available in print and online by subscription.

This core resource abstracts and indexes the international literature in sociology and related disciplines in the social and behavioral sciences. The database provides abstracts of journal articles and citations to book chapters, dissertations, conference papers, and book reviews drawn from over 1,800 serial publications. Beginning in 2002, references cited in the bibliography of the source article are also provided for many entries, as well as links to articles that cite the paper. The entire backfile, starting in 1952, is available online and provides extensive coverage of the literature from the mid-twentieth century.

Dictionaries and Encyclopedias

11. **Dictionary of the Social Sciences.** Calhoun, Craig, editor. New York: Oxford University Press, 2002. 563p. ISBN 095123719.

President of the Social Science Research Council, sociologist and historian Calhoun has compiled a concise, one-volume dictionary that strives to "make social scientific language comprehensible to general readers." The text provides brief (50–500 word) definitions of terms used, and biographical sketches of some 275 notable figures. The essays include brief bibliographies and a 40-page bibliography of core literature in the social sciences is included at the end.

12. **Encyclopaedia of the Social Sciences.** Seligman, Edwin R. A., editor. New York: Macmillan, 1930–1935. 15v.

This seminal reference source remains valuable for the quality of its scholarship and the historical background it provides on the development of the social sciences. Contributors are drawn from the major figures of social research in the twentieth century.

13. **International Encyclopedia of the Social and Behavioral Sciences.** Smelzer, Neil, and Paul B. Baltes, editors. New York: Elsevier, 2001. 26v. ISBN 0080430767.

The publication of this set establishes it as state of the art scholarship in the social sciences, complementing the two previous landmarks in the field, the *Encyclopaedia of the Social Sciences* (entry 12) and the *International Encyclopedia of the Social Sciences* (entry 14). The significance of this new title lies in its integration of the social sciences with other disciplines, particularly the behavioral sciences. The work also reflects "the growth and specialization of knowledge since the 1960s." The advisory board consists of prominent social scientists and anthropology is well represented. Entries are substantial and authoritative, providing a substantive overview as well as in-depth coverage of timely topics. Each entry is followed by a bibliography, and a comprehensive subject and name index is provided in the final volume.

14. **International Encyclopedia of the Social Sciences.** Sills, David L., editor. New York: Macmillan, 1968–1991. 19v. ISBN 0028957105.

Complementing the *Encyclopaedia of the Social Sciences* (entry 12), entries in this encyclopedia reflect the state of the art of post-World War II social science research. Entries include biographical articles of significant contributors to the field, as well as descriptions of the issues, methods, disciplines, intersecting fields, and applications of social and behavioral sciences. Each entry is followed by a bibliography, and a comprehensive subject and name index is provided in the final volume.

15. **New Keywords: A Revised Vocabulary of Culture and Society.** Bennett, Tony, Lawrence Grossberg, and Meaghan Morris, editors. Malden, MA: Blackwell, 2005. 427p. ISBN 0631225684; 0631225692pa.

Updating Raymond Williams' seminal *Keywords: A Vocabulary of Culture and Society* (1976), this volume provides 142 signed entries briefly defining words used to describe social and cultural phenomena, situating their usage within particular schools of thought, and providing some guidance to neophytes trying to understand the subtle implications of these sometimes loaded terms. In addition to the usual suspects (e.g., culture or theory) this volume also explores terms of current interest, like fundamentalism and pornography.

16. **Reader's Guide to the Social Sciences.** Michie, Jonathan, editor. Chicago: Fitzroy Dearborn, 2001. 2v. ISBN 1579580912.

The intent of this guide is to identify seminal literature for over 1,200 concepts and individuals in the social sciences. The alphabetical entries consist of a headnote and bibliography of works to be discussed, followed by an essay that succinctly describes and assesses their contributions to the scholarly literature.

17. **Social Science Encyclopedia.** Kuper, Adam, and Jessica Kuper. 3rd ed. New York: Routledge, 2004. 2v. ISBN 0415320968.

This recent two-volume set updates the authors' previous edition and provides succinct entries for commonly used terms, and includes a brief bibliography for most entries.

Handbooks and Manuals

18. **Dictionary of Statistics and Methodology: A Nontechnical Guide for the Social Sciences.** Vogt, W. Paul. 3rd ed. Thousand Oaks, CA: Sage, 2005. 355p. ISBN 0761988556pa.

Vogt's dictionary of more than 2,000 terms provides clear, accessible definitions of basic statistical concepts and methods in the social sciences and related fields. This volume will be useful for those wanting to interpret and understand statistical research, as well as for the novice wanting to develop a strong foundation of understanding of basic concepts before analyzing their own data.

19. **Making Sense: A Student's Guide to Research and Writing: Social Sciences.** Northey, Margot, Lorne Tepperman, and James Russell. 2nd ed. Toronto: Oxford University Press, 2005. 272p. ISBN 0195421000pa.

The authors of this updated edition, written primarily for an undergraduate audience, provide an overview of how to plan projects, evaluate existing research, and select research design. A useful section includes ethical issues such as informed consent, confidentiality, etc. The second half is a writer's manual, covering topics such as writing essays and research papers.

20. **Oxford Dictionary of the World.** Munro, David, editor. New York: Oxford, 1996. 704p. ISBN 0198661843.

Gazetteers are a common type of reference work, providing information about places and place-names, and providing brief information about the location, demographics, and physical features of a country. Numerous titles are available (e.g., *Chambers World Gazetteer, Cambridge World Gazetteer,* etc.). Munro focuses more on political rather than physical features and notes changes in place names. Handy for ready reference information (with the caveat that printed information can date quickly), this book also includes charts and comparative statistics (e.g., life expectancies) and numerous color maps.

21. **The Sage Encyclopedia of Social Science Research Methods.** Lewis-Beck, Michael S., Alan Bryman, and Tim Futing Liao, editors. Thousand Oaks, CA: Sage, 2004. 3v. ISBN 0761923632.

This three-volume set outlines the purposes and basic principles of social science research methods. The encyclopedia features two major types of entries: definitions that provide a quick explanation of a methodological term; and a more in-depth discussion of the nature, history, application (with an example), and implication of using a certain method. Many entries include a reference list. Each entry is written by an authority in the field and covers both quantitative and qualitative methods. The set is intended for researchers and social science students, but should be accessible to the general reader. Also included are suggested readings and references for future study.

22. **Theses and Dissertations: A Guide to Planning, Research and Writing.** Thomas, R. Murray, and Dale L. Brubaker. Westport, CT: Bergin & Garvey, 2000. 294p. ISBN 0897897463.

This work outlines the basic steps for social science students completing their theses or dissertations. The authors give advice regarding choosing a faculty advisor, collecting information, conducting research, interpreting results, and presenting the final paper to the committee. Each section contains multiple biographical references to further works that will aid students in carrying out various phases of specific types of theses or dissertations. The work includes an outline of an actual dissertation, as well as a bibliography and lengthy index.

23. **Tricks of the Trade: How to Think About Your Research While You're Doing It.** Becker, Howard S. Chicago, IL: University of Chicago Press, 1998. 239p. ISBN 0226041247pa.

Becker, a sociologist well known for his clear and accessible style and his thoughtful methodology, has written the definitive guide to social science research. Drawing on four decades of experience, broad erudition, and specific approaches from a host of disciplines including anthropology, sociology, literature, and philosophy, Becker elucidates the fundamental building blocks of good research methodology. This is one of the few works by a nonanthropologist that makes a regular appearance in the syllabi for courses on fieldwork and ethnography.

Internet Gateways

24. **Intute: Social Sciences.** Available online at <http://www.sosig.ac.uk/>.

Based on the esteemed Social Science Information Gateway (SOSIG), *Intute: Social Sciences* is a Web portal that provides links to an extensive number of quality, librarian-selected, annotated websites. Categories include 16 areas including anthropology, geography, European Studies, politics, psychology, social welfare, sociology, statistics, and women's studies. Part of the UK's Resource Discovery Network, the site also provides a "Social Science Search Engine" that searches over 250,000 social-science related web pages, and the "Social Science Grapevine," offering career development opportunities for social science researchers.

Chapter 2

General Anthropology Reference Sources

Though each of the four subdivisions of anthropology has developed its own emphasis, the principal reference works for the field generally take a holistic approach and serve the entire discipline. Few of the titles that follow, therefore, are specific to cultural anthropology and most also serve physical anthropologists, archaeologists, and linguistic anthropologists. There are, however, a number of reference sources pertaining specifically to these other subfields of anthropology that are treated in Chapter 4.

This chapter is divided into two sections. The first covers ready reference sources, including guides to the literature, dictionaries, encyclopedias, style and writing guides, biographical sources, and Internet gateways. The second section covers bibliographic tools—sources that enable researchers to find and identify publications in anthropology. These include literature reviews and abstracting and indexing databases (including specialized sources for book reviews, dissertations, conference proceedings, and anthropology-related news) as well as bibliographies and published catalogs. While the latter may seem antiquated, the importance of the retrospective literature in anthropology guarantees their continued relevance—at least until there is more robust bibliographic control of older materials in the major online tools.

Ready Reference

Guides to the Reference Literature

25. **"Anthropology."** Ogburn, Joyce L. In *The Social Sciences: A Cross-Disciplinary Guide to Selected Sources*. Nancy L. Herron, editor. 3rd ed. Greenwood, CO: Libraries Unlimited, 2002. pp. 235–257. ISBN 1563089858; 1563088827pa.

Ogburn provides a succinct and useful overview of core reference sources in anthropology, including association and scholarly society information, reviews, and current literature. The introductory essay briefly describes the discipline and the structure and use of the literature in anthropology.

26. **Fieldwork in the Library: A Guide to Research in Anthropology and Related Area Studies.** Westerman, R. C. Chicago: American Library Association, 1994. 357p. ISBN 083890632X.

Westerman's guide covers approaches to finding information and doing literature searches in the four subfields of anthropology and related area studies. Each chapter is divided by type of research materials, such as retrospective materials, current materials, graphic materials, and unpublished materials. Author and title indexes are included.

27. **Introduction to Library Research in Anthropology.** Weeks, John M. 2nd ed. Boulder, CO: Westview, 1998. 401p. ISBN 0813390036.

This substantial volume serves as a guide to library resources in anthropology and related area studies. Library of Congress classification numbers for anthropology, a list of major anthropological collections in the United States and Canada, and information on the Human Relations Area Files (HRAF) are given in appendices. Author, ethnic/cultural group, and geographic index are also provided.

28. **Resources for Anthropology & Sociology Librarians & Information Specialists.** Ogburn, Joyce L., compiler. Available online at <http://www.lib.odu.edu/anss/resources.html>.

Maintained by Joyce Ogburn and hosted by the Anthropology and Sociology Section of the Association of College and Research Libraries, this frequently updated bibliography compiles resources of interest to librarians and information specialists working in these disciplines. Divided into the broad categories of anthropology, sociology, and general social sciences, each section includes citations and links to resources pertaining to topics such as bibliographic control and metadata, information needs, digital resources, publishing, preservation, and reference sources.

Dictionaries, Encyclopedias, and Handbooks

The following includes the major dictionaries, encyclopedias, and handbooks that cover the discipline as a whole. Those interested in ethnographic terminology may also want to consult the *Ethnographic Thesaurus (ET)* (entry 173). Handbooks and other sources relating to methods and practice are listed in Chapter 3. A number of important anthropological encyclopedias are listed in Chapter 7, which covers area and ethnic studies and includes sources related to specific cultural groups or geographic regions. Among the sources listed in that chapter is *The Encyclopedia of World Cultures* (entry 473), an essential ready reference source in the field that provides historical, social, political, linguistic, cultural, and bibliographic information for more then 1,500 cultural groups worldwide.

29. **Anthropological Glossary.** Pearson, Roger. Malabar, FL: R.E. Krieger, 1985. 282p. ISBN 0898745101.

Pearson seeks breadth over depth with 4,000 entries—far more terms than are included in most other anthropological dictionaries. General in scope, the glossary covers archaeology, linguistics, physical, and cultural anthropology and is intended as a concise handbook or on-the-spot reference for terms ranging from names of archaeological sites and ethnic groups to mythological figures. Emphasis is on identification of discrete terms rather than theory. Unfortunately, the crowded layout makes the dictionary difficult to use.

30. **The Cambridge Encyclopedia of Hunters and Gatherers.** Lee, Richard B., and Richard Daly, editors. Cambridge, UK: Cambridge University Press, 1999. 511p. ISBN 052157109X; 0521609194pa.

This unique and highly acclaimed reference work is divided into two parts: (1) more than 50 ethnographies on specific groups arranged according to seven geographical areas of the world, each preceded by thematic essays on the archaeology and recent social history of that area; and (2) topical essays on issues relating to hunters and gatherers. Entries in both sections include sources for further reading and are amply illustrated.

31. **Companion Encyclopedia of Anthropology: Humanity, Culture and Social Life.** Ingold, Tim, editor. London: Routledge, 1994. 1,127p. ISBN 0415021375; 0415286042pa.

Closer to a handbook or reader than to an encyclopedia, this systematic synthesis of the discipline takes a broad look at anthropological issues across disciplines and presents a baseline of anthropological knowledge, as well as an analysis of new areas of study and future trends. All chapters include extensive reference lists with both current and canonical texts. The original content was reissued in 2002 in a paperback edition.

32. **The Dictionary of Anthropology.** Barfield, Thomas, editor. Oxford, UK: Blackwell, 1997. 626p. ISBN 1577180577; 1577180577pa.

Though called a dictionary, this volume is in many ways closer to an encyclopedia. Barfield brings together more than 500 entries of varying length contributed by 125 anthropologists. Topical entries focus on significant anthropological concepts and theoretical approaches and 42 lengthy biographies provide detailed accounts of major figures in the disciplines. A comprehensive cumulative bibliography and ample cross-references between entries enhance the usefulness of this volume. Although coverage of archaeology, biological and linguistic anthropology is slim, this would be a good starting point for ready reference questions in cultural anthropology.

33. **Dictionary of Anthropology.** Seymour-Smith, Charlotte. Boston, MA: G.K. Hall, 1986. 305p. ISBN 0816188173.

Compiled by a British social anthropologist, Seymour-Smith's *Dictionary of Anthropology* is unique among anthropological dictionaries in several aspects. Unlike the other dictionaries, it encompasses only social and cultural anthropology, resulting in a focus that is considerably less diffuse. Seymour-Smith also incorporates entries relating to theory rather than simply identifying ethnographic terms. Coverage of particular schools of thought in cultural anthropology, such as Marxist and feminist theory, is especially useful. Over 1,000 entries, including 150 biographies, range from one sentence to several hundred words. Bibliographical references to over 600 titles provide excellent authority and related reading. This dictionary offers a genuine synthesis of the discipline at the time of publication.

34. **Dictionary of Anthropology.** Winick, Charles. Reprint ed. New York: Greenwood, 1969. 578p. ISBN 0837120942.

Originally compiled in 1956, this classic dictionary with over 5,000 entries contains the largest number of terms of any of the anthropological dictionaries. The terms are derived from all subfields of anthropology and many identify specific objects, mythological figures, and selected ethnic groups, with an emphasis on the vocabulary of physical anthropology, material culture, and religious practice. Definitions are short, ranging from ten to nearly one hundred words, and prominent anthropologists are identified with brief notes. No sources for further reading are provided.

35. **Dictionary of Concepts in Cultural Anthropology.** Winthrop, Robert H. New York: Greenwood Press, 1991. 347p. ISBN 0313242801.

One of a series of three dictionaries exploring the central concepts in anthropology (see also entries 219 and 240), Winthrop's *Dictionary of Concepts in Cultural Anthropology* offers lengthy essays tracing the development of key concepts in the discipline, such as culture, acculturation, and applied anthropology. Bibliographical references are included for those interested in further exploration of the topic at hand. Name and subject indexes are provided.

36. **Dictionnaire de l'Ethnologie et de l'Anthropologie.** Bonte, Pierre, and Michel Izard. Paris: Presses Universitaires de France, 2000. 842p. ISBN 2130506879; 2130544223pa.

Though lacking an edition statement, this volume represents a new compact edition with an entirely new analytical index and 68 additional entries appended to the end of the work. The dictionary is thoroughly grounded in the French perspective and provides medium-length, signed entries focusing on concepts, theory, and approaches. A unique contribution is that the entries explore the ethnographic tradition in specific countries, updated in the 2000 edition to include discussion of ethnographic practice in Australia and Greece. A number of biographies are also included. Most entries include substantial bibliographies.

37. **Encyclopedia of Anthropology.** Birx, H. James, editor. Thousand Oaks, CA: Sage, 2006. 5v. ISBN 0761930299.

This ambitious five-volume encyclopedia, with over 1,200 substantial entries, encompasses all four fields of anthropology and the 300 contributors represent a broad international perspective. It also covers related research areas such as evolution, genetics, geology, linguistics paleontology, psychology, philosophy, and sociology, as well as approximately 200 biographical sketches of prominent anthropologists and others who have influenced the field. Entries are lengthy (ranging from 2 to over 30 pages) and often include chronologies or a narrative account of the development of a particular theory or body of research. Each entry also includes a list of "Further Readings" that are generally more up-to-date than is often the case with reference works this broad in scope. The arrangement is alphabetical, with additional access points provided by a detailed general index in the back and a "Reader's Guide," which classifies entries and sidebars into broad thematic categories ranging from "Applied Anthropology" to "Research/Theoretical Frameworks," at the beginning of each volume.

38. **Encyclopedia of Cultural Anthropology.** Levinson, David, and Melvin Ember, editors. New York: Holt, 1996. 4v. ISBN 0805028773.

Sponsored by Human Relations Area Files at Yale University, this comprehensive encyclopedia provides brief essays summarizing specific topics, methods, concepts, and approaches within the field of cultural anthropology. Bibliographies are included to facilitate further study. Volume 4 includes a list of anthropological periodicals and an index.

39. **Encyclopedia of Social and Cultural Anthropology.** Barnard, Alan, and Jonathan Spencer, editors. New York: Routledge, 2004. 658p. ISBN 0415285585.

Geared toward undergraduates, this encyclopedia compiles over 200 brief essays providing background information on the discipline of anthropology. Brief biographical sketches of more than 200 figures and a glossary of more than 600 terms are also provided at the end of the volume. Contributors were encouraged to write from their own point of view (in order to reflect the diversity of perspectives in this "pluralistic and occasionally fractious discipline") and coverage includes areas of emerging interest such as the anthropology of war and peace. Each entry includes bibliographic references and a subject index is provided. A second edition, with new entries and revisions throughout, is expected in 2009.

40. **The History of Humanity.** De Laet, S. J., editor. New York: Routledge, 1994–2004. 7v. ISBN various.

This seven-volume set covers the entire history of humanity with each volume covering a specific period. The first volume "Prehistory and the beginnings of civilization" (ISBN 0415093058) is of particular interest, but each volume covers archaeology, oral traditions, religion and other topics of potential interest to anthropologists.

41. **Mehrsprachiges Wörterbuch für die Ethnologie: Deutsch, Englisch, Französisch, Spanisch, Portugiesisch, Russisch, Esperanto** (Multilingual Dictionary for Ethnology: German, English, French, Spanish, Portuguese, Russian, Esperanto). Janzing, Gereon. München: LINCOM Europa, 2001. 193p. ISBN 3895862991pa.

Because anthropologists commonly need to read literature published in different countries and in many different languages, a multilingual dictionary of discipline-specific terms can be useful to have on hand. This specialized dictionary includes terms used in particular subfields, such as archaeology and folklore that are generally not included in standard bilingual dictionaries. Janzing has compiled more than 1,200 entries in German, English, French, Spanish, Portuguese, Russian, and also in Esperanto (when available).

42. **Social and Cultural Anthropology: The Key Concepts.** Rapport, Nigel, and Joanna Overing. London: Routledge, 2000. 464p. ISBN 0415181550; 0415181569pa.

Rapport and Overing present 58 entries discussing major concepts in contemporary anthropology, with an emphasis on debates, contentious issues, and the diversity of ways in which anthropologists have understood these concepts over time. As the authors note in their introduction, there is very little overlap between this and Winthrop's *Dictionary of Concepts in Cultural Anthropology* (entry 35), which largely hews to traditional areas of interest, in contrast to Rapport and Nigel's postmodern emphasis. This volume is well indexed with ample cross-references.

43. **WebRef: Anthropology.** Available online at <http://www.webref.org/anthropology/anthropology.htm>.

WebRef has compiled a fairly comprehensive dictionary of more than 1,700 general anthropology terms. Authorship of this and the other subject dictionaries on the site is not clear, although there is a form for reporting "Claimed Copyright Infringement!"

Style and Writing Guides

44. **AAA Style Guide.** American Anthropological Association. Available online at <http://www.aaanet.org/pubs/style_guide.pdf>.

This is the official guide to style and citation format for publications of the American Anthropological Association, which is only available online as a pdf. For the most part, the guidelines follow *The Chicago Manual of Style* but the *AAA Style Guide* includes a number of style and usage rules specific to the field, such as the preferred spelling of "bride-price" and "bridewealth" or the distinction between basketmakers (artisans) and Basket Makers (cultural period).

45. **Style Guides for Authors.** George and Mary Foster Anthropology Library, University of California at Berkeley. Available online at <http://www.lib.berkeley.edu/ANTH/reference/styleguides.html>.

A handy gateway to some of the most commonly used style guides in anthropology that includes links to the *AAA Style Guide* (above), as well as to the style guides of almost 200 individual journals.

Biographical Sources

Indexes

The following list includes some major general-purpose biographical indexes, which are often the best starting point for biographical information on contemporary figures, particularly if you don't have access to the more specialized sources listed under "Collective Biographies" below.

46. **Biographical Directory of Anthropologists Born Before 1920.** Mann, Thomas L., editor. Library-Anthropology Resource Group, compilers. New York: Garland, 1988. 245p. ISBN 082405833X.

With nearly 3,500 entries, this index serves as an excellent source for biographical information on anthropologists born before 1920. Both a directory and an index, this source provides brief entries with information regarding birth and death dates, birthplace, profession and area of specialization, and major contributions, followed by a listing of sources that contain more detailed biographical information. The index was generated by identifying names in the *Encyclopaedia of the Social Sciences* (entry 12), all editions of the *International Directory of Anthropologists* (entry 58), articles from *American Anthropologist* (entry 641) and the *New York Times*, among other reference sources and periodical publications. This methodology has resulted in unusual breadth, but also some striking omissions of significant figures in the discipline (e.g., John Adair, Cora DuBois). The scope and coverage are international, and a useful index by subject or culture group specialty is provided.

47. **Biography and Genealogy Master Index,** Vol. 1-. Detroit, MI: Gale, 1980-. Print cumulations every 5 years with annual supplements. ISSN 0730-1316. Available in print, on CD-ROM, and online by subscription.

Because it indexes hundreds of collected biographies, including retrospective sets such as *Encyclopaedia of the Social Sciences* (entry 56) as well as current sources such as *Who's Who in America*, this source serves as a good starting point for biographical research. Arranged alphabetically, the names are followed by an abbreviated listing of the source(s) that provides the text of the biography. Though not as comprehensive for historical coverage as the *Biographical Directory of Anthropologists Born Before 1920* (entry 46), *BGMI* enables you to quickly determine which publication to consult for biographical information on current and historical anthropologists.

48. **Biography Reference Bank.** New York: H. W. Wilson, 2001-. ISSN not assigned.

Biography Reference Bank contains biographical information on approximately half a million people, from antiquity to the present, with images for a few thousand of the more current entries. It contains the full text of the articles from more than 100 volumes of biographical reference books published by H. W. Wilson, including all the articles from all volumes of *Current Biography,* as well as biographies from other respected publishers, including Macmillan (entry 714), Greenwood (entry 707), and Harvard University Press (entry 708). The subject entry for anthropologists lists more than 900 entries, while more than 1,200 individuals are classified as ethnologists. In addition to the full text biographies, *Biography Reference Bank* also links to book reviews and articles in the Wilson databases (e.g., entry 8), conveniently grouped into books and articles *about* the person, and those *by* the person.

49. **Biography Resource Center.** Farmington Hills, MI: Gale, 1999-. ISSN not assigned.

The *Biography Resource Center (BioRC)* is a comprehensive database of biographical information on over 325,000 people from throughout history, around the world, and across all disciplines and subject areas. It combines more than 415,000 biographies from more than 135 respected Gale sources such as *Encyclopedia of World Biography, Notable Twentieth-Century Scientists,* and *Contemporary Black Biography* with full-text articles from more than 270 magazines. The database supports searches by "occupation," including anthropologist (over 60 listings), ethnologist (52), and ethnomusicologist (95), as well as more sparsely populated categories like ethnographer (15) and ethnobotanist (2 entries—Schultes and Plotkin).

Collective Biographies

Many of the sources listed below, such as *Encyclopaedia of the Social Sciences* (entry 56), are indexed in *Biography and Genealogy Master Index* (entry 47), which can thus serve as a handy guide to locating individual biographical entries in a broad range of sources.

50. **Anthropological Ancestors.** McFarlane, Alan. Cambridge University. Available online at <http://www.alanmacfarlane.com/ancestors/>.

Anthropological Ancestors is an online collection of interviews with leading anthropologists, historians, ethnomusicologists, and others compiled by Alan McFarlane and his team at Cambridge University. The collection is also accessible via the Cambridge University institutional repository <http://www.dspace.cam.ac.uk/>. Videos are in Quicktime, accompanied by handy transcriptions.

51. **Anthropologists and Anthropology: The Modern British School, 1922–1972.** Kuper, Adam. New York: Pica Press, 1973. 256p. ISBN 087663711X.

Kuper provides a critical and historical account of modern British social anthropology through a discussion of the prominent anthropologists in the field from the early 1920s to the 1980s. Subject and name indexes are provided.

52. **Anthropology Biography Web.** Minnesota State University, Mankato. Available online at <http://www.mnsu.edu/emuseum/information/biography/>.

This website provides biographical information about more than 850 anthropologists and scholars from other fields (such as Ernst Mayr) who have made substantial contributions to anthropology. Developed by Minnesota State University students, the quality of the entries varies but all entries include a list of references consulted, which make this a useful starting point for biographical research.

53. **Biographical Dictionary of Social and Cultural Anthropology.** Amit, Vered, editor. New York: Routledge, 2004. 613p. ISBN 0415223792.

This dictionary provides basic biographical information for key figures that have directly engaged socio-cultural anthropology at some point in their careers. Written by anthropologists from all over the world, each entry contains year and date of birth, a short biography, education, fieldwork, and key publications. Four indices are provided: interests, institutions, names, and concepts.

54. **Daughters of the Desert: Women Anthropologists and the Native American Southwest, 1880–1980.** Babcock, Barbara A., and Nancy J. Parezo. Albuquerque, NM: University of New Mexico Press, 1988. 241p. ISBN 0826310877; 0826310834pa.

Based on an exhibit sponsored by the Arizona State Museum and the Southwest Institute for Research on Women, this attractive and compelling collection of biographies, features, essays, and photographs documents the careers of 45 women who made substantial contributions to the anthropology of the American southwest.

55. **Dictionnaire des Ethnologues et des Anthropologues (The Routledge Dictionary of Anthropologists).** Gaillard, Gérald. James Bowman, translator. London: Routledge, 2004. 394p. ISBN 0415228255.

Originally published in France in 1997, this biographical dictionary provides a historical look at the work of prominent anthropologists across the globe within the framework of their peers and schools of thought. Chapters are arranged by national traditions and include details of each anthropologist's life and work, theories, and publications. Each chapter concludes with an extensive bibliography.

56. **Encyclopaedia of the Social Sciences.** Seligman, Edwin R. A., editor. New York: Macmillan, 1930–1935. 15v. ISBN not assigned.

This classic work includes almost 4,000 biographies of prominent social scientists, mostly from the nineteenth and early twentieth century, and only persons deceased at the time of writing were included. Figures deemed more important have longer entries, but most are brief. Entries are indexed in the *Biography and Genealogy Master Index* (entry 47). See entry 12 for full annotation of this source.

57. **International Dictionary of Anthropologists.** Winters, Christopher, editor. Library-Anthropology Resource Group, compilers. New York: Garland, 1991. 823p. ISBN 0824050940.

The librarians and anthropologists who compiled this volume endeavored to contact anthropologists from every country in the world in order to identify the most influential figures worldwide, resulting in unusually broad international coverage. Each of the 725 entries consists of a biographical essay, along with complete bibliographic citations for major works and sources of additional biographical information. Only persons born before 1920 are included. A diversity of indexes (by name, place, ethnicity, institution, and subject) make this a particularly versatile biographical source.

58. **International Directory of Anthropologists.** 5th ed. Chicago: University of Chicago Press, 1975. 496p. ISBN 0266790770.

Although too dated to be useful as a directory, the volumes in this series of successive editions offer a unique record of the professionals in the discipline from the 1920s through the early 1970s and continue to be useful as a source of biographies of international figures.

59. **International Encyclopedia of the Social Sciences.** Sills, David L., editor. New York: Macmillan, 1968–1991. 19v. ISBN not assigned.

Volume 18 of this classic reference source includes substantial biographical essays for approximately 600 prominent social scientists and others whose ideas helped shape the social sciences. The biographies are notable for their analytic (as opposed to descriptive) emphasis and include selective bibliographies. No persons born after 1890 are included. See entry 14 for a full annotation of this source.

60. **Women Anthropologists: Selected Biographies.** Gacs, Ute, editor. Urbana, IL: University of Illinois Press, 1989. 428p. ISBN 0252060849.

Providing detailed biographical essays on 58 women anthropologists born before 1934, this work also includes a bibliography of works by the anthropologist and bibliographical references to her life and work. Though coverage is international, most of the anthropologists profiled are from the United States. The biographies in this collection are not merely a catalog of individual achievements and publications but also provide a sense of each woman as an individual, thus revealing something of the "special nature of being female in the domains of fieldwork research, formal higher education or training, and public life" (preface). The biographies also offer a glimpse at the state of the discipline and social climate at the time when these women were active. Originally published as *Women Anthropologists: A Biographical Dictionary* by Greenwood Press in 1988.

Directories of Individual Anthropologists

Unlike biographical sources that summarize educational and professional highlights from the careers of prominent figures, directories offer condensed information and are typically designed to give little more than an address or intuitional affiliation. Included below are both current and retrospective directories, the latter being useful for historical purposes.

61. **Directory of Practicing Anthropologists.** National Association for the Practice of Anthropology. Available online at <http://www.practicinganthropology.org/directory/>.

This directory includes anthropologists who are members of the National Association for the Practice of Anthropology (NAPA) (entry 759). Listing is not restricted to those practicing outside academia but includes all NAPA members, including college professors. Information provided includes address and phone (business and home), occupation, degrees, languages, geographic and cultural specialties, professional specialties, and publications. The listings can be searched by areas of expertise, employment area, geographic region, languages, and methods as well as by organizational affiliations.

62. **Guide: A Guide to Departments, A Directory of Members.** Arlington, VA: American Anthropological Association. 1995-. Annual. ISSN not supplied. (Continues *AAA Guide*, 1989/90–1994/95 and *AAA Guide to Departments of Anthropology*, 1962/63–1988/89). <http://www.aaanet.org/pubs/guide.htm#eguide>.

More than just a listing of academic departments, this comprehensive directory provides detailed information on the degree programs, faculty, and staff, size, requirements, special programs, and facilities of anthropology departments in over 400 colleges and universities, as well as community colleges. It also identifies more than 90 museums, research institutions, and government agencies in the field, providing information regarding their staff, facilities, publications, etc. A directory of members gives names, addresses and the AAA unit affiliations of the more than 10,000 members of the Association. In addition, statistics pertaining to the growth of the discipline and a listing of dissertations submitted during the previous year are also provided at the back of each volume. Access to the online version is limited to AAA members.

63. **Worldwide Email Directory of Anthropologists (WEDA).** Jarvis, Hugh, editor. Available online at <http://wings.buffalo.edu/WEDA/>.

Hosted by the University of Buffalo and maintained by Hugh Jarvis, *Worldwide Email Directory of Anthropologists (WEDA)* is a searchable directory of individual anthropologists and anthropological institutions (including academic departments, societies, and companies). The web-based directory supports searching by geographical location, research interest, and institution. According the most recent statistics posted at the time of viewing, the database includes approximately 6,000 entries.

Internet Gateways

64. **Anthro.Net.** White, Eric J. University of California, Santa Barbara. Available online at <www.anthro.net>.

The *Anthro.Net* database contains over 40,000 refereed websites and bibliographic references with anthropological content searchable by keyword. The site also organizes resources into regional, topical, and thematic areas for browsing.

65. **AnthroBase.** Partapuoli, Kari Helene, and Finn Sivert Nielsen. Available online at <www.anthrobase.com>.

AnthroBase is a searchable database of "articles, theses, essays, reports, conference papers, fieldnotes, etc., written by anthropologists and others with an interest in social and cultural diversity." Authors retain copyright to their texts. The texts are multilingual and can be browsed by author, title, region, theme, and citation, and collections. The site also includes announcements for upcoming conferences and an extensive dictionary, authored by Finn Sivert Nielsen (Institute of Anthropology, University of Copenhagen) who maintains this site along with his wife and fellow anthropologist, Kari Partapuoli.

66. **Anthropology Resources on the Internet.** American Anthropological Association. Available online at <http://www.aaanet.org/resinet.htm>.

This useful collection of links provided on the American Anthropological Association (entry 745) website is organized into the following categories: "Anthropologists," "Anthropology and Technology," "Biological/Physical Anthropology," "Applied/Practicing Anthropology," "Archaeology Resources," "Ethnography," "Funding Opportunities," "General Resources," "Lists/Discussion Groups," "Literature and Libraries," "Museums," "News and Media," "Organizations and Institutes," "Other AAA Sites," "Resources for Teachers/Professors," and "Visual Anthropology."

67. **Anthropology Resources on the Internet: WWW Virtual Library of Archaeology and Prehistory.** Lutins, Allen, and Bernard Oliver Clist. Available online at <http://www.anthropology-resources.net>.

This gateway provides a comprehensive collection of links to anthropology and archaeology sites, each evaluated on its content, currency, and presentation. Includes a directory of university departments, research institutes, and museums worldwide as well as a collection of links arranged topically and geographically (using the Open Directory Project subdivisions within the United States and the *CIA World Factbook* for the rest of the world). The site was launched in 1995 by Allen Lutins, MA in Archaeology.

68. **Intute: Anthropology.** Available online at <http://www.intute.ac.uk/socialsciences/anthropology/>.

Intute was formed by combining the resources compiled by the venerable *Social Science Information Gateway (SOSIG)* with those from *Altis*, the newest hub in the Resource Discovery Network (RDN) created by a consortium of institutions within the UK post-16 education sector. The anthropology section is a comprehensive selection of links edited by the University of Manchester and the University of Kent at Canterbury.

69. **WWW Virtual Library: Anthropology.** Anthro TECH. Available online at <http://vlib.anthrotech.com>.

Part of the *WWW Virtual Library* organization, this site provides a listing of resources in the many subfields of anthropology and serves as a starting point for finding online information for anthropology, broadly defined. Links are arranged in broad topical categories such as "Applied Anthropology" and "Organizations." The site is maintained by Anthro TECH, a web design and development company that uses ethnographic approaches to technology implementations.

70. **Yahoo Directory: Social Science: Anthropology and Archaeology.** Available online at <http://dir.yahoo.com/Social_Science/Anthropology_and_Archaeology/>.

The Yahoo anthropology page is a fairly comprehensive collection of links related to anthropology and archaeology.

Bibliographic Tools (Finding Publications)

The section focuses on the bibliography of anthropology—those sources that assist the researcher in identifying research and scholarship in the field. The end product of this research can take the form of a book, journal article, dissertation, working paper, report, or conference paper and may have been published recently or in the sixteenth century.

A sizable body of reference material has been developed that identifies and organizes bibliographic references to this research, providing contemporary scholars with access to the work of their colleagues both past and present. Anthropology is notorious, however, for its "fugitive" literature: working papers, special reports, papers appearing in irregularly published series, and so forth. Unfortunately, not all of these have been "captured" in the bibliographic record, and tracking them down often requires the services of a bibliographic sleuth.

Anthropologists frequently utilize internal references in scholarly literature and browse current journals in their area of specialization to develop a body of literature upon which to draw. For students or researchers unfamiliar with the literature or working in a new area, however, indexes and bibliographies provide a good starting point for identifying published research on a specific geographic area, ethnic group, or topic. Published on a continuing basis (though not always as current as researchers may find necessary), indexes provide citations to recent books and/or journal articles and as they cumulate become an organized record of the discipline's published research.

In general, the literature needs of anthropologists are extensive in terms of date, language, and subject. Older materials continue to be relevant and anthropologists use foreign language materials more intensively than any other social scientists (Stenstrom, P. and McBride, R.B. (1979). "Serial Use by Social Science Faculty: A Survey." *College & Research Libraries* 40(5): 426–431). With one foot in the humanities and one foot in the sciences, anthropologists draw on a large literature base and one citation study found that 70 percent of sources cited in anthropology articles were from other fields (Choi, Jin M. (1988). "Citation Analysis of Intra- and Interdisciplinary Communication Patterns of Anthropology in the U.S.A." *Behavioral and Social Sciences Librarian* 6 (3/4): 65–84.). This section focuses on anthropology sources, both current and retrospective, that cover the literature in English and other languages. Sources relevant to specific subfields and research areas are listed in the appropriate chapter or section and often include indexes from other disciplines.

Because anthropology's indexes and abstracts are of relatively recent vintage (the oldest, *Anthropological Index*, began in 1963), published bibliographies and library catalogs provide a mechanism for conducting retrospective literature searches. Their compilers provide a monumental service to the field by identifying and organizing older literature. Bibliographies can include both monographic and periodical literature and generally focus on specific topics or regions. The Human Relations Area Files, for example, has published extensive works such as the *Ethnographic Bibliography of North America* (entry 601) that is now available as part of the *Bibliography of Native North Americans* (entry 600), a regularly updated online database. Most of the bibliographies in this guide are listed by topic or geographic region in the appropriate chapter. Though the heyday of anthropological bibliography has passed in the wake of online databases, and fewer and fewer new titles are being published each year, many of the existing bibliographies continue to be the best way of locating retrospective literature in anthropology.

Literature Surveys and Reviews

71. **Annual Review of Anthropology,** Vol. 1-. Palo Alto, CA: Annual Reviews. 1972-. Annual (print); continuously updated (online). ISSN 0084-6570; 1545-4290e.

This important publication presents critical reviews of published research on topics that have received increasing attention during the previous year within all subfields of the discipline. With approximately 20 articles in each volume, the review serves as a record of the state of the art of specific anthropological investigations and provides substantial topical bibliographies through the extensive lists of cited references. Coverage is international, but with a high percentage of references in English. The online version includes preprints of forthcoming articles and supports full-text searching across the entire backfile (in pdf), which makes it easy to locate a particular author, topic, or keyword. Each print volume provides an author and subject index, and 5-year cumulative indexes are available.

72. **Reviews in Anthropology,** Vol. 1-. Philadelphia, PA: Gorden & Breach. 1974-. Quarterly. ISSN 0093-8157; 1556-3014e.

This publication is comprised entirely of review essays that examine a cluster of books on a particular theme (e.g., "indigenous movements in Latin America" or "Africa bewitched"). The 10–20 essays included in each issue provide an analytical synthesis of the literature on a topic to date and include references. The titles discussed in these review articles have generally been published 1–2 years prior to the review.

Indexes, Abstracts, and Databases

73. **Abstracts in Anthropology,** Vol. 1-. Westport, CT: Greenwood. 1970-. 8/yr. ISSN 0001-3455; 1557-5136e. Available in print and online by subscription.

This periodical index covering the English-language serial literature in anthropology bears the distinction of being the only currently available source that also includes abstracts. The scope includes all areas of anthropology, with numbered issues alternating between cultural anthropology and linguistics and archaeology and physical anthropology. Approximately 300 journals, primarily from the United States, are indexed annually and the time lag between when an article is published and when it is cited is 1–2 years. Some of the titles are highly specialized (e.g., *Romanian Journal of Gerontology and Geriatrics*) and are not likely be found in most college collections. An online version, hosted by EBSCO's MetaPress, was launched in 2005 with coverage starting with Volume 48 (2004). As of this writing, access to the online version was free with any print subscription.

Arrangement of the citations is by discipline, then broad category (kinship, urban anthropology, medical anthropology), with indexes by author and subject. This arrangement is replicated in the online version with the "Browse subjects" option. The subject index can prove frustrating to use, with no cross-references, inconsistent terminology, and lack of specificity (e.g., general headings such as "Women"). Nonetheless, grouping the articles by general category facilitates a review of the literature for researchers using a topical approach, but is less useful for area-studies literature searches.

74. **Anthropological Abstracts,** Vol. 1-. Münster: Lit. 2002-. Annual. ISSN 0173-2986. Available in print by subscription; a partial version is available free online. <http://www.anthropology-online.de>.

Established in 1980 to make German anthropological scholarship accessible to a broad range of scholars and originally published under the title *Abstracts in German Anthropology* (1980–97), this source provides abstracts in English to German-language dissertations, monographs, exhibition catalogs, yearbooks, and articles appearing in over 50 major anthropological and area studies journals. Publication was suspended briefly in the mid-1980s and again in the late 1990s due to financial problems, but it is currently available online and in print (distributed by Transaction Publishers in North America). The online version is open access, with the proviso that the "print issues of *AA* will have about 30% more material than the Internet versions." The print version of Volume 1 (2002) includes content originally issued in the online version of *Anthropological Abstracts* from 1999–2002, with additional material.

This source will be most useful to scholars seeking to broaden their research base through access to the work of their German counterparts. Doctoral students will also appreciate the opportunity to identify articles to translate for their language requirement!

75. **Anthropological Index.** The Anthropology Library at the British Museum, editor. London: Royal Anthropological Institute of Great Britain and Ireland. 1995-. Annual. ISSN 0003-5467. (Continues *Anthropological Index to Current Periodicals in the British Museum Library*, Vol. 15–32, 1977–1994). Available online by institutional subscription, free to individuals. <http://80-lucy.ukc.ac.uk.proxy2.library.uiuc.edu/AIO.html>.

Based on the periodical collection in the Anthropology Library of the British Museum, this title is one of the major indexes in the field, covering over 600 journals worldwide. The scope includes all areas of anthropology, with extensive coverage of Commonwealth countries and Africa. Date coverage is from 1957 to the present. As with many periodical indexes, *Anthropological Index* excludes nonarticle materials such as book reviews, letters, and obituaries. The time lag between an article's publication and its citation in *AI* is generally 2–3 years.

The advanced search provides access by geographic region, which can be further subdivided by subfield: archaeology, cultural anthropology, physical anthropology, and linguistics. This arrangement is well suited for researchers taking an area studies approach because it brings the literature together in one section. It is less workable, however, for topical research, providing no access points other than keyword searches for concepts such as incest taboos or transnationalism.

Individual researchers engaged in educational, noncommercial activities can access the web version at no charge, but institutions are expected to subscribe (and will be asked to do so if the transaction logs show significant traffic from a particular IP range). *Anthropology Plus* (entry 77) provides combined access to this title and Tozzer Library's *Anthropological Literature* (entry 76).

76. **Anthropological Literature.** Cambridge, MA: Harvard University, Tozzer Library. 1979-. Quarterly. ISSN 0190-3373. Available in print, on CD-ROM and online by subscription.

Anthropological Literature (AL) provides access to the contents of approximately 900 of Tozzer's serial publications including journals, proceedings, and irregular series. Because important anthropological literature is published in edited books as well as in periodicals, *AL* also analyses approximately 200 of these collections annually, providing access to individually authored chapters. As in most other anthropological indexes, book reviews, commentaries, letters to the editor, and other communications are not included. Citations appear in the index approximately 1–2 years after their publication. Date coverage includes article citations going back to the early nineteenth century.

The scope of *AL* is international, with particularly good coverage of Central and Latin America, and includes all subfields within anthropology. Because the print version is organized by anthropological subfield, citations for cultural anthropology are listed together irrespective of their geographical or topical focus.

The subject index, however, compensates for the lack of classified arrangement by providing entries for specific ethnic groups and geographic areas as well as in-depth subject terms and ample cross-references.

AL is part of a bibliographic continuum developed by Harvard's Tozzer Library, which includes the *Author and Subject Catalogues of the Tozzer Library* (entry 107), providing access to the library's collection of books through the mid-1980s and to periodical articles from the turn of the century through 1983. *Anthropological Literature (AL)* was established 1979 as a separate periodical index based on the collection, and the *Bibliographic Guide to Anthropology and Archaeology* (entry 110) serves as an annual bibliography of the library's books and other materials received from 1986 to date.

Anthropology Plus (entry 77), available from the Research Libraries Group's CitaDel database service, provides combined access to this title and the British Museum's *Anthropological Index* (entry 75). For a brief period (1983–1988), *AL* was published in microfiche, but paper copy was reinstated in 1989.

77. **Anthropology Plus.** Mountain View, CA: Research Libraries Group. 1993-. Available online by subscription.

This database provides simultaneous access to two of the majors indexes in the field: *Anthropological Literature* (entry 76) from Harvard University and *Anthropological Index* (entry 75) from the Royal Anthropological Institute in the United Kingdom, and thus identifies print materials in all four fields of anthropology and related interdisciplinary research areas published in thousands of journals and monographic series from the nineteenth century to the present. Coverage of the North American and British literature is comprehensive, and core European and Latin American serials are also indexed. As of this writing, *Anthropology Plus* is in the midst of moving from RLG to OCLC first search and will soon be available on its new platform.

78. **AnthroSource.** Berkeley, CA: University of California Press for the American Anthropological Association. 2004-. Available online by subscription. <http://www.anthrosource.net/>.

This portal to the publications of the American Anthropological Association currently provides a full text archive of major AAA journals and bulletins from Volume 1 to the present, and will continue to incorporate additional AAA publications and other collections. Book reviews are included, but not always tagged as such. The interface supports full-text searching across the archive, email alerts, saved searches, and direct links from citations in the pdfs to the full text of the cited article. Journal issues generally appear online prior to distribution in print. Surprisingly, there is a 10-year embargo for institutional subscribers on current issues of *Anthropology News* (entry 98), the AAA's newsletter and primary public outreach organ.

AnthroSource is a cooperative project between AAA and the University of California Press with a steering committee comprised of editors, scholars and librarians. The intention is to create "an evolving, interactive repository of research and communications tools designed to bring the most credible and relevant of anthropological scholarship together in one place and to support a strong community of scholars, teachers, and students in the field" (www.anthrosource.net/, accessed March 13, 2006). Access is free to individual members of the American Anthropological Association.

79. **International Bibliography of Anthropology = Bibliographie Internationale d'Anthropologie,** Vol. 44-. London: Routledge. 1998-. Annual. (Continues *International Bibliography of Social and Cultural Anthropology,* 1955–1997). ISSN 0085-2074. Available in print or on CD-ROM by subscription. Also available online as part of *International Bibliography of the Social Sciences* (entry 4).

One of the subfiles included in the *International Bibliography of the Social Sciences (IBSS)* (entry 4), this may be the most comprehensive international index in anthropology, indexing over 500 periodicals in English and European languages, as well as books, conference proceedings, technical reports, and government publications. Many U.S. anthropological journals are included, but most of the journals indexed are published outside the United States and the United Kingdom and only larger research libraries will have a high percentage of the titles in their collections. Through the time lag for this publication is significant (citations appear approximately 2 years after publication), it remains an excellent index to literature in the field. The focus is primarily on social and cultural anthropology, with physical anthropology, archaeology, and linguistics receiving limited attention.

Use of the print version is facilitated both by its internal arrangement and through the subject index. Organized by category, the citations include references to general studies; materials and methods; morphological foundations; ethnographic studies of specific peoples; social organizations; religion, magic, and witchcraft; material and expressive arts; studies of culture and personality; acculturation; and applied anthropology. Each of these general areas has topical as well as geographic subdivisions. The detailed subject index includes multiple access points for each citation.

80. **List of Publications of the Bureau of American Ethnology, With Index to Authors and Titles.** Washington, DC: Smithsonian Institution Press, 1971. 134p. (*Bulletin / Smithsonian Institution, Bureau of American Ethnology*, 200). Available online at <http://www.sil.si.edu/DigitalCollections/BAE/Bulletin200/200title.htm>.

This source indexes all publications by the Bureau, dating back to 1877, including *Annual Reports, Bulletins, Contributions to North American Ethnology, Publications of the Institute of Social Anthropology,* and other miscellaneous publications. The appearance of the *List of Publications* in 1971 brought to an end all publications under the Bureau name, the *Bulletin* series having been superseded by *Smithsonian Contributions to Anthropology* in 1965.

81. **Thematic List of Descriptors: Liste Thematique des Descripteurs: Anthropologie.** The International Committee for Social Science Information and Documentation. New York: Routledge, 1989. 522p. ISBN 0415017769.

Prepared on behalf of UNESCO by the International Committee for Social Science Information and Documentation as companion volume to the *International Bibliography of the Social Sciences* (entry 4), the Thematic List of Descriptors is useful for locating topical material in that source, as well as for the development of controlled vocabulary for other information systems pertaining to cultural phenomena and artifacts.

Reviews of Indexes

Apart from general sources like *Ulrich's*, abstracting and indexing sources are given scant attention in the published literature. ANSS Reviews (entry 82) helps address this gap for anthropology and sociology resources.

82. ANSS Reviews. Anthropology and Sociology Section of the Association of College and Research Libraries. 1996-. Available online at <http://www.lib.odu.edu/anss/reviews.html>.

Produced by the Anthropology and Sociology Section of the Association of College and Research Libraries, this series of review articles evaluates "abstracts and indexes in all formats to determine their value to the anthropology and sociology community." Sources reviewed include subject specific indexes such as *Anthropological Literature*, as well as reviews of resources whose scope is more general or focused on other disciplines or fields of study, such as *Art and Archaeology Technical Abstracts, Biological Abstracts*, or *Web of Science*. In the latter case, the focus of the reviews is on the coverage and usefulness *vis-à-vis* anthropology and sociology. The reviews are also published in *ANSS Currents*.

Dissertations

See also *Ethnoart: Africa, Oceania, and the Americas: A Bibliography of Theses and Dissertations* (entry 294).

83. Guide: A Guide to Departments, A Directory of Members. Arlington, VA: American Anthropological Association. 1995-. Annual. ISSN not supplied. (Continues *AAA Guide*, 1989/90–1994/95 and *AAA Guide to Departments of Anthropology,* 1962/63–1988/89).

More than just a listing of academic departments, this comprehensive directory also provides a listing of dissertations submitted during the previous year at the back of each volume. See entry 62 for a complete annotation of this source.

84. A Guide to Theses and Dissertations: An International Bibliography of Bibliographies. Reynolds, Michael. Rev. ed. Phoenix, AZ: Oryx Press, 1985. 263p. ISBN 0897741498.

This extensive annotated list of bibliographies of theses and dissertations is arranged by broad subject area. Included are sections on anthropology as well as specific area studies, languages and linguistics, and folklore, among others. The lists are extensive, identifying theses from a broad range of sources. International coverage for identification of theses is particularly good. The section for anthropology, for example, identifies 21 sources, including lists of theses that have been published in serials such as *America Indigena, Sovetskaya Etnografiya, Yearbook of Anthropology*, and *Current Anthropology* and separately published titles such as David McDonald's *Bibliography of Dissertations in Anthropology*

(New Haven, CT: HRAF Press, 1977). Similar extensive lists are provided within area-studies and related disciplines. To further assist the researcher, the citations are briefly annotated, with information as to the scope and number of theses contained in each bibliography. A subject index provides further access through specific country, topic (hygiene), or culture group (Igbos).

85. **Masters' Theses in Anthropology: A Bibliography of Theses from United States Colleges and Universities.** McDonald, David R. New Haven, CT: Human Relations Area Files Press, 1977. 453p. ISBN 0875362176.

This listing of masters' theses in anthropology contains over 3,700 titles of theses accepted from 1898 through 1975. Arranged alphabetically within the major subdivisions of anthropology, information provided includes author, title, date, and institution. Indexes by subject, culture, geographical area, title, and institution provide additional access.

86. **Proquest Dissertations and Theses.** Ann Arbor, MI: Proquest. 2006-. Monthly. (Continues *Proquest Digital Dissertations*, 1999–2006). Available online and on CD-ROM by subscription and in print as *Dissertation Abstracts International, A: The Humanities and Social Sciences*, 1939-.

An essential source for identifying doctoral dissertations completed in accredited North American universities, as well as more than 200 universities elsewhere—although international coverage is spotty. Some masters' theses are also included in the electronic versions. Citations (1861–present) and abstracts (1980–present) are available to all subscribers; online visitors can access the past 2 years' citations and abstracts even without an institutional license. Some abstracts of older dissertations may only be available through the original print version of *Dissertation Abstracts International*.

All versions provide access by author, title keyword and subject; the electronic versions also support searching by advisor, granting institution, date, and abstract keyword. Browsing by subject is provided via a "Subject Tree." Dissertations in anthropology are listed in "Humanities and Social Sciences" under "Social Sciences" and are organized into three subheadings: "Archaeology," "Cultural Anthropology," and "Physical Anthropology." For cultural anthropologists, particularly those in area and ethnic studies, reviewing the literature outside the field is also important, and relevant sections include folklore, history, and sociology (within the "Social Sciences" section); linguistics (within the "Language, Literature, and Linguistics" section); and fine arts and music (within the "Communications and the Arts" section).

87. **Theses Canada Portal.** National Library of Canada. Available online at <http://www.collectionscanada.ca/6/4/index-e.html>.

Theses Canada Portal is the central access point for Canadian theses. At this site, you can search AMICUS, Canada's national online catalogue, for records of all theses in the National Library of Canada's theses collection, which was established in 1965. You can also search and download (for free) the full text electronic versions of Canadian theses and dissertations that were published from the beginning of 1998 to August 31, 2002 (this coverage will continue to expand). All theses in Library and Archives Canada's collection are available on interlibrary loan.

Conference Proceedings

Though the papers delivered at conferences may represent the cutting edge of the discipline, gaining access to them is no simple matter. Many proceedings are not published at all; others may be published as edited collections or special issues of journals, frequently appearing a considerable length of time following the conference. Many conferences are held under the auspices of learned societies and are most easily accessed in library catalogs under the name of the sponsoring society. Proceedings of the American Anthropological Association meetings are not published as a whole, although separate panels and units may publish their papers and abstracts appear in the annual AAA *Abstracts of the Annual Meeting.*

88. **Abstracts of the Annual Meeting.** Washington, DC: American Anthropological Association. 1971-. Annual. ISSN 0160-1873.

In order to provide information about the scholarly exchange at its annual meeting, the American Anthropological Association publishes abstracts of all papers delivered at each meeting. The abstracts appear in program order under the title of the panel and include the author's name and institutional affiliation, title of the paper, and an approximately 75-word summary. The publication is divided into three sections: session abstracts, film and video abstracts, and abstracts of papers. An index of authors and sessions is provided at the back.

89. **Proceedings First.** Dublin, Ohio: OCLC. 1990s-. Monthly. ISSN 0959-4906. Available in print as *Index of Conference Proceedings*, 1964–2003; online by subscription.

The online continuation of the *Index of Conference Proceedings, 1964–2003*, this unique resource indexes citations to proceedings of every congress, symposium, conference, exposition, workshop, and meeting received at The British Library from October 1993 to the present. Each record contains a list of papers presented at each conference and basic bibliographic information for the published proceedings is provided. International coverage, especially for European and Commonwealth countries, is superior. Anthropological conferences are well covered, particularly taking area-studies conferences into consideration.

Book and Media Reviews

Anthropology Specific

Many anthropology journals regularly publish a large number of book reviews, including *Current Anthropology* (entry 661) and *American Ethnologist* (entry 642). Book reviews in the latter can conveniently be searched along with all those appearing in other AAA journals via *AnthroSource* (entry 91). *Reviews in Anthropology* (entry 693) is comprised entirely of thematic reviews of a group of books on a particular topic. For reviews of films, see also *A*

Bibliography of Ethnographic Films (entry 187) which lists more than 1,000 film and video reviews published before 1992.

90. **Anthropology Review Database.** Jarvis, Hugh W. University of Buffalo Department of Anthropology. Available online at <http://wings.buffalo.edu/anthropology/ARD/>.

Perhaps the best place to start for reviews of recent books in anthropology, *Anthropology Review Database (ARD)* is searchable compilation of reviews of anthropological books, films and videos, audio recordings, software, multimedia, and online resources. Sponsored by the University of Buffalo, Department of Anthropology, this freely available resource provides surprisingly broad and timely coverage of current publications and products. Signed, refereed reviews specifically written for *ARD* are included, as well as citations to reviews published in *Current Anthropology, Reviews in Anthropology* and other journals. Date coverage extends from 1990 to present.

91. **AnthroSource.** Berkeley, CA: University of California Press for the American Anthropological Association. 2004-. Available online by subscription. <http://www.anthrosource.net/>.

As a portal to American Anthropological Association (entry 745) journals, *AnthroSource* (entry 78) includes any book review published in the dozen or so AAA journals included in the database. To find reviews, search with the name of the book in quotes or try searching by author name.

General Review Sources

A number of standard book review sources and indexes have good coverage of anthropology; these are listed below with hints on retrieving reviews of interest to anthropologists.

92. **Book Review Digest.** New York: H. W. Wilson. 1906-. Monthly, with annual print cumulations. ISSN 0006-7326; 1076-7045e. Available in print, CD-ROM, and online by subscription.

This standard review source, available in most academic and public libraries, indexes and provides brief excerpts from book reviews appearing in over one hundred general interest and scholarly periodicals from the United States, Canada, and Great Britain. To be included, titles must have been reviewed at least twice in the periodicals indexed. A number of social science titles of interest to anthropologists, such as *Journal of Marriage and Family* and *Contemporary Sociology,* are covered, as well as book review journals like *Booklist, Choice,* and *Kirkus*.

The new online version, *Book Review Digest Plus,* has greatly expanded coverage including reviews drawn from over 8,000 periodicals covered by other Wilson databases, including *Social Sciences Full Text.* The online database also includes full text of many reviews drawn from the Wilson family of databases, all of which can be searched concurrently. The search capabilities of *BRD+,* lauded by reviewers for their power and flexibility, include features like synonym and soundex ("sounds like") searching.

93. **Book Review Index,** Vol. 1-. Detroit, MI: Gale. 1965-. 3/yr., with annual print cumulations. ISSN 0524-0581. Available in print and online by subscription.

This general index to book reviews covers over 450 newspapers, magazines, and journals and is superior to *Book Review Digest* (H.W. Wilson, 1905-) in coverage of specifically anthropology-related sources, though its retrospective coverage is not as deep. Anthropology and area studies are fairly well represented, and as anthropological titles are regularly reviewed in periodicals such as *Choice*, these are identified as well. Arrangement is alphabetical by author of the book review, with an index by title, and the entries include brief citations to review sources.

94. **Combined Retrospective Index to Book Reviews in Scholarly Journals, 1886–1974.** Woodbridge, CT: Research Publications, 1979. 15v. ISBN 084080167X.

This massive index to book reviews in scholarly journals was compiled to compensate for the poor representation of scholarly journals in the major retrospective reviewing sources. The index covers over 400 titles; coverage of anthropology is not as strong as that for area studies. The index provides references to literally thousands of book reviews published from 1886 through 1974. Arrangement is by author's name, with a title index.

95. **PCI Periodicals Contents Index.** Alexandria, VA: Chadwyck-Healey. 1993-. ISSN not supplied. Available online by subscription.

Provides access to the retrospective journal literature beginning in the eighteenth century and does not include current journal literature. To find reviews, under keyword search, enter the title of the book and limit search to "Book reviews only" at the bottom of the page. Some sources are natively available in full-text.

96. **Social Sciences Index.** New York: H. W. Wilson. Monthly. ISSN 0094-4920. Available in print, CD-ROM, and online by subscription.

One of the better sources for book reviews in anthropology, Wilson's *Social Sciences Index* (entry 8) provides access to reviews published in 500 social science journals published from 1907 to present (print) and 1983 to present (electronic). Online searches can be run concurrently against other Wilson databases, including *Book Review Digest* and *Humanities Abstracts* for better coverage of interdisciplinary or general interest topics.

News and Newsletters

97. **Anthropology in the News.** Texas A&M Department of Anthropology. Available online at <www.tamu.edu/anthropology/news.html>.

Maintained by David L. Carlson at Texas A&M, this site provides links to the full-text of anthropology-related news stories from major news and media outlets (CNN, NPR, *New York Times*, *USA Today*), newswires, magazines, and press releases from universities, government agencies, and research institutes.

Only services providing free content are included, though some may require that you register and select a password in order to retrieve articles. It seems a natural fit for an RSS feed, but that functionality was not yet available as of this writing.

98. **Anthropology News,** Vol. 1-. Berkeley, CA: University of California Press for the American Anthropological Association. 1999-. Monthly. ISSN 1541-6151; 1556-3502e.

Published monthly (except June–August), *Anthropology News* is the official newsletter of the American Anthropological Association (entry 745). In addition to carrying brief articles, correspondence, news items, and an extensive list of new publications, the newsletter serves as a vehicle for communication for the individual units within the AAA and offers information on placement opportunities, grants, and forthcoming meetings. A substantial listing of job openings is provided in the "Career Development" section.

Although *Anthropology News* is the public face of the Association, there is a 10-year embargo on current issues for institutional subscribers via *AnthroSource* (entry 78). Highlights from the current issue are posted on the AAA website (http://www.aaanet.org/press/an/index.htm), however, along with an online bulletin board of announcements between issues. *AAA E-News,* featuring brief announcements of awards, fellowships, meetings, etc., is also issued periodically via e-mail to AAA members.

99. **Yahoo! News: Anthropology and Archaeology.** Available online at <http://news.yahoo.com/fc/science/anthropology_and_archaeology>.

This website provides links to anthropology-related news and articles available free on the web. Items are drawn form newswires and major news outlets like the BBC, the *Christian Science Monitor*, and NPR.

Bibliography of Bibliographies

100. **AnthroGlobe Bibliographies.** Ciolek, T. Matthew, editor. Available online at <http://coombs.anu.edu.au/Biblio/biblio_index.html>.

This collection of online bibliographies, arranged by topic or region, is compiled by the editors of the *AnthroGlobe* electronic journal (ISSN 1481-3440). Links to other bibliography gateway sites with an anthropological focus are also provided.

101. **Anthropological Bibliographies: A Selected Guide.** Smith, Margo L., and Yvonne M. Damien, editors. South Salem, N.Y.: Redgrave, 1981. 307p. ISBN 0913178632.

An impressive effort at bringing together published bibliographies within the field of anthropology, this source lists over 3,200 bibliographies that have been separately published as books or articles or that appear as cited references or additional reading lists in anthropological literature. The majority of the citations focus upon area studies and are arranged by a broad geographic category, such as Europe, then further subdivided by region. A section on topical bibliographies covers categories such as material culture, medical anthropology, and anthropological linguistics. A subject index is included. Though researchers doing a literature search would need to consult sources published since the late 1970s, this bibliography provides a good starting place for systematic coverage of the literature prior to that date. The bibliography was one of many projects sponsored by the Library-Anthropology Research Group to further access to the literature of the discipline.

102. **Anthropology Bibliographies.** Department of Anthropology, Texas A&M University. Available online at <http://anthropology.tamu.edu/bibliographies.htm>.
Maintained by the Texas A&M Department of Anthropology, this site provides a frequently updated collection of online bibliographies related to anthropology.

Periodical Bibliographies and Directories

For an annotated listing of core anthropology journals, see Chapter 8.

103. **"Journals of the Century in Anthropology and Archaeology."** Ogburn, Joyce, J., Christina Smith, and Gregory A. Finnegan. *Serials Librarian* 39(4) (2001): 69–78.
An analytic bibliography of the core journals in anthropology and the history and development of the serial literature in anthropology over the last 100 years.

104. **Serial Publications in Anthropology.** Grollig, Francis. X., and Sol Tax, editors. 2nd ed. South Salem, NY: Redgrave, 1982. 177p. ISBN 0913178640pa.
Though other sources are more up-to-date and provide more detailed information, this work covers, by far, the most titles and remains useful for identification and bibliographic verification of lesser known serial publications from across the globe. The strength of this reference book lies not in the depth of information it provides for individual titles (only name, place of publication, and frequency are provided) but rather in its coverage of the "gray literature" that has always flourished in anthropology. In addition to journals, titles of over 3,000 occasional papers, working papers, research bulletins, and other materials published on a continuing (if irregular) basis from all branches of anthropology and area studies are included. The book is arranged alphabetically by title, and additional access is provided by geographic and broad subject indexes.

105. **Ulrich's Periodicals Directory.** New York: R.R. Bowker. 1932-. Annual. ISSN 0000-0175. Available in print, CD-ROM, and online by subscription.
This directory is an indispensable tool for identifying currently published periodicals in all fields; nearly 240,000 periodicals worldwide are listed. Titles can searched or browsed within a number of indices including language, e-vendor,

or subject. The subject "anthropology" includes approximately 1,500 titles in all subfields with cross-references to journals in related areas. Citations provide full title, title history, start year, frequency, publishing body, place of publication, editor, and ISSN. Useful notes indicate advertisement policy, rights and permissions contacts, circulation figures and audience, publisher and ordering information, online, microfilm and other format availability, reviews, and a list of indexes and abstracts that cover a particular journal title. *Abstracts in Anthropology, Anthropological Index* and *Anthropological Literature* are all included among Ulrich's periodical indexes.

An annual print version (limited to active titles plus the last 3 years of ceased titles) is available in addition to the CD-ROM and online versions. The online version provides link to tables of contents, abstracts, full-text, and document delivery options available from cooperating partners, as well as OpenURL links to local library catalogs and online resources. As of this writing, Z39.50 links to local holdings are under development.

106. **World List of Social Science Periodicals: Liste Mondial des Periodiques Specialises dans les Sciences Sociales.** 8th ed. Paris: UNESCO, 1991. ISBN 9230027340.

Focusing specifically on social science titles, this reference source includes fewer titles than *Ulrich's* but provides more information on individual titles by including not only full publishing information (editor, frequency, availability of book reviews, etc.) but also brief abstracts and notes that describe the scope and average number of pages and articles per issue. Arrangement is by country of origin. The subject index lists over 200 titles in cultural anthropology, social anthropology, and ethnology and provides access to specific topics such as ethnic identity. The geographical index offers access to titles having a national or regional focus.

Published Library Catalogs and Guides

A specific type of bibliography, the published library catalog serves as an important, through frequently overlooked, resource in anthropological research. Seemingly arcane to the novice user, the catalogs generally consist of reproduction of printed catalog cards from a specific library providing author, and frequently provide enhanced subject access to its collection. Though library networks have revolutionized access to collections worldwide, the published catalogs nonetheless assist in identifying scholarship in the field, the holdings of a particular library, and sometimes provide more comprehensive retrospective access than online catalogs.

Perhaps more importantly, however, the catalogs can also be used to find materials in one's own library. They represent special collections, so the level of cataloging (particularly assignment of subject headings) can be very detailed and precise, augmenting the more general Library of Congress subject headings used in most libraries. For instance, the *Author and Subject Catalogues of the Tozzer Library* (entry 107) offer extremely detailed subject access by ethnic group, with numerous cross-references. Moreover, many of the published catalogs (such as Tozzer's) do not restrict their coverage to books. Articles in journals and edited books may also be included, making the catalogs periodical indexes as well.

Only *published* catalogs are listed here; major anthropological libraries and archives (and corresponding directories) can be found in Chapter 8. Both published catalogs and library collections pertaining to specific research areas are listed in the appropriate section (e.g., the *Catalogos de la Biblioteca Nacional de Antropologia e Historia* is listed in the Latin America and the Caribbean section of Chapter 7).

107. **Author and Subject Catalogues of the Tozzer Library.** Tozzer Library. 2nd ed. Boston, MA: G.K. Hall, 1988. 1,122 fiche in 8 binders ISBN 0816117314 (Continues *Catalogue of the Library of the Peabody Museum of Archaeology and Ethnology, 1963–1979).*

First issued in 1963, with supplements through 1979, the original *Catalogue of the Library of the Peabody Museum of Archaeology and Ethnology* identified the holdings of the important collection of anthropological resources held by the Tozzer Library (entry 855). In 1988, a second enlarged edition was published on microfiche that cumulates all entries from the first edition and its supplements and combines them with entries through June of 1986. This listing of approximately 1.34 million entries includes books, manuscripts, serials, pamphlets, microform materials, and periodicals held in the Tozzer Library at that point in time. From July 1986 forward, monograph entries have been published in G.K. Hall's *Bibliographic Guide to Anthropology and Archaeology* (entry 110), issued annually and citations to periodical articles are now issued in *Anthropological Literature* (entry 76). Although most of the materials in the printed catalog can now be found in either *Anthropological Literature* or Harvard's online catalog, HOLLIS (http://hollis.harvard.edu/), the *Author and Subject Catalogues* provide the only access to Tozzer's extensive (584 box) pamphlet collection that contains some unique and obscure publications.

The strength of the published catalog comes from the breadth of the collection it encompasses and from the depth of access it provides to that collection. With important holdings form throughout the world, particularly regarding Central America and Mexico, and inclusion of all subfields of anthropology, the collection serves as a rich repository of anthropological scholarship. Access to the collection is enhanced by extensive analytics, i.e., festschriften, conference proceedings, and periodicals received by the library have been indexed by author and subject since the early part of the twentieth century. The author/title catalog contains entries for editor, translator, sponsoring institution, and monograph series. The emphasis of the subject catalog is on ethnic groups, languages, and major archaeological sites. The library's pre-1986 use of specialized subject headings allows for precision searching by individual culture groups (Bemba) or concepts (puberty rites). These subject headings can also be very useful for retrospective searching in HOLLIS and *Anthropological Literature* (entry 76). The printed subject catalog might also be useful for tracing the history of the nineteen subfields of anthropology distinguished within, including cultural, social, medical, psychological, and urban anthropology, among others.

108. **A Catalog to Manuscripts at the National Anthropological Archives.** Smithsonian Institution, National Museum of Natural History Department of Anthropology. Boston, MA: G. K. Hall, 1975. 4v. ISBN 0816111944.

Much of the material in the National Anthropological Archives (entry 853) was collected by the Bureau of American Ethnology between 1879 and 1965. The overwhelming emphasis of the collection, therefore, is on Native Americans. The catalog lists over 6,000 collections of manuscripts, which include vocabularies, grammar notes, correspondence, maps, linguistic tests, journals and field notes, and administrative records of the Bureau of American Ethnology. Other materials include manuscripts from anthropological museums and papers from numerous anthropologists.

The catalog is divided into three sections. The first is a file for manuscripts of Indians of America north of Mexico. Arrangement is alphabetical by tribe, linguistic group, or name of individual, with occasional descriptive headings (e.g., "Eagle dance-Iroquois"). The second section, arranged geographically, consists of manuscripts on peoples not included in the first section. The third section contains manuscript collections arranged by accession number. A small list of drawings is located at the end of the catalog.

More recent additions to the collections can be accessed via the online *Guide to the National Anthropological Archives* (entry 113) and *SIRIS: The Smithsonian Online Catalog* <http://www.siris.si.edu/>.

109. **Dictionary Catalog of the Missionary Research Library, New York.** Missionary Research Library. Boston, MA: G. K. Hall, 1968. 17v. ISBN not assigned.

The Missionary Research Library, a separate library in the Union Theological Seminary in New York, was established by the Foreign Missions Conference of North America and collects works on missions and missionaries throughout the world. In addition to books and an extensive collection of missionary magazines, the library holds extensive files of nineteenth-century magazines, pamphlets, reports, and archives. Nearly 300,000 items, including journal articles and chapters in books, are listed in the catalog, interfiled by author, title, and subject. The early mission reports and descriptions of the societies in which the missionaries worked hold particular interest for anthropologists.

110. **G.K. Hall Bibliographic Guide to Anthropology and Archaeology.** Detroit, MI: Gale. 1999-. Annual. ISSN 0896-8101 (Continues *Bibliographic Guide to Anthropology and Archaeology*, 1988–1998).

This annual bibliography lists all publications (books, serial titles, microforms, manuscripts, maps, film, and video recordings) cataloged during the year by the Tozzer Library at Harvard (entry 855), and updates the second edition of *Author and Subject Catalogues of the Tozzer Library* (entry 107). The *Bibliographic Guide* identifies all items received in the collection beginning in June

1986, while *Anthropological Literature* (entry 76) analyzes the contents of journals and collected works.

This annual bibliography is essentially a supplement to Harvard's library catalog (HOLLIS), with each entry providing a description of the item. Multiple access points are provided, including coauthors, titles, series, and subjects. In an effort to standardize the subject headings to conform to usage in other libraries (which facilitates resource-sharing on a national level), the entries do not use the carefully developed Tozzer Library subject headings but use the Library of Congress subject headings instead. Now that this information is also available online, this print bibliography is primarily useful as a collection-development tool. As of this writing, however, the most recent issue published was the 2003 volume, which appeared in October 2004.

111. **Guide to Anthropological Fieldnotes and Manuscripts in Archival Repositories.** Leopold, Robert, compiler. National Anthropological Archives, Smithsonian Institution. 1999-. Available online at <http://www.nmnh.si.edu/naa/other_archives.htm>.

Complementing the *Guide to the National Anthropological Archives* (entry 113), this volume lists 850 collections of personal papers, anthropological fieldnotes, records of expeditions, fieldschools, conferences, and associations held in archives outside the Smithsonian Institution.

112. **A Guide to Published Library Catalogs.** Nelson, Bonnie. Metuchen, NJ: Scarecrow, 1982. 342p. ISBN 0810814773.

Written by an anthropology subject specialist, this annotated guide to library catalogs provides a useful listing of library catalogs published before 1980. Relevant sections include anthropology (including Native studies), area studies, and related subject fields such as folklore and religion. Entries provide a complete bibliographic citation and a detailed description of the scope and arrangement of each catalog. Because of the number of fields with which anthropology intersects, this description of published library catalogs can identify a wealth of resources for the advanced researcher.

113. **Guide to the National Anthropological Archives, Smithsonian Institution.** Glenn, James R. Rev., editor. Revised and enlarged edition. Washington, D.C.: National Anthropological Archives, 1996. 328p. Available online at <http://www.nmnh.si.edu/naa/guide/_toc.htm> (revised and amended).

Glenn's guide provides descriptions of more than 640 collections of personal papers, fieldnotes, and manuscripts at the National Anthropological Archives (entry 853), which includes primary source material (fieldnotes, correspondence, photographs, sound and video recordings, etc.) collected by prominent anthropologists in the United States. The records of the American Anthropological Association are also included. A complementary publication, *Guide to Anthropological Fieldnotes and Manuscripts in Archival Repositories* (entry 111), lists collections of fieldnotes and manuscripts in other institutions.

A revised and amended version of the *Guide* is available online. Collections in the National Anthropological Archives can also be searched by author/creator, title, subject and keyword on SIRIS, the Smithsonian Institution online catalog (see entry 192). Detailed findings aids for some of the collections are available online at <http://www.nmnh.si.edu/naa/guides.htm>.

114. **Index to Subject Headings.** Library of the Peabody Museum of Archaeology and Ethnology, Harvard University. Rev. ed. Boston, MA: G.K. Hall, 1971. 137p.

Used in conjunction with the *Author and Subject Catalogues of the Tozzer Library* (entry 107), the *Index to Subject Headings* facilitates locating the appropriate term in the subject catalog and is also useful for retrospective searching in *Anthropological Literature* (entry 76) and *Anthropology Plus* (entry 77). These subject headings were devised by the staff of the Peabody Museum Library (now the Tozzer Library, entry 855) to create a list of subject headings tailored to its collection. Terms include geographical names, ethnic groups (based on the *Outline of World Cultures*, entry 485), and specific concepts (e.g., culture change), with numerous cross-references. The subject headings were updated in 1981 (entry 117), but are no longer in use.

115. **The Proper Study of Mankind: An Annotated Bibliography of Manuscript Sources on Anthropology & Archeology in the Library of the American Philosophical Society.** Van Keuren, David K. Philadelphia, PA: American Philosophical Society, 1986. 79p. ISBN 0871693704. Available online at <http://www.amphilsoc.org/library/guides/vank>.

Because few detailed guides to manuscript sources in anthropology are available, this source serves as an excellent guide to the archival collection at the Library of the American Philosophical Society (entry 847). The nearly 150 entries constitute a veritable who's who in anthropology: Benedict, Kroeber, Lowie, Mead, among others. Particularly impressive are the holding of the papers of Boas, Parsons, Sapir, and Radin. The major focus of the collection, however, is Native American linguistics.

Each entry consists of the subject's name, dates, brief biographical sketch, collection name, size of collection, and description. Archival materials include correspondence, fieldnotes, photographs, and manuscripts and are of particular value to historians of anthropology.

116. **Research Catalog of the Library of the American Museum of Natural History.** American Museum of Natural History. Boston, MA: G.K. Hall, 1977. ISBN Author Catalog, 13v, ISBN 0816100640; Classed Catalog, 12v, ISBN 0816102384.

The scope of the American Museum of Natural History Library (entry 846) includes all aspects of natural history (astronomy to zoology), with an important collection in anthropology (particularly physical anthropology and North American ethnology). In addition to books, the catalog provides article-level access to journals, proceedings, and memoirs. Also included are rare books, manuscripts, letters, pamphlets, and museum and government publications, collected from 1877 through the mid-1960s. The classed catalog is arranged by the library's own decimal classification system, and specific topic searching is facilitated by the subject guide.

117. **Tozzer Library Index to Anthropological Subject Headings.** 2nd rev. ed. Boston: G. K. Hall, 1981. 177p. ISBN 0816104050.

To overcome limitations identified in the earlier subject heading list (entry 114) and to keep pace with evolving terminology, a second edition of anthropological subject headings was produced in 1981. Used in conjunction with the second revised edition of the Tozzer Library (entry 855) subject catalog (entry 110), these "custom made" headings provide superior description of and access to the contents of the collection and are also useful for searching for older entries in *Anthropological Literature* (entry 76) and *Anthropology Plus* (entry 77).

Chapter 3
Methods and Practice

This chapter covers the guides to ethnographic research, fieldwork, and ethics, as well as three particular areas of practice defined by their distinctive methodological approaches: applied anthropology, museum studies, and visual anthropology.

Methods

The titles in this section focus on anthropological methods and include handbooks covering general research methods, fieldwork, ethnography and ethics. Specialized titles are treated elsewhere; e.g., *Cross-Cultural Research Methods* addresses cross-cultural research in the tradition of Edward B. Tylor and George Peter Murdock and focuses specifically on using the Human Relations Area Files (HRAF), so it is listed with other HRAF materials in Chapter 7. For the most part, the titles included here are strictly anthropological, but exceptions were made for sources of particular interest from outside the discipline such as the *Oral History Manual* (entry 122).

118. **Analyzing Discourse: Textual Analysis for Social Research.** Fairclough, Norman. London: Routledge, 2003. 270p. ISBN 0415258928; 0415258936pa.
   Fairclough provides a guide for theoretically informed analysis of socially situated texts, be they written, spoken, or multimedia broadcast. A glossary of key terms and theorists (e.g., Bourdieu) is included.

119. **Anthropology: A Student's Guide to Theory and Method.** Barrett, Stanley R. Toronto and Buffalo, NY: University of Toronto Press, 1996. 270p. ISBN 0802008488; 0802078338pa.
   Reprinted in 1998 and 2000, this volume provides a historical overview of theory and method in anthropology. Barrett divides the history of anthropology into three phases: building the scientific foundation, patching the cracks, and demolition and reconstruction. Theory and method are treated in separate chapters for each of these phases. The final section tackles the challenge of qualitative analysis in the post-reconstruction phase and focuses a bit more on how-to than

the preceding chapters. A substantial (23 page) bibliography and indexes by name and topic are also provided.

120. **Finding Culture in Talk: A Collection of Methods.** Quinn, Naomi, editor. New York: Palgrave Macmillan, 2005. 277p. ISBN 1403969140; 1403969159pa.

This handbook presents essays by prominent anthropologists (e.g., Roy D'Andrade, Jane H. Hill, Wendy Luttrell) explicating methods for analyzing discourse and narrative.

121. **Handbook of Methods in Cultural Anthropology.** Bernard, H. Russell, editor. Walnut Creek, CA: AltaMira, 1998. 816p. ISBN 0761991514.

Geared primarily toward students, this compilation of essays is meant to explain and contextualize participant-observation fieldwork, and the various approaches that practicing anthropologists use during empirical anthropological research. Chapters exploring methodological perspectives, information gathering, interpretation, and the presentation and application of anthropological knowledge were contributed by 27 prominent anthropologists, mostly from North America. Author and subject indices are included.

122. **The Oral History Manual.** Sommer, Barbara W., and Mary Kay Quinlan. Walnut Creek, CA: AltaMira, 2002. 129p. ISBN 0759101000; 0759101019pa.

Sommer and Quinlan have created a systematic guide to conducting oral history research, complete with full-size reproducible forms, sample planning documents, checklists, and summary sheets.

123. **Preserving the Anthropological Record.** Silverman, Sydel, and Nancy J. Parezo. 2nd ed. New York: Wenner-Gren Foundation for Anthropological Research, 1995. 254p. ISBN not assigned.

This contributed volume serves as a practical guide to the issues surrounding the preservation of anthropological records (including fieldnotes, audio and visual records, and manuscripts) for individual researchers as well as for the discipline as a whole. Topics range from physical preservation of various formats to ethical considerations in archiving fieldnotes. As of this writing, an online edition <http://www.nmnh.si.edu/naa/copar/bulletins.htm> is being developed by Robert Leopold (Director of the National Anthropological Archives) and other members of the Council for the Preservation of Anthropological Records (entry 839) with funding from the Wenner-Gren Foundation (entry 833).

124. **Research Methods in Anthropology: Qualitative and Quantitative Methods.** Bernard, H. Russell. 4th ed. Walnut Creek, CA: AltaMira, 2006. 803p. ISBN 0759108684; 0759108692pa.

This well-known guide places emphasis on the quantitative approach to anthropological research. Bernard covers methodological topics such as preparing for fieldwork, selection of informants, interviewing, sampling techniques, questionnaire design, writing and managing fieldnotes, conducting a literature search, data analysis and more. Each section offers numerous examples and provides bibliographic references. The emphasis is on behavioral research; humanities-related areas of research receive scant attention. Appendices include a random number table; t and chi square distribution tables; statement of professional and ethical responsibilities from professional associations (including the American Anthropological Association and the Society for American Archaeology) and a guide to software and related resources.

125. **Using Historical Sources in Anthropology and Sociology.** Pitt, David C. New York: Holt, Rinehart and Winston, 1972. 88p. ISBN 003078758.

The purpose of this book "to set out the ways in which historical documents have been, or may be, of use to the cultural or social anthropologist" (preface). Particular emphasis is placed upon integrating documentary sources with fieldwork. Pitt begins with a discussion of historical research and identifies major sources of documentary material. Additional chapters address recording and analyzing data and present a case study on the utilization of historical documents in an anthropological research project. Though some of the descriptions of particular sources and repositories may be dated, the techniques and approaches still pertain.

Fieldwork and Ethnography

In a field long dominated by a few staid handbooks, there is now a diverse and growing set of titles on methods in anthropology, particularly ethnography and fieldwork. This can partly be explained by the fact that ethnography and other hallmarks of anthropological method like participant observation are generating considerable interest in disciplines outside of anthropology. Indeed, Sage recently launched a journal, *Ethnography* (2000-) focusing on ethnographically oriented research that fuses close, rigorous observation with sophisticated theoretical orientation across a wide range of disciplines.

126. **The Chicago Guide to Collaborative Ethnography.** Lassiter, Luke E. Chicago: University of Chicago Press, 2005. 201p. ISBN 0226468895; 0226468909pa.

This handbook explores the theoretical and methodological implications of collaboration with ethnographic subjects as "consultants rather than just informants." Lassiter's text is divided into two sections. The first part of the book provides a historical and theoretical overview of collaboration in U.S. anthropology, while the second focuses on practice and practicalities including ethical dilemmas and the challenges of presenting collaborative work to tenure committees.

127. **Critical Ethnography: Method, Ethics, and Performance.** Madison, D. Soyini. Thousand Oaks, CA: Sage, 2005. 245p. ISBN 0761929150; 0761929169pa.

This handbook focuses on critical ethnography, placing it within the broader ethnographic tradition, and demonstrating the link between theory and practice through fictional case studies. Attention is given to ethical issues, methodological techniques, interpretation, and theoretical concepts (including critical race theory, queer theory, and phenomenology).

128. **Doing Ethnographic Research: Fieldwork Settings.** Grills, Scott, editor. Thousand Oaks, CA: Sage, 1998. 256p. ISBN 0761908919; 0761908927pa.

In this edited volume, experienced researchers working in a wide variety of settings reflect on the challenges of fieldwork and how they managed particular problems encountered in their fieldsites. Lacking an index, this collection may be valuable for the novice ethnographer or for use in a course covering ethnographic methods, but is not useful for ready reference or quick consultation.

129. **Doing Fieldwork: Ethnographic Methods for Research in Developing Countries and Beyond.** Fife, Wayne. New York: Palgrave Macmillan, 2005. 174p. ISBN 1403969086; 1403969094pa.

Fife, a Canadian anthropologist, provides a succinct guide to the "craft" of ethnography, drawing on examples from his own experience in the field. The first two sections cover methods for macro-level research (with chapters on using historical sources, contemporary scholarly sources, and newspapers and government documents) and micro-level research (participant-observation, interviewing, and self-reporting). The final section addresses analysis, creating and testing theory, and "academic and practical writing." The volume is indexed, and includes a handy "methodological check list."

130. **Doing Team Ethnography: Warnings and Advice.** Erickson, Ken C., and Donald D. Stull. Thousand Oaks, CA: Sage, 1998. 70p. ISBN 0761906665; 0761906673pa.

This concise guide to the process of engaging in collaborative ethnography is written by anthropologists and thoroughly grounded in the anthropological tradition, although it challenges longstanding assumptions about the lone ethnographer and the emphasis on individual achievement.

131. **The Ethnographer's Method.** Stewart, Alex. Thousand Oaks, CA: Sage, 1998. 97p. (Qualitative Research Methods Series, 46). ISBN 0761903933; 0761903941pa.

Stewart outlines normative standards for ethnographic research and provides guidelines for presenting ethnographic findings to those outside the field. An appendix provides an "Editorial and Funding Review Checklist for Ethnographic Method" intended to provide a guide to evaluating ethnographic work.

132. **Ethnographer's Toolkit.** Schensul, Jean J., and Margaret D. LeCompte. Walnut Creek, CA: AltaMira, 1999. 7v. ISBN 0761990429.

Each of the seven volumes in this set treats a different aspect of ethnographic research, from interviews and participant observation to social networks and spatial data. An excellent resource for both novice researchers and old hands interested exploring a particular method in depth, these guides strike a balance between being accessible and providing a nuanced perspective on complex methodological, ethical and theoretical issues.

133. **Ethnographic Methods.** O'Reilly, Karen. London and New York: Routledge, 2005. 252p. ISBN 0415321557; 0415321565.

Grounded in the British tradition of rigorous training in the methods and epistemological grounding of ethnographic practice, this handbook provides a concise but comprehensive introduction to the topic. Case studies from student research illustrate particular points and are used as the bases for exploring methodological complexities, providing material of interest to seasoned scholars as well as students.

134. **Ethnographic Research: A Guide to General Conduct.** Ellen, R. F. London and Orlando: Academic Press, 1984. 403p. ISBN 0122371801.

First published in 1984 and reprinted in 1987, this classic handbook reflects the British emphasis on rigorous training in field methodology. Ellen covers ethnographic research, data gathering, and the practical aspects of fieldwork in a format that is suitable for ready reference consultation.

135. **Ethnography.** Bryman, Alan. London: Sage, 2001. 4v. ISBN 0761970916.

These four volumes bring together a collection of key readings on ethnography from classic and contemporary practitioners in anthropology and sociology.

136. **Ethnography: Principles in Practice.** Hammersley, Martyn, and Paul Atkinson. 2nd ed. New York and London: Routledge, 1995. 323p. ISBN 0415086647.

Frequently reprinted and still a standard text for courses covering ethnographic methods, this handbook provides a clear overview of ethnographic practice. While the first chapter grapples with philosophical issues and defines ethnography as inherently reflexive, the remainder of the volume tackles practicalities such as note-taking, listening, and asking questions negotiating access, field relations, and analysis.

137. **Ethnography Step By Step.** Fetterman, David M. 2nd ed. Newbury Park, CA: Sage, 1998. 156p. ISBN 0803928904; 0761913858pa.

Though not unique in the literature, this manual for ethnographers makes a distinct contribution in addressing the concerns of applied anthropologists and those working closer to home as well as the ethnographer in traditional societies. Organized thematically, the guide begins with an overview of theory, research design and related anthropological concepts (emic and etic perspectives, contextualization) and goes on to describe specific methods and techniques, analysis, writing, and ethics. Though the products are rapidly developing and changing, the section on ethnographic equipment briefly addresses the use of the computer as an ethnographic tool and Fetterman has set up a companion web page "Ethnography and the Internet" that provides an updated version of the equipment chapter. Each chapter contains numerous references to recent literature.

138. Field Projects in Anthropology: A Student Handbook. Crane, Julia G., and Micheal V. Angrosino. 3rd ed. Prospect Heights, IL: Waveland Press, 1992. 200p. ISBN 0881336858.

Written primarily for undergraduates and beginning graduate students, this handbook presents a series of projects that represent some of the most commonly used data-collection techniques, such as participant observation, collecting life histories, designing a survey, planning a community study, and others. Each chapter begins with a general introduction and discussion of the field technique in question, providing numerous illustrations (and citations) from actual field situations. A sample project is then proposed and described, followed by a selected annotated bibliography of items useful in describing the topic area and in planning the project. Conceived in general terms (e.g., becoming a participant-observer within a religious group), the projects are particularly applicable for fieldwork courses.

139. Fieldwork. Pole, Christopher J., editor. London: Sage, 2005. 4v. ISBN 1412900301.

A collection of previously published writings by anthropologists and sociologists, this set is useful mostly for the handy arrangement of these articles into thematic groupings, such as "sensitive and stressful situations," "visual methods and fieldwork," and "leaving the field."

140. Globe Trotting in Sandals: A Field Guide to Cultural Research. McKinney, Carol Virginia. Dallas, TX: SIL International, 2000. 337p. ISBN 1556710860.

McKinney, who teaches anthropology at the SIL International's Graduate Institute of Applied Linguistics, provides a practical guide to fieldwork and data collection that blends qualitative and quantitative methods.

141. A Guide to Qualitative Field Research. Bailey, Carol A. 2nd ed. Thousand Oaks, CA: Pine Forge Press, 2007. 214p. ISBN 1412936500.

Geared toward sociologists, this guide to conducting qualitative field research may also be useful to undergraduate and graduate students in anthropology. The section on data analysis techniques, in which Bailey clearly elucidates ten specific techniques (e.g., taxonomies or critical events), is particularly noteworthy.

142. A Handbook for Social Science Field Research: Essays & Bibliographic Sources on Research Design and Methods. Perecman, Ellen, and Sara R Curran. Thousand Oaks, CA: Sage, 2006. 254p. ISBN 1412916801; 141291681Xpa.

A collection of essays from prominent scholars from a wide range of social science disciplines examines research methods from a perspective grounded in real life experiences. The ethics of fieldwork is given particularly attention, both in individual chapters throughout the volume and in a separate chapter. Part I explores "tools" such as archives, case studies, ethnography, oral histories, focus groups, surveys, and combined qualitative and quantitative methods. Part II, "Essentials for conducting research," includes reflections on the essential considerations and background reading for ethnographic fieldwork, case studies, research design, ethics, and maintaining perspective. All chapters include bibliographic essays compiled by the editors that include classic and contemporary sources arranged topically with subheadings highlighting the various types of materials available.

143. **Handbook of Ethnography.** Atkinson, Paul, editor. Thousand Oaks, CA: Sage, 2001. 507p. ISBN 0761964800; 0761964819pa.

With chapters by anthropologists and sociologists from the United States, the United Kingdom, and elsewhere, this volume provides a state-of-the-art overview of current ethnographic practice. The chapters are grouped into three sections covering disciplinary and theoretical contexts, domains and settings, and ethnographic practice—though these distinctions tend to be rather fluid. Each chapter includes a substantial (2–7 page) list of references for further research and a comprehensive index is included at the back of the volume.

144. **In the Field: An Introduction to Field Research.** Burgess, Robert G. London: George Allen & Unwin, 1984. 254p. ISBN 0043120172; 0043120180.

Written by a sociologist with an interest in using ethnographic methods to study contemporary society, this handbook will also be of interest to social anthropologists working in urban settings. Practical, theoretical, and ethical issues are systematically explored. Separate name and subject indexes are appended, along with a lengthy (26 pages) list of references.

145. **Learning a Field Language.** Burling, Robbins. Prospect Heights, IL: Waveland Press, 2000. 112p. ISBN 1577661230.

According to Burling (himself a specialist in anthropological linguistics), discussions of linguistic field methods have usually come from linguists who are more concerned with the analysis and structure of language than with communication. Thus his guide is addressed to anthropologists who are not specialists in linguistics and stresses comprehension and exchange of information. After a brief survey and critique of other field language manuals, he provides practical suggestions on understanding and speaking. Although not exhaustive, the text provides a useful starting point for those entering the field without benefit of a dictionary or grammar of the language. Originally published in 1984, it was reissued in 2000 with minor updates and changes.

146. **Overseas Research: A Practical Guide.** Barrett, Christopher B, and Jeffrey W. Cason. Baltimore, MD and London: Johns Hopkins University Press, 1997. 142p. ISBN 0801855136; 0801855144pa.

This practical guide to overseas research grew out of the need to prepare an interdisciplinary group faculty and students to do fieldwork for a MacArthur/Social Science Research Council program studying local perspectives on regional conflicts. Barret and Cason provide an accessible overview of the logistics of overseas fieldwork through all stages of the process, from funding to post-fieldwork culture shock, obligations, and opportunities. A selected topical bibliography and an index are also provided.

147. **Qualitative Research and Hypermedia: Ethnography for the Digital Age.** Dicks, Bella. Thousand Oaks, CA: Sage, 2005. 200p. ISBN 076196097X.

This guide has a two-fold purpose: to provide the tools, both theoretical and practical, needed "to conduct ethnography in the age of email and the internet" and to introduce readers to technologies available that can facilitate data collection, analysis, and representation.

148. **The SAGE Handbook of Fieldwork.** Hobbs, Dick, and Richard Wright, editors. London; Thousand Oaks, CA: Sage, 2006. 399p. ISBN 0761974458.

Twenty-two contributed chapters explore the ethical, reflexive, and practical dimensions of fieldwork in a representative range of sites across the globe.

149. **Writing Ethnographic Fieldnotes.** Emerson, Robert M., Rachel I. Fretz, and Linda L. Shaw. Chicago, IL: University of Chicago Press, 1995. 254p. ISBN 0226206807; 0226206815pa.

Approaching note-taking and ethnographic writing as a "craft that can be taught," Emerson, Fretz, and Shaw guide novice ethnographers through the process of transforming direct experience and observation first into written fieldnotes and then into finished texts.

Bibliographies

150. **Anthropological Fieldwork: An Annotated Bibliography.** Gravel, Pierre, and Robert B. Marks Ridinger. New York: Garland, 1988. 241p. ISBN 0824066421.

This excellent bibliography annotates 700 books and articles written from the early twentieth century through 1986 that deal with the practical aspects of anthropological fieldwork and includes citations for English, French, and German works. The entries are arranged alphabetically by author; the index is arranged by subject and provides access to specific topics such as ethics, interviewing, preparation for the field, language training, writing and interpretation, and personal accounts. The geographic index identifies works focusing on a particular area. The authors also include works on general anthropological research and methods.

151. **Bibliography of Fieldwork, Research Methods and Ethnography in Sociocultural Anthropology.** Telban, Borut. Available online at <http://coombs.anu.edu.au/Biblio/biblio_fieldwork1.html>.

This Web site provides a selected bibliography organized into several thematic areas: introduction to fieldwork; research methods; ethics; sex, gender and fieldwork; writing ethnography; history and theory; and personal accounts of anthropological fieldwork. Most entries date from prior to 2002.

Ethics

An announcement for the Presidential Session on "Placing Ethics at the Discipline's Center" at the December 2005 American Anthropological Association meeting notes that:

> Anthropology has had a certain ambivalence toward ethics. It is easy to mention prominent anthropologists who model ethical behavior: Mooney at Wound Knee, Boas on race, and, today, Farmer with AIDS. But if we move beyond them, there appears less concern. In the training of students, for example, theory is often highlighted, research ethics much less so.

The situation does seem to be changing, however, and the calling of this special presidential session attests to the fact that ethics is becoming a central topic of discussion within the discipline. There is certainly a growing body of literature, ranging from handbooks and internet gateways to edited volumes that engage ethical dilemmas in the field.

152. **AAA Ethics Homepage.** American Anthropological Association. Available online at <http://www.aaanet.org/committees/ethics/ethics.htm>.

The goal of this site hosted by the American Anthropological Association (AAA) is to provide "resources to assist anthropologists when dealing with ethical issues." Links to the AAA *Code of Ethics* (1998), *Statement on Confidentiality of Field Notes* (2003), *Statement on Ethnography and Institutional Review Boards* (2004), and the *Final Report of the El Dorado Task Force* and associated documents are included. Discussions of ethical issues and links to other resources, including a selection of links to the ethics codes of other associations, are also provided.

153. **Ethical Issues in Archaeology.** Zimmerman, Larry J., Karen D. Vitelli, and Julie Hollowell-Zimmer, editors. Walnut Creek, CA: AltaMira Press in cooperation with the Society for American Archaeology, 2003. 300p. ISBN 0759102708; 0759102716pa.

Signed chapters explore the ethics of archeological fieldwork, museum collection, and cultural resource management from a variety of perspectives. Includes bibliographical references (pp. 263–284) and a comprehensive index.

154. **The Ethics of Archaeology: Philosophical Perspectives on Archaeological Practice.** Scarre, Christopher, and Geoffrey Scarre. Cambridge, UK: Cambridge University Press, 2006. 318p. ISBN 0521840112; 0521549426pa.

This collection of essays written by anthropologists, archaeologists, and philosophers from a number of different countries explores ethical issues and dilemmas inherent in archaeology. Rather than offer simple, prescriptive solutions, the essays explore the complexities and grapple with the underlying issues of how to best serve the needs of science and of local communities, both living and dead.

155. **Handbook on Ethical Issues in Anthropology.** Cassell, Joan, and Sue-Ellen Jacobs, editors. Washington, DC: American Anthropological Association, 1987. 108p. ISBN 0913167193pa. Available online at <http://www.aaanet.org/committees/ethics/toc.htm>.

Though the topic of ethics within the profession has implications beyond fieldwork, most of the discussions and case studies in this handbook involve issues that arise when working in the field. Actual and fictional dilemmas (conflict of interest, substance abuse, ownership of fieldnotes) are presented along with responses and comments. As with most handbooks, this work is less a reference book than a collection of review essays bearing on relevant issues and sources. Included in the appendix is the American Anthropological Association's code of ethics, *The Principles of Professional Responsibility*. The *Handbook* is also reproduced online in the "Ethics" section the American Anthropological Association's (entry 745) website.

156. **Handle With Care: Ownership and Control of Ethnographic Records.** Jaarsma, Sjoerd R., editor. Pittsburgh, PA: University of Pittsburgh Press, 2002. 264p. ISBN 0822957779pa.

In this volume, 14 scholars discuss experiences involving the responsible treatment of cultural property (both tangible and intangible) and repatriation of artifacts. This volume grew out of a conference panel and all of the case studies here deal with Pacific Islands examples, but the issues raised are of broad interest.

157. **Human Subjects Protections and Anthropology.** Plattner, Stuart. Available online at <http://aaanet.org/press/an/infocus/hrp/Plattner.htm>.

From the longtime director of the National Science Foundation Anthropology Program, this web page discusses human subjects protection in anthropology. In addition to providing advice on complying with federal regulations and working with institutional review boards, Plattner discusses the unique considerations that pertain to anthropological research.

Applied Anthropology

Anthropology is a discipline with roots in both the biological and social sciences, and anthropologists have long been involved in gathering knowledge and testing theories relating to the human condition. Using anthropological methods and theories to solve human problems represents an important specialty in the field known as applied or practicing anthropology. Defined as "putting anthropology to use," applied anthropology generally lies outside the academic arena, and applied anthropologists take on roles such as advocates in community development or consultants in public or private agencies.

The standard anthropology reference sources have generally focused more on theory and research than on application, but applied anthropologists are beginning to develop a high profile and a concurrent "control" of the literature. The Society for Applied Anthropology (entry 829) and the AAA's National Association for the Practice of Anthropology (entry 759) have been instrumental in furthering the cause of applied anthropology within the profession. Respectively, they sponsor the journals *Human Organization* (entry 673) and *Practicing Anthropology* (entry 692) and have developed useful reference works such as the *Directory of Practicing Anthropologists* (entry 61).

Literature Surveys and Reviews

158. **Applied Anthropology: An Introduction.** Van Willigen, John. 3rd ed. Westport, CT: Bergin & Garvey, 2002. 285p. ISBN 089789832X; 0897898338pa.

Van Willigen, founder of the Applied Anthropology Documentation Project (entry 169), provides a thorough introduction and overview of the field of applied anthropology. Beginning with a history of its development, he discusses the question of ethics and describes "interventions" in anthropology, including action anthropology, research and development, community development, advocacy anthropology, and the role of the anthropologist in policy studies. The final section focuses on practical aspects of practicing anthropology and making a living with a discussion of the job market for applied anthropologists.

Numerous examples, case studies and references are included throughout. Each section has a list of titles for further reading, and the references are cumulated in a lengthy bibliography. A detailed index rounds out this useful text.

159. **Development Anthropology: Encounters in the Real World.** Nolan, Riall W. Boulder, CO: Westview Press, 2002. 345p. ISBN 0813309840; 0813309832.

Nolan, who currently serves as the Director of the Institute of Global Studies and Affairs at the University of Cincinnati and served for many years on international development projects, provides an excellent overview of the application of anthropological methods and theories to real world problems and social change. Nolan provides an account of the history of international development, an overview of the cycle of development project and some proposals for a rapprochement between the development arena and the academy.

160. **Tourism and Applied Anthropologists: Linking Theory and Practice.** Wallace, Tim. Arlington, VA: National Association for the Practice of Anthropology, 2005. 273p. (*NAPA Bulletin*, 23). ISBN 1931303223.

Part of the ongoing series of substantial bulletins issued by the National Association for the Practice of Anthropology (entry 759) exploring a particular topic or approach of current issue, this collection of papers illustrate the "directions the anthropology of travel and tourism is taking in theory and in practice" (preface).

Series

161. **NAPA Bulletin.** University of California Press for the American Anthropological Association: National Association for the Practice of Anthropology. 1985-. Irregular. ISSN 1556-4789; 1556-4797e.

A peer-reviewed publication of the National Association for the Practice of Anthropology (entry 759), "dedicated to the practical problem-solving and policy applications of anthropological knowledge and methods." Issues published in 2005 tackled topics such as *Tourism and Applied Anthropologists: Linking Theory and Practice* (No. 23) and *Creating Evaluation Anthropology: Introducing an Emerging Subfield* (No. 24).

Indexes, Abstracts, and Databases

162. **PAIS International**, Vol. 1-. New York: Public Affairs Information Service. 1991-. Monthly. ISSN 1051-4015. Available online by subscription.

Beginning in 1991, the well-known *PAIS Bulletin* (1915–1990) and its companion volume, *PAIS Foreign Language Index (1971–1990),* merged to form *PAIS International*. Unlike most current affairs foreign and domestic indexes, *PAIS International* covers not only journals but monographs, agency reports, and foreign and domestic government documents. In addition to over 1,400 English-language journals, materials published in French, German, Italian, Portuguese, and Spanish are included, with brief abstract-type notes.

Through this index is not designed to identify anthropological scholarship, its coverage of policy-oriented literature in economics, sociology, and political science, particularly with regard to developing countries, makes it a useful tool for background or applied research.

Handbooks and Manuals

163. **Anthropology in Practice: Building a Career Outside the Academy.** Nolan, Riall W. Boulder, CO: Lynne Rienner Publishers, 2003. 213p. ISBN 1555879578; 1555879853pa.

Drawing on his experience working for international development agencies, Nolan (Director, Institute of Global Studies and Affairs, University of Cincinnati) provides an eminently practical guide for anthropologists (and anthropologists-in-training) interested in pursuing careers outside the academy. He offers advice to those still in school on academic training and graduate study, as well as more general advice on the job search, career development, and tips for successfully advancing the anthropological perspective in policy and planning. Sample resumes, cover letters, and an appendix of resources that includes websites of potential employers are among the tools Nolan provides to make the job search easier.

164. **Anthropology in Use: A Source Book of Anthropological Practice.** Van Willigen, John. Boulder, CO: Westview, 1991. 254p. ISBN 0813382505.

This unique source is at once a bibliography, a directory, and a literature review. Van Willigen describes research projects in which anthropology has been applied to real world problems and lists any associated publications. He also provides a timeline of relevant legislation and appointments of anthropologists to administrative or policy positions.

165. **Applied Anthropology: Domains of Application.** Kedia, Satish, and John Van Willigen, editors. Westport, Conn. Praeger, 2005. 370p. ISBN 0275978419; 0275978427pa.

Satish and Van Willigen invited a diverse group of professionals to reflect on how applied anthropology can and has contributed to various areas of practical application including business and industry education, environment, health and medicine, and the resettlement of displaced peoples. One of the intended purpose of the volume is to suggest ways that people with anthropological backgrounds can apply their training to other, seemingly unrelated fields, but it also serves as a useful introduction to the areas discussed (including the anthropology of health and medicine, environment, education, and nutrition).

166. **Training Manual in Development Anthropology.** Partridge, William, editor. Washington, DC: American Anthropological Association, 1984. 122p. (Special Publication of the American Anthropological Association and the Society for Applied Anthropology, no. 17). ISBN 0913167029.

This manual was written to help practicing anthropologists become more effective in their work on international development projects (such as those sponsored by the World Bank or the U.S. Agency for International Development). The first section discusses anthropology in the context of development: the role of the anthropologist, project planning and design, implementation, and monitoring and evaluation. The second part presents brief case studies. The third section provides a useful annotated bibliography of more than 200 books, articles, and reports arranged by topic (education, women's roles) and geographic area.

167. **Working with Indigenous Knowledge: A Guide for Researchers.** Grenier, Louise. Ottawa: International Development Research Centre, 1998. 115p. ISBN 0889368473.

Geared toward to development professionals, this guide will be of interest to applied anthropologists interested in exploring "what indigenous knowledge can contribute to a sustainable development strategy that accounts for the potential of the local environment and the experience and wisdom of the indigenous population" (Book jacket). Grenier weaves together theory, practice, and examples from the field to provide a state-of-the-art review of research on indigenous knowledge.

Bibliographies

168. **Anthropology in Use: A Bibliographic Chronology of the Development of Applied Anthropology.** Van Willigen, John. Pleasantville, NY: Redgrave, 1980. 150p. ISBN 0913178667.

Beginning with a citation to a directive from Pope Gregory in A.D. 596 concerning the conduct of missionaries with regard to pagan sacrifices, this annotated bibliography provides a chronological record of "anthropology put to use." Its purpose is to document the history of applied anthropology and to identify existing case studies that may have applicability to other projects. The material cited includes over 300 books, journal articles, and dissertations as well as more elusive literature such as technical reports. Access to specific authors, agencies, topics and geographic regions is provided through the indexes.

Libraries, Archives, and Special Collections

169. **Applied Anthropology Documentation Project**
c/o John van Willigen
Special Collections and Digital Programs
King Building
University of Kentucky
Lexington, KY 40506
(859) 257-8611

Because documents produced by applied anthropologists are generally not available through traditional publishing outlets such as journals and books, they become "fugitive" literature—difficult to identify and gain access to. This material, however, is valuable not only for understanding specific projects and the roles of the anthropologist, but as a record for the field of applied anthropology itself. In order to provide access to these materials, the Society for Applied Anthropology established the Applied Anthropology Documentation Project in 1978. Project staff collects and organizes the written materials produced by practicing anthropologists in the course of their work, including technical reports, social impact assessments, conference papers, practicum and internship reports, curriculum materials, legal briefs, pamphlets, and proposals. Typical examples include a report of health practices of the Bhils or a survey of the nutritional status of children in a Brakna village. Materials are cataloged using Library of Congress subject headings and are accessible through the OCLC library network and available through interlibrary loan. New materials are cited in *Practicing Anthropology* (entry 692) and in the new publication section of *Anthropology News* (entry 98). The Applied Anthropology Documentation Project welcomes donated materials but did not have a website as of this writing.

Internet Gateways

170. **Public Anthropology.** Borofsky, Robert. Available online at <http://www.publicanthropology.org>.

Maintained by Robert Borofsky, Professor of Anthropology at Hawaii Pacific University, this website includes publications related to applied anthropology, an archive of student-authored summaries of articles in core journals, and a photo gallery.

Museum and Cultural Heritage Studies

The relationship between museums and anthropology is longstanding. The first departments of anthropology generally grew up alongside museums such as the Peabody Museum at Harvard and prominent anthropologists like Boas spent the early parts of their careers as museum curators. Museums are intimately involved with the collection and preservation of ethnographic and archaeological artifacts, sponsor primary research through laboratories and research centers, and seek to educate the public. The titles here represent a small sample of reference sources that relate to anthropology and museums, with a particularly selective section on handbooks and manuals. (See also the "Museum Directories" section of Chapter 8.)

Guides to the Reference Literature

171. **Keyguide to Information Sources in Museum Studies.** Woodhead, Peter, and Geoffrey Stansfield. 2nd ed. London: Mansell, 1994. 224p. ISBN 1884964117; 0720121515.

A standard source for information on museums and museum studies, the first edition of this title was named a *Choice* "Outstanding Academic/Reference Book" in 1989. Like the other titles in this series (one of which, *Keyguide to Information Sources in Archaeology* (entry 198) was also authored by Woodhead), this volume provides an overview of the field, an annotated bibliography of key publications and a directory of organizations. The bibliography and directory were both updated extensively from the first edition and now include broader international coverage.

172. **The Museum: A Reference Guide.** Shapiro, Michael Steve, editor. New York: Greenwood, 1990. 385p. ISBN 0313236860.

In the introduction, Shapiro asserts that the literature on museums remained "substantially disorganized" for many years, making it virtually inaccessible to all but the museum community. This reference guide is intended to redress the situation by offering authoritative essays that provide an introductory historical narrative, survey of sources, and bibliographic checklist of additional titles that relate to specific types of museums and issues pertaining to museum studies.

In addition to the chapter on natural history museums (which includes anthropology), relevant chapters include those addressing museum collections, exhibits, museum education, and the public and the museum. The book concludes with an extensive listing of over 200 museum directories organized geographically, a directory of museum archives and special collections, and a selective list of museum publications.

Dictionaries and Encyclopedias

173. **Ethnographic Thesaurus (ET).** American Folklore Society, in partnership with the American Folklife Center at the Library of Congress. 2005. Available online at <http://www.afsnet.org/thesaurus/>.

The Ethnographic Thesaurus "is a comprehensive controlled list of terms to be used in describing ethnographic research collections . . . and to classify cultural information" ("About the Ethnographic Thesaurus"). Still in the early stages of development as of this writing, this joint project by American Folklore Society and the American Folklife Center at the Library of Congress (with funding from the Mellon Foundation) promises to provide an invaluable tool for anyone who works with ethnological collections. A fairly sophisticated interface (and underlying data structure) allows terms to be viewed in an alphabetic, hierarchical, or rotated display. The site also includes a useful compilation of links to online thesauri <http://www.afsnet.org/thesaurus/thesauri.html> that is an excellent starting point for research on ethnographic terminology in specific domains (e.g., clothing, geographic, or material culture).

Handbooks and Manuals

174. **The Archaeologist's Manual for Conservation: A Guide to Non-Toxic, Minimal Intervention Artifact Stabilization.** Rodgers, Bradley A. New York: Kluwer, 2004. 214p. ISBN 0306484668; 0306484676pa.

Rodgers provides a step-by-step manual for stabilizing artifacts as they are excavated, as well as for objects already held in museum collections. Chapters detail methods for handling specific materials (wood, iron, copper, glass, ceramic, composite artifacts, organics, textiles, and leather) and each opens with a handy flowchart. The artifact conservation procedures outlined here will be of interest to all museum professionals charged with the long-term care and preservation of material culture.

175. **Curating Archaeological Collections: From the Field to the Repository.** Sullivan, Lynne P., and S. Terry Childs. Walnut Creek, CA: AltaMira, 2003. 150p. (*Archaeologist's Toolkit*, 6). ISBN 0759100241pa; 0759104026.

The sixth volume in AltaMira's *Archaeologist's Toolkit*, this guide covers all aspects of curation from acquisition, cataloging, storage to display. Sullivan and Childs also discuss the history of archeological curation in the United States, current legislation, and ethical issues surrounding the acquisition and display of cultural artifacts.

176. **Introduction to Museum Work.** Burcaw, George Ellis. 3rd ed. Lanham, MA: AltaMira, 1997. 237p. ISBN 0761989250; 0761989269pa.

Endorsed by the Documentation Center of the International Conference of Museums as exemplary of museum training, this has long been a standard reference book for practicing museum professionals as well as a standard classroom textbook. The basics of museum building and design, finances, and day-to-day operation are covered.

177. **Legal Primer on Managing Museum Collections.** Malaro, Marie C. 2nd ed. Washington, DC: Smithsonian Institution Press, 1998. 507p. ISBN 1560987626; 1560987871pa.

Although not addressing anthropological museums specifically, this handbook on museum personnel addresses important legal aspects of collection management that have implications for ethnological collections. Relevant sections include acquisitions policies (including removing objects from their country of origin), disposal and deaccessioning, incoming and outgoing loans, care of the collection, insurance and public access. Each chapter provides an overview of the issues and provides specific examples and appropriate legal references.

178. **New Museum Theory and Practice: An Introduction.** Marstine, Janet, editor. Rev ed. Malden, MA : Blackwell, 2006. 332p. ISBN 1405105585; 1405105593pa.

Twelve chapters by 14 archivists, conservators, curators, scholars, and teachers engage the central issues in museum practice and theory. Geared toward graduates and advanced undergraduates in museum studies and related areas, this text provides an accessible overview of state of the art practice in the field.

Bibliographies

179. **Bibliographies.** International Council of Museums. Available online at <http://icom.museum/biblio_list.html>.

A topically organized list of bibliographies pertaining to various aspects of museum practice provided by the International Council of Museums.

Internet Gateways

180. **Council for Museum Anthropology.** Available online at <http://www.nmnh.si.edu/anthro/cma>.

The Council for Museum Anthropology's (entry 754) website includes a listing "Sites of Interest to Museum Professionals" and a directory of programs offering museum training for anthropologists based on a survey of course and programs conducted in 1996.

181. **UNESCO Culture Sector.** Available online at <http://portal.unesco.org/culture>.

This site brings together resources created and complied by UNESCO's Culture Sector related to their mission of "promoting cultural diversity, with special emphasis on the tangible and intangible heritage."

Visual Anthropology

Visual anthropology has long been a distinct field of study with a well-developed literature. Internationally, the Commission on Visual Anthropology (entry 806) publishes the journal *Visual Anthropology* (entry 695) while the AAA Society of Visual Anthropology produces the *Visual Anthropology Review* (entry 696).

Literature Survey and Reviews

182. **The Visual Culture Reader.** Mirzoeff, Nicholas, editor. 2nd ed. London: Routledge, 2002. 737p. ISBN 0415252210; 0415252229pa.

This reader brings together key articles and specially commissioned pieces exploring visual communication from a variety of disciplinary perspectives, arranged thematically and accompanied by suggestions for further reading. The introductory section explores the development of visual studies in the context of globalization and digital culture.

Handbooks and Manuals

183. **Doing Visual Ethnography: Images, Media, and Representation in Research.** Pink, Sarah. 2nd ed. Thousand Oaks, CA: Sage, 2006. 196p. ISBN 1412923476; 1412923484pa.

This handbook explores the use (and potential use) of visual media in ethnographic research. In addition to traditional media, such as photography, film, and video, Pink also considers emerging forms of electronic and hypermedia.

184. **The Future of Visual Anthropology: Engaging the Senses.** Pink, Sarah. London and New York: Routledge, 2006. 166p. ISBN 0415357640; 0415357659pa.

This volume presents a collection of essays (some published or presented previously, others written expressly for this volume) by Sarah Pink examining the current practice of visual anthropology, its historical development and possibilities for empirical, methodological and theoretical advancement within the field. Pink is particularly interested in exploring the impact of the "wide range of visual and digital technologies that have transformed visual research and analysis" within anthropology and closely allied research areas in the humanities and the social sciences. The usefulness of this volume as a reference work is further enhanced by a 12-page list of references and a comprehensive index.

185. **Principles of Visual Anthropology.** Hockings, Paul, editor. 3rd ed. Berlin; New York: Mouton de Gruyter, 2003. 562p. ISBN 311017930X.

The third edition of this classic handbook covers film and videography in anthropological research; the uses of still photography, archives and videotape, as well as ethnographic film and its relations with cinema and television.

186. **Working Images: Visual Research and Representation in Ethnography.** Pink, Sarah, Laszlo Kurti, and Ana Isabel Afonso, editors. London; New York: Routledge, 2004. 224p. ISBN 0415306418; 041530654Xpa.

Chapters by prominent visual anthropologists "explore how old and new visual media can be integrated into contemporary forms of research and representation." Working with media ranging from drawings, photographs and film to cartoons and online technologies, the authors draw upon their fieldwork experiences to demonstrate the use of visual methods to both produce and communicate cultural knowledge.

Bibliographies

187. **A Bibliography of Ethnographic Films.** Husmann, Rolf. Göttingen: Lit, 1992. 335p. (Göttinger Kulturwissenschaftliche Schriften, no. 1). ISBN 3894733527.

Husman has collected and organized over 3,000 references (including 1,000 film reviews) to publications on ethnographic films. This comprehensive bibliography covers the European literature as thoroughly as it does the North American. The citations are divided into useful categories (book and articles, reports of conferences/symposia/festivals, film catalogs/filmographies/bibliographies and film reviews) and indexed by film title, film author, film and book reviewer, geographical regions and ethnic groups.

Libraries, Archives, and Special Collections

188. **Guide to the Collections of the Human Studies Film Archives.** Wintle, Pamela, and John P. Homiak. Washington: National Museum of Natural History, Smithsonian Institution, 1995-. Available online at <http://www.nmnh.si.edu/naa/guide/film_toc.htm> (revised version of the printed edition; accessed October 19, 2006).

Founded in 1975, the Human Studies Film Archives (HSFA) is an internationally recognized center within the Smithsonian devoted to collecting, preserving, documenting, and disseminating ethnographic and anthropological moving image materials in all formats. The HFSA's collection includes nearly 8 million feet of original ethnographic film and video footage.

The guide to the HFSA collection is available online and periodically updated in that format. Within the guide, film and video titles are organized by major geographical area with individual titles listed chronologically thereunder. Two-letter prefixes denote geographical area. Films can also be located through geopolitical, ethnic group, and subject indexes.

Media and Film Catalogs

189. **Anthropology Review Database.** Jarvis, Hugh W. University of Buffalo Department of Anthropology. Available online at <http://wings.buffalo.edu/anthropology/ARD/>.

The *Anthropology Review Database* (see entry 90 for full annotation) includes reviews of anthropological films and videos, audio recordings, software, multimedia and online resources, as well as books.

190. **Films for Anthropological Teaching.** Heider, Karl G., and Carol Hermer. 8th ed. Arlington, VA: American Anthropological Association, 1995. 324p. ISBN 0913167657.

Lists and annotates 3,000 films useful for teaching anthropology with indexes by geographical area, topic, name, and film title.

191. **Haddon: The Online Catalogue of Ethnographic Footage 1895–1945.** Oxford University, Economic and Social Research Council. 1996-. Available online at <http://www.bodley.ox.ac.uk/external/isca/haddon/HADD_home.html>.

This web-based database contains records of over 1,500 films and lengths of film footage shot between 1895 and 1945. Most of the material is documentary and was shot outside of Western Europe. This collection is virtual; the films in the catalog are housed in institutions around the world.

192. **SIRIS Image Gallery.** Smithsonian Institution. Available online at <http://sirismm.si.edu/siris/sirisimagegallery.htm>.

The *SIRIS* (Smithsonian Institution Research Information System's) *Image Gallery* contains over 110,000 electronic images from several archival repositories at the Smithsonian. Although this is just a small sample of the images available in the collections held by the Smithsonian, it provides large and rich selection of images that is useful for a variety of purposes. The images can be browsed by the repository where they are held or by their physical format.

Image Sources

193. **ARTstor.** New York: ARTstor, 2003-. Available online by subscription.

ARTstor is a digital library of images associated with information and software tools designed for classroom and research use. The database currently contains approximately 400,000 images from a wide range of cultures and time periods that can be search, browsed, and downloaded. The emphasis is on high arts and architecture, but this resource may be of interest to those exploring various aspects of visual culture. Collections of particular interest to anthropology include Native American Art and Culture from the National Anthropological Archive, the Huntington Archive of Asian Art and Mellon International Dunhuang Archive.

194. **OAIster.** University of Michigan Digital Library Production Service. <http://oaister.umdl.umich.edu/o/oaister/>.

OAIster provide a single point of access to digital resources dispersed across repositories worldwide and can provide a convenient point of access to visual resources of interest to anthropologists. A search on "Nasca or Nazca" returned over 200 results, ranging from a 3D-model of the Nasca lines based on remote sensing data from the ETH (Eidgenossische Technische Hochschüle Zurich) E-Collection to an image of a "Mummy mask or Huaco-picture" held in the University of Michigan Museum of Anthropology. Searches can be scoped to return only images, audio, video, data, or text.

195. **Pictures of Record (UM Image Source).** Ann Arbor, MI: University of Michigan, Ann Arbor. <http://images.umdl.umich.edu/cgi/i/image/image-idx>.

This website provides a gateway to visual images held in University of Michigan's digital collection. It is notable for the extent of the images available, as well as the easy-to-browse categories (by topic or collection) and handy features (including the ability to create personal portfolios of photos that can be held for later reference, shared with others, or used in the classroom). The site is open to the public, but UM affiliates are granted extra privileges.

Internet Gateways

196. **Ur-List: Web Resources for Visual Anthropology.** Biella, Peter. Center for Visual Anthropology at the University of Southern California. Available online at <http://www.usc.edu/dept/elab/urlist/index.html>.

Biella's excellent gateway to visual anthropology resources is comprehensive and well-organized. Almost 400 sites are cross-indexed into 22 subject categories.

197. **Visual Anthropology.net.** Ethnodoc. Available online at <http://www.visualanthropology.net/>.

This excellent website provides a gateway to news and online resources related to visual anthropology. The listing of new films, books, festivals, and conferences is particularly useful. The website is produced by Ethnodoc, a cultural association based in Matera, Italy, that provides support for cultural heritage projects, with a special focus on anthropology of visual communication, ethnographic film, ethnographic photography, digital pictures.

Chapter 4
Subfields of Anthropology

The discipline of anthropology developed from investigations of the entire spectrum of the human experience, ranging from biological origins and physical variations to linguistic, social, and cultural phenomena. Since the mid-twentieth century, the focus of anthropological inquiry has become increasingly specialized, dividing into the subfields: sociocultural anthropology, biological (or physical) anthropology, linguistic anthropology, and archaeology. Although this book focuses primarily on sociocultural anthropology, this chapter provides a brief overview of the major reference sources in the other three subfields in order to provide a basic introduction to information sources in the discipline as a whole.

Archaeology

Though the methodologies and focus of archaeology differ significantly from those of ethnology, both disciplines are concerned with social and cultural traditions and the processes involved in sociocultural change and development. Archaeology encompasses two distinct scholarly traditions: classical archaeology, concerned with the study of the civilizations of Ancient Greece and Rome, and prehistoric archaeology, which seeks to reconstruct the life-ways of peoples from the emergence of man to the advent of written history. This section focuses on reference sources in prehistoric rather than classical archaeology, although some titles overlap. The titles included here represent a highly selective sample, limited to basic sources that orient the new student to the field or present the material in a way that is particularly useful to scholars familiar with the topic at hand.

Professional societies in archaeology include, among others, the Society for American Archaeology, which publishes the journal *American Antiquity*, and the Archaeology Section of the American Anthropological Association, which publishes the monographic series *Archeological Papers of the American Anthropological Association*.

Guides to the Reference Literature

198. **Keyguide to Information Sources in Archaeology.** Woodhead, Peter. New York: Mansell, 1985. 219p. ISBN 0720117453.

Despite its age, this guide can still be a useful starting point for library research in archaeology. Woodhead provides bibliographic essays on the scope and history of archaeology, the organization of the discipline, the origins and utilization of archaeological information, current awareness strategies, and overall research strategies for scholars in the discipline—all of which remain relevant. Of more limited utility as the citations become increasingly dated, however, is the annotated bibliographical listing of over 700 archaeological reference sources.

Literature Surveys and Reviews

199. **Archaeology at the Millennium: A Sourcebook.** Feinman, Gary M., and T. Douglas Price, editors. New York, NY: Kluwer, 2001. 508p. ISBN 0306464527.

This volume brings together contributions from Canadian, Mexican, and American archaeologists discussing state-of-the-art research and emerging trends with a focus on New World archaeology.

Indexes, Abstracts, and Databases

200. **AATA Online: Abstracts of International Conservation Literature.** Los Angeles, CA: J. Paul Getty Trust. 2002-. Quarterly. ISSN 0004-2994. Available online. <http://aata.getty.edu>.

This free online database sponsored by the Getty Trust provides abstracts from over 400 journal titles, as well as books, reports, conference proceedings, dissertations, audiovisual, and select digital materials dealing with the technical aspects of art and archaeology in general. *AATA* covers literature published from 1932 to present, with abstracts in English or the language of the original. Content is drawn from all volumes of *Art and Archaeology Technical Abstracts* (AATA) and its predecessor, *IIC Abstracts*, issued from 1955 to 2002. In addition, the index includes 1,600 abstracts published by the Fogg Art Museum and the Freer Gallery of Art, 1932–1955.

201. **eHRAF Collection of Archaeology.** New Haven, CT: Human Relations Area Files. 1998-. Available online by subscription. <http://www.yale.edu/hraf/collections.htm>.

Following the format and approach of *eHRAF Collection of Ethnography* (entry 481), *eHRAF Collection of Archaeology* provides transcriptions of core current and retrospective sources, subject-indexed to the paragraph level, for all cultures covered. As of this writing, 50 archaeological traditions are covered, but the collection is growing steadily with approximately eight new files (each with more than 10,000 pages) released every year. Each file is comprised of sources compiled by scholars and generally includes five to seven site reports, a "Tradition Summary" providing a cogent overview of the regional and cultural traditions (e.g., PostClassic Maya or Middle Paleolithic Egypt) and an evaluation of each of the sources included in the file. The cultures included represent prehistorical cultures from across the globe, and can be browsed by geographic region.

The full-text of each source is included, but in a re-keyed format that intersperses the index terms with the original text, lacks good visual navigational clues, and cannot be easily printed. The usefulness of *eHRAF* is thus limited to an aid in locating relevant passages—researchers wanting to read extended passages will need to consult the original texts. Unlike the ethnography collection, the *Collection of Archaeology* was released only as an electronic resource and does not include any previous print or microfiche installments.

202. **FRANCIS.** Institut de l'Information Scientifique et Technique du Centre National de la Recherche Scientifique (INIST-CNRS) and the Getty Research Institute (GRI). 1984-. Monthly. ISSN 1161-0395. Available on CD-ROM and online by subscription.

FRANCIS is an excellent source for citations to articles and book chapters on world prehistory from the origin of humans to non-European art and archaeology. Over 600 archaeological and multidisciplinary journals are analyzed, with particularly good coverage of Western European publications. For a more complete annotation of this source, see also entry 3.

203. **Geobase.** New York: Elsevier. 1980-. ISSN 0953-9611; 0954-0504. Available online by subscription.

This index identifies the journal literature in earth sciences, ecology, geosciences, development studies, geomechanics, human geography, and oceanography. Whereas *GeoRef* focuses specifically on geological publications and includes materials published back to 1785, *Geobase* includes literature from related fields and includes materials published since 1980.

204. **GeoRef.** Alexandria, VA: American Geological Institute. 1969-. ISSN 0197-7482. Available on CD-ROM and online by subscription. <http://www.agiweb.org/georef/index.html>.

Particularly useful for geoarchaeologists, lithic specialists, as well as archaeologists interested in dating techniques and stratigraphy, this index to geological literature includes citations from more than 3,500 journals in 40 languages. It also contains references to book chapters, maps, conference papers, technical reports, dissertations, and theses. A limited number of citations include abstracts. Production of the print version, *Bibliography and Index of Geology (1969–2006)*, ceased in 2006. The American Geological Institute link given above lists all currently available formats and vendors.

205. **Historical Abstracts.** Santa Barbara, CA: ABC Clio. 1955-. ISSN 1528-3445. Also available online 1969-.

While *Historical Abstracts* is mainly relevant to archaeologists, cultural anthropologists and ethnohistorians may also benefit from the citations this index provides to historical literature dealing with world history (exclusive of North America) from 1450 forward. For coverage of the history of the United States and Canada, see the sister database *Historical Abstracts, America History and Life* (entry 570).

206. **The National Archeological Database (NADB).** Archeology and Ethnography Program, National Park Service. Available online at <http://www.cast.uark.edu/other/nps/nadb>.

This site sponsored by the U.S. National Park Service contains three modules: *Reports*, *MAPS*, and *Permits*. *NADB-Reports* is a "bibliographic inventory of over 350,000 reports on archeological investigation and planning . . . this gray literature represents a large portion of the primary information available on archeological sites in the U.S." *NADB-MAPS* provides GIS layers related to archeological data, including maps showing "national distributions of cultural and environmental resources across the United States." *NADB-Permits* provides information about significant federally sponsored archaeological and paleontological research projects via a database of over 3,000 permits issued by the Department of the Interior under the Antiquities Act of 1906 and the Archaeological Resource Protection Act of 1979, as well as a few "permits issued after the granting authority was delegated to individual federal agencies in 1984."

207. **Outline of Archaeological Traditions.** Peregrine, Peter N., editor. New Haven, CT: Human Relations Area Files, 2001. 55p. ISBN not assigned.

A companion to the *eHRAF Collection of Archaeology* (entry 201), this text is "an attempt to catalog all known archaeological traditions, covering the entire globe and the entire prehistory of humankind." Each entry provides the name of the tradition; the approximate time period for the tradition; brief information on the tradition's location and salient characteristics; and the tradition's alphanumeric code used in the *eHRAF Collection of Archaeology* (entry 201).

Biographies

(Also see "Biographical Sources" in Chapter 2.)

208. **Encyclopedia of Archaeology: The Great Archaeologists.** Murray, Tim, editor. Santa Barbara, CA: ABC-Clio, 1999. 2v. ISBN 1576071995.

Arranged chronologically from William Camden (1551–1623) to David Clarke (1938–1976), entries begin with a brief overview of each archaeologist's main contributions, followed by an in-depth but accessible examination of their life and work. Each entry ends with a list of references that facilitate further study. An index appears at the end of the second volume, as well as a epilogue on writing archaeological biographies.

Atlases

209. **Atlas of Archaeology.** Aston, Mick, and Tim Taylor. New York: DK Publishing, 1998. 208p. ISBN 0789431890.

In the first part of this atlas, chronologically presented site excavations offer the student an illustrated guide to the complete archaeological process, from excavation to analysis. The sites chosen span the globe and encompass time periods from Olduvai Gorge (1.7 million years ago) through the industrial age. The second part is a very useful gazetteer listing more than one thousand sites, arranged by geographical region. A glossary, bibliography, and index are also included at the end of the volume.

210. **The Atlas of Past Worlds: A Comparative Chronology of Human History 2000 BC–AD 1500.** Manley, John. London: Cassell, 1993. 224p. ISBN 0304319813.

This generously illustrated source contains selective coverage of global archaeology from 2000 BC to around AD 1500. The atlas is organized by themes—early religion, subsistence, change, and urbanization. Within each section, selected sites are discussed. It includes a combined site and subject index.

211. **The Atlas of World Archaeology.** Bahn, Paul G, editor. New York: Checkmark Books, 2000. 208p. ISBN 0816040516.

This atlas summarizes archaeological scholarship of the development of human societies worldwide. Drawing on state-of-the-art knowledge in the field, the authors provide global and regional views of prehistory that are both accessible and scholarly. The atlas is organized into three sections—early humans, postglacial expansion, and the rise of regional civilizations. Each of these sections has subsections focusing on broad regions (e.g., Africa or East Asia), particular features or themes. Superb illustrations, in color as well as black and white, and numerous timelines accompany the maps. A glossary, detailed index, and list of references father enhance the usefulness of this outstanding reference source.

212. **Past Worlds: The Times Atlas of Archaeology.** New York: Crescent Books, 1995. 319p. ISBN 0517121743.

First published by Times Books Limited in 1988, this well-illustrated large-format reference work provides an overview of the methods, interpretations, and analyses that concern archaeologists. More an encyclopedia than an atlas, it provides articles on overarching topics such as human origins, food, textiles, and disease followed by essays covering specific archaeological traditions across the globe. A glossary and index to sites are also provided.

213. **The World Atlas of Archaeology.** Boston, MA: G.K. Hall, 1985. 423p. ISBN 0816187479.

With nearly 100 essays, outstanding graphics, a glossary of technical terms, and an index to site names and topics, this atlas continues to be of interest despite its age. It is organized primarily by geographic region, with sections on Oceania, the Americas, Africa, Asia/India, and the Near East which include numerous maps, essays on historical background, primary archaeological investigations, and special topics relevant to each area, such as nomadism or apartheid. The bibliography is comprehensive and includes topical subdivisions such as "Women in the Paleolithic."

Dictionaries, Encyclopedias, and Handbooks

214. **Archaeological Method and Theory: An Encyclopedia.** Ellis, Linda, editor. New York: Garland, 2000. 705p. ISBN 0815313051.

This source provides a comprehensive overview of archaeological methods and theories written by prominent researchers from across the globe. Alphabetically arranged essays address topics such as the archaeological site formation processes, site discovery, excavation, site and object documentation, on-site conservation and packaging, and post-excavation analysis. Some biographies also are provided. Each entry includes a bibliography of sources. A comprehensive subject index and a subject guide that groups thematically related entries aid in the location of information on a given topic.

215. **Archaeological Objects Thesaurus.** Archaeological Objects Thesaurus Working Party. Available online at <http://www.mda.org.uk/archobj/archcon.htm>.

Created by the Archaeological Objects Thesaurus Working Party, this glossary is part of their efforts to create "common principles for the recording of object names within the archaeological profession and related disciplines" (Foreword).

216. **Companion Encyclopedia of Archaeology.** Barker, Graeme, editor. New York: Routledge, 1999. 2v. ISBN 0415064481.

This two-volume set provides the reader with 29 substantial signed essays describing archaeological theory, methods, and practice and summarizing major discoveries within the discipline. Like the *Companion Encyclopedia of Anthropology* (entry 31), it is more of a reader or handbook than an encyclopedia. All chapters include references for further research and the second volume includes a comprehensive index.

217. **The Concise Oxford Dictionary of Archaeology.** Darvill, Timothy. Oxford: Oxford University Press, 2002. 506p. ISBN 0192116495; 0192800051pa.

Darvill, a professor of archaeology at Bournemouth University, U.K., provides brief but scholarly entries defining 4,000 terms relating to the archaeology of Europe, the Americas, and parts of the Old World. Entries define concepts, techniques and tools, cultural phases, theoretical models, and artifacts, as well as providing basic information about institutes, organizations and individual biographies. Appendices include a timeline for cultural periods in the Americas, charts of stratigraphic subdivisions in Europe and North America, and chronologies of the British Bronze Age, Egyptian dynasties, Roman emperors, and English rulers to 1066.

218. **A Dictionary of Archaeology.** Shaw, Ian, and Robert Jameson, editors. Oxford, UK: Blackwell, 1999. 624p. ISBN 0631174230.

This dictionary is "based on the premise that archaeology is a process rather than simply a body of knowledge" (preface) and the 1,500 entries of varying length and scope explore the "challenges, ambiguities and theoretical context of archaeology." Coverage of classical archaeology is omitted in favor of geographical areas less commonly encountered in the reference literature such as China, Japan, and Oceania. This focus on lesser known regions and thoughtful consideration of theoretical issues in the context of archaeological practice make it a unique addition to the somewhat crowded field of general archaeology dictionaries. The alphabetical entries, written by 40 prominent archaeologists from around the world, are well-written and provide a list of sources for further research. High-quality graphics, including maps, chronologies and drawings, add to the overall appeal. The usefulness of this volume, however, is seriously diminished by the lack of indexing. Ample cross-references help counterbalance this shortcoming, but it still can be difficult to locate relevant entries.

219. **Dictionary of Concepts in Archaeology.** Mignon, Molly Raymond. Westport, CT: Greenwood, 1993. 364p. ISBN 0313246599.

One of a series of three dictionaries exploring the central concepts in anthropology (see also entries 35 and 240), this volume provides lengthy entries describing the historical context and current meaning of 72 important archaeological concepts (e.g., culture, lithics, stratigraphy). Entries are detailed, with extensive bibliographies. The sources referred to are well-known sources which provide access to a large portion of the literature, or reflect recent trends in the field.

220. **Encyclopedia of Archaeology: History and Discoveries.** Murray, Tim, editor. Santa Barbara, CA: ABC-Clio, 2001. 3v. ISBN 1576071987; 157607577Xe.

In this companion to the two-volume *Encyclopedia of Archaeology: The Great Archaeologists* (entry 208), Murray provides a more topical approach to the field. This three-volume set is geared toward undergraduates and covers major archaeologists, countries, sites, traditions, methods, and theories. Articles are cross-referenced and well-illustrated.

221. **Encyclopedia of Prehistory.** Peregrine, Peter N., and Melvin Ember, editors. New York: Kluwer, 2001. 9v. ISBN 0306462648.

This set, prepared in conjunction with Human Relation Area Files (entry 709), includes basic information on all archaeologically known cultures, and is intended to provide a basis for comparative research. The first eight volumes cover different regions of the world (e.g., Africa or Oceania) and the ninth volume provides a detailed cumulative index and tables arranging all archaeological traditions in chronological order and in order of regional descent. Each volume also includes its own index and maps. Entries provide an overview of major archaeologically known cultures highlighting subsistence practices, sociopolitical organization, and material industries. All entries are written by prominent anthropologists and include bibliographies of core sources.

222. **Encyclopedic Dictionary of Archaeology.** Kipfer, Barbara Ann, compiler. New York: Kluwer, 2000. 708p. ISBN 0306461587.

With a total of 7,000 entries, this is the largest and most comprehensive dictionary of its kind with a very good balance of New World and Old World coverage. In short, pithy entries, Kipfer defines the terms and techniques of archaeology and describes the major premises, important concepts, and scientific methods used in the field. Other useful features include a glossary of archaeological abbreviations, a bibliography, supplementary list of archaeological sites and terms and a section on "writing and archaeology" that provides a timeline of the development of writing systems worldwide.

223. **Handbook of Archaeological Methods.** Maschner, Herbert D. G., and Christopher Chippindale, editors. Lanham, MD: AltaMira Press, 2005. 2v. ISBN 0759100780.

This practical handbook brings together 37 substantial articles, written by prominent archaeologists, covering a range of methodological topics, including fieldwork (logistics and data collection, excavation, remote sensing), analysis (dating techniques, statistics, modeling), the management of cultural resources, data curation, funding, communicating results, and working with and for indigenous communities. Useful as both a reference source and a methodological handbook, selected chapters will likely appear on reading lists for upper level undergraduate and graduate courses.

224. **Handbook of Archaeological Sciences.** Brothwell, Don R., and A. Mark Pollard, editors. New York: Wiley, 2001. 762p. ISBN 0471984841; 0470014768pa.

The *Handbook of Archaeological Sciences* provides an overview of the diverse sciences comprising the study of the human past. Fifty-nine essays by an international team of contributors are organized under eight broad headings: dating, quaternary palaeoenvironments, human palaeobiology, developments in biomolecular archaeology, resource exploitation, archaeological prospection, conservation science in the archaeological context, and statistical and computer applications. Access to this rich content is enhanced by a general index as well as indexes by site, species name, and taxonomic group.

225. **Manuals in Archaeological Method, Theory, and Technique.** New York: Kluwer, 2002-. ISSN: 1571-5752.

This series of manuals launched in 2002 provides in-depth explorations of specific archaeological methodologies. Volumes already published include *Archaeological Survey* (2002), *Lithic Analysis* (2003), and *Mortuary Monuments and Burial Grounds of the Historic Period* (2004).

226. **The Oxford Companion to Archaeology.** Fagan, Brian, editor. Oxford: Oxford University Press, 1996. 844p. ISBN 0195076184.

This encyclopedia provides 700 entries describing major archaeological sites and regions, as well as the history, methods, and theories of the discipline. The contributors are international authorities in the field and most of the entries are thorough, well-written, and include references. Like many encyclopedias, however, this volume suffers from a lack of uniformity. The length of the entries varies considerably and the coverage is uneven (e.g., there is an entry for Sicily, but not for Cambodia). The maps and timelines provide useful information, but are not cross-referenced to the corresponding entries in the main text.

227. **Penguin Archaeology Guide.** Bahn, Paul G., editor. Rev. ed. London: Penguin, 2001. 494p. ISBN 0140293086; 0140514481.

The first edition of this work was published under the title *Collins Dictionary of Archaeology*, and an abridged edition, entitled *The New Penguin Dictionary of Archaeology*, appeared in 2004. Bibliographic confusion notwithstanding, this dictionary provides a comprehensive overview of archaeological artifacts, sites, and regions, as well as theory, methods, and central figures in the discipline. Almost 3,000 brief entries (1–3 paragraphs) alphabetical entries are included from a team of contributors including archaeologists from the United States, United Kingdom, Canada, Australia, South Africa, and Russia. Useful for ready reference, this dictionary eschews common terms such as "cave" or "figurine" and avoids broad terms that would be covered in encyclopedic sources, such as "subsistence patterns" or "agriculture." In addition, Bahn provides regional maps of important sites and a list of suggested readings arranged by topic and geographical region at the back of the volume.

Directories

228. **America's Ancient Treasures: A Guide to Archaeological Sites and Museums in the United States and Canada.** Folsom, Franklin. 4th rev., enl. ed. Albuquerque: University of New Mexico Press, 1993. 459p. ISBN 082631449X; 0826314503pa.

Folsom's guide provides an alphabetical listing of excavated and protected prehistoric sites and prehistory museums in the United States and Canada. Each section gives an overview of prehistoric periods of a particular region. Entries include the location, brief description, and administrative agency responsible for the site. A glossary of terms, a listing of archaeological organizations, and a comprehensive index are also provided at the back of the volume.

Bibliographies

229. **Archaeology: A Bibliographical Guide to the Basic Literature.** Heizer, Robert F., Thomas R. Hester, and Carol Graves. New York: Garland, 1980. 434p. ISBN 0824098269.

This classic bibliography provides an extensive listing of nearly 5,000 unannotated citations to the important literature in the field from the nineteenth century through the late 1970s. The detailed topical arrangement (that compensates somewhat for the absence of a subject index) includes references concerning the nature, purpose, and history of archaeology; the work of the archaeologist; kinds of archaeology (prehistoric, salvage, underwater); common kinds of sites (kill sites, mounds); fieldwork methods; analysis (skeletal analysis, dating methods, use of computers); interpretation (population movements, language) and archaeology as a profession. Coverage is international and includes books and important journals.

Series

230. **Understanding Ancient Civilizations (series).** Santa Barbara, CA: ABC-Clio, 2004-. ISSN not assigned.

This ongoing series published by ABC-Clio provides overviews of archaeological civilizations, from the Maya to the Mesopotamians. The volumes are targeted toward the general reader, but provide rich detail and substantial bibliographies that are excellent starting points for further exploration. All volumes are also available online in e-book format.

Internet Gateways

231. **ArchNet.** Archaeological Research Institute at Arizona State University. Available online at <http://archnet.asu.edu/>.

Hosted and maintained by the staff at the Archaeological Research Institute at Arizona State University, this is one of the most useful archaeology sites on the web. The comprehensive collection of links to websites and online resources is organized into four main areas: regional views, topical selection, educational and research resources, and institutions and organizations. Specific subject areas include archaeometry, botanical analysis, ceramics, collection management, ethnohistory, ethnoarchaeology, faunal and zooarchaeology, geoarchaeology, GIS/cartography/mapping, historic archaeology, human origins, lithics, and remote sensing. The site also provides links to electronic journals, publishers, and archaeology-related newsgroups and listservs.

232. **World Atlas of Archaeology on the Web.** Hirst, K. Kris. Available online at <http://archaeology.about.com/od/worldarchaeology/index.htm>.

This frequently updated site provides a geographically organized gateway to scholarly sites on archaeology. Most of the sites listed are hosted by academic institutions or scholarly organizations.

233. **WWW Virtual Library: Archaeology.** Available online at <http://vlib.org/Archaeology>.

Part of the *WWW Virtual Library* organization, this site provides a single gateway to the various virtual libraries related to archaeology including *ArchNet* (entry 231), as well as separate gateways covering archaeology in the United Kingdom, Europe, and worldwide.

Biological Anthropology

While maintaining close ties to the natural sciences, particularly biology and medicine, biological (or physical) anthropology retains its connection to the study of mankind through its investigation of the relationship between the human physical condition and culture. Its concerns are broad and varied and include the analysis of human remains and artifacts (including forensics); the study of human evolution, anatomy, genetics, adaptations and ecology; and primate studies.

As in cultural anthropology, there are a number of increasingly specialized professional associations in which biological anthropologists can become involved. One of the primary organizations, the American Association of Physical Anthropologists, publishes the *American Journal of Physical Anthropology*. The American Anthropological Association (entry 745) also includes the Biological Anthropology Section among its units.

The titles listed below do not include the full range of reference works in the natural sciences relevant to research in biological anthropology but focus instead upon representative works that offer a basic orientation to the field. For information on the diverse career options available to those with training in this subfield, see *A Guide to Careers in Physical Anthropology* (entry 859) in the final chapter.

Literature Surveys and Reviews

234. **Human Evolution: A Guide to the Debates.** Regal, Brian. Santa Barbara, CA: ABC-Clio, 2004. 357p. ISBN 1851094180; 1851094237e.

Written for a general audience, this synthetic overview of the research on human evolution traces the history development of the theory of evolution in general and human evolution in particular. Most of this will be familiar to anthropologists, but the volume provides a well-balanced background for nonspecialists and neophytes.

235. **Yearbook of Physical Anthropology,** Vol. 1-. New York: Wiley. 1943-. Annual. ISSN 0096-848X.

Published once a year as a supplement to *American Journal of Physical Anthropology*, this yearbook contains essays on developments within the field of physical anthropology.

Indexes, Abstracts, and Databases

236. **Biological Abstracts,** Vol. 1-. Philadelphia: Thomson BIOSIS. 1926-. Bimonthly. ISSN 0006-3169. Available in print, on CD-ROM and online by subscription.

Biological Abstracts is an extensive international abstracting service that indexes biology journals not covered by the standard anthropology indexes. Topics of interest to anthropologists include physical anthropology, ethnobiology, evolution, paleobiology, paleozoology, resource management and conservation, among others. Judicious subject indexing allows for very specific subject access by concept (e.g., variation in body size) as well as by geographic region or culture group. Extensive annotations report research findings. Though the information presented is outside the general scope of cultural anthropology, medical and applied anthropologists (among others) will find this source a useful complement to anthropological indexes.

237. **PrimateLit.** Wisconsin Primate Research Center and Washington National Primate Research Center. 2001-. Bimonthly. Available online. <http://primatelit.library.wisc.edu/>.

This free online database identifies scholarly literature on all aspects of primate-related research, including journal articles, books, meeting abstracts, technical reports, dissertations, and book chapters from 1940 to the present. Subject indexing well-attuned to the needs of researchers in the field makes it easy to identify literature related to a particular concept, species/taxon, and geographic area. *Current Primate References (CPR)* is a subset of *PrimateLit*, offering a broad subject approach to recently indexed citations. This outstanding resource is a collaborative project of the Wisconsin Primate Research Center, the Washington National Primate Research Center and the University of Wisconsin-Madison Libraries.

238. **Zoological Record,** Vol. 1-. London: Zoological Society of London. 1864-. Annual (print); monthly (online). ISSN 0144-3607. Available in print and online by subscription. <http://www.biosis.org/>.

A comprehensive index to over 6,000 international publications in zoology and animal science, *Zoological Record* is very useful for research in primatology and paleoanthropology, but does not cover modern humans. Sources are indexed include journals, newsletters, conference proceedings, and books. Includes author, subject, geographical, palaeontological, and systematic indexes. As of this writing, the online version covers 1978–present.

Dictionaries and Encyclopedias

(See also *Encyclopedia of Prehistory*, entry 221)

239. **The Cambridge Encyclopedia of Human Evolution.** Jones, Steve, Robert Martin, and David Pilbeam, editors. New York: Cambridge University Press, 1992. 506p. ISBN 0521323703.

An eclectic encyclopedia covering the evolution of the human species, drawing heavily from the fields of genetics, morphology, physiology, and behavior.

Signed entries are extensively illustrated. Appended are brief biographies of historical figures in evolutionary biology, maps of key archaeological sites, a glossary of relevant terms, a lengthy classified bibliography for further reading, and a detailed general index.

240. **Dictionary of Concepts in Physical Anthropology.** Stevenson, Joan C. Westport, CT: Greenwood Press, 1991. 432p. ISBN 0313247560.

One of a series of three dictionaries exploring the central concepts in anthropology (see also entries 35 and 219), this volume contains 75 lengthy entries providing in-depth discussions of major concepts in physical anthropology. Each entry gives the current meaning of a concept, traces its "historical origins and connotative development," and provides a substantial list of references to related works. Subject and name indexes are provided.

241. **The Encyclopedia of Evolution: Humanity's Search for Its Origins.** Milner, Richard. New York: H. Holt, 1993. 483p. ISBN 0805027173 .

Originally published in 1990 by Facts on File, this encyclopedia provides an accessible, semipopular treatment of human evolution more appropriate for undergraduates than researchers. The coverage of issues and controversies provide a useful introduction to human origins and development. A foreword by Stephen J. Gould and brief biographies of significant figures are also included. Separate subject, name, and place indexes are provided at the back.

242. **Encyclopedia of Human Evolution and Prehistory.** Delson, Eric, Ian Tattersall, John A. Van Couvering, and Alison S. Brooks, editor. 2nd ed. New York: Garland, 1999. 753p. ISBN 0815316968.

Written to be accessible to those with no prior knowledge of the subject, this one-volume reference work is useful to both students and scholars of human evolution and paleontology. The book is alphabetically arranged with nearly 800 signed entries ranging from brief definitions of technical terms to lengthy essays on topics such as evolutionary theory, primatology, and Paleolithic archaeology.

The encyclopedia is well organized for ready reference use; the generous use of cross-references brings related material together; and a detailed list of all articles by topic identifies entries in general categories such as human fossils or primates. Although written by experts in the field, content of the essays is balanced, with a range of opinion provided on controversial or disputed issues. The accompanying references to books and articles generally date from the 1990s. Introductory material includes a brief overview of human evolution and prehistory, a subject list by topic, a classification of the primates, and a time line. Numerous maps, photos, charts, tables and other illustrations further enhance the utility of this valuable reference source.

243. **History of Physical Anthropology: An Encyclopedia.** Spencer, Frank, editor. New York: Garland, 1997. 2v. ISBN 0815304900.

In this excellent encyclopedic synthesis, Spencer has collected a cogent and comprehensive set of essays written by international experts on topics related to the history of physical anthropology. Entries include a list of sources for further research, including primary sources and the location of relevant archival materials. Attention is given to the development of the discipline in specific countries, and more than 300 biographies of major and minor figures worldwide are provided. There is much here of interest to those studying the history of science as well as to physical anthropologists doing retrospective literature reviews.

Handbooks and Manuals

244. **Fundamentals of Forensic Anthropology.** Klepinger, Linda L. Hoboken, NJ: Wiley-Liss, 2006. 185p. ISBN 0471210064.

This handbook lays out the fundamentals of paleoanthropology and the identification of human fossil remains. The first part provides an overview of forensic anthropology and a history of the development of this specialization within anthropology. The second part serves as a manual of methods for assessment and identification of human skeletal remains. The final section deals with the area popularized by the *CSI* television series, "Principal Anthropological Roles in Medical-Legal Investigation."

245. **The Human Fossil Record.** Schwartz, Jeffrey H., Ian Tattersall, and Ralph L. Holloway, editors. New York: Wiley-Liss, 2002. 4v. ISBN 0471678643.

Authoritative and comprehensive documentation of the fossil evidence relevant to the study of our evolutionary past. Fossil remains from major sites are carefully documented with the salient morphological characteristics highlighted. Organized alphabetically by site name, each entry includes clear descriptions, outstanding photos, illustrations, references to the literature and an overview of the site, context, and dating.

Bibliographies

246. **Ecce Homo: An Annotated Bibliographic History of Physical Anthropology.** Spencer, Frank. Westport, CT: Greenwood Press, 1986. 495p. ISBN 0313240566.

The subtitle of this classic bibliography does not do justice to its scope because the aim of the book is "to reveal not only the historic development of inquiry into the nature of the origin and variation of our species, but also the underlying thematic continuity of anthropological thought" (preface). Thus the citations serve essentially as a literature review, providing identification, analysis, and synthesis of research and theory in physical anthropology from ancient times through the mid-twentieth century.

The bibliography is divided into four time periods: Ancient, Medieval, Renaissance, and Early Modern (eighteenth century, nineteenth century, and twentieth century). An introductory essay (with references) provides an overview of the prevailing theoretical and research orientation of the time and is followed by lengthy critical annotations of the writings of scholars in the field, in roughly chronological order. An index to names is provided and the subject index affords access by specific topic (e.g., gorillas, skin color, *Australopithecus*).

247. **Field Primatology: A Guide to Research.** Wolfe, Linda D. New York: Garland, 1987. 288p. ISBN 0824085523.

This classic work focuses on the publications of researchers who have conducted behavioral studies of free-ranging primates and synthesizes the literature into an annotated bibliography of over 1,000 books and articles from anthropology, animal behavior, ecology, and related scientific disciplines. Topics include general primate studies, prosimians, New World monkeys, Old World monkeys, and apes. Although the subject index is somewhat limited, it does provide access to citations on concepts such as communication, dominance, and territoriality.

Internet Gateways

248. **ALFRED: The ALlele FREquency Database.** Kidd, Kenneth K. Yale University. Available online at <http://alfred.med.yale.edu/alfred/index.asp>.

Originally funded by NSF and curated by the lab of Dr. Kenneth Kidd at Yale University, this website links allele frequency data from well-defined populations to ethnographic and molecular data, as well as to the corresponding literature. As of October 21, 2006, ALFRED included 3,670 polymorphisms, 516 populations and 84,915 frequency tables. Holdings are keyword searchable and can be browsed by chromosomal loci or by geographic area via an interactive map. Compiled from disparate sources into a single archive with a user-friendly interface, the data collected on this site are very useful for research and teaching in biological anthropology and human population genetics.

Linguistic Anthroplogy

Linguistic anthropologists are concerned with theoretical issues such as language universals, the classification of language groups, and language and world view. Linguistics is a relatively small, but very salient, subfield of anthropology. The study of language and communication practices is thoroughly integrated into sociocultural anthropology. Indeed, it is part and parcel of ethnographic practice, which by definition involves extended periods of fieldwork and thorough integration into daily life—including verbal and nonverbal communication—at the fieldsite.

Although there are several general linguistics associations relevant to anthropologists, the Society for Linguistic Anthropology (entry 767) was established as a unit of the American Anthropological Association to foster communication within the field. Beginning in 1991, the society began issuing *the Journal of Linguistic Anthropology* (entry 682) that serves as an important vehicle for the publication of specifically anthropological studies.

Because reference materials on linguistic anthropology have been covered by Anna DeMiller's excellent *Linguistics: A Guide to the Reference Literature* (entry 249) that includes a section devoted to "anthropological linguistics," the titles listed here are limited to those that have appeared since DeMiller's guide was published in 2000, as well as a few essential titles that are of particular relevance to anthropology (e.g., *Dictionary of Worldwide Gestures*, entry 256 and *World's Major Languages*, entry 265) that were covered in other sections of DeMiller's guide.

Guides to the Reference Literature

249. **Linguistics: A Guide to the Reference Literature.** DeMiller, Anna L. 2nd ed. Englewood, CO: Libraries Unlimited, 2000. 396p. ISBN 1563086190.

The only bibliographic guide to the reference sources in linguistics, DeMiller's volume covers the core literature in the field, including websites. Over 1,000 entries spanning 1957–1998 judiciously identify and describe the most useful English language reference sources in linguistics and related fields. A small number of French, German, and Russian works are also included. The guide is divided into three sections: "General Linguistics," "Allied Areas," and "Languages." All of these contain material of interest to linguistic anthropologists, but the "anthropological linguistics" section in the chapter on "Allied Areas" is particularly relevant, as well as the section on sociolinguistics.

Literature Surveys and Reviews

250. **A Companion to Linguistic Anthropology.** Duranti, Alessandro, editor. Malden, MA: Blackwell, 2004. 625p. (Blackwell Companions to Anthropology, 1). ISBN 0631223525; 1405144300pa.

This state of the art survey of linguistic anthropology consists of 22 essays by respected scholars exploring theory and method in the study of language and culture. The essays are grouped thematically into chapters on speech communities, contact and variation, performance, subjectivities and intersubjectivities, and "the power in language." A general index and bibliography enhance the usefulness of this volume as reference source. This is one of the few reference sources geared specifically toward the field of linguistic anthropology.

Indexes, Abstracts, and Databases

251. **Linguistics and Language Behavior Abstracts (LLBA),** Vol. 19-. La Jolla, CA: CSA. 1985. Quarterly. ISSN 0888-8027. (Continues *Language and Language Behavior Abstracts,* 1967–1984). Available in print, on CD-ROM and online by subscription.

This international interdisciplinary indexing and abstracting service provides summaries of scholarly articles on linguistics and language behavior from books, book reviews, journal articles, and dissertations. *LLBA* indexes approximately 2,000 journals from a variety of disciplines including anthropology, communication, education, psychology, linguistics, and philosophy. More than 30 languages are represented with good coverage of subject areas of interest to anthropologists, including anthropological linguistics, language and cognition, comparative linguistics, psycholinguistics, and nonverbal communication. A keyword index provides access by language, ethnic group, and specific subject.

252. **MLA International Bibliography,** Vol. 1-. New York: Modern Language Association of America.1921-. Annual (print); 10 times/year (online). ISSN 0024-8215. Available in print, on CD-ROM and online by subscription.

The official index of the Modern Languages Association, *MLA International* covers linguistics as well as literature, and has very good coverage of American Indian languages. 3,500 journals written in English, French, German, Spanish, Italian, Portuguese, a Scandinavian language, and Dutch are included, as well as monographs, series, dissertations, bibliographies, and proceedings. As of this writing, the online edition covers 1963–present. See also entry 436 for a full annotation.

Atlases

253. **The World Atlas of Language Structures.** Haspelmath, Martin, Matthew S. Dryer, David Gil, and Bernard Comrie, editors. Oxford; New York: Oxford University Press, 2005. 695p + CD ROM. ISBN 0199255911.

This essential new tool for comparative linguistics provides 142 world maps and numerous regional maps showing the geographical distribution of linguistic structures. Features of grammar and pronunciation (such as the number of genders, color categories, or tenses) are charted for more than 400 languages. Each map is accompanied by an essay describing the feature in question and analyzing its geographic distribution. The accompanying CD-ROM allows users to zoom in on a particular region, map multiple features to examine possible correlations, and create other types of customized maps.

Dictionaries and Encyclopedias

254. **The Cambridge Encyclopedia of Language.** Crystal, David. 2nd ed. Cambridge, England: Cambridge University Press, 1997. 480p. ISBN 0521550505; 0521559677pa.

With the aim of illustrating the enormous diversity of the world's languages, this one-volume encyclopedia presents an excellent overview of major topics of investigation in the study of language. The author eschews dictionary format, organizing the discursive essays into three basic themes. Part 1 is concerned with popular ideas about language (function, equality of languages); Part 2 deals with language and identity, including the question of dialects; and Part 3 is devoted to essays on the structure of language and on the languages of the world, including topics such as language families, change, pidgins, and creoles. This edition introduces new topics such as machine translation and updates language distributions, statistics on languages spoken, etc., to reflect changes in geopolitical border since the first edition was published in 1987. Richly illustrated, the encyclopedia also includes charts, tables, a glossary and lists of references for additional reading. Overall, this volume provides an engaging overview of the study of language for both the expert and the enthusiast.

255. **A Dictionary of Linguistics & Phonetics.** Crystal, David. 5th ed. Malden, MA: Blackwell, 2003. 508p. ISBN 063122663X; 0631226648pa.

An updated and expanded edition of a previously issued title by a prominent linguist, this dictionary succinctly defines and discusses over 2,000 terms. Although many of the terms are technical, important theories and issues are also discussed. In addition to definitions, entries often include examples, diagrams, ample cross-references, and a list of references for further reading. The breadth of terms and clarity of definitions enhance the utility of this dictionary to those unfamiliar with linguistic terminology.

256. **Dictionary of Worldwide Gestures.** Bäuml, Betty J., and Franz H. Bäuml. 2nd ed. Lanham, MD: Scarecrow Press, 1997. 510p. ISBN 0810831899.

More an index than a dictionary, this interesting reference tool draws from a source list of nearly 1,000 books and articles encompassing ethnography, folklore, geography and literature to identify and describe culturally transmitted (semiotic) gestures. Useful for comparative studies, entries are arranged by parts of the body involved and included a description of the gesture, its meaning and a citation to the source from which the entry was taken. The second edition incorporates additional sources, expands the commentary and rectifies a significant shortcoming of the previous edition by providing many more illustrations of the gestures under consideration.

257. **The Encyclopedia of Language and Linguistics.** Asher, R. E., editor. Oxford: Pergamon Press, 1994. 10v. ISBN 0080359434.

This massive set provides a comprehensive and in-depth overview of the field, aimed at scholars and specialists. The final volume includes a substantial (100 page) glossary, a list of languages of the world, indexes by subject and names, and a list of entries classified by broad topical area, including "Anthropology and Language."

258. **Encyclopedia of Linguistics.** Stazny, Phillip, editor. New York: Fitzroy Dearborn, 2005. 2v. ISBN 1579583911.

This two-volume encyclopedia provides a general overview for the non-specialist to linguistics, focusing on theoretical issues, major figures, languages, and geographic distributions. Approximately 500 essays with bibliographies are included. The essays are arranged alphabetically, but a thematic table of contents groups related entries.

259. **Encyclopedic Dictionary of Semiotics.** Sebeok, Thomas Albert, editor. 2nd ed. New York: Mouton de Gruyter, 1994. 3v. ISBN 3110142295.

Semiotics, the study of signs and sign-using behavior, has obvious relevance for the anthropological study of language and communication. Sebeok, a renowned scholar of semiotics, has coordinated the efforts of over 200 scholars worldwide to produce this exhaustive reference work. Over 400 signed entries, ranging in length from a paragraph to over 20 pages, include historical background and present usage of terms, biographies of deceased prominent scholars in semiotics, and discussions of the impact of semiotics on other fields.

260. **International Encyclopedia of Linguistics.** Frawley, William J., editor. 2nd ed. Oxford; New York: Oxford University Press, 2003. 4v. ISBN 0195139771.

The updated and revised edition of this comprehensive and technically sophisticated work is of particular interest to anthropologists. Frawley, who identifies as both an anthropologist and a psychologist, focuses on the intersection of linguistics with the social and behavioral sciences. Ethnolinguistics, anthropological linguistics, and sociolinguistics and other major fields of studies are all treated in-depth, while shorter entries define technical terms or provide brief biographies highlighting the contributions of major scholars, such as Edward Sapir. A significant portion of the work outlines the major languages and language families both in terms of their structural features as well as their geographical distribution, number of speakers and interintelligibility. Up-to-date bibliographies, ample cross-references, a synoptic outline, and a detailed index all enhance the usefulness of this excellent reference source.

261. **Linguistics Encyclopedia.** Malmkjćr, Kirsten, editor. 2nd ed. London: Routledge, 2002. 643p. ISBN 0415222095; 0415222109.

This one-volume encyclopedia provides a scholarly overview of the major theories and approaches in linguistics. Information about individual scholars is located in entries dealing with particular theories or schools of thought. Intended as a companion to the *Compendium of the World's Languages* (entry 262), this volume does not cover languages or language families.

Handbooks and Manuals

262. **Compendium of the World's Languages.** Campbell, George L. 2nd ed. London: Routledge, 2000. 2v. ISBN 0415202981.

This companion to *The Linguistics Encyclopedia* (entry 261) provides detailed information about languages and language families, living and extinct, and provides somewhat broader coverage than Comrie's *The World's Major Languages* (entry 265).

263. **Ethnologue: Languages of the World.** Gordon, Raymond G., Jr., editor. 15th ed. Dallas, TX: SIL International, 2005. 1,272p. ISBN 155671159X. Available online at <http://www.ethnologue.com/web.asp>.

Though the original intent of this reference work was to identify the languages/dialects into which the Bible had not yet been translated, it also serves as an extremely useful ready reference tool cataloging 6,912 languages and dialects throughout the world. Arranged by geographical region and country, *Ethnologue* identifies the languages spoken in each region. The information provided includes alternative names, language family, dialects, estimated number of speakers, and literacy. The main text is accompanied by the computer-generated "Language Name Index" and "Language Family Index." The latter lists dialect chains and networks according to mutual intelligibility, while the "Language Name Index" lists over 39,000 names associated with the world's languages, identifying all the alternate language and dialect names. The usefulness of this name index extends beyond its function of indexing *Ethnologue*; it lists an average of five alternate names for the almost 7,000 recognized world languages and therefore serves as a ready reference source for identifying a named language that may not appear in other classified lists or indexes.

The free web edition contains "all the content of the print edition" and can be searched by country, language family, or language name files to find demographic and linguistic information. Hypertext links between these three basic access points facilitate broadening and narrowing of searches.

264. **The Languages of the World.** Katzner, Kenneth. 3rd ed. New York: Routledge, 2002. 384p. ISBN 0415250048; 041525003X.

This single-volume provides detailed descriptions of over 200 languages, including written examples of the language, its history, major characteristics, language family, dialects, and loan words in English. A large table in the front of the book lists 600 of the world's languages, locating each within its family, subgroup, branch, and subbranch. Also includes a country-by-country list of languages spoken.

265. **The World's Major Languages.** Comrie, Bernard, editor. New York: Oxford University Press, 1987. 1,025p. ISBN 0195205219.

This impressive work is a collaborative project by over 40 linguists. More than 50 major languages and language families are thoroughly described and analyzed. Historical, sociological, and linguistic information is presented for each language, along with extensive descriptions of each language's phonological and graphic systems, morphology, syntactic patterns, and word formation. Bibliographic notes and extensive references follow each chapter, though these are now rather dated. This publication was the basis for the more detailed treatments in the *Routledge Language Family Descriptions* series.

Archives and Special Collections

266. **A Catalog of the C.F. and F.M. Voegelin Archives of the Languages of the World.** Urciuoli, Bonnie. Bloomington, IN: Archives of Traditional Music, Indiana University, 1988. 8v. ISBN OCLC: 17857575.

Established within the Archives of Traditional Music at Indiana University (entry 431), the C.F. and F.M. Voegelin Archives of the Languages of the World contain the world's largest collection of recorded languages. The volumes contain an inventory list of the collections that provides language/dialect name, collector, collection accession number, and a description of the collection. For the researcher seeking primary material, this catalog identifies the holdings of an important linguistic archive.

267. **Speech Accent Archive.** Weinberger, Steven H. George Mason University. Available online at <http://accent.gmu.edu/>.

The speech accent archive "uniformly presents a large set of speech samples from a variety of language backgrounds. Native and non-native speakers of English read the same paragraph and are carefully transcribed" (from the website, accessed April 3, 2006). As of this writing, the archive includes over 500 sample recordings in Quicktime format, with detailed linguistic and demographic background information on each speaker. The archive can be browsed by the first language of the speaker or by region of the world and selection made based on basic demographic information. This freely available website provides a rich source of primary data for linguists, language instructors, and others interested in the variations in English pronunciation across the globe.

Research Areas

Chapter 5

The cross-fertilization between anthropology and other disciplines such as psychology and education continue to evolve, and diverse theoretical and topical concerns—such as transnational/global anthropology and the anthropology of food and nutrition—establish themselves as additional areas of specialization. There is little consensus within the discipline as to the classification or terminology for these areas. Research areas such as environmental anthropology and medical anthropology have emerged, defying obvious placement within the "four subfields" model. The *Author and Subject Catalogues of the Tozzer Library* (entry 107) recognizes 19 subfields of anthropology, including folklore, ethnomusicology, anthropology of religion, ethnography, and others. Other schemes have placed specializations with distinctive theoretical and methodological approaches, such as psychological, urban, and economic anthropology, under the umbrella of cultural anthropology (Honigmann, John J. *Handbook of Social and Cultural Anthropology*. Chicago: Rand McNally, 1973).

In this guide, most widely recognized research areas have been included in this chapter, not including humanities-related fields (covered in Chapter 6) and applied anthropology, museum studies, and visual anthropology (Chapter 3), which are treated separately due to their distinctive methodological orientations. Not all specializations have developed a body of reference literature (e.g., symbolic and interpretive anthropology), so the list of research areas treated below is not exhaustive.

Agriculture, Food, and Nutrition

The IUAES Commission on Food and Food Problems (entry 788) takes an applied approach to the anthropology of food and nutrition. *Ecology of Food and Nutrition* (1971-) is an international journal that approaches food, nutrition, and agriculture from a broadly ecological perspective and includes a number of anthropologists on its editorial board. The anthropology of food also includes studies that approach food and foodways as a cultural signifier, as folklore, or as something that is "good to think." Food can provide a window into the social world that ramifies from breaking bread at the dinner table to global commodities trading.

Literature Surveys and Reviews

268. **"The Anthropology of Food and Eating."** Mintz, Sidney W., and Christine M. Du Bois. *Annual Review of Anthropology* 31 (2002): 99–119. ISSN: 0084-6570.

Arguing that the study of food and eating is important "both for its own sake... and because the subfield has proved valuable for debating and advancing anthropological theory and research methods," Mintz (a landmark figure in Caribbean anthropology who has had a long-standing interest in food) and Du Bois trace the anthropology of food beginning with early studies, but focusing primarily on contemporary research. They provide a bibliographic essay on ethnographic studies of food and eating organized into seven subcategories: classic ethnographies of food and foodways; single commodities and substances; food and social change; food insecurity; eating and ritual; eating and identities; and instructional materials.

269. **"Food and Globalization."** Phillips, Lynne. *Annual Review of Anthropology* 35 (2006): 37–57. ISSN: 0084-6570.

Phillips reviews the literature on food and globalization, tracing two strands of research: food as a commodity and food as a focal point in ideas about globalization.

Indexes, Abstracts, and Databases

270. **Agricola**, Vol. 1-. Baltimore, MD: U.S. National Agricultural Library. 1970-. ISSN 0897-3237. Available on CD-ROM and online. <http://www.nal.usda.gov>.

Useful for research on cross-cultural agricultural practices, ethnobotany, and development-related topics, *Agricola* covers the vast literature of the agricultural sciences. All books, journals, dissertations, theses, microforms, audiovisuals, software, and technical reports received in the National Agricultural Library are indexed, including items published in the fifteenth century. The database supports searching for books, journal articles, or both simultaneously. This database is available for free on the website <http://www.nal.usda.gov> or can be licensed on various platforms. The print version ceased in 1996.

271. **CAB Abstracts**, Vol. 1-. Cambridge, MA: CABI Publishing. 1973-. ISSN not assigned. Available on CD-ROM and online by subscription.

Useful for topics related to ethnobotany, ethnopharmacology, human nutrition, and rural sociology, *CAB Abstracts* indexes the worldwide agricultural literature. Publications from over 125 countries in more than 50 languages are included, with particularly good coverage of publications from Western Europe and the United Kingdom. Nearly 9,000 journals titles are indexed, along with conference proceedings, books, technical reports, and selective patents.

272. **Native American Ethnobotany Database.** Moerman, Dan. University of Michigan-Dearborn. Available online at <http://herb.umd.umich.edu/>.

Moerman, a Professor of Anthropology at the University of Michigan-Dearborn, provides database of nearly 80,000 plants used by Native Americans as food, medicine, dyes, and for other purposes. The plant names link to the *USDA Plant Database*.

Dictionaries, Encyclopedias, and Handbooks

273. **The Cultural Feast: An Introduction to Food and Society.** Bryant, Carol A., Kathleen M DeWalt, Anita Courtney, and Jeffrey H. Schwartz. 2nd ed. Belmont, CA: Thomson/Wadsworth, 2003. 446p. ISBN 0534525822.

Written by a group of professors and public health officials, this textbook examines the "complex matrix of technological, social, and ideological factors that influence human food systems and the impact that diet has on our social, political and economic structures" (preface). Specific sections address subjects ranging from the diet of early hominids to hunger in a global perspective. A detailed index aids in locating information on a particular topic or cultural group and a thirty page list of references facilitates further research.

274. **Edible Medicines: An Ethnopharmacology of Food.** Etkin, Nina L. Tucson, AZ: University of Arizona Press, 2006. 301p. ISBN 0816520933.

Etkin, who holds a dual appointment as professor in anthropology and in the School of Medicine at the University of Hawaii, presents a wide-ranging account of the medicinal properties of foods in specific cultural contexts. With excellent general and scientific name indexes, this volume serves as a handy reference for anthropologists, nutritionists, and others interested in the physiological effects of food and the cultural dynamics of food choice. Foodies will enjoy features like an eight-page appendix highlighting the salient features of "Some Common Spices." The reference list runs almost twenty pages and serves as a unannotated bibliography of the ethnopharmacological literature.

275. **Encyclopedia of Food and Culture.** Katz, Solomon H., editor. New York: Scribner, 2003. 3v. ISBN 0684805685.

Edited by an anthropologist with assistance from a culinary historian, this three-volume encyclopedia provides a sociocultural perspective on food and food-related practices from the paleolithic to the present day. The set includes over 600 signed articles, varying in length from 1–10 pages, with current bibliographies. The table of contents lists 27 topical areas, arranged alphabetically, including feasts and festivals, obesity, regions and culture, religion, and staple foods. Biographies of important individuals in food history are also included. A large number of interesting illustrations, tables and charts that present statistical data on food consumption and import/exports further enrich this unique reference source. A detailed index and the logical, intuitive organization of the entries make this one of the more useful food-related encyclopedias and its broad scope is ideally suited to the interests of anthropologists.

Bibliographies

276. **A Bibliography of Foodways, Zooarchaeology, and Faunal Identification on Historical Sites.** Hampton, William, compiler. Available online at <http://www.mtsu.edu/~kesmith/TNARCHNET/Pubs/foodbib.html>.

This online bibliography is weighted toward the archaeological perspective, but also includes some interesting bibliographies on topics related to contemporary foodways.

277. **Human Food Uses: A Cross-Cultural, Comprehensive Annotated Bibliography.** Freedman, Robert L. Westport, CT: Greenwood Press, 1981. 552p. ISBN 0313229015.

(See entry 278)

278. **Human Food Uses: Supplement.** Freedman, Robert L. Westport, CT: Greenwood Press, 1983. 387p. ISBN 0313234345.

Developed "for scholars and scientists requiring data on various aspects of food in human culture" (preface), this comprehensive bibliography includes more than 9,000 citations to books, articles, government reports, theses and dissertations, and conference proceedings in Western languages. The book is arranged alphabetically; users must depend on the keyword index for access to citations on particular topics (e.g., obesity, coca) and cultures. The index is less useful for the latter because some categories are too broad and thus contain an unwieldy number of references (e.g., over 700 references to Native North Americans). Entries range from scientific studies of cultivation to food use in ceremonies.

The supplement expands upon the original work, identifying and annotating over 4,000 additional sources. The keyword index is better organized and provides geographic and topical subdivisions under terms for more precise access, though some geographic entries remain too large.

279. **Melting Pot: An Annotated Bibliography and Guide to Food and Nutrition Information for Ethnic Groups in America.** Newman, Jacqueline M. 2nd ed. New York: Garland, 1993. 240p. ISBN 0824077563.

Conceptually, this title is related to ethnic studies, medical anthropology, and the anthropological study of food and culture. Newman addresses food, nutrition, and health-related dietary concerns of the major ethnic groups in the United States. Many of the entries are technical in nature (e.g., breast cancer and diet among Japanese Americans), emanating from literature in the fields of health and nutrition, and are of potential interest to medical and physical anthropologists. Numerous citations, however, deal with sociocultural aspects of food within the context of Black, Hispanic, Native American, Middle Eastern, and Asian American societies. Over 500 annotated references to books and articles are organized by ethnic group. Unfortunately, no subject index is provided.

280. **World Food Habits: English-Language Resources for the Anthropology of Food and Nutrition.** Dirks, Robert. Illinois State University. Available online at <http://lilt.ilstu.edu/rtdirks/>.

Created and maintained by Robert Dirks, Professor Emeritus of Anthropology at Illinois State University, this website compiles thematic and regional bibliographies of English-language sources related to the anthropology of food and nutrition. Bibliographies by subject include "Cannibalism," "Feasts and Festivals," "Food and Social Identity," "Infants and Children," "Linguistic Studies," "Prehistoric Diets," etc. Articles that are available online or have online abstracts or reviews are linked directly from the site.

Internet Gateways

281. **Anthropology of Food.** Centre d'Edition Numérique Scientifique du CNRS. Available online at <http://www.aofood.org/>.

This website is the home of the open access web journal the *Anthropology of Food* (1999-), produced and published by a network of European academic researchers interested in the social science of food. The site also provides a collection of links related to food and culture, including webliographies, professional associations, research institutes, and journals.

Art and Material Culture

Anthropologists have frequently focused on the arts and artistic traditions of the societies they study. Their interest lies less with the objects themselves than with the application of anthropological theory, which ranges from cultural diffusion to structural principles of artistic production. Through scholarship on the anthropology of art is allied more closely with symbolic and cognitive anthropology than with art history, the anthropologist and the art historian frequently play complementary roles and can benefit from sharing each other's literature. Reflecting a growing interdisciplinary interest in material culture and social artifacts, the *Journal of Material Culture* (entry 683) was launched in 1996 and draws on art history, design, and museology as well as anthropology and archaeology. Visual anthropology, a related but methodologically and theoretically distinct area of study, is covered in Chapter 3.

Guides to Reference Literature

282. **Indigenous Architecture Worldwide: A Guide to Information Sources.** Wodehouse, L. Detroit, MI: Gale, 1980. 392p. ISBN 0810314509.

Wodehouse, an architect, has provided a useful bibliography on vernacular architecture around the world. Over 500 books, encyclopedia articles, dissertations, and periodical articles (primarily from *National Geographic* and *Architectural Review*) are organized by geographic region or country and briefly annotated. The section on Africa, for example, lists general works and citations to the indigenous architecture of countries ranging from Algeria to Zimbabwe. The subject index provides access by specific topic, such as building elements (doors, roofs, floors), materials (adobe, bamboo, earth), and types of residential architecture (huts, platform dwellings, tents).

Literature Surveys and Reviews

283. **The Anthropology of Art.** Layton, Robert. 2nd ed. New York: Cambridge University Press, 1991. 258p. ISBN 0521363675.

This examination of art, from the perspective of an anthropologist, provides a cultural context and framework that art historians typically neglect. Focusing on the art of "other" (i.e., non-European) cultures, Layton explores aesthetic traditions, art and social life, imagery and style, art and visual communication, and creativity of the artist. Situating the discussions within specific cultures, primarily Africa, the Pacific Islands and North America, he provides numerous citations to the literature of anthropologists (such as Boas) who have explored the artistic expressions of the cultures they studied. The book concludes with a bibliography and index by subject, culture group, and personal name.

284. **The Anthropology of Art: A Reader.** Morphy, Howard, and Morgan Perkins. New York: Blackwell, 2006. 576p. ISBN 1405105615.

Reflecting on both the history and contemporary practice of the anthropology of art, this collection of readings includes classic articles from Boas and Levi-Strauss to articles on contemporary tourist art. Sections include "Framing the Discipline;" "Primitivism and Art/Artifact;" "Aesthetics across Cultures;" "Form Style, and Meaning;" "Marketing Culture;" and "Contemporary Artists." A total of 30 articles and excerpts of the work of notable anthropologists of art, dating from 1955 to 1998, is included.

285. **Art as Culture: An Introduction to the Anthropology of Art.** Hatcher, Evelyn Payne. 2nd ed. Westport CT: Bergin & Garvey, 1999. 337p. ISBN 0897896289.

As the preface states, this book is not about objects of art themselves, as much as it is about the ideas that people have had about art as part of the human condition. It describes what is meant by the anthropology of art, and in particular the "who, what, where, when, how" questions that practitioners hope to answer. Art objects and ethnographic examples are used to illustrate the author's points.

286. **Encyclopedia of Hair: a Cultural History.** Sherrow, Victoria. Westport, CT: Greenwood Press, 2006. 455p. ISBN 0313331456.

This unique reference source examines hair and hairstyles as a cultural signifier across cultures and through time. Essay-length entries (with references to further readings, ample cross-references and illustrations in color and black and white) describe the social-historical aspects of hair care and styling worldwide, with an emphasis on Western traditions and the United States. A comprehensive bibliography, arranged by type of resource (books, journal articles, and websites), makes this an excellent starting point for research on the cultural significance of hair.

287. **Handbook of Material Culture.** Tilley, Chris, editor. London: Sage, 2006. 556p. ISBN 1412900395.

This handbook provides an overview of material culture studies as a theoretical and conceptual field, surveying its theories, domains, production, performance, and traditions of study. From food to housing, clothing and monuments, people's relation to the material world is explored. Also included are critical debates in the field, such as the politics and poetics of representing, displaying and conserving cultural materials.

288. **"The World in Dress: Anthropological Perspectives on Clothing, Fashion, and Culture."** Hansen, Karen Tranberg. *Annual Review of Anthropology* 33 (2004): 369–392. ISSN: 0084-6570.

Hansen provides both a thematic and regional overview of recent anthropological research on clothing and fashion. She also traces shifting theoretical paradigms that have increasingly focused on the study of dress as a phenomena worthy of study in and of itself.

Indexes, Abstracts, and Databases

289. **Art Index,** Vol. 1-. New York: H.W. Wilson. 1929-. Quarterly. ISSN 0004-3222. Available in print and online by subscription.

Covering approximately 300 domestic and foreign periodicals, yearbooks and museum bulletins, this venerable index provides a useful tool for accessing ethnological topics from the perspective of art history. Coverage for area studies is particularly good, and citations under the heading "Ethnology" identify articles with a specifically anthropological focus. Additional areas of interest to anthropologists are the citations relating to photography, filmmaking, and museology.

290. **Bibliography of the History of Art.** Los Angeles, CA, and Paris: Getty Research Institute and the Institut de l'Information Scientifique et Technique (INIST). 1973-. Available online by subscription.

The *Bibliography of the History of Art* (BHA) database grew out of the merger of the primary international indexes to research in art history, the *International Repertory of the Literature of Art* (RILA) and the *Repertoire d'art et d'archaeologie*. The online database covers materials published from 1973 to present, and includes the fine, applied, and decorative arts, material culture, photography, and the visual arts aspect of performing arts. The indexes are bilingual (French and English) and coverage is extensive, with citations to journal articles, monographs, collections of essays and book chapters, conference proceedings and exhibition catalogs.

291. **Ethnoarts Index.** Seattle, WA: Data Arts. 1984-1998. ISSN 0893-0120.

Though it ceased in 1998, *Ethnoarts Index* provides retrospective bibliographic coverage of published research with citations to books, periodical articles, exhibition catalogs, dissertations and conference papers, primarily in English and other Western European languages. Approximately 800 unannotated references are included in each volume. Arrangement is by broad geographical area, with indexes by author and subject. Particularly impressive is the broad range of material indexed, including a significant amount of "gray literature" in the form of museum publications, working papers, etc. Continues *Tribal Arts Review*, 1984–1988. For publication information regarding the periodicals cited, readers are referred to the companion title *Serials Guide to Ethnoart* (entry 293).

Dictionaries and Encyclopedias

292. **Dictionary of Art.** Turner, Jane, editor. New York: Grove, 34v. ISBN 1884446000. Also available online as *Grove Art Online.*

While this significant reference work focuses heavily on the Western notion of "fine arts," the set nonetheless offers excellent background on the arts of many of the world's indigenous cultures. The extensive articles are often accompanied by color photographs or images, and the online version seamlessly links related topics. This massive undertaking took several years and several hundred contributors (including several anthropologists) to compile. Extensive bibliographies and a thorough index further enhance its usefulness.

Directories

293. **Serials Guide to Ethnoart.** Burt, Eugene C. New York: Greenwood, 1990. 368p. ISBN 0313273324.

Subtitled *A Guide to Serial Publications on Visual Arts of Africa, Oceania, and the Americas*, this directory provides information on over 700 serials relevant to the study of the arts of indigenous peoples. The list was generated from serials in the disciplines of art, anthropology, natural history, museology and ethnomusicology, among others. Arrangement is alphabetical by serial title; and entries include former title, publisher and address, frequency, cost, focus, beginning date of publication, language, illustrations, book reviews, advertising, notices and a rating indicating the relative importance of the title for ethnoart research. Though this guide has not been updated, it remains useful for identifying specialized and elusive publications in the ethnoarts.

Bibliographies

Note: Because separately published bibliographies of the arts of specific peoples are too numerous to identify here, only selected general bibliographies are included.

294. **Ethnoart: Africa, Oceania, and the Americas: A Bibliography of Theses and Dissertations.** Burt, Eugene C. New York: Garland, 1988. 191p. ISBN 0824075455.

Utilizing over 30 sources, including bibliographies of theses and dissertations from Australia, France, Great Britain, Germany, and countries in Africa, Burt has compiled an extensive record of graduate research on the arts of indigenous peoples. The book is organized by region and subdivided by specific ethnic group; entries include author, title, degree and date, and number of pages. The discipline in which the degree was earned, however, is not included, nor are citations annotated. The author's assertion that interest in ethnoart has burgeoned since mid-century is borne out in the size and scope of this bibliography, which identifies over 1,300 theses and dissertations. The subject index reflects the diversity of topics covered from analyses of basketry techniques to aesthetic preferences and tourist art.

295. **Masks from Antiquity to the Modern Era: An Annotated Bibliography.** Inhaber, Herbert. New York: Routledge, 2003. 313p. ISBN 081833603.

This bibliography includes over 1,200 citations to books, catalogs, dissertations, periodical articles, and nonprint media relating to masks. Each entry provides bibliographic information and an annotation. Entries are arranged alphabetically by author, but include geographic and subject headings. Also included is a brief list of museums from around the world that have mask collections. Illustrations include 16 plates of masks collected by the author, a collector, and student of masks.

Cognitive Anthropology

Influenced by cognitive psychology, linguistics, and structural anthropology, cognitive anthropology focuses on the concept of culture as an ideational system, that is, a system of categories, rules, and organizing principles common to a given culture. The perspectives from cognitive anthropology gave rise to the "new ethnography," which attempts to record the view from inside another culture. Though much research has been conducted within the theoretical framework of cognitive anthropology, few systematic reviews or surveys have been produced. As cognitive anthropologists share common ground with both linguists and psychologists, however, they can utilize sources in these fields.

A few of the sources listed below (e.g., *Encyclopaedia of the History of Science, Technology, and Medicine in Non-Western Cultures*, entry 298) do not take a strictly cognitive approach—focusing on cross-cultural studies of scientific practices, but not necessarily the underlying systems of classification that inform those practices. They are nevertheless included because they bring together information about systems of knowledge and categorization across cultures that are highly relevant to research in cognitive anthropology.

Literature Survey and Reviews

296. **Categorical Impulse: Essays on the Anthropology of Classifying Behaviour.** Ellen, R. F. Berghahn Books, 2005. 224p. ISBN 1845450175 .

In his lengthy introduction to this collected volume, Ellen traces the development of anthropological studies of classification and argues that there has been a substantial rapprochement between the British constructionist tradition exemplified by Mary Douglas and American ethnosemantics presented by Harold Conklin and Brent Berlin. The essays from leading scholars in the field show how the scholarly debate on this subject has unfolded since the 1960s.

297. **Culture & Cognition: Implications for Theory and Method.** Ross, Norbert. Thousand Oaks, CA: Sage, 2004. 203p. ISBN 0761929061; 076192907Xpa.

Ross brings together cognitive anthropology and cognitive psychology to create a roadmap for research in the study of the interrelation between cultural processes and thinking and behavior.

Dictionaries and Encyclopedias

298. **Encyclopaedia of the History of Science, Technology, and Medicine in Non-Western Cultures.** Selin, Helaine, editor. Dordrecht: Kluwer, 1997. 1,117p. ISBN 0792340663.

Selin, a librarian with an impressive record of publication on science and medicine across cultures, has brought together nearly 600 articles by more than 300 contributors describing astronomy, ethnobotany, mapmaking, medicine, philosophy, and science across cultures. Contributors include historians of science and scientists, as well as anthropologists. An updated and expanded edition, entitled *Encyclopaedia of the History of Non-Western Science: Natural Science, Technology and Medicine*, is expected in 2007. Selin has also edited a monographic series, *Science across Cultures* (entry 301), that explores some of these topics in greater depth.

Bibliographies

299. **Bibliography of Anthropology of Quantification.** Lawless, Robert. Available online at <http://coombs.anu.edu.au/Biblio/biblio_numbers.html>.

Lawless has created a handy online bibliography of ethnographic studies of quantification and indigenous mathematics. Most of the citations are to English-language publications.

300. **Folk Classification: A Topically Arranged Bibliography of Contemporary and Background References through 1971.** Conklin, Harold C. New Haven, CT: Department of Anthropology, Yale University, 1980. 521p. ISBN 0913516023.

Identifying and organizing the work of cognitive anthropologists with regard to indigenous systems of classification, this classic bibliography lists over 5,000 citations to books and articles dealing with principles of classification including kinship, ethnobotany, ethnozoology, ethnomedicine, orientation, color, and sensation.

301. **Science Across Cultures: An Annotated Bibliography of Books on Non-Western Science, Technology, and Medicine.** Selin, Helaine. New York: Garland, 1992. 431p. ISBN 0815308396.

This annotated bibliography lists sources dealing with science (including astronomy, ethnobotany, mathematics, medicine, navigation, and other sciences and technologies) in cultures worldwide.

Series

302. **Science Across Cultures: the History of Non-Western Science (series).** Selin, Helaine, editor. Dordrecht: Kluwer, 2000-. ISSN: 1568-2145.

This series publishes collections of essays focusing on topics related to cross-cultural studies of science and knowledge. Past volumes include *Astronomy Across Cultures* (2000), *Mathematics Across Cultures: The History of Non-Western Mathematics* (2000), *Medicine Across Cultures: History and Practice of Medicine in Non-Western Cultures* (2003), and *Nature Across Cultures: Views of Nature and the Environment in Non-Western Cultures* (2004).

Economic Anthropology

Originally focusing on small-scale, traditional economics, economic anthropology is concerned with the broad issues of production, distribution, and exchange in comparative perspective as well as with the ethnographic description of specific economic systems, and the interplay between global economic systems and local communities. Indeed, economic anthropology can be difficult to untangle from some strands of global and transnational anthropology and a number of titles listed in the "Urban, National, and Transnational Anthropology" section of this chapter are highly relevant to economic anthropology.

Though anthropologists may borrow concepts and constructs from the field of economics, the vast reference literature of economics holds relatively little scholarship of direct relevance to the anthropologist. The literature generated by economic anthropologists has, however, been synthesized into several useful (if somewhat dated) bibliographies. The Society for Economic Anthropology (entry 831) facilitates the exchange of ideas in the field.

Literature Surveys and Reviews

303. **"The Anthropology of Money."** Maurer, Bill. *Annual Review of Anthropology* 35 (2006): 15–36. ISSN: 0084-6570.

This review article traces recent research in anthropology and other social sciences on money and finance. Maurer argues for looking at the pragmatic and performative aspects of monetary exchange and circulation as a corrective to the usual semiotic approach. He concludes "that the new anthropology of money is taking a different tack. The continual 'discovery' and then subsequent decomposition of money's supposedly unique attributes are themselves integral to money, to its own analytical abstractions, and to those social scientists trying to catch up behind it" (p. 29).

304. **Economic Anthropology.** Gudeman, Stephen, editor. Cheltenham; Northampton, MA: Elgar, 1998. 576p. ISBN 1858987598.

This volume brings together a selection of classic and contemporary papers exploring the intersection between anthropology and economics. The collection provides an excellent overview of the development of the discipline of economic anthropology from 1922 to 1998.

Handbooks and Manuals

305. **A Handbook of Economic Anthropology.** Carrier, James G. Northampton, MA: Elgar, 2005. 584p. ISBN 1843761750.

This handbook provides an accessible, but rigorous, introduction to the anthropological study of economic processes, institutions, and daily life throughout the world. Sections on orientations, elements, circulation, integrations, issues, and regions bring together articles on topics ranging from households to post-socialist economies. Topics are treated concisely, but suggestions for further reading provide a springboard to more in-depth research. This volume is also useful for tracing the contributions of particular figures that have been influential in the field.

Bibliographies

306. **Economic Anthropology.** Plattner, Stuart, editor. Stanford, CA: Stanford University Press, 1989. 487p. ISBN 0804716455; 0804717524pa.

The essays in this classic overview of economic anthropology reflect the expertise of 12 economic anthropologists as they define, describe, and analyze the parameters of economic anthropology. Chapters range from a discussion of the economic behavior of hunters and gatherers to trade and markets in developing urban areas to women in economic institutions. Each chapter provides a review of the literature and addresses basic issues on the topic, providing numerous bibliographic citations.

307. **Economic Anthropology 1940–1972: An Annotated Bibliography.** Van der Pas, H. T., compiler. Oosterhout, Netherlands: Anthropological Publications, 1973. 221p. ISBN not assigned.

Written to provide access to the early literature of economic anthropology, this detailed and comprehensive bibliography provides annotations of over 500 books and articles appearing during a 30-year period. The annotations are lengthy and well written, providing a concise synopsis of each entry. Arrangement is chronological. The scope is international, but the majority of the entries are from English-language publications. An index by author and geographic area/ethnic group is provided, but no specific subject or topical access is available.

308. **Social Science Bibliography on Property, Ownership, and Possession: 1580 Citations from Psychology, Anthropology, Sociology, and Related Disciplines.** Rudmin, Floyd W., Russell W. Belk, and Lita Furby. Monticello, IL: Vance Bibliographies, 1987. 134p. (*Public Administration Series Bibliography*, P-2294). ISBN 1555905749.

Although not strictly focusing upon economic anthropology, this bibliography contains a considerable number of relevant citations. The subject index includes topics such as acquisition, comparative economics, exchange and trade, and social functions of property, as well as nearly 300 citations dealing specifically with ethnographic aspects of property and procession and subdivided into seven geographic regions. The unannotated citations identify books and articles from the nineteenth century through the mid-1980s and incorporate ethnographic and sociological perspectives as well as legal, economic, and political analyses.

Education

The fields of anthropology and education converge on several levels. Pedagogical concerns constitute one plane, and because many anthropologists are also teachers, they are involved with issues such as curriculum development and content. Comparative education represents another level at which the disciplines meet. Applied anthropologists in particular may be involved in addressing the educational needs of specific cultural groups or of peoples in developing countries. In a more theoretical vein, anthropologists study "educational culture," the nature of those institutions charged with transmitting the information deemed valuable and important to members of a society. Formal and informal educational systems exert a powerful influence on the individual and the society and play a critical role in the transmission of culture.

Interest in anthropology and education is evidenced by the establishment of the American Anthropological Association's Council on Anthropology and Education (entry 755), which publishes the journal *Anthropology and Education Quarterly* (entry 648).

Guides to the Reference Literature

309. **Education: A Guide to Reference and Information Sources.** O'Brien, Nancy P. 2nd ed. Englewood, CO: Libraries Unlimited, 2000. 189p. ISBN 1563086263.

In a clearly written and well-organized text, O'Brien provides a guide to the voluminous reference literature in the field education. In addition to presenting general reference works such as indexes, financial aid directories, and statistical sources, she identifies and describes works on specific topics. Bibliographies and handbooks on multilingual and multicultural education, comparative education and international, educational testing and measurement, and the history, philosophy, and psychology of education are of particular note.

Literature Surveys and Reviews

310. **"Highlights and Overview of the History of Educational Ethnography."** Yon, Daniel A. *Annual Review of Anthropology* 32 (2003): 411–429. ISSN: 0084-6570.

This essay "identifies and reviews key trends and theoretical orientations that have shaped the field of educational ethnography from the period of its inception to the closing decade of the twentieth century" (abstract).

Indexes, Abstracts, and Databases

311. **Education Index,** Vol. 1-. New York: H.W. Wilson. 1929-. Monthly, with annual print cumulations. ISSN 0013-1385. Available in print and online by subscription.

Though the coverage is more limited than in other educational indexes, this venerable reference source has greater retrospective coverage and it provides useful references relating to the teaching of anthropology, comparative educational systems, and anthropology as an academic discipline. Relevant subject headings include "Fieldwork," "Educational Anthropology," "Ethnology," and "Cultural Relativism." The back files covering 1929–1983 are available separately as *Education Index Retrospective*. Wilson also provides different levels of access to the same content: *Education Index* has indexing only for some 750 journals, *Education Abstracts* provides abstracts as well as indexing for those titles, and *Education Full Text* provides full text going back to 1996 from approximately 300 of the 750 journals indexed.

312. **ERIC (Educational Resources Information Center).** Washington, DC: U.S. Department of Education. Available online. <http://www.eric.ed.gov/>.

ERIC combines the print indexes *Resources in Education* and *Current Index to Journals in Education* into one extensive database. Indexing articles from over 700 journals in education and a wide variety of other fields, this comprehensive source is useful for accessing material that bridges anthropology and education. From culture-biased tests to ethnographic studies of school students, this source also includes curriculum materials for teaching anthropology. Relevant headings include "Educational Anthropology," "Cross-cultural Studies," "Museums," and "Area Studies," among others. ERIC can be accessed for free via the government-sponsored site listed above, but many libraries chose to license access from a vendor to provide a common interface and for better search and retrieval functionality.

Environmental Anthropology

Anthropology's holistic orientation and focus on human social interaction *in situ* has meant that an environmental perspective can be found in many strands of anthropological practice, albeit not always explicitly articulated. There is, however, an active body of research that identifies itself as environmental or ecological anthropology. The Anthropology and the Environment Section (entry 747) of the American Anthropological Association provides a forum for anthropologists interested in ecology, the environment and environmentalism and the journal *Human Ecology* (entry 672) focuses on the "complex and varied interactions between people and their environment" from a primarily anthropological perspective.

Literature Survey and Reviews

313. **"Environments and Environmentalisms in Anthropological Research: Facing a New Millennium."** Little, Paul E. *Annual Review of Anthropology* 28 (1999): 253–284. ISSN: 0084-6570.

This review articles focuses on two major strands of anthropological research on the environment: ecological anthropology and the anthropology of environmental movements.

314. **Human Adaptability: An Introduction to Ecological Anthropology.** Moran, Emilio. 2nd ed. Westview Press, 2000. 446p. ISBN 081331254X.

Moran, one of the preeminent figures in environmental anthropology, provides a synthesis of the systems approach to ecological anthropology in this well-received volume, now in its second edition. The crux of this approach is a focus on human adaptability and human-habitat interaction. Moran's bibliography runs nearly 80 pages and is useful in its own right as an entry point into the literature of environmental anthropology and that one of its major intellectual forbearers, cultural ecology.

Ethnohistory

Anthropologists and historians share extensive scholarly involvement in area studies and also utilize similar methodologies such as oral history. The field of ethnohistory applies the methods of historiographic research to the study of cultural and social processes. It involves developing histories that include a holistic perspective incorporating the lived experience and knowledge of people in a particular time and place.

The journal *Ethnohistory* (entry 664) published by The American Society for Ethnohistory (entry 809) brings together anthropologists and scholars from other disciplines (e.g., geography and history) interested in the ethnohistorical method of developing histories informed by ethnography, linguistics, archaeology, and ecology, with a particular emphasis on the ethnohistory of the Americas.

Guides to Reference Literature

315. **Handbook for Research in American History: A Guide to Bibliographies and Other Reference Works.** Prucha, Francis Paul. 2nd ed. 1994. 214p. ISBN 0803237014; 0803287313pa.

Prucha's guide to reference literature in American history, written by a noted historian and Native American studies scholar, provides useful general information on the utilization of newspapers, manuscripts, state and local materials, legal sources, and atlases and maps. The first edition was hailed as "an excellent tool for historians of all interests and levels of experience" and the revised second edition is equally successful in providing a guide to research in an increasingly online environment. Chapters on reference sources in social history, women, racial and ethnic groups, as well as regional material and travel accounts, will be of particular interest to anthropologists.

Series

316. **The Ethnohistory Series.** Wallace, Anthony, and Lee V. Cassanelli, series editors. Philadelphia: University of Pennsylvania Press, 1985-. ISSN not assigned.

Launched in the mid-1980s by Anthony Wallace and Lee Cassanelli, two of the major names in ethnohistory, this series from the University of Pennsylvania Press selectively publishes monographs in the field. The series is published in conjunction with Pennsylvania's long-standing Ethnohistory Program, established in 1976 to "explore the areas of intellectual convergence between historians engaged in the 'new' social history and anthropologists interested in a diachronic approach to the study of social and symbolic forms" (website).

Evolutionary Anthropology

Standing at the crossroads of sociocultural and biological anthropology, evolutionary anthropology involves the application of evolutionary theories to the analysis of human behavior and culture. The Evolutionary Anthropology Society of the American Anthropological Association (entry 745) provides a forum for anthropologists interested in evolutionary perspectives on human behavior and publishes the journal *Human Nature*.

Literature Surveys and Reviews

317. **Evolutionism in Cultural Anthropology: A Critical History.** Carneiro, Robert L. Boulder, CO: Westview Press, 2003. 322p. ISBN 0813337658; 0813337666pa.

Carneiro, one of the most prominent contemporary proponents of cultural evolutionary theory, traces the cross-fertilization of cultural anthropology and evolutionary theory from nineteenth-century theorists (Spenser, Morgan, Tylor, etc.) to the present day. This comprehensive and erudite account will be of interest to historians of anthropology and graduate students grappling with the intellectual genealogies of the discipline, as well as those interested in cultural evolution.

Series

318. **Origins of Human Behavior and Culture (series).** Borgerhoff Mulder, Monique, and Joe Henrich, editors. Berkeley, CA: University of California Press, 2006-. ISBN various.

This series focuses on evolutionary approaches to the study of human and primate societies. Interdisciplinary approaches to studying behavior and culture (both past and present) in terms of adaptive significance, mechanism, ontogeny, and phylogenetic history are featured. The first volume, *Behavioral Ecology and the Transition to Agriculture* (2006) is a collection of essays applying the framework of human behavioral ecology to the transition from foraging to farming in the New and Old Worlds.

History of Anthropology

The rich and abundant literature of anthropology provides a fertile field for historians of the discipline. Fortunately for those interested in the history of anthropology, there have been many successful attempts at organizing and synthesizing these materials—represented here by a highly selective sample.

Literature Surveys and Reviews

319. **Fieldwork and Footnotes: Studies in the History of European Anthropology.** Vermeulen, Han F., and Arturo Alvarez Roldán. London; New York: Routledge, 1995. 261p. ISBN 0415106559; 0415106567pa.

Drawing on papers presented at several workshops on the history of anthropology in Europe, this collection offers a corrective to the usual focus on Anglo-American (and perhaps French) scholarship when discussing cultural anthropology. The essays included here examine anthropological practice and the development of the discipline in Poland, Slovenia, Spain, Germany, and elsewhere. The approaches to the subject are rather diverse and the collection as a whole provides only partial glimpses into the whole of European anthropology, but it provides an excellent starting point for further exploration.

320. **A History of Anthropological Theory.** Erickson, Paul A., and Liam Donat Murphy. 2nd ed. Orchard Park, NY: Broadview Press, 2003. 283p. ISBN 1551115263.

Erickson and Murphy give a concise overview of the history of anthropological theory in the United States and also provide a useful chronology and bibliography. Given its scope and level of treatment, this is probably more appropriate for undergraduates than graduates, but it provides a solid and very readable introduction to the subject and its index makes it handy for ready reference. A companion volume, *Readings for a History of Anthropological Theory* (2001), provides a selection of texts illustrating the themes discussed here.

321. **A History of Anthropology.** Eriksen, Thomas Hylland, and Finn Sivert Nielsen. London; Sterling, VA: Pluto Press, 2001. 207p. ISBN 074531385Xpa; 0745313906.

Written by social anthropologists Erikson (U. of Olso) and Nielsen (U. of Copenhagen), this volume provides a concise history of the discipline of anthropology spanning precursors in early Greece through the 1990s. The coverage is detailed enough to provide a handy overview for advanced students, and the lengthy bibliography and a detailed index makes it a useful reference source.

Handbooks and Manuals

322. **European Anthropologies: A Guide to the Profession.** Rogers, Susan Carol, Thomas M. Wilson, and Gary W. McDonogh, editors. Arlington, VA: American Anthropological Association, 1996. 66p. ISBN 0913167762.

This volume was intended to foster links between "American anthropologists of Europe and their European colleagues" (introduction), but is now useful mainly for its documentation of anthropological practice in specific European countries. The first part of the volume is comprised of short profiles describing the history and practice of sociocultural anthropology in 21 European countries. The second half provides addresses of major institutions and organizations and selected publications for each country. A useful table of "Approximate Terminological Equivalents" is provided, listing terms used in Britain, France, Germany, and Sweden. Volume 2 was intended to provide the same treatment for archaeology (a separate discipline in many European countries) but this follow-up volume has not yet been published.

Bibliographies

323. **Ecce Homo: An Annotated Bibliographic History of Physical Anthropology.** Spencer, Frank. Westport, CT: Greenwood Press, 1986. 495p. ISBN 0313240566.
(See entry 246)

324. **History of Anthropology Bibliography.** Erickson, Paul A. rev ed. Halifax, Nova Scotia: St Mary's University, 1991. ISBN not supplied.
This unannotated bibliography of approximately 3,000 citation complements and updates the earlier publication by Kemper and Phinney (*The History of Anthropology: A Research Bibliography*. New York: Garland, 1977). The revised edition includes all titles from the first edition, supplements, and new works and material not previously identified. A third edition, produced in 1998, is only held by a handful of libraries.

Entries are arranged alphabetically with indexes by author, topic, geographic area, and names of individuals. Given the large number of citations, however, the index can prove cumbersome because many of the terms are too general (e.g., physical anthropology has over 50 entries). Citations include books and journal articles and consist of secondary sources, i.e., works *about* anthropology or *about* anthropological research.

Series

325. **Histories of Anthropology Annual.** Darnell, Regna, and Frederic W. Gleach, editors. Lincoln, NE: University of Nebraska Press. 2006-. ISSN 1557-637X.
This new annual publication "is dedicated to the proposition that there is a diversity in the history of anthropology as a disciplinary specialization... that is not reaching its appropriate audiences. *HOAA* will assemble such diverse efforts and make them more visible and accessible" (introduction). Not surprisingly, the inaugural volume covers a diversity of themes, from the influence of Herbert Spenser to anthropology and the Cold War.

326. **History of Anthropology.** Handler, Richard, editor. Madison, WI: University of Wisconsin Press. 1983-. ISSN 0891-9348.
Founded by George W. Stocking, a noted historian of anthropology, this monograph series continues to provide a respected outlet for scholars reflecting on the history of the discipline. Each volume in the series is devoted to a specific theme and features a collection of articles by noted anthropologists that offer a

succinct overview and review of the literature as well as identify important issues and trends.

Marriage and Family

Studies of kinship and households have long been a hallmark of sociocultural anthropology. The sources listed below are largely separate from that tradition, but do provide a jumping off point for research on marriage and families worldwide. In addition to the sources listed below, many of the publications sponsored by the Human Relations Area Files (entry 817), including *eHRAF Collection of Ethnography* (entry 481) and the *Encyclopedia of World Cultures* (entry 473), provide a rich source of cross-cultural information on marriage, family, and kinship worldwide.

Indexes, Abstracts, and Databases

327. Family and Society Studies Worldwide: An International Perspective on the Family & Society. Baltimore, MD: National Information Services Corporation (NISC). 2001-. Monthly. Available on CD-ROM and online by subscription.

Published in association with the National Council on Family Relations (NCFR), this database now encompasses content drawn from three sources: (1) *Family and Society Studies* (1970–present) a comprehensive index to research, policy, and practice literature in family studies, human ecology, human development, and social welfare, with bibliographic records from over two thousand professional journals, books, popular literature, conference papers, government reports, and other sources; (2) *Australian Family & Society Abstracts* (1980–present), which covers the Australian literature and includes links to many full-text reports; and (3) *U. S. Military Family Resource Center Documents Database,* which covers a wide range of publications (articles, reports, chapter, dissertations, etc.) dealing with policy and research on military families and family programs.

Dictionaries and Encyclopedias

328. International Encyclopedia of Marriage and Family. Ponzetti, Jr. James J. 2nd ed. New York: Macmillan, 4v. ISBN 0028656725.

This updated four volume encyclopedia "is a compendium surveying the shared patterns and amazing variation in marriage and family life in a rapidly changing multicultural world" and is designed for use by general readers as well as scholars and students seeking information on global family lifestyles. Users can look for information by subject (e.g. adoption, later life families, stress) or by country name (though not every country is included). A comprehensive and detailed index is provided in Volume 4.

329. **Marriage Customs of the World: From Henna to Honeymoons.** Monger, George P. Santa Barbara, CA: ABC-Clio, 2004. 327p. ISBN 1576079872; 1576079880e.

Covering ground no other current reference source approaches, Monger (a folklorist and museum conservator based in East Anglia, England) examines the rites and practices associated with marriage across the world. More than 200 alphabetical entries explore topics (e.g., adultery, trousseau) or geographic regions (e.g., Afghanistan, Zulu weddings).

Medical Anthropology

The social and cultural aspects of health and disease hold profound implications for anthropologists. Though considered by some as a branch of applied anthropology, medical anthropology is more appropriately viewed as a biocultural discipline whose practitioners are concerned with both the biological and sociocultural aspects of health and disease. Thus the scope of medical anthropology ranges from etiological and epidemiological studies to ethnographic studies of traditional medical systems to analyses of a society's world view, social systems, and values based upon the society's perception and treatment of disease. Mental health and ethnopsychiatry frequently bridge both medical and psychological anthropology but will be considered here under "Psychological Anthropology."

Medical anthropologists have established several professional societies, which include the IUAES Commissions on Medical Anthropology and Epidemiology (entry 793) and on the Anthropology of AIDS (entry 798) and the American Anthropological Association's Society for Medical Anthropology (entry 768). Relevant journals include *Culture, Medicine, and Psychiatry* (entry 660), *Medical Anthropology* (entry 688), and *Medical Anthropology Quarterly* (entry 689).

Though anthropological interest in theoretical aspects of cross-cultural medical systems has been longstanding, only recently has the literature of medical anthropology taken on its own identity. Not surprisingly, research in medical anthropology involves the use of medical literature, and reference works such as dictionaries, histories of medicine, and indexes are useful sources for anthropologists to consult.

Guides to Reference Literature

330. **Information Sources in the Medical Sciences.** Morton, Leslie T. 4th ed. New York: Bowker-Saur, 1992. 608p. ISBN 0862915961.

To the uninitiated, the corpus of medical literature can be truly daunting. Although the anthropologist may have little need to identify journals, or textbooks dealing with surgery or anesthesia, medical anthropologists may find useful the good, basic introduction to general medical reference sources (as well as specialized titles) provided by Morton. The guide begins with a discussion of primary sources of information and strategies for research. This is followed by a discursive bibliography of medical indexes, abstracts, bibliographies and reviews, dictionaries, handbooks, and sources on terminology and nomenclature.

Though the specialized chapters (e.g., pediatrics, clinical medicine, obstetrics, and gynecology) identify sources geared toward medical personnel, several cite useful overview texts and journals relevant to medical anthropology, notably the chapters on public health, tropical medicine, psychiatry, and pharmacology. Few of the works specifically address traditional medicine or medical anthropology—the utility of this guide lies in the sources and strategies it offers for using medical literature.

Literature Surveys and Reviews

331. **"Anthropology and Circumcision."** Silverman, Eric K. *Annual Review of Anthropology* 33 (2004): 419–445. ISSN: 0084-6570.

Silverman reviews the anthropology of male and female circumcision over the last 100 years and offers his own analysis of gender symbolism surrounding male circumcision in the Judeo-Christian traditions and in current debates over female circumcision in sub-Saharan Africa and elsewhere.

332. **Medical Anthropology: Contemporary Theory and Method.** Sargent, Carolyn Fishel, and Thomas M. Johnson, editors. Rev. ed. Westport, CT: Praeger, 1996. 557p. ISBN 0313296588; 0275952657pa.

Sargent and Johnson provide an introduction to medical anthropology and a "state-of-the-art" survey organized into five sections, encompassing theoretical perspectives, medical systems, health issues in human populations, methods in medical anthropology, and policy and advocacy. Within each section, individual chapters trace major developments, define current parameters, and discuss future directions. The topics addressed in the 19 chapters, such as clinically applied anthropology, the professionalization of indigenous healers, and culture and disease, bear witness to the expansion and diversity of medical anthropology in the 1990s and offer an excellent overview of central issues in the field.

Indexes, Abstracts, and Databases

333. **MEDLINE.** Bethesda, MD: National Library of Medicine, 1966-. Available online by subscription or free as *PubMed* <http://www.pubmed.gov>.

The premier medical index, *MEDLINE* identifies and organizes medical literature published in books, journals, and reports and incorporates content from *Index Medicus*. Directed toward medical and public health personnel, this source will be of interest to medical and biological anthropologists. Coverage is worldwide, but most records are from English-language sources or have English abstracts. *MEDLINE* is sometimes packaged with other medical resources like *CINAHL* and *EMBASE* and is freely available through *PubMed*, a service of the U.S. National Library of Medicine that includes over 16 million citations from *MEDLINE* and additional biomedical journals. *PubMed*'s search engine can be used to link to over 700 journals for full text articles if access is permitted via a library subscription or the content is open access.

334. **Population Index.** Princeton, NJ: Office of Population Research, Princeton University, 1937-2000. ISBN ISSN 0032-4701. Available in print and online at <http://popindex.princeton.edu>.

This specialized index provides abstracts of articles, books and technical reports on population, family planning, health care and policy issues. The online database, maintained by the Population Information Program at Johns Hopkins University with assistance from Princeton University, covers materials published between 1986 and 2000.

Dictionaries and Encyclopedias

335. **Encyclopedia of AIDS: A Social, Political, Cultural, and Scientific Record of the HIV Epidemic.** Smith, Raymond A., editor. New York: Penguin, 2001. 782p. ISBN 0140514864.

Smith, a research scientist at the HIV Center for Clinical and Behavioral Studies at the New York State Psychiatric Institute, has compiled a comprehensive and multi-faceted snapshot of the AIDS epidemic and its social, political, and medical ramifications. Signed articles written by 181 contributors from around the world cover topics of interest to anthropologists, including epidemiology, culture and society, and the global epidemic. A good starting point for research, all entries include pointers to related entries, key words for searching online resources and suggestions for further reading.

336. **Encyclopedia of Medical Anthropology: Health and Illness in the World's Cultures.** Ember, Carol R., and Melvin Ember, editors. New York: Kluwer, 2004. 2v. ISBN 0306477548.

This two-volume set produced in conjunction with the Human Relations Area Files (HRAF) (entry 709) explores the social and cultural context of medical beliefs and practices. The first volume contains 53 essays on topics related to general medical concepts and perspectives: medical systems; political, economic, and social issues; sexuality, reproduction, and the life cycle; and health conditions and diseases. The second volume provides portraits of health and illness in 52 cultures from around the world, with every cultural region and varied levels of sociopolitical complexity represented. Each chapter includes a list of references for further research.

337. **Encyclopedia of Plague and Pestilence: From Ancient Times to the Present.** Kohn, George Childs. Rev. ed. New York: Facts on File, 2001. 454p. ISBN 0816042632.

With more than 700 entries, this source is a compendium of information concerning the major epidemics and outbreaks of disease, both past and present, throughout the world. The work chronicles the origins of each disease, their cause, whom they affected, and the significant results. Arranged geographically by disease, entries contain cross-references within the text and a list of further readings that are also included in a comprehensive bibliography. A timetable of plague and pestilence and a detailed general index are also provided.

338. **Medical Anthropology Glossary.** O'Neil, Dennis. Behavioral Sciences Department, Palomar College, San Marcos, California. Available online at <http://anthro.palomar.edu/medical/glossary.htm>.
Part of the *Cultural Anthropology Tutorials*, an excellent set of topical study guides geared toward undergraduate students, this glossary defines terms in the context of medical anthropology.

Handbooks and Manuals

339. **Training Manual in Applied Medical Anthropology.** Hill, Carole E. Washington, DC: American Anthropological Association, 1991. 237p. ISBN 0913167460.
Not a technical training manual as the title might imply, this text serves primarily to prepare the practicing anthropologist for a career in medical anthropology. Chapters include topics such as applied anthropology and public health, medical anthropology and medical education, and anthropologists in hospitals. Each chapter outlines the field, detailing the range of possibilities for an anthropologist's input. Case studies and examples are provided, as well as a discussion of necessary skills and information on getting a job. In addition to bibliographical references following each chapter, an annotated resource bibliography provides citations to books, articles, and reports dealing with the practice of medical anthropology.

Bibliographies

340. **AIDS and Anthropology Bibliography.** AIDS and Anthropology Working Group, American Anthropological Association. Available online at <http://puffin.creighton.edu/aarg/bibliography/index.html>.
Based on *The AIDS Bibliography: Studies in Anthropology and Related Fields* (entry 341), this online bibliography includes all 1,663 citations from that work, as well as additions from other sources including the Center for AIDS Prevention Studies' (CAPS) online bibliography and bibliographical updates from the *Aids and Anthropology Bulletin*. Currently, the bibliography includes more than 4,000 citations covering all aspects of AIDS of interest to anthropologists. In addition to the web-published version (arranged alphabetically by author), the bibliography is also available for download as an ascii or EndNote (Version 8) file.

341. **The AIDS Bibliography: Studies in Anthropology and Related Fields.** Bolton, Ralph, and Gail Orozco, editors. Arlington, VA: Commission on AIDS Research and Education, American Anthropological Association, 1994. 126p. ISBN not assigned.

In order to provide access to the widely dispersed literature on AIDS, Bolton and Orozco have compiled nearly 2,000 citations to the literature documenting research being done in anthropology and other closely related fields. The entries in this volume have since been incorporated into the web-based *AIDS and Anthropology Bibliography* (entry 340), but can still be purchased in the original print format form the American Anthropological Association (entry 745).

342. **Resources for Third World Health Planners.** Singer, Peter, and Elizabeth McKenney Titus. New York: Trado-Medic Books, 1980. 155p. ISBN 0932426115; 0932426123pa.

Having reviewed the anthropological, psychiatric, medical, and specialized literature in the area of traditional healing, Singer and Titus organized the citations into selected subject categories "to provide a scholarly and practical information base upon which to develop further action programs involving traditional practitioners" (preface). The categories include critique of folk medicine; cultural milieu; disease concepts and models; folk-modern contact; and professional practitioners/shamans, among others. The second section provides citations organized by broad geographic area and specific culture group.

The breadth of coverage is impressive; the authors consulted not only North American bibliographic sources and databases, but also did extensive research in the Ethnological Missionary Museum at the Vatican library and in the Pontifical Biblioteca Missionaria in Rome. Over 1,800 unannotated entries to books, articles, and reports are listed. As with other bibliographies in medical anthropology, however, a specific subject index is not provided.

Internet Gateways

343. **Demographic and Health Surveys.** Measure DHS. Available online at <http://www.measuredhs.com>.

This site hosted by Measure DHS (a public-private partnership funded by USAID and private donors) provides an excellent collection of information pertaining to health, nutrition, HIV, and population in 75 countries. It includes survey instruments and data collection tips, data sets (with customizable report generators and queries), publications, country profiles, and a "topics" section that pulls together information on subjects of current interest such as biomarkers or HIV.

Political and Legal Anthropology

Political anthropology is concerned with the study of the organization and management of the public affairs of a society. Although political anthropology was originally conceived as the study of non-Western political systems, that differentiation no longer holds true. Concerns of political anthropologists include origin of the state and development of political institutions, distribution of power, and conflict and dispute. These concerns are represented by the American Anthropological Association's Association for Political and Legal Anthropology (entry 749) and the IUAES Commission on Folk Law and Legal Pluralism (entry 787).

Literature Surveys and Reviews

344. **"Anthropology and International Law."** Merry, Sally Engle. *Annual Review of Anthropology* 35 (2006): 99–116. ISSN: 0084-6570.

Merry defines the scope of contemporary international law as including "war and the treatment of combatants and noncombatants in wartime; international peace and security; the peaceful settlement of disputes; economic arrangements and trade agreements; the regulation of the global commons such as space, polar regions, and the oceans; environmental issues; the law of the sea; and human rights." This review article examines the role of anthropological theory in understanding these processes and reviews ethnographic studies of specific sites within the "complex array of norms, principles, and institutions that constitute international law and legal regulation" (preface).

345. **Law and Anthropology: A Reader.** Moore, Sally Falk. Malden, MA: Blackwell, 2005. 371p. ISBN 1405102276; 1405102284.

Moore, a respected name in contemporary anthropology, augments this collection of previously published essays with her own rich interpretation of themes and trends. The essays are organized into three major groupings: "Early Themes that Re-appear in New Forms," "The Early Classics of Legal Ethnography," and "Present Thematic Approaches." She closes the volume with one of her own lectures: "Certainties Undone: Fifty Turbulent Years of Legal Anthropology, 1949–1999," given as the 2001 Huxley Memorial Lecture to the Royal Anthropological Association.

346. **"Madening States."** Aretxaga, Begoña. *Annual Review of Anthropology* 32 (2003): 393–410. ISSN: 0084-6570.

This article reviews recent research on state power and the ways that the state "becomes a social subject in everyday life" particularly through violence, sexuality, and desire.

347. **Political Anthropology: An Introduction.** Lewellen, Ted C. 3rd ed. Westport, CN: Praeger, 2003. 262p. ISBN 0897898907; 0897898915pa.

Lewellen describes his book as "a painless overview . . . not a scholarly monograph, nor a state of the art summary, nor, heaven forbid, a survey of the literature" (preface). His protests notwithstanding, the text serves as a succinct summary of the development of political anthropology over the past 50 years, an examination of its theoretical structure and a review of the contributions of its main formulators.

(He succeeds, however, in making it painless.) Each chapter contains numerous bibliographic references and an annotated list of suggested readings. A glossary, bibliography, and index are provided.

348. **Political Anthropology: Power and Paradigms.** Kurtz, Donald V. Boulder, CO: Westview Press, 2001. 251p. ISBN 0813338034; 0813338042pa.

Kurtz (Professor Emeritus of Anthropology at the University of Wisconsin-Milwaukee) provides an overview of the history and development of political anthropology as a distinct area of interest within anthropology. As such, the focus is primarily on theoretical orientations and approaches, but Kurtz is careful to demonstrate how these tools have been used in the field. The substantial (22 page) bibliography provides a useful introduction to the literature of political anthropology.

349. **"Violence, Terror, and the Crisis of the State."** Nagengast, Carole. *Annual Review of Anthropology* 23 (1994): 109–136. ISSN: 0084-6570.

Written in 1994, this article looks at the interplay between globalization and the crisis of the nation state, ethnic violence, and terror and provides an excellent review of the burgeoning anthropological literature on the topic.

Indexes, Abstracts, and Databases

350. **CIAO: Columbia International Affairs Online.** New York: Columbia University Press. 1997-. Monthly. Available online by subscription. <http://www.ciaonet.org/>.

Developed as a collaborative effort between the Columbia University libraries and Columbia University Press with funding from the Mellon foundation, *Columbia International Affairs Online (CIAO)* is a comprehensive source for theory and research in international affairs. It provides full-text access a wide range of scholarship from 1991 to the present that includes working papers from university research institutes, occasional papers series from NGOs, foundation-funded research projects, and proceedings from conferences. Not all content is full-text; some books and articles include only abstracts.

351. **PAIS International,** Vol. 1. New York: Public Affairs Information Service. 1991-. Monthly. ISSN 1051-4015. Available online by subscription.

(See entry 162)

Bibliographies

352. **The Anthropology of War: A Bibliography.** Ferguson, R. Brian, and Leslie E. Farragher. New York: Guggenheim Foundation, 1988. 361p. ISBN not supplied.

In the introduction, Ferguson analyzes trends in the anthropological interest in war and points to the dramatic upsurge in the number of publications on warfare by anthropologists from the 1960s through 1986. In an attempt to organize and synthesize the literature on the topic, he has compiled a classified bibliography of over 1,500 unannotated citations to books and journal articles. Focusing on "non-modern warfare," Ferguson excludes developments associated with the spread of European control (e.g., the advent of gunpowder), although "anthropological approaches to contemporary war, and studies of slave, peasant, and tribal insurrections" are included (preface). Organizations of the citations into topical chapters, such as a social organization and war, the psychology of collective violence, belief systems and cognitive orientations, and ritual and war, among others, precludes a subject index.

Psychological Anthropology

Anthropological interest in human behavior has given rise to the area of specialization known as psychological anthropology. Broad in scope, its concerns have evolved from culture and personality studies, strongly influenced by psychoanalytic and behaviorist theory to comparative studies of child development, abnormal behavior, perception and cognition, learning, memory, and states of consciousness—to name a few.

Psychological anthropologists are represented by the American Anthropological Association's Society for Psychological Anthropology (entry 769), which publishes the journal *Ethos* (entry 668). Within the discipline of psychology, the related field of cross-cultural psychology has also established professional societies, such as the International Association for Cross-Cultural Psychology (entry 820).

Guides to Reference Literature

353. **Psychology: A Guide to Reference and Information Sources.** Baxter, Pam M. Englewood, CO: Libraries Unlimited, 1993. 219p. ISBN 0872877086.

Focusing on reference sources in psychology and related disciplines, this annotated bibliography covers over 600 selected sources. Of particular interest is the section covering anthropology sources and special topics such as "Comparative Psychology and Ethnology."

Indexes, Abstracts, and Databases

354. **PsycINFO.** Washington, DC: American Psychological Association. 1927-. Monthly. ISSN 0033-2887. Available in print as *Psychological Abstracts*; on CD-ROM and online by subscription.

An indispensable research tool for behavioral and social scientists, this index identifies articles, books and dissertations in psychology and related subjects, including medicine, psychiatry, sociology, education, linguistics, and other areas.

Coverage is worldwide, and includes references and abstracts to dissertations from over 1,400 journals in more than 30 languages, and to book chapters and books in the English language. Over 50,000 references are added annually. Popular literature is excluded. *PsycINFO Historic* covers 1887–1966. An extensive and carefully constructed thesaurus provides controlled vocabulary including numerous terms relevant to anthropological research such as culture, ethnology, religion, social organization, social processes, and others.

Dictionaries and Encyclopedias

355. **Dictionary of Multicultural Psychology: Issues, Terms, and Concepts.** Hall, Lena E. Thousand Oaks, CA: Sage, 2005. 179p. ISBN 0761928227; 0761928235pa.

Written from a psychological perspective and intended to provide psychologists working with multicultural populations a basic orientation to cross-cultural psychology, some of the explanations provided here will no doubt seem naive or misinformed to anthropologists familiar with the topics at hand. Nonetheless, this volume will be of interest to some and signals a new rapprochement between the disciplines.

356. **Encyclopedia of Human Emotions.** Levinson, David, James J. Ponzetti, Jr., and Peter F. Jorgensen. New York: Macmillan, 1999. 2v. ISBN 0028647661.

Written primarily to introduce students and the general public to topics related to human emotions, some parts are very technical and intended for scholars unfamiliar with particular subject areas. This two-volume set contains 146 entries that address specific emotions or behavioral expression of emotion; review conceptual, thematic, and theoretical issues; describe the role of emotions in society and the human experience; or identify important contributors to this field of study. Each entry includes a bibliography of sources and a comprehensive bibliography and a subject index are provided at the end of the second volume. Contributors include representatives from psychology, psychiatry, sociology, anthropology, biology, medicine, history, communication, and the arts.

357. **International Encyclopedia of the Social and Behavioral Sciences.** Smelzer, Neil, and Paul B. Baltes, editors. New York: Elsevier, 26v. ISBN 0080430767.

This comprehensive social science encyclopedia has particularly good coverage of psychological topics and approaches. For a full annotation, see entry 13.

Handbooks and Manuals

358. **Clinician's Guide to Cultural Psychiatry.** Tseng, Wen-Shing. San Diego: Academic Press, 2003. 493p. ISBN 0127016333.

The purpose of this text is to aid in clinical training of psychiatrists and clinical psychologists in the area of culture-oriented clinical practice. This work is derived from the *Handbook of Cultural Psychiatry* (Academic Press, 2001), with a focus on extracting information most relevant to clinical practice and adding 29 case vignettes to complement the discussion. Topics addressed include cultural dimensions of stress and illness, general disorders, clinical assessment and care, psychotherapy, and drug therapy, as well as culturally competent assessment, care, and psychotherapy related to working with various ethnic groups common in the United States. Each section concludes with a list of references organized by subject, and the text contains a subject index.

359. **Handbook of Cross-Cultural Psychology.** Berry, John W., Ype H. Poortinga, and Janak Pandey, editors. 2nd ed. Boston: Allyn and Bacon, 1997. 3v. ISBN 0205160743; 0205160751; 020516076X.

This three-volume handbook assembles in one place the key findings of cross-cultural psychologists and, as such, serves as a state-of-the-art review. Each of the volumes deals with a theme or topic, including history and theory of cross-cultural psychology; for example, methodology, including cross-cultural surveys and holocultural research methods; basic processes (e.g., cross-cultural approaches to cognition); development (e.g., cross-cultural research on infancy); social psychology; and psychopathology. The essays provide an excellent review of the literature and offer lengthy bibliographies. Name and subject indexes are provided for each volume.

360. **The Handbook of Culture & Psychology.** Matsumoto, David, editor. New York: Oxford University Press, 2001. 458p. ISBN 0195131819.

Topical essays by distinguished scholars "provide an account of the current state of cross-cultural psychology across a wide range of topics that are representative . . . of the discipline" (preface). Each chapter presents a state-of the art review of the theoretical and empirical literature on that topic, an evaluation of that literature, and a vision of the future work needed in that area. The usefulness of this handbook is further enhanced by a detailed index and extensive reference lists with both classic and current publications (some citations were to items "in press").

361. **Psychology of Cultural Experience.** Moore, Carmella C., and Holly F. Matthews. Cambridge; New York: Cambridge University Press, 2001. 247p. (*SPA Publication*, no. 12). ISBN 0521803195; 0521005523pa.

This collection of essays published by the Society for Psychological Anthropology focuses on "the relationship of individual experience to culture, and chart a new research agenda for psychological anthropology in the twenty-first century" (book jacket). The authors draw on their fieldwork experiences across the globe and employ a variety of approaches, including person-centered ethnography, activity theory, attachment theory, and cultural schema theory.

Bibliographies

362. Anthropological and Cross-Cultural Themes in Mental Health: An Annotated Bibliography, 1925–1974. Favazza, Armando R., and Mary Oman. Columbia, MO: University of Missouri Press, 1977. 386p. ISBN 0826202152.
(See entry 363)

363. Themes in Cultural Psychiatry: An Annotated Bibliography, 1975–1980. Favazza, Armando R., and Ahmed D. Faheem. Columbia, MO: University of Missouri Press, 1982. 194p. ISBN 0826203779.

The two preceding bibliographies deal with the extensive literature that bridges the disciplines of anthropology and psychiatry. In order to treat the study of human behavior within a cultural context, numerous cross-cultural and specific-culture studies are included. Mental health is defined broadly and encompasses virtually all aspects of psychology.

Following its general introduction and overview, *Anthropological and Cross-Cultural Themes in Mental Health* provides over 3,600 annotated citations to English-language articles in a chronological arrangement. A comprehensive subject index provides access to specific culture groups as well as to topics such as aggression, child rearing, intelligence, sex, and suicide, among many others.

Themes in Cultural Psychiatry identifies articles and books on cultural psychiatry published since the previous bibliography. With a similar format and focus, this supplement also includes books, non-English-language journals, and greater coverage of anthological (rather than predominantly psychological) journals.

Series

364. Culture, Mind, and Society (series). New York: Palgrave Macmillan for the Society for Psychological Anthropology. 2002-. ISSN not provided.

Established by the Society for Psychological Anthropology in 2002, this series publishes works that "illuminate the workings of the human mind, in all of its psychological and biological complexity, within the social, cultural, and political contexts that shape thought, emotion, and experience." Volumes published include *American Individualisms: Child Rearing and Social Class in Three Neighborhoods* (2004) and *Finding Culture in Talk: A Collection of Methods* (2005).

Religion

From studies of rites and ceremonies, rituals and cosmologies to symbolic and conceptual studies, the spiritual aspects of the world's cultures have long commanded anthropologists' attention and the *Journal of Ritual Studies* (entry 684) provides a venue for current scholarship in this area. The anthropology of religion constitutes a vital and much-researched area of anthropological enquiry, and the related area of mythology boasts an equally impressive body of literature (see the section on "Folklore and Mythology" in Chapter 6). The titles included here are therefore highly selective, with an emphasis on the study of non-Western religious expression.

Literature Surveys and Reviews

365. **Anthropology of Religion: A Handbook.** Glazier, Stephen D., editor. Westport, CT: Greenwood, 1997. 542p. ISBN 0313283516.

The volume is a collection of readings on "the key findings and methods in the anthropology of religion" (introduction). The book is divided into four sections: "Looking at Religion Anthropologically" identifies issues in religious studies that hold particular interest for anthropologists; "The Study of Ritual" looks at ritual in general, and in Africa, India, Japan, and the United States, including Native America; "Little and Great Traditions" takes a comparative view of Islam, Hinduism, and Buddhism; and "Shamanism and Religious Consciousness" explores shamanic practices and altered states. Together the chapters provide a general overview, but little synthesis.

366. **Ordered Universes: Approaches to the Anthropology of Religion.** Klass, Morton. Boulder, CO: Westview, 1995. 177p. ISBN 0813312132.

In this text, Klass explores religion as a cultural universal, and includes general topics such as definitions of religion, religious institutions, and the relationship between belief and values, as well as specifically anthropologically focused material such as witchcraft, shamanism, ritual, etc. The scope includes religious expressions and movements from traditional to industrialized societies, and provides a succinct introduction to an increasingly timely topic.

367. **Religion and Anthropology: A Critical Introduction.** Morris, Brian. New York: Cambridge University Press, 2006. 350p. ISBN 0521617790.

Morris provides the most recent text devoted to the anthropology of religion. Beginning with a discussion of shamanism, he moves on to cover the world's major religions and explores individual and comparative belief systems and practices. Case studies of selected groups are profiled (e.g., Zar cults in northern Somalia, popular Hinduism), as the variety of religious expression is explored. Millennial, contemporary pagan and new age spiritualism are also covered in this wide-ranging overview.

Indexes, Abstracts, and Databases

368. **Religion Index.** Chicago: American Theological Library Association. 1949-. ISSN 0149-8428. Available in print and online by subscription.

Over 300 periodicals in Western languages (German sources are particularly well represented) are indexed. The focus is on theology and Western religions, particularly Protestant Christianity. Nonetheless, this reference source provides selective access to anthropology-related scholarship within the discipline of religious studies. The index is organized by subject; relevant headings include "Anthropology and Religion" "Mythology," and "Missions" among others. Articles on specific areas or peoples are included under both general and specific headings (e.g., "Indians of Central America—Religion," "Mayas—Religion").

Dictionaries, Encyclopedias, and Handbooks

369. **Encyclopedia of Religious Rites, Rituals, and Festivals.** Salamone, Frank A., editor. New York, NY: Routledge, 2004. 487p. ISBN 0415941806.

Ranging from puberty rites in West Africa to Star Trek conventions (!), this lively but scholarly encyclopedia provides 130 entries treating religious ritual from a variety of perspectives, with global coverage. Each article is followed by suggestions for further reading, and a useful index brings related ideas together. Illustrated sidebars highlight specific primary source materials, chronologies, etc., and complement the text.

370. **Religious Holidays and Calendars: An Encyclopedic Handbook.** Bellenir, Karen, editor. 3rd ed. Detroit, MI: Omnigraphics, 406p. ISBN 0780806654.

This revised and expanded edition provides information about the core beliefs and practices of over 20 major religions. The first section is devoted to the history of calendars, which discusses the development of lunar and solar calendars and calendar reforms, while the second part is divided into chapters that cover the rituals, festivals, and observances of specific religions and sects. The appendix provides a chronology and extensive list of titles for further reading.

371. **Shamanism: An Encyclopedia of World Beliefs, Practices, and Cultures.** Mariko Namba, Walter, and Eva Jane Neumann Fridman. Santa Barbara, CA: ABC-Clio, 2004. 2v. ISBN 1576076458.

A substantial and scholarly treatment of shamanism worldwide with nearly 200 entries by anthropologists, historians, and religious studies' scholars. Divided into two sections, the first covers topics and themes ranging from "Animal Symbolism" to "Witchcraft and Sorcery." The second section is arranged by broad region and includes both a general overview and entries covering specific practices and cultural groups, both contemporary and historical. All entries are cross-referenced and include suggestions for further reading.

372. **Traditional Festivals: A Multicultural Encyclopedia.** Roy, Christian. Santa Barbara, CA: ABC-Clio, 2005. 2v. ISBN 1576070891.

The festivals included here are primarily religious in nature, and include profiles of 150 feast days and ritual observances from the world's major cultures. Festivals are situated in their historical, geographic, and cultural context. Both historical and contemporary festivals are considered, and the entries often provide comparative information that reflects the influence of cultural transmission.

The text is supplemented by photographs and illustrations, and a bibliography is included with each article. The appendices include a chronology of major feasts and festivals by religion and culture area.

Bibliographies

373. **Bibliography of New Religious Movements in Primal Societies.** Turner, Harold W., editor. Boston: G.K. Hall, 1977. 5v. ISBN 0816179271.

These extensive bibliographies identify books, articles, and dissertations on religious movements, including cults and sects, which have arisen within native societies. Each volume is devoted to a broad geographic area (Africa, North America, Oceania, Latin America, Europe, and Asia), and includes introductory essays, citations with descriptive annotations, and indexes by author, ethnic group, and movement.

374. **Shamanism: A Selected Annotated Bibliography.** DeMiller, Anna L. Available online at <http://www.lib.odu.edu/anss/shamanism.html>.

DeMiller, a librarian, compiled a selective, annotated bibliography of reference works and monographs on shamanism. She identifies major works that have been published, primarily since the 1980s. Individual articles appearing in journals are not included, though she identifies the primary journals devoted to the scholarly study of shamanism.

Sexuality and Gender Studies

Closely allied and frequently overlapping with the anthropology of women, research on sex and gender in anthropology has a long history going back at least as far as Mead's cross-cultural studies of sex and temperament. Recent research has broadened to include queer and Lesbian, Gay, Bisexual, and Transgender (LGBT) studies, studies of masculinity, sexworkers, and sex tourism and a distinct reference literature has begun to emerge that covers these areas of research.

The Society of Lesbian and Gay Anthropologists of the American Anthropological Association (entry 778) promotes LGBT research and also serves as a forum for gay and lesbian anthropologists within the Association.

Guides to Reference Literature

375. **Reader's Guide to Lesbian and Gay Studies.** Murphy, Timothy F., editor. Chicago, IL: Fitzroy Dearborn Publishers, 2000. 720p. ISBN 1579581420.

With nearly 500 signed bibliographic essays, this volume serves as a reference guide to existing academic literature on topics relevant to gay and lesbian studies. Each entry provides a brief overview of a particular issue, person, period, or topic and lists the key scholarly sources to consult for further information.

The guide includes a general index, a booklist index and both an alphabetical and thematic list of entries.

376. **A Research Guide to Human Sexuality.** Lichtenberg, Kara Ellynn. New York: Garland, 1994. 497p. ISBN 0815308671.

Lichtenberg provides comprehensive guide to the multidisciplinary literature on human sexuality and a directory of libraries and organizations active in the field. Although the sources listed were published between 1982 and 1993, the guide continues to offer some useful pointers on terminology, primary source material, and approaches to starting the research process in a field where the literature is dispersed across a number of disciplines.

Literature Surveys and Reviews

377. **Same Sex, Different Cultures: Exploring Gay and Lesbian Lives.** Herdt, Gilbert. Boulder, CO: Westview Press, 1997. 224p. ISBN 0813331633; 0813331641pa.

Herdt, director of the Human Sexuality Studies Program and professor of Anthropology at San Francisco State University, provides an overview of homosexuality and same sex relationships in cultures, both historical and contemporary, across the globe. Although none of these are treated in depth, Gilbert provides a glimpse of the diversity of sexual practices and attitudes worldwide and provides citations to further readings for those who want to delve deeper.

378. **"Trafficking in Men: The Anthropology of Masculinity."** Gutmann, Matthew. *Annual Review of Anthropology* 28 (2000): 509–529. ISSN: 0084-6570.

As Gutmann notes in the opening sentences of this review essay, "Anthropology has always involved men talking to men about men. Until recently, however, very few within the discipline of the 'study of man' had truly examined men as men." He then goes on to review the literature on men as engendered subject, categorize the four major approaches to the study of masculinity and sketch some of the areas of topical interest in anthropological studies of men.

Indexes, Abstracts, and Databases

379. **Gender Studies Database.** National Information Services Corporation (NISC). 1972-. Quarterly. Available on CD-ROM and online by subscription.

This database combines NISC's *Women's Studies International* (entry 405) and *Men's Studies* (entry 382) databases.

380. **Gender Watch.** Proquest. 1998-. Quarterly. Available online by subscription.

This full-text database covers academic and scholarly journals, magazines, newspapers, newsletters, pamphlets, and NGO special reports back to the 1970s.

Subject areas include business, education, literature and the arts, health sciences, history, public policy and contemporary culture with a focus on the United States.

381. **GLBT Life.** Ipswich, MA: EBSCO. 2002-. Continually updated. Available online by subscription.

GLBT Life provides access to the scholarly and popular literature related to gay, lesbian, bisexual, and transgender issues. It fully indexes and abstracts 80 core periodicals and selectively covers thousands of other titles. Lifestyle and regional publications are included (e.g., *Washington Blade, Bay Area Reporter*), as well as grey literature, bibliographies, case studies, and selected dissertations. Also available with full text.

382. **Men's Studies Database.** National Information Services Corporation (NISC). 1990-. Available on CD-ROM and online by subscription.

Indexing more than 225 serials, this niche database provides multidisciplinary coverage of men's identity and experience and includes journal articles, book reviews, books, book chapters, theses, dissertations, bulletins, newsletters, and online resources from 1990 to the present.

383. **Sexual Diversity Studies: Gay, Lesbian, Bisexual & Transgender Abstracts.** National Information Services Corporation (NISC). 1997-. Available on CD-ROM and online by subscription.

This database provides citations and abstracts of articles, reviews, and essays appearing in almost 600 sources, including journals, magazines, newspapers, newsletters, books, proceedings, reports, dissertations, websites, and multimedia sources dealing with gay, lesbian, bisexual, and transgendered communities. Continues *Gay & Lesbian Abstracts* and is also available as part of the *Gender Studies Database* (entry 379).

Dictionaries and Encyclopedias

384. **The Continuum Complete International Encyclopedia of Sexuality.** Francoeur, Robert T., Raymond J. Noonan, and Beldina Opiyo-Omolo, editors. Rev. ed. New York: Continuum, 2004. 1,419p. ISBN 0826414885.

This updated edition of this reference work provides a dense compilation of current information about sexuality and sexual practices in 64 countries worldwide. Although coverage is clearly biased toward European countries, the breadth is nonetheless impressive. The country profiles were compiled by a panel of 27 experts, with natives or area studies experts serving as the lead author. The profiles follow a standard outline (including "Important Ethnic, Racial, and/or Religious Minorities") and include a list of references and additional readings. This encyclopedia provides an incomparable source of current information for cross-cultural studies of sexuality.

385. **Encyclopedia of Lesbian and Gay Histories and Cultures.** Zimmerman, Bonnie, and George Haggerty, editors. New York: Garland, 2000. 2v. ISBN 0815319207; 0815333544.

In two separate, but complementary, volumes Zimmerman (Women's Studies, San Diego State University) and Haggerty (English, University of California-Riverside) provide an overview of gay and lesbian histories and communities. The subject guide provided at the front of each volume includes a heading for "anthropology" that points to entries with some sort of anthropological dimension.

386. **Encyclopedia of Sex and Gender: Men and Women in the World's Cultures.** Ember, Carol R., and Melvin Ember, editors. New York: Kluwer, 2003. 2v. ISBN 030647770X.

Published in conjunction with the Human Relations Area Files (entry 481), this encyclopedia takes a decidedly anthropological approach to issues of sex and gender that sets it apart from other similar titles. The first volume is divided between 22 topical essays (grouped under three themes: "Cultural Conceptions of Gender," "Gender Roles, Status, and Institutions," and "Sexuality and Male-Female Interaction") and an alphabetical listing (A–K) of culture groups. The second volume finishes the culture-by-culture listing (L–Z). A glossary and subject and alternate culture name indexes are also included.

387. **Men and Masculinities: A Social, Cultural, and Historical Encyclopedia.** Kimmel, Michael, and Amy Aronson, editor. Santa Barbara, CA: ABC-Clio, 2004. 2v. ISBN 1576077748; 1576077756e.

Reflecting a growing interest in studies of masculinity, this encyclopedia explores male gender roles. Approximately 400 one-to-two page signed articles examine particular individuals, historical events, the arts, pop culture and psychological or cultural processes that both challenge and reflect particular constructions of masculinity. Almost all examples are drawn from the U.S. experience.

Urban, National, and Transnational/Global Anthropology

Though urban anthropology is concerned with the application of anthropological research techniques and methods to the study of people living in cities, in a broader sense it encompasses research on large-scale societies. Urban anthropology developed as a consequence of the rapid transformation of rural groups into city dwellers and focuses on topics such as recent immigrants to cities, rural-urban networks, voluntary associations that facilitate adjustment, and culture change. More recently, research in this area has focused on the interplay of the global and the local and the transnational flow of people, commodities and capital.

Urban and transnational anthropologists contribute to and benefit from urban studies research conducted by their colleagues in sociology, geography, and city planning and consequently can draw upon a broad literature base. A number of relevant professional associations have been formed, notably the American Anthropological Association's Society for Urban, National and Transnational/Global Anthropology (entry 776), which publishes *City and Society* (entry 655), and the IUAES Commission on Urban Anthropology (entry 804). The journal *Urban Anthropology and Studies of Cultural Systems and World Economic Development* (entry 694) serves as another forum for communication. See also "General Area and Ethnic Studies" in Chapter 7 for additional relevant sources.

Literature Survey and Reviews

388. **The Anthropology of Development and Globalization: From Classical Political Economy to Contemporary Neoliberalism.** Edelman, Marc, and Angelique Haugerud, editors. Malden, MA: Blackwell, 2005. 406p. ISBN 0631228799; 0631228802pa.

Like *Anthropology of Globalization: A Reader*, this volume brings together articles from some of the leading anthropologists interested in global social and economic flows. Indeed, some of the same authors appear in both volumes (e.g. Ferguson, Friedman). This volume, however, has a somewhat broader scope, tracing the current interest in globalization back to its roots in classical political economy and forward into various thematic areas (e.g., Comaroff and Comaroff on millennial capitalism or Escobar on post-development).

389. **Anthropology of Globalization: A Reader.** Inda, Jonathan Xavier, and Renato Rosaldo, editors. Malden, MA: Blackwell, 2002. 498p. ISBN 0631222324; 0631222332.

This volume brings together key articles by notables like Appadurai, Gupta, Ferguson, Abu-Lughod, and Scheper-Hughes as well as some substantial synthesis and reflection by Inda and Rosaldo whose "Introduction: A World in Motion" runs 35 pages. A comprehensive index enhances the usefulness of the reader as a reference source. An updated and revised edition of this seminal volume is scheduled for publication in Spring 2007.

390. **"The Local and the Global: The Anthropology of Globalization and Transnationalism."** Kearney, M. *Annual Review of Anthropology* 24 (1995): 547–565. ISSN: 0084-6570.

Kearney provides a concise review of the anthropological literature on the global flows of immigrants, populations, information, capital, and commodities in transnational spaces.

391. **"Urbanization and the Global Perspective."** Smart, Alan, and Josephine Smart. *Annual Review of Anthropology* 32 (2003): 263–285. ISSN: 0084-6570.

In this review article, Smart and Smart review anthropological research on late capitalist cities, after first reviewing what the global perspective means within anthropology and how it affects anthropological research on urbanization.

Dictionaries and Encyclopedias

392. Encyclopedia of Diasporas: Immigrant and Refugee Cultures around the World. Ember, Melvin, Carol R. Ember, and Ian Skoggard, editors. New York; London: Kluwer, 2004. 2v. ISBN 0306483211.

Another excellent reference source focusing on a topic of current interest created under the auspices of Human Relation Area Files (entry 817), this encyclopedia provides a rich and nuanced view of mass migrations and refugee cultures informed by the anthropological perspective. The signed entries were contributed by team of international experts and include topical essays, as well as descriptions of particular diasporas and diasporic communities.

393. Encyclopedia of Urban Cultures: Cities and Cultures around the World. Ember, Melvin, and Carol R. Ember. Danbury, CT: Grolier, 2002. 4v. ISBN 0717256987.

Following the highly successful approach of *Countries and their Cultures* (entry 467), the Embers have edited another excellent cross-cultural reference source covering a topic of compelling contemporary importance. Produced under the auspices of the Human Relations Area Files (entry 817), this four-volume set provides an anthropologically informed look at 240 urban centers worldwide. Each city is treated an individual entry providing a basic "orientation" (location, population, attractions, languages) to the metropolitan area and tracing its history, infrastructure and political, economic, and cultural life. In addition, topical essays discuss subjects like health and disease or describe patterns of urbanization in a particular region.

394. The History of Human Populations, Volume II: Migration, Urbanization, and Structural Change. Harris, P. M. G. Westport, CT: Praeger, 2003. 553p. ISBN 0275971910.

This is the second volume of a three part series that focuses on forms of change in human population history. Harris examines the historical literature related to three major population trends across the globe: free migration, involuntary migration and the slave trade, and urbanization. Tables and figures accompany the text and the volume includes and index. An extensive bibliography points to additional sources of information.

Bibliographies

395. Industrial Anthropology: A Selected Annotated Bibliography. Pennbridge, Julia N. Washington, DC: Society for Applied Anthropology, 1984. 229p. ISBN not supplied.

Although dated, Pennbridge's well-annotated bibliography on industrial ethnology fills a definite gap in the literature and is of use to applied anthropologists as well as to those studying contemporary subcultures. Over 800 citations to books and articles are organized into sections on theory, industry, and society, organization as social-technical-economic system, workers, managers, methodology, and literature reviews. Acknowledging that the line between industrial anthropology and the sociology of work is unclear and that the literature on industrial social psychology, management, and economics is likewise related, Pennbridge does not limit her citations to strictly anthropological literature. Cross-cultural studies are included, and the focus is international. A detailed subject index provides additional access by specific topic (alienation, productivity), industry (mining, fishing), or geographic region.

396. **Urban Anthropology in the 1990s: A Collection of Syllabi and an Extensive Bibliography.** Glasser, Irene, and Lawrence B. Breitborde. Rev. ed. Washington, DC: Society for Urban Anthropology, 1996. 340p. ISBN not supplied.

This revised and expanded edition compiles 49 course syllabi from both graduate and undergraduate courses and provides an extensive bibliography of urban studies research of relevance to anthropologists. The syllabi are arranged into three sections: (1) General Urban Anthropology Courses; (2) Geographically-Focused Courses; and (3) Topically-Focused Courses.

Media, Film, and Images

397. **Urban Life on Film and Video: A Collection of Reviews for the Teaching of Urban Anthropology.** Glasser, Irene, editor. Washington, DC: Society for Urban Anthropology, 1995. 55p.

This volume brings together reviews of 34 films that can be used in teaching urban anthropology. Many of the reviews also include suggested readings and classroom discussion questions. The reviews are arranged by topic and country.

Women

There is, of course, considerable overlap between women's studies/feminist ethnography and studies of sexuality and gender. The anthropology of women is treated separately here in recognition of the distinct body of literature on women, as well as the theoretical contributions and symbolic importance of women's studies as a distinct field of research. Anthropological studies of women have included examination of the status and role of women across cultures as well as considerations of male bias in ethnography (and the corresponding scarcity or misinterpretation of women's perspectives).

Several associations reflect the ties between women's studies and anthropology, including the IUAES Commission on the Anthropology of Women (entry 802), the International Women's Anthropology Conference (entry 822), and the American Anthropological Association's Association for Feminist Anthropology (entry 748).

Guides to Reference Literature

398. **Women's Studies: A Recommended Bibliography.** Krikos, Linda A., Cindy Ingold, and Catherine Loeb. 3rd ed. Westport, CT: Libraries Unlimited, 2004. 828p. ISBN 1563085666.

This is third in a series of bibliographies that serve as a basis for identifying a core collection of in-print, English-language publications relating to women. Organized around academic disciplines and types of literature, the anthropology section includes annotated titles that present historical and contemporary ethnographic studies focusing on women. Following the same format and scope as its predecessors, the 2004 edition provides a selection of nearly 100 titles published between 1986 and 1999 under the heading "anthropology, cross-cultural studies and international studies." Selections reflect both theoretical issues and ethnographic studies of women in specific cultures.

Literature Surveys and Reviews

399. **Feminism and Anthropology.** Moore, Henrietta L. Minneapolis, University of Minnesota Press, 1988. 246 p. ISBN 0816617481; 0816617503pa.

In this classic overview of the principal theoretical issues and concerns defining the anthropology of women, Moore touches upon gender and status, kinship, women's work, women's lives, and women and the state. Each chapter offers a general synthesis and analysis of the literature, and extensive notes and bibliography are included.

400. **Feminist Anthropology: A Reader.** Lewin, Ellen, Editor. Malden, MA; Oxford: Blackwell, 2006. 460p. ISBN 1405101954; 1405101962pa.

In this collection of classic and current essays exploring key themes emerging from feminist anthropology, Lewin endeavored to avoid duplicating essays collected elsewhere and focused on "substantive and ethnographic writings." The collection is divided into five thematic sections, each with an introduction and an in-depth bibliographic essay.

401. **Feminist Anthropology: Past, Present, and Future.** Geller, Pamela L., and Miranda K. Stockett, editors. Philadelphia: University of Pennsylvania Press, 2006. 226p. ISBN 0812239407.

In this volume, Geller and Stockett (both archaeologists interested in sex and gender in pre-Colombian Mesoamerica) invited contributors from all of the subfields of anthropology to reflect on issues related to sex and gender. The focus here is on how these issues have been theorized within anthropology, with attention to three central issues: critical revisioning of old interpretations, working within the academy, and the critique of heteronormativity.

402. **"Histories of Feminist Ethnography."** Visweswaran, Kamala. *Annual Review of Anthropology* 26 (1997): 591–621. ISSN: 0084-6570.

Feminist ethnography, a term of recent vintage, nonetheless has already come to define a specific interdisciplinary methodological tradition. In this review essay, Viswessan traces how "changes in the conception of gender define the historical production of feminist ethnography in four distinct periods" between the late nineteenth century and the present.

Indexes, Abstracts, and Databases

403. **Contemporary Women's Issues.** Gale Group. 1992-. Weekly. Available online by subscription.

A collection of full-text sources with excellent coverage of health and human rights globally. Includes research reports and fact sheets from nonprofit groups; governments; NGOs; and international agencies, as well as journal and magazine articles, book reviews, pamphlets, and newsletters. Coverage is international, but mostly English language.

404. **Studies on Women and Gender Abstracts.** Abingdon, Oxfordshire: Carfax Publishing/Taylor & Francis.1983-. ISSN 0262-5644; 1467-596X. Available in print and online by subscription.

This British publication indexes a wide variety of international books and journal articles with detailed abstracts and good coverage of the anthropological literature. The online version provides coverage from 1995 forward.

405. **Women's Studies International,** Vol. 1-. National Information Services Corporation (NISC). 1972-. Monthly (online); Quarterly (CD-ROM). Available on CD-ROM and online by subscription.

This database combines ten different women's studies databases and bibliographies, including *Women, Race And Ethnicity: A Bibliography, 1970–1990* and *Women's Studies Abstracts,* both incorporated in 2003. Primarily covers scholarly journals, books, and book reviews related to women's studies with some popular magazines and other publications. Coverage is international, but the primary focus is journals published in the United States, United Kingdom, and Canada. Although the citations do not draw heavily from anthropological literature, the index nonetheless identifies important interdisciplinary works on topics of interest to anthropologists involved in women's and gender studies.

Atlases

406. **The Penguin Atlas of Women in the World.** Seager, Joni, and Isabelle Lewis. 3rd ed. New York: Penguin, 2003. 128p. ISBN 0142002410.

A unique reference source, this atlas "maps the world of women" to illustrate patterns that statistical tables or narratives may obscure. The maps and tables are divided into categories, including marriage, motherhood, work, resources, and welfare; individual topics focus on young brides, population policies, contraception, labor force, earnings, education, and voting behavior, among others. The innovative use of maps, charts, and other graphics assists in visually representing problems and issues. Sources for the statistics and a bibliography are provided.

Dictionaries and Encyclopedias

407. **Encyclopedia of Sex and Gender: Men and Women in the World's Cultures.** Ember, Carol R., and Melvin Ember, editors. New York: Kluwer, 2003. 2v. ISBN 030647770X.
(See entry 386)

408. **Encyclopedia of Women and Gender: Sex Similarities and Differences and the Impact of Society on Gender.** Worell, Judith, editor. San Diego, CA: Academic Press, 2001. 2v. ISBN 0122272455.
This encyclopedia provides comprehensive coverage of many topics covered by current research and scholarship on the psychology of women and gender. Though the primary focus is psychological, many of the signed articles offer insights from related disciplines, including anthropology, sociology, and communications. Special attention is paid to such issues as multicultural diversity in human experience; including nationality, economics, sexuality, and racial/ethnic variables. Content is organized alphabetically by title.

Bibliographies

409. **Motherhood and Reproduction: An International Bibliography.** Schemberg, Annegret. Canberra, Australia: Gender Relations Project, Research School of Pacific and Asian Studies, The Australian National University, 1995. 338p. ISBN 0731518764.
This bibliography focuses primarily on the early stages of motherhood: pregnancy, childbirth, and infancy. Closely related topics such as abortion, reproductive rights, and puberty rites are covered less thoroughly. The bibliography includes recent books, chapters, articles, papers, and theses, drawn mainly form the anthropological and sociological literature, but relevant publications from related areas (such as psychology, health and demography) are also included. The first section include general and theoretical works, while the remaining sections cover broad geographical regions such as "Mexico, Central and South America" and the "Pacific."

Other Topics

Aging

410. **Aging and Cultural Diversity: New Directions and Annotated Bibliography.** Strange, Heather, and Michele Teitelbaum. South Hadley, MA: Bergin and Garvey Publishers, 1987. 350p. ISBN 0897891031.

This annotated bibliography contains references to books and articles, primarily from the United States. Although anthropological journals are represented, many of the citations derive from the literature of sociology, family studies, gerontology, and social work—with which anthropologists may be less familiar. Arranged topically, the bibliography includes general works; specific studies of aging in single ethnic, national, racial, or regional groups; studies comparing two or more ethnic groups; and single and cross-cultural studies. A subject index provides access by specific topic (e.g., menopause, suicide).

Alcohol Use

411. **"Alcohol: Anthropological/Archaeological Perspectives."** Dietler, Michael. *Annual Review of Anthropology* 35 (2006): 229–249. ISSN: 0084-6570.

This review traces new trends in anthropological research on alcohol use in the twenty years since the publication of Dwight B. Heath's (1987) *Annual Review* article.

412. **Alcohol Use and World Cultures: A Comprehensive Bibliography of Anthropological Sources.** Heath, Dwight B., and A. M. Cooper. Toronto, Ont.: Addiction Research Foundation, 1981. 248p. ISBN 0888680457pa.

Compiled with the aim of "providing easier and more comprehensive access to the large, diverse, and widely scattered literature that deals with alcoholic beverages in relation to human behavior among various populations throughout the world" (preface), this bibliography identifies over 1,300 citations from the late nineteenth century to 1979. The focus is on the sociocultural component of alcohol use rather than physiological reactions across cultures. Books and journal articles are the majority of citations, but reports, dissertations, and conference papers are also included. The arrangement is alphabetical, but an index of subjects allows for identification by tribal/ethnic group or country as well as by terms (e.g., beer, ritual).

Death and Dying

413. **Death and the Afterlife: A Cultural Encyclopedia.** Taylor, Richard P., editor. Santa Barbara, CA: ABC-Clio, 2000. 438p. ISBN 0874369398.

Written by a religious studies scholar, this encyclopedia provides a more in-depth look at cross-cultural customs and beliefs relating to death and the afterlife than the other recent encyclopedias on this topic. The scope is wide, covering prehistoric times to the present, but most of the entries do not stray far beyond Near Eastern and Judeo-Christian religious and cultural traditions.

414. **Encyclopedia of Death and Dying.** Howarth, Glennys, and Oliver Leaman, editors. London: Routledge, 2001. 534p. ISBN 0415188253.

Reflecting the burgeoning interest in death and dying across the social sciences, Howarth (sociology, U. of Sydney, Australia) and Leaman (philosophy, U. of Kentucky) have compiled a wide-ranging encyclopedia that looks at death and dying in different cultures and religions, as well as in history and literature. Nearly 400 signed entries, written by academics from the United Kingdom, United States, and Australia, are arranged alphabetically and amply cross-referenced.

415. **Macmillan Encyclopedia of Death and Dying.** Kastenbaum, Robert, editor. New York: Macmillan, 2003. 2v. ISBN 002865689X.

This two-volume set include signed entries discussing topics related to the process of death and dying. In addition to subjects directly related to death (autopsy, cemeteries, ghosts, etc.), the encyclopedia also covers topics about how people deal with death through different religious and medical practices.

Disasters

416. **"Anthropological Research on Hazards and Disasters."** Oliver-Smith, Anthony. *Annual Review of Anthropology* 25 (1996): 303–328. ISSN: 0084-6570.

Disaster, defined here as "a process/event involving the combination of a potentially destructive agent(s) from the natural and/or technological environment and a population in a socially and technologically produced condition of vulnerability," is an area of growing research interest in anthropology. This review article traces three major research threads in the anthropological research on disasters and hazards: (1) a behavioral and organizational response approach, (2) a social change approach, and (3) a political economic/environmental approach that focuses on the historical-structural dimensions of vulnerability to hazards, particularly in the developing world. Oliver-Smith also traces the contributions applied anthropology has made to disaster management and recent research on risk assessment and perception.

Names and Naming

417. **Personal Names and Naming: An Annotated Bibliography.** Lawson, Edwin D. New York: Greenwood Press, 1987. 185p. ISBN 0313238170.

This bibliography provides a unique compilation of research on the content and process of personal names and naming. The briefly annotated citations derive from books and journal articles and identify English-language studies on naming throughout the world. Anthropology, linguistics, onomastics literature, and other social science disciplines are represented. The book is organized topically. The largest section focuses on ethnic, national, and regional names from nearly 70 societies/regions worldwide. Other topics include folklore and names, gods and names, length and meaning of names, naming process, psychology and names, to mention but a few. In addition to the classified arrangement, a detailed subject index is provided.

Online Communities and the Internet

418. **"The Anthropology of Online Communities."** Wilson, Samuel M., and Leighton C. Peterson. *Annual Review of Anthropology* 31 (2002): 449–467. ISSN: 0084-6570.

Wilson and Peterson provide a review of anthropological research on online communities and Internet. They argue that the new technologies are cultural products "embedded in existing practices and power relations of everyday life" and are therefore amenable to anthropological analysis.

Humanities Related Fields

Chapter **6**

Though anthropology is typically considered a social science, anthropologists lay claim to a humanistic tradition through their studies of the spiritual and creative aspects of the world's cultures. This chapter introduces reference materials in the humanities that closely relate to anthropology, including ethnomusicology, folklore and mythology, and performance studies. Other related areas include linguistics (see Chapter 4), as well as art and material culture and religion, which are covered in Chapter 5. Anthropology's humanistic approach is represented professionally by the Society for Humanistic Anthropology (entry 765), which publishes *Anthropology and Humanism* (entry 649).

General Humanities Sources

Guides to Reference Literature

419. **The Humanities: A Selective Guide to Information Sources.** Blazek, Ron, and Elizabeth Smith Aversa. 5th ed. Englewood, CO: Libraries Unlimited, 2000. 603p. ISBN 1563086018.

For students and scholars in anthropology who do research in related humanities disciplines, this guide presents an excellent introduction to library research strategies and bibliographic sources in philosophy, religion, mythology and folklore, visual arts, performing arts, and language and literature. For each discipline, the authors provide a chapter on how information is organized and used, and include contact information for libraries and special collections, as well as electronic sources. The corresponding chapters on library materials include full descriptions of bibliographic guides, indexes, dictionaries and encyclopedias, handbooks, directories and biographical sources, and databases in specific humanities fields.

Indexes, Abstracts, and Databases

420. **Arts and Humanities Citation Index.** Philadelphia: Institute for Scientific Information. 1978-. ISSN 0162-8445. Available online by subscription.

With extensive coverage—over 1,300 core journals are fully indexed and 5,100 titles are partially indexed—the *Arts and Humanities Citation Index* provides an unparalleled resource for citations to current literature in the humanities. Similar in organization to the *Social Sciences Citation Index* (entry 7), *AHCI* provides access to humanities scholarship by author and keyword-in-title and enables researchers to identify which articles are cited within core journal literature in the humanities. While the print version is no longer being published, the online version has been enhanced by links to the full text of selected cited articles.

421. **Humanities Index.** New York: H.W. Wilson. 1975-. ISSN 0095-5981. Available in print and online by subscription.

A basic index for college libraries, this title indexes over 400 core periodicals from all areas of the humanities and selected titles from the social sciences. In addition to identifying relevant journal articles from religion, folklore, and philosophy, among other disciplines, the index provides access to recent scholarship on the literary and creative aspect of anthropology, such as writing ethnography. Continues *Social Sciences and Humanities Index* (1966–1974) and *International Index* (1907–1965).

Internet Gateways

422. **Voice of the Shuttle UCSB.** Liu, Alan. University of California, Santa Barbara. Available online at <http://vos.ucsb.edu/browse.asp>.

Launched in 1994, the mission of this website is " to provide a structured and briefly annotated guide to online resources that at once respects the established humanities disciplines in their professional organization and points toward the transformation of those disciplines as they interact with the sciences and social sciences and with new digital media." The anthropology section is somewhat eclectic, but appears to be updated frequently and is well-organized. Of particular interest are pages covering emerging interdisciplinary areas such as cultural studies, cyberculture, and the technology of writing.

Ethnomusicology

Ethnomusicology, the study of musical systems in non-Western contexts, has obvious relevance for anthropological research as the social and cultural context of musical expression engages both ethnomusicologists and anthropologists. The Society for Ethnomusicology (entry 832) has long represented the field and publishes the journal *Ethnomusicology* (entry 666).

Guides to Reference Literature

423. **Ethnomusicology: A Guide to Research.** Post, Jennifer C. New York: Routledge, 2004. 470p. ISBN 0415938341.

Post has done an outstanding job of selecting and organizing reference sources pertinent to the study of ethnomusicology. Beginning with guides to the literature, she casts a wide net and includes core sources in folklore and fieldwork as well as regional guides. Other formats include encyclopedias and dictionaries; bibliographies, discographies, and filmographies; indexing and abstracting tools; journals and serial publications; audio, film and video recordings; and a classified selection of books on the music of genres (blues); regions (West Africa) and cultures (Jewish traditions).

Literature Surveys and Reviews

424. **The Study of Ethnomusicology: Thirty-One Issues and Concepts.** Nettl, Bruno. New ed. Urbana and Chicago, IL: University of Illinois Press, 2005. 513p. ISBN 0252072782.

Noted musicologist Bruno Nettl provides both a history and an overview of the field of ethnomusicology. In lively prose, he explores the study of ethnomusicology and discusses past and present practice, with emphasis on topics of contemporary relevance, such as women's roles. A generous number of bibliographic citations (nearly 960 items) are cited in the text.

Indexes, Abstracts, and Databases

425. **Music Index,** Vol. 1-. Warren, MI: Harmonie Park Press. 1949-. ISSN 0027-4348. Available in print and online by subscription.

A major resource for music research, *Music Index* cites articles from over 350 journals in the field of music. The index is arranged by specific subject, and research on ethnomusicology is well represented. The general heading "Ethnomusicology" as well as specific subject headings ("American Indian Dance") provide access to contents of journals such as *Ethnomusicology* (entry 666) and *African Music* and offer good international coverage of the music of the world's indigenous peoples.

426. **RILM Abstracts,** Vol. 1-. New York: RILM. 1967-. ISSN 0033-6955. Available in print and online by subscription.

RILM is one of the standard indexes in the field of musicology; each issue offers approximately 200 citations relating to ethnomusicology. Entries are grouped within the ethnomusicology section and include abstracts of books, articles, reviews, dissertations, and catalogs. Coverage of sources as well as content is truly international. General works in ethnomusicology (theory, methodology) are included in addition to the studies of the music of specific peoples or area. A detailed subject index offers access by specific topic or culture group.

Dictionaries and Encyclopedias

427. **New Grove Dictionary of Music and Musicians.** Sadie, Stanley, and John Tyrrell. 2nd ed. New York: Grove, 2001. 29v. ISBN 1561592390. Also available online as *Grove Music Online*.

One of the most significant additions to this new edition of a venerable reference work is the broadening of its coverage of music beyond the traditional Western focus. Thus it includes hundreds of survey articles on non-Western music, incorporating them into the mainstream of musical scholarship. Also included is a lengthy "Index of Terms Used in Articles on non-Western, Folk Music, and Kindred Topics" that gives brief definitions and article references. The online version is enhanced by audio clips, as well as links that tie related articles together.

Bibliographies

428. **Ethnomusicology,** Vol. 1-. Bloomington, IN: Society for Ethnomusicology. 1953-. Quarterly. ISSN 0014-1836.

In each issue of the journal *Ethnomusicology* (entry 666), the "Current Bibliography" section provides an extensive listing of current citations, including journal articles, books, recordings, and films and videos. The material is arranged by category and general titles are followed by specific area studies, including Africa, the Americas, Asia and Oceania and Europe. Though it is difficult to determine how many journals are indexed, the bibliography appears to have good international coverage. This bibliography/discography/filmography is relatively recent, citing articles from the preceding 1–2 years and serves as an excellent current awareness source for scholarship in the field.

429. **Ethnomusicology Research: A Select Annotated Bibliography.** Schuursma, Ann Briegleb. New York: Garland, 1992. 173p. ISBN 082405735X.

This useful bibliography lists nearly 500 English language publications that have appeared since 1960 dealing with ethnomusicology as a field of research. Though many of the entries describe and analyze specific musical cultures, the annotations focus on methods, theories, and approaches to research. The entries are organized in five categories: history of the field; theory and method; fieldwork method and technique; musical analysis; and publications from related fields such as anthropology and linguistics that have been influential in ethnomusicology. Dance and popular music are excluded.

Libraries, Archives, and Special Collections

430. **Archive of Folk Culture**
American Folklife Center
Library of Congress
101 Independence Ave. SE
Washington, DC 20540-4610
(202) 707-5510
<http://www.loc.gov/folklife/archive.html>
The Archive of Folk-Song was established in 1928 to maintain a national collection of manuscripts and recordings of American folk songs and traditional music. The archive's mission broadened to include all aspects of folklore, prompting a name change in 1981 to the Archive of Folk Culture. Serving as a national repository for primary source material on American folklore, spoken word as well as music, the archive holds an extensive collection of Native American, regional, and ethnic music.

431. **Archives of Traditional Music**
Indiana University
Morrison Hall 117 & 120
Bloomington, IN 47405
(812) 855-4679
<http://www.indiana.edu/~libarchm/>
According to its website, the Archives of Traditional Music at Indiana University is the largest university-based ethnographic sound archive in the United States. Its holdings cover a wide range of cultural and geographical areas, and include commercial and field recordings of vocal and instrumental music, folktales, interviews, and oral history, as well as videotapes, photographs and manuscripts. Archives holdings document the history of ethnographic sound recording, with formats from wax cylinders through digital technologies. The collection includes over 2,000 field collections provided by anthropologists, linguists, ethnomusicologists and folklorists throughout the world.

Discographies and Catalogs

432. **Smithsonian Global Sound.** Washington, DC: Smithsonian, 2006. Available online at <http://www.smithsonianglobalsound.org/>.
Smithsonian Global Sound (SGS) is a virtual discography of the world's musical and aural traditions. SGS partners with Folkways Records and other labels, and with institutions around the world (e.g., International Library of African Music, and the Archives and Research Center for Ethnomusicology in New Delhi) to document, record, archive, catalog, and digitize music and other verbal arts and distribute them via the Internet. Royalties go to artists and institutions, and honor the intellectual property rights of composers, musicians, and producers.

In addition to recordings, the database provides narrative description and images that "connect recordings to their social contexts."

Recordings can be downloaded for a nominal fee. There is no charge, however, for students and faculty fortunate enough to be affiliated with a library that subscribes to the *Smithsonian Global Sound for Libraries* (available from Alexander Street Press).

Folklore and Mythology

As a hybrid discipline, folklore has roots in both the social sciences and the humanities and its ties to anthropology run long and deep. Through the study of traditional beliefs and customs, and oral and artistic expressions, folklore is often considered a type of autobiographical ethnography through which a group expresses shared values and articulates a sense of group identity. Folklore has developed a substantial library of reference works and the titles below represent selected core resources. Though many reference titles from other fields such as art and material culture, European ethnology, ethnobotany, music and religion intersect with folklore, this section is more narrowly focused on verbal arts and is limited to "classic" reference works, current indexes, and representative bibliographies. With its roots in oral tradition, mythology is included here, though related titles can be found in the section on religion in Chapter 5.

Anthropologists have historically made significant contributions to the American Folklore Society (entry 808), and its publication, the *Journal of American Folklore* (entry 678).

Guides to Reference Literature

433. Folklore and Folklife: A Guide to English-Language Reference Sources. Steinfirst, Susan. New York: Garland, 1992. 2v. ISBN 0815300689.

Listing more than 1,400 titles in eight thematic sections, this important guide encompasses the breadth of folklore studies. A bibliographic essay introduces each section and discusses the major issue, trends, and scholarship of each genre (e.g., belief systems). The annotations are both descriptive and evaluative. International sources are well represented (e.g., motif indices) and the work serves as an excellent guide for identifying scholarship and library resources for pursing in-depth folklore studies.

Literature Surveys and Reviews

434. Mythography: The Study of Myths and Rituals. Doty, William G. 2nd ed. Tuscaloosa, AL: University of Alabama Press, 2000. 577p. ISBN 0817310053.

Defining mythography as "the application of critical perspectives to mythological materials" (preface), Doty focuses on modern approaches to myths and rituals and on the major schools of interpretation that still have viability for critical study. Chapters include functional contexts, symbolic approaches, structuralism and psychological approaches, among others. In addition to a lengthy list of references, a classified introductory bibliography assists in organizing the voluminous "classic" literature on the topic.

Indexes, Abstracts, and Databases

435. **Internationale Volkskundliche Bibliographie. International Folklore Bibliography. Bibliographie Internationale des Arts et Traditions Populaires.** Basel, Switzerland: G. Krebs. 1939-. Annual. ISSN 0074-9737.

This extensive bibliography covers books and articles on folklore from cultures around the world, with a strong European emphasis. The detailed table of contents in German, English, and French provides access to entries arranged by general categories (arts and crafts) with subdivisions (pottery, textiles, woodwork). Citations represent both folklore and folklife (beliefs and customs as well as material culture, including foodways and technology). The index is particularly useful for its coverage of European regional ethnography. Though the bibliography is issued annually, the significant delay in publication limits its utility as an index to currently published literature.

436. **MLA International Bibliography.** New York: Modern Language Association of America.Vol. 1-. 1921-. Annual (print) ISSN 0024-8215. Available in print, on CD-ROM, and online by subscription.

Because early folk narrative and ballad scholarship took a distinctly literary approach, the scholarly literature was indexed in the *MLA International Bibliography*, an indexing source devoted primarily to literary studies. Beginning in 1970, folklore scholarship was organized into its own section within the *MLA*. The tradition of indexing folklore books, articles, and dissertations continued even after folklore adopted a more anthropological approach; thus through the *MLA* one can access literature dealing with customs and traditions as well as myth, legend, and folktale. The scope is international, though North American and European studies predominate. Ethnology-related coverage prior to 1970 is limited, and before 1981 citations were listed only by broad subject area (e.g., "Material Culture"). An annual subject volume was added in 1981, however, and access to specific terms and topics, such as folk belief systems, is now provided.

437. **World Folklore and Folklife.** Westport, CT: Greenwood. 2005-. Available online by subscription.

With an increasingly rich array of image, sound, and full text, databases defy classification into standard reference categories. Greenwood's *World Folklore Online* is no exception. Covering the range of verbal and performance arts that constitutes folklore studies, the interface provides easy access by keyword and the ability to browse by subject (music, foodways, folk medicine, etc.) or region (North America, Africa, etc.). Searches yield the full text of articles from more than 60 folklore-related reference works (primarily Greenwood titles), as well as the full text of folk and fairy tale collections, multimedia resources, images, web links, etc. Essentially, this source is a super-encyclopedia and a collection of folklore texts and materials. Not for the serious scholar, this database is part of Greenwood's *Daily Life Online* set of digital social history products aimed at a general or undergraduate audience.

Thematic Indexes

438. **Archetypes and Motifs in Folklore and Literature: A Handbook.** Garry, Jane, and Hasan El-Shamy, editors. Armonk, NY: M.E. Sharpe, 2005. 515p. ISBN 0765612607.

Based upon Stith Thompson's canonical folklore classification index *Motif-Index of Folk-Literature* (entry 439), Garry and El-Shamy have selected the most important archetypes and motifs in folk literature and offer 66 essays on topics such as food taboos, creation myths, ghosts and other revenants, and others. Each essay contains a bibliography with references to related scholarly sources. Though the number of motifs and tale types is limited (considering that there are thousands to choose from) and the authors address a scholarly audience, the topics they chose have a broad general interest.

439. **Motif-Index of Folk-Literature: A Classification of Narrative Elements in Folktales, Ballads, Myths, Fables, Mediaeval Romances, Exempla, Fabliaux, Jest-Books and Local Legends.** Thompson, Stith. Rev. ed. Bloomington, IN: Indiana University Press, 1955-1958. 6v. ISBN 023338875.

Early folklore scholarship was concerned almost exclusively with the study and classification of narratives collected from oral tradition. A motif index classifies specific narrative elements, such as a particular action (blowing down a house), object (glass slipper) or character (wicked stepmother). Thompson painstakingly analyzed hundreds of narratives transcribed from oral tradition and systematically analyzed thousands of plot elements, identifying the texts from which they come. Citations to the texts are included in the accompanying bibliography of source books and articles. The index is international in scope, and Native American mythology and legends are particularly well represented.

440. **Tale-Type and Motif-Indexes: An Annotated Bibliography.** Azzolina, David. New York: Garland, 1987. 105p. ISBN 0824087887.

Although the Thompson *Motif-Index of Folk-Literature* (entry 439), and the Aarne-Thompson *Types of the Folktale* (entry 441) are perhaps the most widely known, they represent but two of many published tale-type and motif indexes. Azzolina has compiled an annotated bibliography of over 186 of these essential reference tools for scholars of folktales. The bibliography is international in scope and includes items in a wide range of languages. In a lengthy introduction, Azzolina details the history of tale-type and motif indexes and describes their value in the context of folklore scholarship. Entries are arranged alphabetically by author; there are separate subject and geographic indexes. The informative annotations carry occasional references to reviews.

441. **Types of the Folktale: A Classification and Bibliography.** Aarrne, Antii, and Stith Thompson. 2nd ed. Helsinki: Suomalainen Teideakatemia, 1961. 588p.

A standard reference source for folk narrative scholarship, the tale-type index classifies stories by plot or storyline, allowing for cross-cultural comparisons of texts. Referred to as the Aarne-Thompson Index, this classic folklore reference source identifies the basic kinds of tales collected from oral traditions and categorizes them under major headings. Within each heading, plot types are established, such as that of the Cinderella story. A bibliography of the published versions of the texts, which were collected and transcribed from oral traditions, is also provided.

Dictionaries, Encyclopedias, and Handbooks

442. **Clowns & Tricksters: An Encyclopedia of Tradition and Culture.** Christen, Kimberly A., and Sam K. Gill, editors. Santa Barbara, CA: ABC-Clio, 1998. 271p. ISBN 0874369363.

Christen and Gill have compiled a fascinating study of more than 200 clown and trickster characters throughout history and across cultures. The introductory essay discusses the cool reception that studies of humor have traditionally received in the scholarly world, but notes the importance of humorous stories for understanding and explaining the human condition. The entries place the characters or stories within specific cultural contexts, and discuss the similarities and differences in their representations. Written in lively narrative form, the book nonetheless represents solid scholarship and includes a 17-page bibliography.

443. **Facts on File Encyclopedia of World Mythology and Legend.** Mercatante, Anthony S. 2nd ed. New York: Facts on File, 2004. 2v. ISBN 0816047081.

At two volumes, a dictionary of the world's mythology and legend cannot aspire to be comprehensive. Though this source contains over 3,000 entries, coverage is necessarily selective and entries are brief. Many entries have cross-references, and an annotated bibliography is included. The cultural and ethnic group index is inconsistent, but the set is useful for ready reference.

444. **Folk and Fairy Tales: A Handbook.** Ashliman, D. L. Westport, CT: Greenwood, 2004. 268p. ISBN 0313328102.

Ashliman's handbook takes a scholarly, classical approach to the study of Indo-European folk and fairy tales. The book begins with a review of tale types and classification schemes, then presents 40 short tales arranged by type (e.g., cautionary tale, urban legend, etc), followed by commentary and analysis that illustrate, for instance, how the story changed over time. Includes a useful glossary and a lengthy bibliography of print and online resources.

445. **Funk and Wagnalls Standard Dictionary of Folklore, Mythology, and Legend.** Leach, Maria, editor. New York: Funk and Wagnalls, 1949. 2v. ISBN 0062505224.

This standard ready-reference title has been issued in several reprints. With the intention of providing a "cross section . . . of the spiritual content of the world's cultures," the editors compiled a representative sampling of mythological figures, legends, customs, festivals, and rituals from throughout the world. The essays range in length from a paragraph to several pages and provide a succinct description and discussion of each term. In addition to ready reference identification of terms and concepts, numerous signed survey articles (e.g., Melanesian mythology) are also provided.

446. **Greenwood Encyclopedia of World Folklore and Folklife.** Clements, William, editor. Westport, CT: Greenwood, 2006. 4v. ISBN 0313328471.

As this extensive and engaging set illustrates, folklore is not about quaint practices that are paraded for tourists, but it embodies the traditional beliefs and practices that define a culture. The well-written articles in this impressive collection wed past and present, and provide a window on the cultural diversity of the world's people. The set begins with essays on 39 issues and concepts in folklife studies (e.g., diffusion, hybridization). Each volume is devoted to a broad geographic area, with articles on ethnic or culture groups that discuss historic traditions, oral culture, material culture (including foodways) and belief systems. Bibliographies, black-and-white illustrations and a comprehensive index are also provided.

447. **International Dictionary of Regional European Ethnology and Folklore.** Erixon, Sigurd, and Åke Hultkrantz, editors. Copenhagen: Rosenkilde and Bagger, 1960–1965. 2v.

This classic source provides definitions of general ethnological concepts, as well as folklore-specific terms. The first volume (now mainly of historic interest) focuses on concepts and approaches to regional ethnography, useful for elucidating concepts and approaches current at the time it was written.

448. **Larousse Dictionary of World Folklore.** Jones, Alison. Edinburgh: Larousse, 1995. 493p. ISBN 0752300121.

Like the *Funk & Wagnall's Standard Dictionary of Folklore, Mythology, and Legend* (entry 445), this dictionary focuses on folkloric characters, motifs and archetypes, rather than concepts in folklore studies. The 1,500 brief essays cover themes from around the world. The appendices are particularly useful, including a bibliography of suggested reading, a biographical guide to 37 notable folklorists, an international directory of folklore-related museums, and a calendar of festivals and events.

449. **Storytelling Encyclopedia: Historical, Cultural, and Multiethnic Approaches to Oral Traditions around the World.** Lemming, David Adams, editor. Phoenix, AZ: Oryx, 1997. 543p. ISBN 1573560251.

This encyclopedia on a popular topic discusses classic stories, storytellers, scholars in the field, recurrent themes and motifs, and significant characters. The oral traditions of many cultures and geographic areas are included, as well as articles on the art of storytelling. More than 700 encyclopedic entries are arranged alphabetically, and many offer a brief bibliography to guide readers to additional sources.

Directories

450. **Folklife Sourcebook: A Directory of Folklife Resources in the United States.** Bartis, Peter, compiler. 2nd ed. Washington, DC: Library of Congress, 1994. 165p. ISBN 0844405213.

Though over a decade old, Bartis' sourcebook is a useful guide to federal and other public agencies, archives, professional societies, publishers and educational programs in the field of folklore and folklife studies. Contact and descriptive information is provided, and although the publication predates the inclusion of websites, users can easily use the listings to find additional information that may be available on the Internet.

Bibliographies

Note: Since the number and variety of bibliographies in folklore is extensive, this section includes only a highly selective listing of representative titles with an emphasis on North America.

451. **Contemporary Legend: A Folklore Bibliography.** Bennett, Gillian, and Paul Smith. New York: Garland, 1993. 340p. ISBN 0824061039.

Urban legends are among the most recognizable examples of contemporary oral tradition. Their popularity as a research topic is reflected by this bibliography of 1,100 topical entries. Most of the sources are in English, and the potential for cross-cultural research is limited, but the bibliography provides an excellent starting point for this popular topic.

452. **Handbook of World Mythology (Series).** Santa Barbara, CA: ABC-CLIO, 2000. ISBN (various).

As of 2005, this series had produced ten titles, representing a diversity of historical, and cultural areas: Classical, Chinese, Egyptian, Hindu, Japanese, Inca, Mesoamerican, Native American, Norse, and Polynesian. Each title in the series provides a lengthy introductory essay that surveys the specific mythological system. The alphabetical entries describe significant beliefs, mythological characters, and events. Lengthy introductory essays survey the evolution of mythological systems, and an annotated bibliography gives suggestions for further reading.

453. **Oral-Formulaic Theory and Research: An Introduction and Annotated Bibliography.** Foley, John Miles. New York: Garland, 1985. 718p. ISBN 0824093089.

Oral-formulaic theory is one of the primary theoretical concepts in the study of oral tradition, and Foley provides a history of scholarship and research from its beginnings through the early 1980s. The extensive, annotated bibliography includes international coverage and contains citations in multiple languages.

Libraries, Archives, and Special Collections

454. **American Folklife Center**
Library of Congress
101 Independence Ave. SE
Washington, DC
20540-4610
<www.loc.gov/folklife>

If the Smithsonian's National Museum of American History is America's attic, the American Folklife Center at the Library of Congress is its parlor. Over 4,000 collections of photos and films, song and dance, ballad and tales, and stories ranging from slave narratives to personal accounts of 9/11 have been preserved and organized for current and future generations who want to listen to America's music and stories. In recent years, the scope has broadened to include not only national traditional life, but the culture life of communities from many regions of the world. The materials from the Folklife Center are increasingly available via its website, which serves as a rich primary source for folklorists, anthropologists, cultural historians and anyone who appreciates hearing a good story.

Regional folklore

455. **African Folklore: An Encyclopedia.** Peek, Philip M., and Kwesi Yankah, editors. New York: Routledge, 2004. 593p. ISBN 041593933X.

The scope of "folklore" in this encyclopedia includes not only a rich variety of spoken arts, such as myths, tales, riddles, and songs, but a range of cultural practices and traditions as well. Of particular note are entries on body arts (hairstyles, clothing, piercing) and material culture. The editors treat folklore as a current and evolving phenomenon, as reflected by entries on popular culture, such as "Radio and Television Drama." Topics are situated within a social and historical context, and many include photographs and illustrations. The useful appendices list material from the Field and Broadcast Sound Recording Collections at the Indiana University Archives of Traditional Music (entry 431), a selected filmography, and a list of dissertations and theses on African folklore written in the United States between 1929 and 1984.

456. **Afro-American Folk Culture: An Annotated Bibliography of Materials from North, Central and South America and the West Indies.** Szwed, John F., and Roger D. Abrahams. Philadelphia: Institute for the Study of Human Issues, 1978. 2v. (Publications of the American Folklore Society, Bibliographical and Special Series, Vol. 31–32). ISBN 0915980800.

By any measure, Szwed and Abrahams have put together an important reference work that assembles a wealth of information relating to nearly all aspects of traditional culture of African diaspora peoples throughout the Americas. The first volume is devoted to North America; the second focuses on the Caribbean and Central and South America. More than 5,000 citations, drawn primarily from books and articles, are organized by country and arranged alphabetically, necessitating heavy reliance on the subject index. The authors' conception of folk culture is rich and eclectic, ranging from material culture (food, basketry) to expressive arts (blues, narratives) to customary traditions and beliefs (carnival, funeral, superstitions). The result is an exhaustive bibliography that serves as an excellent starting point for research on African-American culture.

457. **American Regional Folklore: A Sourcebook and Research Guide.** Mood, Terry Ann. Santa Barbara, CA: ABC-CLIO, 2004. 476p. ISBN 1576076202.

This sourcebook and annotated bibliography includes all genres of American regional folklore. The first two chapters provide useful guidance on doing folklore-related research in libraries, museums, historical societies, and local organizations. Part Two provides an annotated bibliography of both classic and contemporary sources on American folklore, arranged by region. Indexed by subject/author.

458. **Dictionary and Catalog of African American Folklife of the South.** Pyatt, Sherman E., and Alan Johns. Westport, CT: Greenwood, 1999. 188p. ISBN 0313279993.

African American folklife and lore has been a rich field of study among folklorists and anthropologists. This book identifies major contributions of the past century, including the pioneering work of Lomax, Hurston, Hughes and Herskovits, and supplements the existing scholarship through personal interviews. The first section is a dictionary of topics and subjects, with content based on personal interviews with individuals currently or recently living in the South. The second section is an unannotated catalog of print sources and selected recordings, divided into seven broad chapters (e.g., folk music). The book concludes with a directory of resources, including festivals, libraries and archives, and state folklore programs.

459. **South Asian Folklore: An Encyclopedia: Afghanistan, Bangladesh, India, Nepal, Pakistan, Sri Lanka.** Claus, Peter J., Sarah Diamond, and Margaret Ann Mills, editors. New York: Routledge, 2003. 710p. ISBN 0415939194.

It is difficult to meet the challenge of presenting a rich and diverse topic such as folklore, within an equally rich and diverse cultural and geographic area as South Asia, particularly in a single volume work. The authors acknowledge this difficulty and their admittedly selective inclusion of a wide range of cultural practices results in an eclectic collection of concepts and topics. The 500 entries fall into three broad categories: general concepts, case studies, and definitions. The broad scope, however, limits its usefulness.

Internet Gateways

460. **Ethnographic Resources Related to Folklore, Anthropology, Ethnomusicology, and the Humanities.** Library of Congress, American Folklife Center, 2006. Available online at <http://www.loc.gov/folklife/other.html>.

An excellent resource provided by the American Folklife Center, this gateway provides links to a wealth of American oral and musical traditions. A rich source of sound and images, this eclectic collection offers unparalleled access to primary and secondary sources, such as Native American music, oral histories of veterans, articles on popular traditions (yellow ribbons, Halloween) and more.

Performance Studies and Dance

A relative newcomer to the academy, performance studies spans a number of disciplines, with particularly strong ties to communications. The titles below provide a representative sampling of the types of resources that are produced by practitioners who share a common interest in the culture of performance.

Literature Surveys and Reviews

461. **The Body, Dance, and Cultural Theory.** Thomas, Helen. New York: Macmillan, 2003. 262p. ISBN 0333724313.

Through a series of case studies, this book explores theories of the body and performativity, particularly in the context of cultural studies. Thomas looks at dance as a social (e.g., rave/club culture) and artistic practice, and explores the ideas of identity and performance.

462. **Dance in the Field: Theory, Methods, and Issues in Dance Ethnography.** Buckland, Theresa, editor. New York: St. Martin's Press, 1999. 223p. ISBN 0312223781.

This international collection of essays discusses the methodology and theory of the study of dance and movement as cultural phenomena, with a focus on ethnography as a research strategy. It brings together the several related fields including folklore, ethnomusicology, and sociology, as it addresses issues ranging from documentary techniques to ethics.

463. **Performance Studies: An Introduction.** Schechner, Richard. New York: Routledge, 2002. 288p. ISBN 0415146208.

This text provides a cogent introduction to the emergent field of performance studies. Transcending disciplinary and genre boundaries, performance studies look at aspects of human behavior such as ritual, cultural performances (storytelling, singing, etc.). Centering on the written and spoken word, as well as the movements and body, Schechner offers an overview of a field with considerable relevance for anthropologists.

464. **Performance Studies Reader.** Bial, Henry. New York: Routledge, 2004. 329p. ISBN 0415302412.

This anthology of readings presents an overview of the character of contemporary studies of performance. Encompassing ritual, performance processes, and global and intercultural performance, among other topics, the readings are theoretical rather than descriptive, and capture the scholarly perspective on a wide range of verbal and non-verbal performances.

Dictionaries and Encyclopedias

465. **International Encyclopedia of Dance.** Cohen, Selma Jean, editor. New York: Oxford University Press, 6v. ISBN 019509462.

Thanks to its broad scope and international list of contributors, indigenous dance traditions of specific countries and cultures are well-represented in this encyclopedic set. Articles of general interest, such as dance research and methodology, are also included. With extensive illustrations, bibliographies and cross references, this reference source provides an excellent background and starting point for the study of dance in all its forms.

Bibliographies

466. **The Music and Dance of the World's Religions: A Comprehensive, Annotated Bibliography of Materials in the English Language.** Rust, Ezra Gardner. Westport, CT: Greenwood, 1996. 446p. ISBN 0313295611.

As this work illustrates, the intersection of religion with music and dance provides a rich area for anthropological inquiry. Well-organized and indexed, the bibliography includes citations to musical genres (e.g., chants), concepts (e.g., transmission), and examinations of the religious and ceremonial music of specific groups (e.g., Asian-Americans). The author identifies scholarly publications from the literature of anthropology, ethnic studies, religion, musicology, and related fields to provide references and annotations for nearly 4,000 studies.

Chapter 7

Area and Ethnic Studies

One of anthropology's most important approaches has been the study of specific tribal, ethnic, or national groups. Anthropological research originally focused on non-Western societies and although this emphasis has weakened in recent years, anthropologists continue to maintain a high profile in area studies scholarship. The breadth and depth of the culture-area approach is reflected by the considerable number of ethnographic monographs and journal articles that have been published and by the numerous retrospective bibliographies that reflect this work. Of the 8,000 bibliographies listed in *Anthropological Bibliographies: A Selected Guide* (entry 101), for example, nearly 75 percent have an area-studies focus.

The sections that follow, therefore, represent a highly selective listing of available sources. Each section is organized to enable the user to identify the core reference literature in area studies, broadly defined by continent or geographic region. Although many of the titles are not specific to anthropology (e.g., the indexes and abstracts have an area studies focus, but cover multiple disciplines), all have significant ethnological content. With a few exceptions, the selections below focus on broad cultural or geographic regions rather than on specific countries or peoples.

General Area and Ethnic Studies

Dictionaries, Encyclopedias, and Handbooks

467. **Countries and Their Cultures.** Ember, Melvin, and Carol R. Ember, editors. New York: Macmillan, 2001. 4v. ISBN 0028649508.

While there are multiple reference sources that provide basic demographic and historical data on the countries of the world (e.g., *Europa Yearbook, Statesman's Yearbook*, etc.), the anthropologists who have edited this set focus not just on country portraits, but on their cultures. Over 200 social scientists contributed articles that highlight each distinctive national culture, as well as ethnic subcultures. The resulting set is useful for comparative research, and as an overview of the way of life rather than a compilation of facts. A bibliography of source materials is provided for each article.

468. Cross-Cultural Statistical Encyclopedia of the World. Parker, Philip M. Westport, CT: Greenwood, 1997. 4v. ISBN 0313297681.

Though anthropologists are not typically 'number crunchers,' this encyclopedic compilation of a massive number of statistics provides a handy ready reference source for comparative statistical information. The four volumes in this set include statistical portraits of religious cultures (70 groups); linguistic cultures (460 groups); ethnic cultures (400 groups); and national cultures (230 groups). Though the statistics are over a decade old, sources are provided so that researchers can identify titles to consult for more recent data.

469. Culture and Customs (Series). Westport, CT: Greenwood, 1998. Also available online by subscription as *World Cultures Today*.

The *Culture and Customs* series is divided into geographical areas that currently include the Middle East, Latin America and the Caribbean, Europe, Asia, and Africa. Within each region, individual volumes focus on specific countries (e.g., Somalia, Vietnam, Ireland). Each book in the series follows the same format, with background information, followed by chapters on religion and worldview; literature and media; art, architecture, and housing; cuisine and traditional dress; gender roles, marriage, and family; social customs and lifestyle; and music and dance. A bibliographic essay is provided at the end. This is not a scholarly work that examines ethnic complexities, but with large brush-strokes, it paints basic portraits of national cultures for the general audience. This series is available online as *World Cultures Today*, part of Greenwood's *Daily Life Online* set of digital social history products.

470. Dictionary of Race, Ethnicity and Culture. Bolaffi, Guido, editor. Thousand Oaks, CA: Sage, 2003. 355p. ISBN 0761968997.

The fluid concepts of race, ethnicity, culture, and related terms are defined and discussed in this scholarly work. Historical background and etymology of a wide range of terms, both European and American are included. Over 200 terms, ranging from boat people to cybernazis are discussed. Entries are encyclopedic, comprising 1–5 pages, and each is followed by a list of bibliographic references.

471. Encyclopedia of Diasporas: Immigrant and Refugee Cultures around the World. Ember, Melvin, Carol R. Ember, and Ian Skoggard, editors. New York: Kluwer, 2004. 2v. ISBN 0306483211.

(See entry 392)

472. Encyclopedia of the Stateless Nations: Ethnic and National Groups around the World. Minahan, James. Westport, CT: Greenwood Press, 2002. 4v. ISBN 0313316171.

Defining and identifying "stateless nations" is a daunting task, and according to one reviewer, estimates of national groups run as high as 9,000. Minahan has therefore been highly selective in his choice of entries. Updating his previous *Nations without States*, he includes 150 groups. While the introduction states only that the resident people must identify themselves as a separate nation, it is not clear what criteria he used for inclusion. Nonetheless, the entries are solid, including general background, an essay on the history and status of the group, and a bibliography. Appendices provide a list of independence declarations, geographical distribution, and national organizations.

473. **Encyclopedia of World Cultures.** Levinson, David, editor. Boston, MA: G.K. Hall, 1991–1996. 10v. with supplement (2002). ISBN 081688840X.

This outstanding reference source provides lengthy descriptions written by prominent scholars of approximately 1,500 cultural and ethnic groups including a large number of immigrant groups, such as Korean-Americans. The ethnographic summaries cover demography, linguistic affiliation, history and cultural relations, settlements, economy, kinship, marriage and family, sociopolitical organization, and religion, and provide a short bibliography of core sources. The outline of the essays follows that of the "Cultural Summary" included with every eHRAF file, but the *Encyclopedia of World Cultures* presently covers far more cultures than are included in *eHRAF Collection of Ethnography* (entry 481).

Each volume covers a specific geographic area and is prefaced with maps showing the distribution of cultural groups in that region. A useful ethnonym index that cross-references alternate names for a given cultural group, and the names of related groups and subgroups, is provided at the back of each volume. Each volume also includes an appendix with a list of films about cultural groups in that region. Detailed cumulative indexes and a glossary are provided in Volume 10. The supplementary volume issued in 2002 includes descriptions of 65 additional cultural groups.

474. **Ethnic Diversity within Nations (Series).** Santa Barbara, CA: ABC-CLIO, 2003. ISSN various.

Ethnic tensions and conflicts are often inseparable from the study of ethnic groups, and this new series examines the ethnic complexity of modern nation-states around the world. At the time of printing, six titles are currently available, focusing on Canada, the former Soviet Union, Nigeria, the former Yugoslavia, Iran, and South Africa. Each title in the series explores historical forces that gave rise to the current situation and explores political, economic, and cultural underpinnings. A chronology and annotated bibliography are also included.

475. **Ethnic Groups Worldwide: A Ready Reference Handbook.** Levinson, David. Phoenix, AZ: Oryx, 1998. 436p. ISBN 1573560197.

Anthropologist Levinson provides a thumbnail sketch of ethnic groups from around the globe. Divided into four sections (Africa, Americas, Asia/Pacific, and Europe), entries are then arranged alphabetically by country. A profile is provided for each ethnic group that describes its history, social status, and relations with the dominant population. The source materials, which are included in individual bibliographies, draw from primary resources such as government data and research reports, as well as scholarly literature. Background materials were drawn from governmental publications, research reports, and scholarly writings.

476. **Ethnic Relations: A Cross-Cultural Encyclopedia.** Levinson, David, editor. Santa Barbara, CA: ABC-CLIO, 1994. ISBN 0874367352.

Levinson tackles the issue of racial and ethnic conflicts from the perspective of a cultural anthropologist. Signed articles provide definitions and discussions of 53 concepts such as ethnic cleansing and xenophobia, as well as profiles of 38 ethnic conflicts, most recently from the early 1990s. Entries are arranged alphabetically, and the appendix includes an annotated international directory of ethnic organizations as well as a substantial bibliography.

477. **Worldmark Encyclopedia of Cultures and Daily Life.** Gall, Timothy L., editor. Detroit, MI: Gale, 1998. 4v. ISBN 0787605522.

Arranged by four geographic regions (Africa, Americas, Asia and Oceania, and Europe), the volumes in this set focus on 500 of the world's major culture groups. (By comparison, Levinson's *Encyclopedia of World Cultures*, entry 473, covers more than 1,500). Each of the entries follows roughly the same format, with an introduction situating each group geographically, politically, and linguistically, then focusing on aspects of culture and daily life such as folklore, religion, family life, foodways, arts, etc. Emphasis is on salient cultural traits and current living conditions. Maps, photographs, and bibliographies complement the text.

Human Relation Area Files (HRAF)

The Human Relations Area Files (HRAF) are a specially organized repository of information on the world's cultures, providing historic and descriptive data on over 400 ethnic, national, and religious groups around the world. The files are used primarily by social scientists doing comparative cross-cultural research and quantitative analysis, though they may also be utilized by individuals seeking data on a specific group or cultural activity.

To use the files effectively, one must understand how they are organized. In order to facilitate cross-cultural comparison, the researchers at HRAF devised an elaborate retrieval system to identify and organize information on specific human activities (e.g., communication, food consumption, political behavior) known as the *Outline of Cultural Materials* (or OCM, entry 484), which is used in conjunction with a geographical classification of cultural groups worldwide called the *Outline of World Cultures* (or OWC, entry 485). For each group, data is drawn from published books, articles, dissertations and reports that are organized geographically and by activity category.

Originally produced in print, and then in microfiche, since 1995 new additions to the files are available only via the *eHRAF Collection of Ethnography*. To check which cultures are covered by HRAF in what formats, see the "Human Relations Files Collection of Ethnography: Collection List For All formats" available online at http://www.yale.edu/hraf/collections.htm.

In recent years, HRAF has also become a major sponsor of reference publications, working with publishers to produce encyclopedias that cover topics of current interest from an anthropological perspective. Examples of include the *Encyclopedia of Diasporas: Immigrant and Refugee Cultures around the World* (entry 392) or *Encyclopedia of Medical Anthropology: Health and Illness in the World's Cultures* (entry 336). In addition to these topically themed works, HRAF has also sponsored titles that provide global coverage of peoples and cultures, both contemporary (*Encyclopedia of World Cultures*, entry 473) and past (*Encyclopedia of Prehistory*, entry 221).

478. **Atlas of World Cultures: A Geographical Guide to Ethnographic Literature.** Price, David H. Newbury Park, CA: Sage, 1989. 156p. ISBN 0803932405.

Based on HRAF's *Outline of World Cultures* (entry 485) and utilizing OWC codes, the *Atlas of World Cultures* is both an atlas and a bibliography, providing geographic location and bibliographic information for over 3,500 cultural and ethnic groups. Forty-one outline maps identify the approximate location of each group. The 1,237-item bibliography provides citations to books, articles, reports, archival materials, and maps and atlases representing the "classic" ethnographic literature for the groups identified. By using the index, the user can look up a culture group, find the group's location on a map and identify relevant ethnographic literature.

479. **A Basic Guide to Cross-Cultural Research Using the HRAF Collections.** Ember, Carol R., and Melvin Ember. New Haven, CT: Human Relations Area Files, 1997. 22p. Available online at <http://www.yale.edu/hraf/basiccc.htm>.

Updating the 1988 *Guide to Cross-Cultural Research Using the HRAF Collections*, this brief text provides orientation on using *HRAF* for cross-cultural research and an explanation of how HRAF is organized. Includes a discussion of basic steps in research from formulating the research question(s) to analyzing the results.

480. **Cross-Cultural Research Methods.** Ember, Carol R., and Melvin Ember. Lanham, MD: AltaMira Press, 2001.164p.

This handbook, coauthored by the executive director and the president of the Human Relations Area Files (HRAF), serves as a primer on cross-cultural research methods in the tradition of Edward B. Tylor and George Peter Murdock. An appendix provides a guide to "Using the Human Relations Area Files," including eHRAF.

481. **eHRAF Collection of Ethnography** (Human Relations Area Files). New Haven, CT: Human Relations Area Files, 1950. Available online by subscription.

A specially organized collection of thousands of mostly primary sources on more than 400 cultures worldwide, HRAF can be useful for anyone looking for background information or specific data on a particular ethnic group, culture, or country, as well as by those investigating subjects such as architecture, kinship, political structure, or gender on a comparative cross-cultural basis. Organized geographically by culture and subject thereunder, HRAF provides detailed subject (and keyword, in the online version) access to texts within and across cultures. HRAF is sometimes the only source for English translations of key anthropological monographs published in other languages.

All HRAF installments published since 1995 are available only via the *eHRAF Collection of Ethnography*, while many older installments (issued 1950–1994) are available only in print or microfiche. To check which cultures are covered by HRAF in what formats, see the "Human Relations Files Collection of Ethnography: Collection List For All formats" at <http://www.yale.edu/hraf/collections_body_ethnoallformats.htm>. All cultures issued on the short-lived CD-ROM version are also included in *eHRAF* online. Cultures that are covered in both the microfiche/print and electronic versions generally do not include the same complement of full text sources across both formats because the updated eHRAF version incorporates new works and discards some of the old sources. Moreover, a small number of sources originally issued in print were never converted to microfiche due to copyright issues and may exist only in the print files.

The print and microfiche versions provide photoreproductions of the sources. *eHRAF* also provides the full-text of each source, but in a re-keyed format that intersperses the index terms with the original text, lacks good visual navigational clues, and cannot be easily printed. The usefulness of *eHRAF* is thus limited to an aid in locating relevant passages—researchers wanting to read extended passages will want to consult the original texts.

482. **HRAF Source Bibliography: Cumulative.** New Haven, CT: Human Relations Area Files, 1976-. 2v (looseleaf).

A culture-by-culture listing of the texts included in the Human Relations Area Files, arranged by OWC code (entry 485) and indexed by author and "area" (broad geographic region). A small number of authors and titles are omitted from the indexes. Minnesota State University Library independently provides the complete source bibliographies for Africa and North America online at <http://www.lib.mnsu.edu/lib/files/files.html>.

483. **Index to the Human Relations Area Files.** National Museum of Ethnology, Osaka Japan. New Haven, CT: Human Relations Area Files, 1988. 31microfiche.

Compiled by the National Museum of Ethnology in Osaka, Japan, this index is a complete "subject index to the sources (books, articles, manuscripts, etc.) processed into the ... cultural data archive through December 1986" (Introduction) updating the *Index to the HRAF Files, Supplement I* (Steffens 1979) and *Index to the Human Relations Area Files* (Naroll and Morrison 1972).

484. **Outline of Cultural Materials.** Murdock, George Peter. 5th ed. New Haven, CT: Human Relations Area Files, 2000. 267p. ISBN 0875366546.

The *Outline of Cultural Materials* (OCM) is comprehensive classification scheme used by HRAF to index ethnographic and archaeological texts by subject.

Cross references are provided along with scope notes. An alphabetical index is also provided that uses terms common to all social science disciplines and thus facilitates use for those less familiar with anthropological terminology. The fifth edition reflects changes made in subject-indexing the new *eHRAF Collection of Archaeology*, as well as shifts in ethnographic research interests.

485. **Outline of World Cultures.** Murdock, George Peter. 5th ed. New Haven, CT: Human Relations Area Files, 1983. 259p. ISBN 0875366643pa.

This companion guide to the Human Relations Area Files provides geographical classification of all cultural groups worldwide. Each group is assigned a code consisting of two letters and a number. All known cultures are listed, but not all cultures listed in the *Outline of World Cultures* (OWC) are included in *HRAF* since development of the files is ongoing.

Bibliographies

486. **Scarecrow Area Bibliographies (Series).** Lanham, MD: Scarecrow Press, 1992-. ISBN (various).

Published since 1992, this series currently contains 20 titles focusing on geographic areas (e.g., Southern Africa, Caribbean) or countries (Japan, China). Each title in the series attempts to provide a balanced and representative bibliography (primarily books) about the region. The number of entries ranges from 3,000 to 6,000 titles and concentrates on the social sciences and humanities. Reference sources are highlighted and key topics typically include social life and customs, economic conditions, history, and environment, among others. Language is primarily in English but also include Western European languages when applicable.

487. **World Bibliographical Series.** Santa Barbara, CA: ABC-CLIO. 1979–2000. ISSN various.

Titles in this series serve as bibliographic guides to sources of information on a wide range of topics for individual countries or regions (e.g., the Arctic). Over 150 volumes have been published, covering all areas of the world. Each volume serves as a selective, annotated guide to English-language books, government documents, and other sources dealing with topics such as current economics and politics. Particularly useful are sections on reference works, bibliographies, newspapers and periodicals. Major libraries, museums, and archives for each country are also profiled.

Libraries, Archives, and Special Collections

488. **School of Oriental and African Studies Library**
    University of London
    Thornhaugh Street, Russell Square

London WC1H 0XG
Tel: +44 (0)20 7637 2388

The SOAS Library is one of the world's most important academic libraries for the study of Africa, Asia, the Middle East, and the Pacific. It houses over 1.2 million volumes, with significant special collections at its campus in central London. The library also holds an important collection of archives and manuscripts, and is particularly strong in missionary accounts and economic and business information.

Internet Gateways

489. **Global Gateway: World Culture & Resources.** Washington, DC: Library of Congress, 2006. Available online at <http://international.loc.gov/intldl/intldlhome.html>.

The Library of Congress has produced an extraordinary portal to worldwide internet resources on world cultures. The primary sections of this extensive website include information about the international collections, links to LC's area studies reading rooms, selected items of importance and exhibits from the Library's collections, research guides and databases, research opportunities, international cybercasts, and "Portals to the World." This page identifies and provides links to e-resources selected by LC subject experts, offering a well-organized and extensive collection of websites relevant to understanding the culture and current political situation in the world's countries.

490. **Native Web: Resources for Indigenous Cultures around the World.** Available online at <www.nativeweb.org/>.

Within its "Resource" section, this extensive web portal provides links by subject to over 30 categories of internet resources, including anthropology and archaeology, food, religion, libraries and archives, organizations, and native travel and eco-tourism. Each of these web pages then provides a selected and annotated list of links to free internet resources. Coverage is international, and the variety and range of relevant and useful links is amazing.

Africa

(See also Middle East and Islam)

The continent of Africa has been the focus of considerable anthropological research and boasts one of the most extensive bodies of ethnographic literature available. African anthropologists can take advantage of numerous bibliographies that identify retrospective research and of the well-organized reference literature on current African-studies scholarship.

The International African Institute (entry 819) has been instrumental in sponsoring seminal works on African anthropology, including the extensive

Ethnographic Survey of Africa (entry 502), the *Africa Bibliography* (entry 494), and the journal *Africa* (entry 639). In the United States, the African Studies Association (entry 807) serves as a vehicle for interdisciplinary communication within the field and publishes the journal *African Studies Review*.

Guides to the Reference Literature

491. **African Studies Companion: A Resource Guide & Directory.** Zell, Hans M. 3rd ed. Lochcarron: Hans Zell Publishers, 2003. 545p. ISBN 0954102916.

Providing quick and easy access to a wide range of information for African studies, Zell has produced a useful directory and guide to the literature. He has annotated over 150 general reference sources, as well as current indexes and bibliographies and identified over 150 relevant journals. Descriptions of Africana holdings of major libraries and documentation centers are included, as well as directories of Africana publishers and vendors throughout the world, organizations concerned with Africa (including African studies associations), and foundations, donor agencies, and awards.

492. **Northern Africa: A Guide to Reference and Information Sources.** Skreslet, Paula Youngman. Englewood, CO: Libraries Unlimited, 2000. 405p. ISBN 1563086840.

In the preface, the author delineates the geographic scope of her work: 14 nations in the areas along the Mediterranean and North Atlantic seas, the Western Sahara, and countries along the Horn of Africa. Entries cover reference literature on the history, politics, society, and culture of the peoples in this critical region. The book is divided into three sections: general works, area studies (by subject) and country/regional works. The annotations provide substantial information about the titles identified, and indexes facilitate access to specific authors and titles. The subject index includes geographic, ethnographic, and language names as well as topics.

493. **Reference Guide to Africa: A Bibliography of Sources.** Kagan, Alfred. 2nd ed. Lanham, MD: Scarecrow, 2005. 222p. ISBN 081085208X.

This second edition of a well-received guide includes more titles related to North Africa and Islam, and a greater emphasis on Internet and web-based resources. Part one provides a selected and annotated list of core Africana-related reference sources such as bibliographies and indexes, statistics, etc. Part two has a subject orientation, describing resources on general topics ranging from development to music.

Indexes, Abstracts, and Databases

494. **Africa Bibliography.** Blackhurst, Hector, editor. Edinburgh: Edinburgh University Press. 1984-. Annual. ISSN 0266-6731.

Indexing nearly 600 periodicals and approximately 125 collected works annually, *Africa Bibliography* provides excellent coverage of current literature in English and Western European languages. The bibliographic citations are organized by region and country, encompassing the entire continent of Africa, and are subdivided by discipline and topic. Sections include anthropology and archaeology; health and medicine; food and nutrition; arts; religion and philosophy; and social anthropology and sociology. Book reviews appearing in the journals are also indexed. Issued annually, the publication is relatively current, identifying literature generally published the previous year.

495. **Bibliography of Africana Periodical Literature.** Bullwinkle, Davis, editor. Available online at <http://www.africabib.org/africa.html>.

The efforts of dedicated librarian and Africana researcher Davis Bullwinkle result in this free online database that indexes over 280 journals in English and other languages, published in over 22 countries, that specialize in African studies. Journals are indexed from the first date of publication (a few date from the nineteenth century) through the present, or until they have ceased. The database is easy to use, with numerous access points, including a clickable map of Africa that limits the search results to specific countries.

496. **Quarterly Index of African Periodical Literature.** Nairobi: Library of Congress. 1991. <lcweb2.loc.gov/misc/qsihtml>.

Since 1991 the Office of the African and Middle Eastern Division of the Library of Congress in Nairobi has published a free index to over 300 journals from 29 African countries, primarily from eastern, southern, and western Africa. According to the website, "Journals have been selected in order to cover subject areas not found in widely available literature (e.g., prisons) and to include organizations that do not frequently circulate their publications (e.g., non-governmental organizations)." The search engine is rudimentary, but effective, and identifies articles and reports that would otherwise be difficult to find. Citations are provided, but not the full text.

Atlases

497. **Cultural Atlas of Africa.** Murray, Jocelyn. Rev. ed. New York: Checkmark Books, 1998. 240p. ISBN 0816038139.

A distinguished list of scholars consulted on this handsome, clearly written and informative work. The publication has features of an encyclopedia as well as an atlas. The first section consists of overview essays on the physical and cultural background of the continent followed by chapters on languages and peoples, religions, arts, music and dance, as well as issues such as education and literacy and the African diaspora. The book is lavishly illustrated and has numerous maps. The essays present a broad summary for the general reader. The third section profiles the nations of Africa, organized by region. Each summary offers vital statistics, a detailed map, and an overview of history and politics. Titles suggested for further reading derive mainly from a historical (rather than ethnological) perspective. A gazetteer and index by subject, proper name and ethnic group are also provided.

Dictionaries, Encyclopedias, and Handbooks

498. **African Ethnonyms: Index to Art-Producing Peoples of Africa.** Biebuyck, Daniel P., Susan Kelliher, and Linda McRose. New York: G.K. Hall, 1996. 378p. ISBN 0783815328.

The subtitle "art-producing" people is somewhat misleading since this work does not involve the production of artwork (and which cultures don't produce art?) and does not appear to be exclusive. Ethnonyms, the names of peoples or ethnic groups, have long presented a challenge for researchers. As in other regions, sub-Saharan Africa is home to a multitude of distinct traditional cultures, the names of which are not uniform. Variant pronunciation and spelling, or misunderstanding of the words the cultures use to refer to themselves, present difficulties for researchers in identifying the most appropriate name and spelling. The compilers have undertaken the worthwhile task of unifying and organizing these name variations into a single alphabetically arranged list, with cross-references. They worked from published research literature and their bibliography exceeds 1,000 titles, resulting in a useful and unique resource.

499. **Encyclopedia of Africa South of the Sahara.** Middleton, John, editor. New York: C. Scribner's Sons, 1997. 4v. ISBN 0684804662.

This well-received set provides excellent coverage of contemporary historical, political, and cultural topics on sub-Saharan Africa, with an emphasis on the post-independence period. Relative to comparable reference works, a significant number of contributors (nearly one third of nearly 900) are African. Entries vary in length and many are substantial and include references for further reading. Appendices include an essay on research about Africa by non-Africans, a chronology, and a listing of about 1,000 names of ethnic groups.

500. **Encyclopedia of African Peoples.** Lye, Keith, compiler. New York: Facts on File, 2000. 400p. ISBN 0816040990.

This one-volume encyclopedia provides a handy ready reference source on the peoples of Africa. The scope includes contemporary as well as historical cultures, and over 1,000 ethnic groups and 53 countries are profiled. Smaller groups have brief entries, but larger groups are covered in greater detail as to their language, life-ways, social structure, and cultural practices. Chronologies, and biographies of 300 notable Africans are provided, and the volume is richly illustrated.

501. **Encyclopedia of Precolonial Africa: Archaeology, History, Languages, Cultures, and Environments.** Vogel, Joseph O., and Jean Vogel, editors. Walnut Creek, CA: AltaMira, 1997. 605p. ISBN 0761989021.

This encyclopedia set provides a survey of the archaeology, history, linguistics, and culture of the indigenous peoples of pre-colonial sub-Saharan Africa. Five major themes are treated: "African Environments" (e.g., geology, geography); "Histories of Research" (e.g., archaeology, historiography); "Technology" (e.g., stoneworking, metallurgy); "People and Culture" (e.g. ethnic groups, languages, rituals); and "Prehistory" (e.g., evolution, political development). Each of the nearly 100 articles contains a useful bibliography. An index is provided, and numerous tables and illustrations complement the text.

502. **Ethnographic Survey of Africa (Series).** Forde, Daryll, editor. London: International African Institute, 1950–1974. ISBN various.

In 1945, the International African Institute (entry 819) became engaged in the preparation and publication of an ethnographic survey of Africa. The purpose of the series was to present, in a brief and readable form, a summary of ethnographic information concerning the native peoples of Africa at the time of early contact with anthropologists. The series is divided into seven sections: Western, Northeastern, East Central, Madagascar, West Central, Congo, and Southern Africa. Within the series, individual titles on specific ethnic and regional groups, such as *The Gisu of Uganda* (1959) and *Peoples of the Lake Nyama Region* (1950) were written by specialists in the field. Each title in the series follows a basic pattern and includes geographic, demographic, historical, and ethnographic information. Chapters describe the culture's language and literature, economy, political and social organizations, life cycle, religion, and expressive culture (e.g., dress, dance). The text is amply footnoted, and an extensive bibliography is provided at the back, as well as a detailed map showing the group's geographic distribution.

Over 50 titles were published through the mid-1970s, with the greatest emphasis on West Africa. Volumes in this series are generally considered the most comprehensive sources of "classic" ethnographic information on the peoples of Africa and are based on extensive research in published material as well as on original field studies.

503. **The Peoples of Africa: An Ethnohistorical Dictionary.** Olson, James S. Westport, CT: Greenwood, 1996. 681p. ISBN 0313279187.

Olson's handbook includes basic information on more than 1,800 ethnic groups as well as their subgroups and clans. His coverage aims to be comprehensive, and he has not limited the scope to the largest or most representative ethnic groups. The tradeoff however is brevity. Each entry provides the geographic location, brief demographic data, and a thumbnail ethnographic sketch. Bibliographic references cite sources, and see references connect variant spellings and names.

Directories

504. **Répertoire International des Etudes Africaines** (International Directory of African Studies Research). Baker, Philip, compiler. 3rd ed. London: H. Zell, 1994. 319p. ISBN 1873836368.

This directory identifies over 1,800 organizations and research institutes concerned with the African continent. Arrangement is by country with organizations listed alphabetically. The amount of detail for each entry varies, and is not necessarily consistent. Each entry provides basic contact information (address, phone number, director, etc.) but some entries offer additional details, such as founding date, staff members, area of research, or publications. Indexes by subject, organization title, ethnic/language group, publications, and personnel.

Published Library Catalogs and Guides

505. **Guide to African-American and African Primary Sources at Harvard University.** Burg, Barbara A., Richard Newman, and Elizabeth E. Sandager. Phoenix, AZ: Oryx Press, 2000. 217p. ISBN 1573563390.

Distinguished scholar Henry Louis Gates provides the introduction to this useful guide. At the time of publication of this title, many of Harvard's unique collections of Africana and African-Americana were uncataloged or inadequately identified in the library's online catalog. Burg and her associates bring to light the contents of 845 collections of original works and microforms. Entries vary in length, but provide descriptive detail. An index to subjects and formats (e.g., photographs) is provided.

Libraries, Archives, and Special Collections

506. **Melville J. Herskovits Library of African Studies**
Northwestern University
1970 Campus Drive
Evanston, IL 60208-2300
847-467-3084
<www.library.northwestern.edu/africana/>

The Herskovits Library at Northwestern University offers a significant collection of books, journals, and archival and manuscript collections in over 300 African languages, as well as English and Western European languages. The library is named for Melville Herskovits, a distinguished anthropologist who founded Northwestern's Program in African Studies in 1948, and his collection laid the basis for this distinguished resource center.

Internet Gateways

507. **Africa South of the Sahara: Selected Internet Resources.** Fung, Karen. 2006. Available online at <library.stanford.edu/africa/>.

With multiple access points (links organized by region, country, or topic), this well-designed portal also has a search feature that enables users to search across websites by keyword (e.g., Twi). Hundreds of the Africa-related sites on a wide variety of subjects have been carefully chosen, organized, and annotated, making this website an excellent starting point for Africana on the Internet.

Asia

Attempting to synthesize the anthropological reference literature for an area as huge and diverse as the continent of Asia presents a considerable challenge. Numerous national and international associations have been established to promote the study of specific areas within Asia. The Association for Asian Studies (entry 812) provides a broad base for international and interdisciplinary scholarly exchange, particularly through its *Journal of Asian Studies* (entry 680). A number of area-specific associations have also been established, and several journals specialize in specific countries or regions within Asia, including *Chinese Sociology and Anthropology* (entry 654) and *Eastern Anthropologist* (entry 663), among others.

Literature Surveys and Reviews

508. **Anthropology of Asia (Series).** Malarney, Shaun, series editor. New York: Routledge, 2003-. ISBN (various).

Titles in this timely series cover aspects of Asian ethnography such as the tea ceremony in Japan, the globalization of Chinese food, modernity in Thailand, and cultural dynamics of megastores in Hong Kong. At the time of printing, 15 titles are available, and each stands as a testament to anthropology's continuing relevance in the modern world.

509. **Asian Anthropology.** Breman, Jan van, Eyal Ben-Ari, and Syed Farid Alatas, editors. New York: Routledge, 2005. 249p. ISBN 0415349834.

The anthology provides a useful overview of current issues in Asian anthropologies and anthropologies in Asia. Following an introductory overview, individual sections focus on East Asia, South Asia, and Southeast Asia, and chapters discuss the state of the art (or science) of anthropology in specific countries (e.g., "Korean anthropology: A search for a new paradigm").

510. **Indigenous Peoples of Asia.** Barnes, R. H., Andrew Gray, and Benedict Kingsbury, editors. Ann Arbor, MI: Association for Asian Studies, 1995. 539p. ISBN 0924304146.

Despite the daunting scope, which includes nearly all of the continent of Asia, this important collection of essays blends ethnography with political science as it focuses on the contemporary oppressions of indigenous peoples resulting from militarization, plundered resources, forced relocation, and cultural genocide.

511. **The Making of Anthropology in East and Southeast Asia.** Yamashita, Shinji, Joseph Bosco, and J. S. Eades, editors. New York: Berghahn Books, 2004. 374p. ISBN 157181258X.

The primary focus of this collection of essays is on "Asian anthropologies" within the global community of anthropologists. The first article introduces the reader to Asian anthropologies, foreign, native, and indigenous. Subsequent essays treat both the discipline of anthropology and the nature of anthropological studies in China, Japan, Korea, and Malaysia.

Indexes, Abstracts, and Databases

512. **Bibliography of Asian Studies.** Ann Arbor, MI: Association for Asian Studies. 1971. ISSN 0067-7159. Available online by subscription.

This important index identifies recent scholarship in Western languages on East, South, and Southeast Asia in the humanities and social sciences, drawing from Western language periodicals, monographs, chapters in edited volumes, conference proceedings and festschriften. Anthropological titles figure prominently among the more than 700 journals indexed. The bibliography began in 1956, as an annual issue (September) of the *Journal of Asian Studies*. From 1971 to 1991 it was published as an annual index. Now only available online, the *Bibliography of Asian Studies* includes all of the citations from the annual print volumes, and scholarship from 1991 forward. Books, however, are no longer indexed.

Dictionaries, Encyclopedias, and Handbooks

513. **Encyclopedia of Modern Asia.** Levinson, David, and Karen Christensen, editors. Detroit, MI: Thomson/Gale, 2002. 6v. ISBN 0684806177.

With an international board of leading scholars and over 700 authors from 65 countries, this cross-disciplinary encyclopedia includes over 3,000 articles focusing on Asian history, politics and culture since 1850. Signed articles are provided on individual countries as well as topics such as the role of women, ethnic and religious conflicts, migrations, tourism, human rights issues and others. The geographic scope is broad, ranging from the Muslim countries of Southeast Asia to the Central Asian republics and the Turkic nations of western Asia. The set is nicely illustrated with maps and photographs, and has a substantial index, bibliographies for further reading, and a lengthy reader's guide.

Internet Gateways

514. **PAIR: Portal to Asian Internet Resources.** University of Wisconsin, 2006. Available online at <digicoll.library.wisc.edu/PAIR/>.

Created as part of the U.S. Department of Education's Title VI grant for "Technological Innovation and Cooperation for Foreign Information Access," this extensive web portal provides links to more than 6,000 professionally selected, cataloged, and annotated online resources, covering all of Asia. An "atlas" search provides access to Internet resources by country, and the subject list offers 25 topical areas, including development, popular culture, society, and religion. This portal provides an excellent starting point for free, quality Internet resources relating to all aspects of Asian studies.

East Asia

Internet Gateways

515. **CEAL: Council on East Asian Libraries.** 2006. Available online at <http://wason.library.cornell.edu/CEAL/>.

An excellent starting point for finding Internet-based information on East Asian Studies, this portal represents the collective work of East Asian studies librarians in North America. In addition to providing links to the Digital Asia Library and subject resources for Asian Studies (in non-Asian languages), the website offers a link to an "Ask an East Asian Studies Librarian" reference service.

South Asia

Indexes, Abstracts, and Databases

516. **ICSSR Journal of Abstracts and Reviews: Sociology and Social Anthropology,** Vol. 1-. New Delhi: Indian Council of Social Science Research. 1972-. Semi-annual.

Sponsored by the Indian Council of Social Science Research (ICSSR), this periodical index covers 50 journals in the fields of anthropology and sociology from India, the United States and the United Kingdom. Classified by broad topics, subjects include social research theory and methodology, culture, religion, life cycle, and women's studies, among others, with a focus on India. Complete bibliographic citations are provided, and articles are summarized in well-written annotations. Selected book reviews relating to South Asian anthropology and sociology are reproduced in their entirety. Because the time lag between an article's publication and the publication of the abstracts may be over three years, its utility as a current awareness source is limited. Though this title may not be widely available in the U.S. libraries, it provides a useful resource for South Asian cultural anthology.

Dictionaries, Encyclopedias, and Handbooks

517. **Oxford India Companion to Sociology and Social Anthropology.** Das, Veena, editor. New Delhi: Oxford University Press, 2003. 2v. ISBN 0195645820.

This reference work brings together contributions from 60 eminent scholars to provide an overview of the social anthropology of the Indian subcontinent.

Beginning with concepts and contexts of Indian society, subsequent sections include cultural landscape (lifestyle, language), religions, education and human development, economic arrangements, and political institutions and processes. A significant contribution to South Asian studies, this timely source provides an excellent starting point for understanding contemporary issues.

518. **People of India Project.** Singh, K. S., series editor. New Delhi: Anthropological Survey of India, 1992-. ISBN (various).

Sponsored by the Anthropological Survey of India, this extensive series currently includes 72 volumes focusing on specific states, regions, and peoples of India. The individually titled ethnographic surveys include cultural, linguistic, and biological traits of ethnic groups across the Indian subcontinent.

Bibliographies

519. **Anthropological Bibliography of South Asia.** Fürer-Haimendorf, Elizabeth von. Paris/The Hague: Mouton, 1958–1970. 3v.

(See entry 520)

520. **Anthropological Bibliography of South Asia.** Kanitar, Helen A., compiler. Paris/The Hague: Mouton, 1976. 346p.

The combined volumes of the *Anthological Bibliography of South Asia* provide nearly 13,000 unannotated citations to books, periodical articles, and theses in Western languages. Citations range from the mid-nineteenth century until 1970 and cover India, Pakistan, Bangladesh, Sri Lanka, Nepal, Sikkim, and Bhutan. The geographically based sections are subdivided by broad subject categories, including cultural and social anthropology, material culture, folklore, archaeology, and physical anthropology and archaeology are deleted. Together, these volumes comprise a definitive bibliography of the scholarship on South Asian anthropology through the 1960s.

Southeast Asia

Literature Surveys and Reviews

521. **The Modern Anthropology of South-East Asia: An Introduction.** King, Victor T., and William D. Wilder. New York: Routledge, 2003. 384p. ISBN 0415297516.

This introductory text situates Southeast Asian anthropology within the general field of anthropological inquiry, and begins with a look at issues during and following decolonization. Other chapters are devoted to identity, ethnicity, and nationalism; ecology and the environment; gender and the sexes, and social organization. A list of ethnic groups is provided in the appendix, and bibliographic references are supplied.

Indexes, Abstracts, and Databases

522. **Excerpta Indonesica,** Vol. 1–66. Leiden: Documentation Centre for Modern Indonesia. Koninklijk Instituut voor Taal-en Volkenkunde. 1970–2002. 2/yr. ISSN 0046-0885.

Published by the Royal Institute of Linguistics and Anthropology, the index offers abstracts of selected periodical articles and books in the social sciences and humanities on Indonesia. Numerous anthropological journals are included among the titles indexed. Approximately 200 citations, indexed by author and subject, are provided in each issue.

Dictionaries, Encyclopedias, and Handbooks

523. **Encyclopaedia of the South-East Asian Ethnography: Communities and Tribes.** Bisht, Narendra S., and T. S. Bankoti, editors. Delhi: Global Vision, 2004. 2v. ISBN 8187746963.

This set provides descriptive summaries of 188 ethnic groups from 14 Southeast Asian countries: Burma, Brunei, Cambodia, East Timor, Hong Kong, Indonesia, Laos, Macau, Malaysia, Philippines, Singapore, Taiwan, Thailand, and Vietnam. Written by scholars in the field, each entry addresses physical, historical, social, political, economic, religious, and cultural information. The latter includes social organization, social life, marriage and the family, religion, and arts, among other topics. This set pulls together many ethnic groups that are relatively obscure and provides a useful summary of ethnic groups in this culturally diverse area.

524. **Ethnic Groups of Insular Southeast Asia.** LeBar, Frank M. New Haven, CT: Human Relations Area File Press, 1972–1975. 2v. ISBN 0875364039.

This ethnographic survey of the peoples of insular Southeast Asia covers Indonesia, the Andaman and Nicobar Islands, and Madagascar, as well as the Philippines and aboriginal peoples of Taiwan. The descriptive summaries, with accompanying bibliographies, synonymies, and ethnolinguistic maps, focus on the traditional cultures of over 100 ethnic groups as described in the literature prior to 1970. Providing a body of "systematically arranged data for comparative use as well as a base from which to project studies of recent change" (preface), the information provided follows the same general format: orientation (overview), settlement patterns, economy, kin groups, marriage and family, sociopolitical organization, and religion, with numerous bibliographic references throughout.

525. **Ethnic Groups of Mainland Southeast Asia.** LeBar, Frank M., Gerald C. Hickey, and John K. Musgrave. New Haven, CT: Human Relations Area File Press, 1964. 248p.

This survey of the peoples of mainland Southeast Asia provides concise ethnographic descriptions of the major ethnic groups through the early 1960s. Information on over 150 societies is included along with ethnographic maps and indexes to ethnic group names. The volume is organized by region: the first part includes Sino-Tibetan peoples, followed by Austroasiatic, Tai-Kadai, and Malayo-Polynesian groups. Systematically organized, the information includes basic identification and location, settlement pattern and housing, economy, kin groups, marriage and family, sociopolitical organization, and religion. Numerous bibliographic references provide a review of the literature.

Bibliographies

526. **Bibliography of Indonesian Peoples and Cultures.** Kennedy, Raymond. 2nd ed. New Haven, CT: Human Relations Area Files, 1962. 207p.

The preface of the first edition (1945) states that "the bibliography here published represents a close approximation to complete coverage of all extant books and periodical articles concerning the peoples and cultures of Indonesia." With the growth in interest in the region following World War II, the second edition no longer made the claim. Acknowledging the scarcity of Indonesian publications as well the difficulty of differentiating anthropological titles from those in areas such as urban development, education, or economics, the bibliography remains extensive nonetheless. Over 11,600 unannotated books and articles (over half in Dutch) are arranged by islands and island groups, then by ethnic groups. Through the emphasis is on cultural anthropology, the scope is broad and includes selected titles in related social science and natural history fields as well. With no subject index, however, and diffuse scope, the bibliography provides a record of the scholarship but not necessarily easy access to it. The bibliography is updated through the 1970s in LeBar (entry 524).

527. **Bibliography of the Peoples and Cultures of Mainland Southeast Asia.** Embree, John Fee, and Lillian Ota Dotson. New York: Russell and Russell, 1972. 621p.

Originally published in 1950, this reprint focuses on ethnographic studies of the peoples of mainland Southeast Asia. The books and periodical articles covered date from the nineteenth century through 1949. Emphasis is on the modern period rather than on historical studies and includes peoples of Assam, Chittagong, Burma, Thailand, Laos, Cambodia, Vietnam, and the ethnic groups of South China. The depth of historical coverage gives this work continued utility despite its age.

Australia and the Pacific

The islands of the Pacific are home to a myriad of cultures, many of which have been documented extensively in the ethnographic literature. Numerous anthropological bibliographies have been published on Melanesia, Micronesia, and Polynesia, as well as on specific regions within these areas, such as Fiji, the Gilbert Islands, and the Hawaiian Islands Likewise, the indigenous peoples of Australia have been the focus of considerable anthropological research. The following list of sources, therefore, is highly selective and focuses on major retrospective and current-awareness reference works.

Continuing anthropological interest in the Pacific is reflected by the numerous professional associations that focus on the region, including, among others, the Association for Social Anthropology in Oceania, the Australian Institute of Aboriginal Studies (entry 815), and the Polynesian Society (entry 827). Important journals in the field include *Oceania* (entry 690) and the *Journal of the Polynesian Society* (entry 686).

Literature Surveys and Reviews

528. **Pacific Islands Studies: A Survey of the Literature.** Jackson, M., editor. Westport, CT: Greenwood, 1987. 244p. ISBN 0313235287.

Not strictly a survey of ethnographic literature, this extensive bibliographic essay takes a broad approach and identifies key social science literature pertinent to Pacific peoples. The volume includes more than 1,800 books and journals articles and is divided into four major sections: Polynesia, Micronesia, Melanesia, and Australia. Within each section, a narrative overview incorporates citations to published research on the history, geography, language, politics, and cultures of the area in general, as well as on specific islands/territories. Much of the literature dates from the 1970s through the mid-1980s, though references include older classic literature as well.

Indexes, Abstracts, and Databases

529. **Australian Institute of Aboriginal and Torres Strait Islander Studies, Annual Bibliography.** Canberra: the Institute, 1972-. Annual. ISSN 1320-1158.

This annual publication is organized primarily by geographic area (New South Wales, Northern Territory, Tasmania, Western Australia, etc.). The bibliography indexes pamphlets, books, and periodical articles on all aspects of aboriginal studies. The geographic areas are subdivided by topic, including social and cultural anthropology, material culture and art; linguistics; health, disease, and psychology; prehistory and history; education; and community organization, among others. Over 150 primarily English-language periodicals are indexed, with good representation of anthropological titles. A total of nearly 1,800 unannotated citations appear in each annual issue, many of which are not duplicated in the standard anthropology indexes.

530. **Hawai'i Pacific Journal Index.** Manoa, HA: University of Hawai'i Library. Available online at <http://libweb.hawaii.edu/uhmlib/databases/hpji.html>.

This free online index to journals published in or about Hawai'i and the Pacific covers the social sciences, humanities, and natural history. It currently covers over 200 journal titles in a database of over 20,000 articles. Indexing typically includes the full run of each journal.

531. **South Pacific Periodicals Index.** Suva, Fiji: Pacific Information Center. 1976-. Irregular. ISSN 1011-5110.

This index continues the *Bibliography of Periodical Articles Relating to the South Pacific*, which was published from 1976–1982. Based on the periodical holdings of the University of the South Pacific Library, the citations in the bibliography relate to island cultures in the South Pacific. Entries are broadly arranged, with general works under the heading Oceania, and area-specific works under Melanesia, Micronesia, and Polynesia. Within each region, the citations are arranged by broad topic, including anthropology (encompassing ethnology, ethnomusicology, folklore, linguistics), archaeology, religion, nutrition, education, sociology, tourism, and others. Over 200 journals in the natural and social sciences are indexed, for a total of approximately 700 unannotated citations per issue.

Dictionaries, Encyclopedias, and Handbooks

532. **Aboriginal Tribes of Australia.** Tindale, Norman B. Berkeley, CA: University of California Press, 1974. 405p. ISBN 0520020057.

This handbook offers a detailed discussion of the ecology, nomenclature, and structure of Australian aboriginal cultures. The first part focuses on the people and the land, with a description of the geography and climate as well as social factors such as family and community patterns, travel and trade, food, etc. Part 2 consists of a listing of Australian aboriginal tribes with a list of alternative names and spellings. The description of geographic boundaries and range are illustrated on an accompanying map. Tasmanian tribes are included in an appendix, and a general bibliography is provided.

533. **New to New Zealand: A Guide to Ethnic Groups in New Zealand.** Bell, Daphne, editor. 3rd ed. Auckland: Reed Books, 2001. 123p. ISBN 0790008092.

While the indigenous population of New Zealand has received significant attention in the anthropological literature, information on immigrants groups and other ethnic minorities are less well represented. Bell remedies this situation by providing a concise guide to the country's more recent peoples and cultures.

534. **Oceania: The Native Cultures of Australia and the Pacific Islands.** Oliver, Douglas L. Honolulu, HI: University of Hawai'i Press, 1989. 2v. ISBN 0824810198.

This survey focuses on the cultures of the Pacific Islanders before European contact. Clearly written and well-organized, the text begins with a background discussion covering the natural setting, population and physical types, languages, archaeology, and ethnology of the region. In the second part, Oliver synthesizes the existing ethnographic literature and provides a general description/summary of major activities, such as foodways and food gathering, housing, transportation, warfare, sex and reproduction, and life cycle. Cultural generalizations as well as exceptions or variations between cultures are discussed. The third part focuses on social relations and within the five major sections (Australia, Polynesia, Micronesia, Melanesia, and Fiji), he describes kinship systems, male-female relationships, and general social organization of specific culture groups within these regions. The text is supplemented with maps and line drawings, copious notes, an extensive bibliography, a "Subject and Peoples Index," and an index to cited authors.

535. **Taonga Tuku Iho: Illustrated Encyclopedia of Traditional Maori Life.** Reed, A. W., and Buddy Mikaere. Revised ed. Auckland, N.Z.: New Holland, 2002. 208p. ISBN 1877246905.

First published in 1963 as *An Illustrated Encyclopedia of Maori Life*, this fully revised and updated new edition is useful for ready reference or as a basic text. The Maori title translates to "treasures from the past that have been handed down to us" and the guide focuses heavily on pre-European Maori life. References to the works of early anthropologists and ethnologists are included, as well as the overviews of the social, cultural, and spiritual lives of the Maori. The text is complemented by detailed line drawings and color and black and white photographs.

Bibliographies

Note: Because the large number of bibliographies on individual cultures and regions within the Pacific constitutes a reference book in its own right, the titles here represent a highly selective sample of the literature available.

536. **Australasia and South Pacific Islands Bibliography.** Thawley, John. Lanham, MD: Scarecrow, 1997. 587p. ISBN 0810832402.

The entries in the bibliography focus on Australia, Melanesia, Micronesia, and Polynesia. The nearly 6,000 references cover only books published through the latter part of the twentieth century, most of which are in English. Coverage is multidisciplinary, and includes the sciences, social sciences, and humanities. The work is organized by region, country, island/ethnic group, and subject. There is no subject index, however. An appendix lists relevant journals and computer databases. Because of the focus on books, the work is useful as a collection development or assessment tool for Pacific studies collections.

537. **Bibliography of Publications on the New Zealand Maori and the Moriori of the Chatham Islands.** Taylor, C. R. H. Oxford, England: Clarendon Press, 1972. 161p. ISBN 0198181566.

This book revises and updates the New Zealand and the Maori section of Taylor's *Pacific Bibliography* (entry 539). Subject headings were expanded from 26 to over 40, with greater emphasis on issues such as education, political and administrative considerations, and race relations. As in the original volume, books as well as articles are cited, with broad international coverage, and a detailed author and subject index is provided.

538. **The Kula: A Bibliography.** Macintyre, Martha. New York: Cambridge University Press, 1983. 90p. ISBN 0521232031.

Through not as general is scope as other bibliographies in this section, this title bears noting because it represents an extensive synthesis of research on a much-studied aspect of Melanesian culture. The kula is a complex exchange system practiced within Milne Bay Province, originally documented by Bronislaw Malinowski. The bibliography is divided into eight sections: Bronislaw Malinowski on the kula; government publications and reports; historical material; anthropological material; archaeological material; Massim art and aesthetics of kula objects; films; and museum collections. The entries (over 600) are selectively annotated and provide an exhaustive complication of the literature.

539. **Pacific Bibliography: Printed Matter Relating to the Native Peoples of Polynesia, Melanesia and Micronesia.** Taylor, Clyde Romer Hughes. 2nd ed. Oxford, England: Claredon Press, 1965. 692p.

Despite its date, this extensive bibliography of books and articles on Pacific cultures serves as a basic source for historical ethnography. Citations are divided into four sections: Oceania in general, Polynesia, Melanesia, and Micronesia. Sections are further subdivided by more than 20 subjects such as family organization, religion, culture contacts, and material culture. Coverage of foreign language materials is extensive, and the index by author and subject facilities identifying works on a specific topic. The portion on the Maori was updated and released as a separate publication in 1972 (entry 537).

Libraries, Archives, and Special Collections

540. **Bernice Pauahi Bishop Museum Library**
   1525 Bernice Street
   Honolulu, Hawai'i 96817
   (808) 847-3511
   <http://www.bishopmuseum.org/research/library/libarch.html>

Founded in 1889, the Bishop Museum is the paramount museum for Oceana and the leading museum concerned with collections and research in the culture and natural history of the Pacific Basin. The museum's trust stipulated that it be a "scientific institution for collection, preserving, storing, and exhibiting specimens of Polynesian and kindred antiquities, ethnology, and natural history" and sponsor and publish the results of its investigations. The anthropology section is one of five departments; its publications include the *Bernice P. Bishop Museum Bulletin, Occasional Papers of the Bernice P. Bishop Museum*, and *Pacific Anthropological Records* (series).

Considered the leading collection in the Western Hemisphere, the library's collection reflects the historical and contemporary research emphases of the Bishop Museum, i.e., the natural and cultural history of the Pacific. Areas of concentration include archaeology, ethnology, linguistics, voyages, exploration, and museology. Strong special collections include photographs and manuscript archives as well as nineteenth-century Hawai'ian-language newspapers and the Fuller Collection of Pacific Books (on anthropology). The library maintains an impressive map collection as well as extensive serial holdings and is open to the public.

541. **Libraries of Asia Pacific Directory.** Conference of Directors of National Libraries of Asia and Oceania. Available online at <http://www.nla.gov.au/lap/>.

This online directory of libraries provides users with information about the location, services, and collections of libraries in Asia and the Pacific region. Its goal is to provide a single access point, and links to the library websites are provided when available.

542. **National Library of Australia**
Canberra, ACT 2600 AUSTRALIA
Telephone: + 61 2 6262 1111
<http://www.nla.gov.au/>

The National Library of Australia has one of the world's most significant collections of primary and secondary sources on the indigenous peoples of the Pacific region, including New Zealand, Papua New Guinea, Melanesia, Micronesia, and Polynesia. The library includes a strong research-level collection of printed material as well as photographs, manuscripts, maps, and microform collections.

Internet Gateways

543. **Australian Institute of Aboriginal and Torres Strait Islander Studies.** Available online at <http://www.aiatsis.gov.au/library/links>.

The Library of the Australian Institute of Aboriginal and Torres Strait Islander Studies provides a useful website of links to sources for indigenous studies from the Pacific region. Organized by subject (human rights, language and linguistics, art), the site is one of several that select and organize related web-based information.

Europe

Because its original focus centered on non-Western peoples, anthropology does not have a strong Europeanist tradition. Early folklorists, however, were involved with the collection and analysis of the expressive culture of rural European societies, believing the customs, narratives, songs and beliefs to be relics of an earlier time. Scholarship on traditional European peoples has generally been subsumed under folklore and the term *regional ethnology* was coined to describe the discipline that studies the national "folk" culture of Europe (see the "Folklore and Mythology" section in Chapter 6).

The once salient simple/complex, rural/urban, and traditional/modern dichotomies that held sway have been abandoned by contemporary anthropologists, however, and Europeanist anthropology is experiencing a significant development.

The AAA's Society for the Anthropology of Europe was established in 1986, and with the critical issues of immigration, assimilation, and ethnic conflict on the European continent, cultural anthropologists are finding fertile ground for study.

Literature Surveys and Reviews

544. **The Anthropology of Europe: Identity and Boundaries in Conflict.** Goddard, Victoria A., Joseph Llobera, and Chris Shore, editors. Providence, RI: Berg, 1994. 310p. ISBN 0854969012.

Beginning with an historical survey of anthropological studies of European communities, this collection of essays explores the notions of Europe as a culture area, the construction of European identity, and nationalism. The intellectual and social developments in European anthropology are explored, and specific case studies (e.g., identity in Gibraltar) are provided.

545. **Appetites and Identities: An Introduction to the Social Anthropology of Western Europe.** Delamont, Sara. New York: Routledge, 1995. 254p. ISBN 0415062535.

In her exploration of the cultural diversity of western Europe, Delamont explores a variety of issues such as food, tourism, migration, housing, religion, and language. Primarily ethnographic in approach, the text provides descriptive and comparative summaries. The extensive bibliography serves as a useful review of the literature through the early 1990s.

546. **"Europeanization."** Borneman, John, and Nick Fowler. *Annual Review of Anthropology* 26 (1997): 487–514.

As the introduction points out, Europe is comprised of 32 nations and 67 languages (not including dialects). Formation of the European Union, however, raises the question of a "European" identity. The authors explore this notion, primarily through the lens of language, money, tourism, sex, and sport. The extensive bibliography of this ethnology of Europeanization provides a useful review of relevant literature.

Indexes, Abstracts, and Databases

547. **American Bibliography of Slavic and East European Studies.** Urbana, IL: American Association for the Advancement of Slavic Studies, 1956-. Available online by subscription.

This online bibliography indexes the major English-language publications and selected foreign language materials published in the United States and Canada relating to Slavic and Eastern European studies. Publications include books, journal articles, government and research reports, dissertations, and book reviews. Brief abstracts are provided and the database supplies a limited number of full text articles. Published since 1956, online availability begins in 1990.

548. **FRANCIS.** Paris: Institut de l' Information Scientifique et Technique du Centre National de la Recherche Scientifique (INIST-CNRS), 1984-. Available online by subscription.

The FRANCIS database is one of the premier indexes of social sciences and humanities literature from Europe. With an international scope and multiple subject areas, the index is particularly useful for identifying European scholarship on topical issues. For a complete annotation of this source, see entry 3.

549. **Historical Abstracts.** Santa Barbara, CA: ABC-Clio. 1969-. Quarterly. ISSN 0363-2717. Available in print and online by subscription.

While *Historical Abstracts* is mainly relevant to archaeologists, cultural anthropologists and ethnohistorians may also benefit from the citations this index provides to historical literature dealing with world history from 1450 forward.

550. **Internationale Bibliographie der Zeitschriftenliteratur.** Osnabrueck, Germany: F. Dietrich. 1896-. Monthly. ISSN 1618-923X. Available in print and online by subscription.

IBZ, as it is known, is an international, interdisciplinary bibliography of academic periodical literature in the arts and social sciences. Available online from 1983, it indexes over 11,000 journals. Subject access is available in German and English through keyword searching as well as by controlled vocabulary. Like its French counterpart FRANCIS (entry 3), IBZ is useful for casting a net beyond North America to identify current and retrospective scholarship, particularly from the European continent.

Dictionaries, Encyclopedias, and Handbooks

551. **Ethnohistorical Dictionary of the Russian and Soviet Empires.** Olson, James S., Lee Brigance Pappas, and Nicholas Charles Pappas, editors. Westport, CT: Greenwood Press, 1994. 840p. ISBN 0313274975.

More than 450 ethnic groups form the cultural landscape of Central Eurasia that was part of the former Russian empire and subsequently the Soviet Union. This handbook provides historical background on these diverse peoples. Alphabetically arranged entries range from a short paragraph to several pages, and include bibliographies with English language sources. Though the focus rests more on historical development than culture, the handbook is useful for providing background information on the large number of ethnic groups in this complex region.

552. **Ethnopolitical Encyclopaedia of Europe.** Cordell, Karl, and Stefan Wolff, editors. New York: Macmillan, 2004. 708p. ISBN 0333971248.

Although this work may seem more relevant to political science or geography than to ethnology, it is useful for identifying ethnic groups that are indigenous to Europe. They may be minorities within a state (e.g., Bretons in France) or transcend national boundaries (e.g., the Sami in northern Europe). Non-European immigrant groups, such as Africans, are not included. The signed articles are organized by country or region, and include bibliographical references. Maps and tables of treaties and conventions are also included.

553. The Times Guide to the Peoples of Europe. Fernández-Armesto, Felipe, editor. London: Times Books, 1994. 416p. ISBN 0723006245.

Subtitled "The Essential Handbook to Europe's Tribes," this one-volume handbook edited by a professor of global studies, describes more than 100 European ethnic groups. Essays typically include information about the history, language, religion, and social structure of both familiar and less-commonly known peoples.

Bibliographies

554. Circum-Mediterranean Peasantry: Introductory Bibliographies. Sweet, Louise Elizabeth, and Timothy J. O'Leary. New Haven, CT: Human Relations Area Files, 1969. 106p.

Though dated, this historically relevant bibliography offers a general introduction to the area and bibliographic essays that review the major anthropological issues and investigations through the mid-twentieth century. The geographic scope includes countries of Southern Europe, the Baltic, and North Africa.

555. Europe: A Selected Ethnographic Bibliography. Theodoratus, Robert J. New Haven, CT: Human Relations Area Files, 1969. 544p.

Despite its age, this bibliography remains important for its coverage of non-English-language scholarship on the ethnology of European peoples. Organized by country and subdivided by culture groups (e.g., Bretons, Walloons), all areas within Europe are represented, with the exception of the Caucasus Mountain region and Finno-Ugric and Turkic peoples. The time period focuses on the "modern period", or nineteenth and twentieth centuries, and citations include materials published in many European languages. Over 1,000 unannotated references are included, but unfortunately no subject access is provided.

556. Selected Bibliography of the Anthropology and Ethnology of Europe. Ripley, William Zebina. Boston: Boston Public Library, 1899. 160p.

Included for historical purposes, this nineteenth century bibliography contains nearly 2,000 titles on the anthropology of the peoples of Europe. Entries are arranged alphabetically. The scope includes all areas of anthropology but emphasizes physical anthropology. Citations include journal articles and books in Eastern and Western European languages. The cursory subject index is most useful for identifying studies on specific countries.

Internet Gateways

557. Eurominority: Portal of European Stateless Nations and Minorities. Organization for the European Minorities. Available online at <http://www.eurominority.eu/ >.

This website provides basic information on stateless nations, native peoples, national, cultural and linguistic minorities, ethnic groups, areas with strong identity and autonomist or separatist tendencies in Europe. Though the website appears to be in the early stage of development, and the thrust is primarily political in nature, it promises to provide a broad range of information and to host indigenous voices.

Middle East, North Africa, and Islam

Though the Middle East has a rich and well-documented history, fewer ethnographic sources are available. Numerous general encyclopedias, atlases and histories summarize the area's cultural achievements (particularly archaeology), but reference sources specific to cultural anthropology are relatively scarce. With the burgeoning interest in this strategically important area however, the sources below offer a good starting point for the armchair ethnologist.

Middle Eastern and Islamic studies are represented in numerous institutes and associations worldwide. In the United States, the Middle East Studies Association (entry 825) is active in promoting scholarship and communication across disciplines and publishes the *International Journal of Middle East Studies*.

Guides to the Reference Literature

558. **The Modern Middle East: A Guide to Research Tools in the Social Sciences.** Simon, Reeva S. Boulder, CO: Westview, 1978. 283p. ISBN 089158059X.

Though it doesn't include current references, this guide provides a useful overview of core reference works for Middle Eastern studies. The first section enumerates the major general bibliographies in the field (including 31 printed library catalogs) and bibliographies for specific countries and regions, including Afghanistan, Turkey, and North Africa. A list of the major periodicals and newspapers is provided along with standard reference tools such as encyclopedias and handbooks, directories, bibliographical sources, and indexes and abstracts. Brief annotations are provided, and a subject index assists in locating sources on particular topics.

Literature Surveys and Reviews

559. **Islam in World Cultures: Comparative Perspectives.** Feener, R. Michael, editor. Santa Barbara, CA: ABC-Clio, 2004. 387p. ISBN 1576075192.

Rather than focusing on politics or doctrine, this collection of scholarly essays highlights the diversity of Islamic cultures in various parts of the world, including Turkey, the Arab Middle East, Shi'ite Iran, South and Central Asia, China, Indonesia, Ethiopia, South Africa, and the United States. Muslim communities in Europe and West Africa, however, are not included. A useful annotated bibliography of scholarly print materials and Internet resources for each topic is also included, as well as a glossary and index.

560. **The Middle East and Central Asia: An Anthropological Approach.** Eickelman, Dale F. 4th ed. Upper Saddle River, NJ: Prentice Hall, 2002. 384p. ISBN 0130336785.

This title provides a contemporary survey of the basic concepts and issues in the anthropology of the Middle East, Central Asia, and North Africa. Rather than taking a regional, ethnographic approach, Eickelman focuses on contexts and constructs, with chapters on village studies, pastoral nomadism and urbanization, the concept of tribe, kinship and family relationships, religion and state, gender and ethnicity. Each chapter includes illustrations and detailed bibliographic references. A list for further reading, a glossary, and a subject index are also provided.

561. **"Zones of Theory in the Anthropology of the Arab World."** Abu-Lughod, Lila. *Annual Review of Anthropology* 18 (1989): 267–306.

In an extensive overview essay, Abu-Lughod analyzes research trends in Arabic ethnology through the late 1980s, emphasizing the contributions to anthropological theory that have emerged from Middle Eastern research. Over 100 citations to historical research are provided.

Indexes, Abstracts, and Databases

562. **Index Islamicus,** Vol. 1 -. Leiden: Brill. 1956-. Annual. ISSN 0308-7395. Also available online.

Index Islamicus began in 1956 as a retrospective catalog of articles on Islamic subjects in periodicals and other collective publications from the collection of the University of London's School of Oriental and African Studies, covering articles written from 1905 to 1955. Subsequent supplements were published, and the index later became an annual publication, which is now available online. This important source has grown in size and scope, reflecting the strategic importance of the Middle East and Islamic studies. With citations dating to 1905, records in the database cover nearly 100 years of publications on the world of Islam. Material cited includes works written on the Middle East, Muslim areas of Asia and Africa, and Muslim minorities elsewhere. Over 3,000 journals are regularly monitored for inclusion of their articles and book reviews in the database. Books are indexed to article and chapter level, and conference proceedings are also included. Focusing on the social sciences and humanities, this source is indispensable for scholars of Islamic cultures.

563. **Middle East: Abstracts and Index,** Vol. 1-. Pittsburgh, PA: Library Information and Research Services. 1978-. ISSN 0162-766X.

Over 700 journals in the humanities and social sciences are indexed for references to all areas of the Middle East. Fields of interest include anthropology, archaeology, art and among others, with a heavy emphasis on current affairs. The index is organized by country, with a subject index to specific topics or disciplines such as anthropology. A lengthy abstract is provided for each entry.

Dictionaries, Encyclopedias, and Handbooks

564. **The Central Middle East: A Handbook of Anthropology and Published Research on the Nile Valley, the Arab Levant, Southern Mesopotamia, the Arabian Peninsula, and Israel.** Sweet, Louise E., editor. New Haven, CT: Human Relations Area Files Press, 1971. 323p. ISBN 0875361072.

This handbook represents provides a survey of the cultural diversity of the indigenous peoples and cultures of specific regions within the Middle East. Five sections, each written by a specialist in the field, represent the major regions and sociocultural groups: the Nile Valley (Egypt and the Sudan); the Arab Levant (Syria, Jordan, Lebanon); Southern Mesopotamia (Iraq); the Arabian Peninsula (Saudi Arabia, Persian Gulf); and Israel. Topics covered in each chapter include an overview of agriculture, political organizations, social stratification, kinship groups, life cycles, religion, arts, and language. Bibliographic references are amply provided in the text, and an annotated bibliography of core books and articles (through 1970) follows each section.

565. **Encyclopedia of Women and Islamic Cultures.** Joseph, Suad, editor. Leiden, MA: Brill, 2003. 6v. (projected). ISBN 9004132473.

The scope of this projected six-volume set is far-reaching, as it seeks to include the diversity of Islamic women in the Middle East, Central and Southeast Asia, the Far East and Africa, as well as Muslim women in non-Muslim societies and non-Muslim women living in Islamic cultures. Historical as well as contemporary, the encyclopedia seeks to examine all aspects of women's lives. The first volume focuses on sources and methods, while subsequent volumes are topically focused, covering family law and politics; family, body, sexuality and health; economics, education, mobility and space; and practices, interpretations and representations. Substantive, scholarly articles also have extensive bibliographic references. An index volume is projected when the set is complete.

566. **Muslim Peoples: A World Ethnographic Survey.** Weeks, Richard V., editor. 2nd ed. Westport, CT: Greenwood, 1984. 953p. ISBN 0313233926.

This book provides insight into the world's Muslim people—where they are and how they live. Ethnographic profiles of over 19 ethnic/linguistic groups that are totally or partly Muslim are included. The essays are arranged alphabetically by ethnic group form the Acehnese to the Yoruk; each essay situates the group geographically and linguistically and recounts its historical involvement with Islam. The ethnographic details on each culture include a description of the social structure, cultural customs, religious practices, and daily life. Though some essays provide more historical detail than others, each has significant ethnographic content, reflecting the anthropological background of the scholars who contributed. A brief bibliography of books, articles follows each entry.

Bibliographies

567. Cultural Anthropology of the Middle East: A Bibliography. Strijp, Ruud. Kinderhook, NY: E.J. Brill, 1992. 2v. ISBN 9004096043.

This extensive bibliography includes monographs and articles written from 1965 to 1987 relating to the cultural anthropology of Muslim peoples in the Middle East, North Africa and the Mediterranean, and Asia. Citations identify research literature written in English, French, or German. The volumes are divided into two sections (anthropological studies and related studies), and subdivided by country. Annotations for the books provide descriptive detail to convey the scope of the work.

Libraries, Archives, and Special Collections

568. Libraries with Major Middle East Collections. Columbia University Libraries. Available online at <http://www.columbia.edu/cu/lweb/indiv/mideast/cuvlm/LIBS.html>.

This portal to library collections contains links to 15 libraries worldwide with strong holdings on the Middle East (e.g., Harvard, University of London's School of Oriental and African Studies, University of Chicago). Users are directed to information about these collections, and provided a link whenever possible to each institution's online catalog.

Internet Gateways

569. Middle East Studies Internet Resources. Columbia University Libraries. Available online at <http://www.columbia.edu/cu/lweb/indiv/mideast/cuvlm/>.

One of several useful portals to Middle East studies, this well-designed resource provided by Columbia University Library's Middle East and Jewish Studies Department, provides an excellent launching pad for Internet resources. Sections include sets of links to online bibliographies, library collections (see 568), news sources, resources by region and country, and subjects such as food, languages, minorities, music, and religion. In addition, links are provided to resources such as publishers, scholarly associations, directories, and graphics and images.

North America and the Arctic

Representing over a century of scholarly inquiry, the anthropological literature on North America is truly extensive. Most ethnographic research has focused on Native Americans, while other ethnic groups have fallen under the purview of sociology and history. Increasingly however, Ethnic Studies has come into its own and anthropologists are making important contributions.

Numerous international, national, and local organizations are devoted to the study of Native Americans, such as the International Congress of Americanists (entry 821) and the Plains Anthropological Society (entry 826). The National Association for Ethnic Studies was established in 1972, and provides an interdisciplinary forum for scholars concerned with national and international dimensions of ethnicity.

Though Arctic peoples are not limited to North America, because a significant amount of anthropological scholarship has involved the Arctic, these resources have been included within this section.

Ethnic Studies

Indexes, Abstracts, and Databases

570. **America, History and Life.** Santa Barbara, CA: ABC-Clio. 1964-. Quarterly. ISSN 0002-7065. Available in print and online by subscription.

Published since 1964, this resource indexes articles, book and media reviews, and dissertations in American history and related disciplines. Consulting this index enables researchers in anthropology to identify articles in American studies, popular culture, women and gender studies, and multicultural studies that are not covered in anthropological literature.

571. **Chicano Database.** Berkeley, CA: University of California, Berkeley, Ethnic Studies Library. 1967-. Quarterly. Available online by subscription.

This database grew out of the *Chicano Periodical Index* and specialized indexes compiled by the Ethnic Studies Library at the University of California, Berkeley. Originally focusing on Mexican-Americans, the database expanded in the early 1990s to encompass the broader Latino experience of Cuban Americans, Puerto Ricans, and immigrants from Central America. The index provides citations to journal articles, books, chapters, and selected newspaper articles. Subject strengths include arts, bilingual education, gender studies, religion, folklore, language, psychology, and social policy.

572. **Ethnic NewsWatch.** Ann Arbor, MI: ProQuest. 1990-. Available online by subscription.

This interdisciplinary, bilingual (English and Spanish) full-text database covers 200 contemporary newspapers, magazines, and journals from ethnic, minority, and Native presses in the United States and provides a viewpoint not always represented in the mainstream media. Examples of titles covered include *Akwasasne Notes* (Native Americans), *Arab American News,* and *Black Child.* Coverage begins in 1990.

573. **International Index to Black Periodicals.** Cambridge, UK: Chadwick-Healey. 1998-. Available online by subscription.

Though many of the journals included in this database are available through other vendors (e.g., JSTOR), this index focuses solely on scholarship devoted to African-American, African, and Caribbean peoples. Over 150 core titles are included, with a substantial number of full-text articles provided. The content is multidisciplinary and international in scope. Retrospective coverage for some titles dates to the early twentieth century.

Dictionaries, Encyclopedias, and Handbooks

574. **Africana: The Encyclopedia of the African and African American Experience.** Appiah, Anthony, and Henry Louis Gates, Jr., editors. 2nd ed. New York: Oxford University Press, 2005. 5v. ISBN 9780195170559. Also available online as part of the *Oxford African American Studies Center.*

This notable encyclopedia was compiled by two of the most prominent names in contemporary Africana and African-American scholarship, and the advisory board and contributors are equally impressive. This new edition features over 4,400 articles, ranging from several paragraphs to multiple pages, many with bibliographies. Full-color photographs, maps, charts, and other illustrations enhance the text. The scope includes the history and cultures of Africa and the African diaspora as well as the African American experience.

575. **American Immigrant Cultures: Builders of a Nation.** Levinson, David, and Melvin Ember, editors. New York: Macmillan, 1997. 2v. ISBN 0028972082.

This extensive reference work, edited by anthropologists long associated with the Human Relations Area Files, provides cultural profiles of 161 ethnic groups who came to America, whether by choice or by force (indigenous peoples are not included). Groups are defined on the basis a distinct cultural identity based on ancestry, race, religion and language, or various combinations of these factors. Articles include defining features of the group, cultural variations, demographic data, immigration and settlement history, discrimination, language, and attitudes towards assimilation. Each article concludes with references and a bibliography.

576. **Asian American Encyclopedia.** Ng, Franklin, and John D. Wilson. New York: Marshall Cavendish, 1995. 6v. ISBN 1854356771.

This set focuses primarily on the immigration experience of Asian Americans, providing background on the history and culture of their countries of origin as well as their experience in the United States. Over 2,000 entries are provided, ranging from brief definitions to extended essays. The test is illustrated with photographs (mainly historical) and also provides charts, tables, and maps as well as an extensive bibliography. Since arrangement is alphabetical, the index is particularly important for finding information embedded within articles on specific ethnic groups.

577. **Cambridge History of the Native Peoples of the Americas.** New York: Cambridge University Press, 1996-2000. 3v. ISBN various.

Combining history, anthropology, and archaeology, this set provides a comprehensive survey of the history and culture of the indigenous peoples of the Western Hemisphere. Volume 1 focuses on the native peoples of North America from their arrival to the present, focusing on their adaptations to the environment and to political oppression. Volume 2 provides an overview of native civilizations in the Mesoamerican region, with a focus on archaeology and culture. The third volume represents the first major survey of research on native peoples of South America since Julian Steward's landmark *Handbook of South American Indians* (see 625).

578. **Encyclopedia of Canada's Peoples.** Magocsi, Paul Robert, editor. Toronto: University of Toronto Press, 1999. 1,334p. ISBN 0802029388.

Nearly a decade in the making, this handbook chronicles the rich multiethnic heritage of Canada—another nation of indigenous peoples and immigrants. An impressive list of contributors and advisors covers 119 ethnic groups. Aboriginal peoples are divided into 13 groups such as Algonquians, Iroquoians, etc., and other groups range from the early Acadians to the relatively recent Arabs. Each entry follows approximately the same format, discussing origins, migration and settlement patterns, community life, economics and politics, and culture. Bibliographic references are provided for each entry.

579. **Encyclopedia of Contemporary American Culture.** McDonogh, Gary W., Robert Gregg, and Cindy H. Wong, editors. New York: Routledge, 2001. 839p. ISBN 0415161614.

While most reference books devoted to U.S. culture look at ethnic, racial, or regional cultures, this work looks at contemporary American culture as a whole. The focus is on mass/popular culture, and the dynamic processes that shape it. Entries are organized around 35 thematic topics, and include a wide variety of topics relevant to the study of contemporary American culture (e.g., body art). Ample cross-references and bibliographies round out this engaging resource.

580. **Gale Encyclopedia of Multicultural America.** Galens, Judy, Anna Sheets, and Robin V. Young. 2nd ed. Detroit, MI: Gale, 2000. 3v. ISBN 0810391635.

This reference source combines features of an encyclopedia, directory, and sourcebook as it profiles over 150 ethnic and minority groups in the United States (including 12 Native American groups, and ethno-religious cultures such as Jews and Amish). The articles emphasize culture in addition to providing historical information, and each concludes with a list of organizations, museums and research centers, media and suggestions for further reading. The text also includes photographs and an extensive index.

581. **Greenwood Encyclopedia of American Regional Cultures.** Ferris, William, editor. Westport, CT: Greenwood, 2004. 8v. ISBN 0313332665.

Regional differences in the United States typically focus on linguistic variations such as accent and terminology. This set illustrates the rich variety of regional cultural manifestations including architecture, food, folklore, and music. Each volume is devoted to a specific region (e.g., Southwest, Pacific) and shares a common format. Essays within each volume are thematically organized into 13 topical sections with signed articles and an index.

582. **Harvard Encyclopedia of American Ethnic Groups.** Thernstrom, Stephan, editor. Cambridge, MA: Belknap Press of Harvard University, 1980. 1,076p. ISBN 0674375122.

The bible of American ethnic studies, this important work draws upon the expertise of over 150 scholars in sociology, history, geography, anthropology, folklore, and area studies to produce an excellent overview of ethnic groups in the United States. Arranged alphabetically, more than 160 ethnic groups (Native American tribes are treated as a group in the section on American Indians) are represented in lengthy essays that discuss geographic origins and immigration history, language, religion, kinship ties, shared traditions and values, material and expressive culture, settlement and employment patterns, as well as internal and external perceptions of distinctiveness. Selected maps and tables are included and an extensive bibliography concludes each essay. Thematic essays deal with folklore, health beliefs and practices, assimilation and pluralism, and concepts of ethnicity, among others.

583. **Nation of Peoples: A Sourcebook on America's Multicultural Heritage.** Barkan, Elliott Robert. Westport, CT: Greenwood, 1999. 583p. ISBN 0313299617.

Unlike other titles in the section that cover a large number of ethnic groups (e.g., *Harvard Encyclopedia of American Ethnic Groups*, entry 582), this sourcebook concentrates on selected ethnic groups with a significant presence in the United States, including Native Americans. One of its strengths is that a majority of the essays appear to have been written by scholars belonging to the ethnic group they discuss. Framed in the context of current debates about multiculturalism, assimilation and education, each of the essays address common themes such as settlement patterns, interethnic relations, and cultural traditions. Each essay concludes with a bibliography.

584. **New Americans (Series).** Westport, CT: Greenwood, 1997-. ISBN various.

Responding to the burgeoning interest in the study of ethnic groups within the United States, Greenwood press instituted this series in the late 1990s. To date, 16 titles have been published, including Arab-, Mexican-, Korean-, and Vietnamese-Americans. Each title in the series investigates the immigrant experience of these ethnic groups and explores their patterns of immigration, assimilation and adaptation, cultural and religious traditions, the role of women and family and topics relevant to each group.

Bibliographies

585. **A Comprehensive Bibliography for the Study of American Minorities.** Miller, Wayne Charles, and Faye Nell Vowell. New York: New York University Press, 1976. 2v. ISBN 0814753736.

Though the purpose of this massive bibliography is to "provide a single source in which students of American minorities may find ample English-language materials to facilitate their research" (preface), coverage of Asian-Americans is notably weak. Nonetheless, the authors have done a useful job of identifying and organizing the anthropological literature on African-Americans, Native Americans (treated as a group), and "hyphenated Americans" from individual countries in the Middle East, Latin America, and Europe. Each section begins with a bibliographic essay detailing the history of the group in the United States. Citations are then arranged topically by subjects including history, sociology and anthropology, education and language, religion, biography, and literature and the arts. In all, nearly 30,000 briefly annotated citations to books and articles are provided, dating from the early part of the century through the early 1970s. A comprehensive index to all works by author and title is included.

Native Americans

Guides to Reference Literature

586. **American Indian Studies: A Bibliographic Guide.** White, Philip M. Englewood, CO: Libraries Unlimited, 1995. 163p. ISBN 1563082438.

Publications on Native Americans remain a growth industry, which is amply demonstrated by this annotated guide that identifies and describes numerous reference sources published from 1970 through the early 1990s. Entries are organized by categories such as guides, directories, dictionaries and encyclopedias, bibliographies, biographical sources, dissertations, government publications, microform collections, and computer databases. Periodicals, newspapers, and newsletters are also included. The useful introduction provides guidance in using Library of Congress classification and subject headings systems to locate books by topic.

587. **The Columbia Guide to American Indians of the Northeast.** Bragdon, Kathleen J. New York: Columbia University Press, 2001. 292p. ISBN 0231114524.

(See entry 588)

588. **The Columbia Guide to American Indians of the Southeast.** Perdue, Theda, and Michael D. Green. New York: Columbia University Press, 2001. 325p. ISBN 0231115709.

The first in a series organized by region, these Columbia Guides provide a good overview and starting point for research. Each title attempts to summarize the history and culture of native peoples of a region of the United States, highlighting historical and contemporary issues and controversies, and identifying current areas of research. Of particular note are the sections entitled, "Resource Guide to Research and Theory," which identifies and annotates primary and secondary resources, including a core bibliography, reference works, archives and museums, media, and web-based sources.

Dictionaries, Encyclopedias, and Handbooks

589. **Encyclopedia of American Indian Costume.** Paterek, Josephine. Denver, CO: ABC-Clio, 1994. 516p. ISBN 0874366852.

Though this reference work is specialized, it has been included in this guide because it identifies, organizes, and synthesizes a wealth of scholarship on Native American and Inuit material culture relating to costume. The scope is broader than clothing arts, and includes hairstyles, masks, body decorations and more. The text is divided into ten cultural regions and individual tribes. An appendix provides details and diagrams explaining how specific items of clothing were constructed, and the copious black and white illustrations (primarily from museum collections) further enhance the text.

590. **Encyclopedia of Native North America.** Green, Rayna. Bloomington, IN: Indiana University Press, 1999. 213p. ISBN 0253335973.

Written by folklorist Rayna Green (of Cherokee descent), this notable encyclopedia aptly demonstrates that Native American culture is not frozen in the nineteenth century. Richly illustrated and engagingly written, the text explores issues and themes in Native American history and culture. Excerpts of stories, songs, quotes, and first-person accounts enliven the articles and provide an insider's perspective.

591. **Encyclopedia of North American Indians.** Hoxie, Frederick E., editor. New York: Houghton Mifflin, 1996. 756p. ISBN 0395669219.

In a crowded field of reference books on Native North Americans, historian Hoxie's encyclopedia stands out for its extensive inclusion of contributions by Native American scholars. Contributors hail from the fields of anthropology, history, Native American Studies, and related social sciences, and include a mix of perspectives. Nearly 500 articles, ranging in length from a few paragraphs to multiple pages, cover particular tribes (many written by tribal members), notable people, specific events, and specific topics (e.g., cradleboards). Articles are signed, and many include a bibliography. Historical as well as contemporary topics are addressed, and the text is supplemented by maps and black and white illustrations.

592. **Encyclopedia of the Arctic.** Nuttall, Mark, editor. New York: Routledge, 2005. 3v. ISBN 15759584365.

An international team of 375 experts served as contributors to this distinguished set. The scope is broad and interdisciplinary, covering 28 subject areas, including anthropology, geography, history, politics, and the environment, among others. Alphabetically arranged, signed essays range in length from a paragraph to several pages, and include bibliographies. Anthropological topics include discussions of archaeology and history, as well as material culture and social life and customs. Written for an academic rather than a popular audience, this set organizes and synthesizes existing scholarship on an area of longstanding interest to anthropologists.

593. **Gale Encyclopedia of Native American Tribes.** Malinowski, Sharon, editor. Detroit, MI: Gale, 1998. 4v. ISBN 0787610852.

With no shortage of reference books devoted to Native Americans, this relative newcomer for the general audience provides numerous articles written or reviewed by Native American authors or tribal leaders. The resulting set profiles 400 native groups, predominantly from North America, but also including Latin America and the Pacific, and offers both historical and current information. Ample black-and-white illustrations complement the text, which is supplemented by a list of federally recognized tribes in the United States and Canada, and a glossary.

594. **Handbook of American Indians North of Mexico.** Hodge, Frederick W. Washington, DC: Government Printing Office, Vol. 2, 1907–1910. (Smithsonian Institution, Bureau of American Ethnology, Bulletin 30). ISBN 0837119839.

In addition to providing ready reference information (on specific tribes, arts, customs, individual Indian leaders, etc.), the work serves as an organized compendium of 19th century scholarship on Native Americans and can serve as a starting point for research on North American Indians. Its references "form practically a bibliography of the tribe for those who wish to pursue the subject further" (preface). Arranged alphabetically, entries range from brief descriptions to essays of several columns, followed by bibliographic references. Illustrated with photos and line drawings, the book also provides a detailed subject index. This title represents a definitive state of the art of Native American scholarship at the turn of the century.

595. **Handbook of North American Indians.** Sturtevant, William C., editor. Washington, DC: Smithsonian Institution Press, 1978-. 20v. (projected). ISBN various.

Volumes published as of 2006 include Vol. 4, Indian-White Relations (1988); Vol. 5, Arctic (1984); Vol. 6, Subarctic (1981); Vol. 7, Northwest Coast (1990); Vol. 8, California (1978); Vol. 9, Southwest. Pt. 1 (1979); Vol. 10, Southwest, Pt. 2 (1983); Vol., 11, Great Basin (1986); Vol. 12, Plateau (1998); Vol. 13, Plains (2001); Vol. 14, Southeast (2004); Vol. 15, Northeast (1978) Vol. 17, Languages (1996).

Forthcoming volumes include Vol. 1, Introduction; Vol. 2, Indians in Contemporary Society; Vol. 3, Environment, Origins, and Population; Vol. 16, Technology and Visual Arts; Vol. 18, Biographical Dictionary; Vol. 19, Biographical Dictionary; Vol. 20, Index.

When completed, this set will stand as definitive source for anthropological scholarship on Indians north of Mesoamerica. Each volume is well edited and presents approximately 50 chapters by well-established scholars in the field. The organization of the geographically based volumes generally follows a similar pattern: coverage of historical, linguistic, and environmental issues; profiles of individual tribes; and contemporary concerns. Each volume is well designed with clear black-and-white photographs and illustrations and a lucid text. The handbook is accessible to the general reader, but the specialist will likewise find the set useful. Each essay contains numerous citations, which are cumulated into a bibliography of several hundred citations. Thorough indexing allows for detailed topical access to the contents.

596. **Macmillan Encyclopedia of Native American Tribes.** Johnson, Michael G. 2nd ed. New York: Macmillan, 1999. 288p. ISBN 0002863499.

Specific tribes are the focus of this one-volume encyclopedia, and Johnson provides information on 400 separate tribes, with an emphasis on contemporary culture. Nicely illustrated, the text also includes almanac and directory information, such as lists of pow-wows, festivals, and holidays, museums, and websites relating to Native Americans.

597. **Native America Today: A Guide to Community Politics and Culture.** Pritzker, Barry M. Santa Barbara, CA: ABC-Clio, 1999. 453p. ISBN 1576070778.

While many reference books continue to profile historic Native Americans, this handbook focuses on the issues faced by contemporary peoples. The first section focuses on the current status of arts, health and education, land ownership, natural resources, and religion, among other issues. The second section provides profiles of 32 active tribes and groups, noting topics of most concern to each of them. The final section, "Documents: Acts of Congress, Executive Orders, Court Decisions, Laws, and Resolutions," reproduces political documents that are relevant to current issues. A bibliography is provided and appendices list the names of federally recognized tribes and those who have petitioned for federal recognition, also included is a list of indigenous peoples of Canada, and maps of federal Indian lands.

598. **Native American Encyclopedia: History, Culture, and Peoples.** Pritzker, Barry M. New York: Oxford University Press, 2000. 591p. ISBN 019513897X.

Pritzker sets out a daunting task: covering the history and culture of the native peoples of North America in a single volume. His strategy is to divide North America into ten broad geographically based culture areas. Within each section, he provides a brief overview of the area, followed by tribal name (and its pronunciation and meaning) and brief historical and contemporary information. The volume is richly illustrated, but unfortunately the photographs favor historical representations and don't adequately include contemporary manifestations of Native cultures.

599. **Native North American Almanac: A Reference Work on Native North Americans in the United States and Canada.** Champagne, Duane, editor. Detroit, MI: Gale, 1994. 1,275p. ISBN 0810388650.

Though referring to itself as an almanac, this title combines the features of a handbook, encyclopedia, and directory. Each of the 17 sections treats a specific topic such as culture areas, law, religion, education, etc. Each section contains articles of varying lengths, a bibliography, and a directory of relevant museums, community organizations, etc., as appropriate. At nearly 200 pages, the Chronology section is particularly extensive. Emphasis is on the twentieth century, and the scope includes both the United States and Canada.

Bibliographies

600. **Bibliography of Native North Americans.** Murdock, George Peter, and M. Marlene Martin. New Haven, CT: Human Relations Area Files, 1990-. Available online by subscription.

This online database contains the citations from the eight volumes of the *Ethnographic Bibliography of North America* (entry 601) as well as the supplement (entry 602) and additional new citations. Content covers citations to literature about native peoples of North America published from the sixteenth century to the present.

601. **Ethnographic Bibliography of North America.** Murdock, George Peter. 4th ed. New Haven, CT: Human Relations Area Files Press, 1975. 5v. ISBN various. Also available online as the *Bibliography of Native North Americans*.

A monumental work, the fourth edition of this important bibliography contains approximately 28,000 citations to ethnographic materials on Native Americans through 1972. References to published books and articles, theses and dissertations, ERIC documents, and government documents are included, but publications in non-Western languages, maps, unpublished manuscripts, and audiovisual materials are omitted. Though emphasis is on ethnographic research, selected citations to fiction and poetry are also included. The work is arranged by broad geographic area, subdivided by specific ethnic groups. Unfortunately, this extensive bibliography offers no subject or author access: the sole access point is by ethnic group. (See also entries 600 and 602).

602. **Ethnographic Bibliography of North America, Supplement.** Martin, M. Marlene, and Timothy J. O'Leary. New Haven, CT: Human Relations Area Files Press, 1990. 3v. ISBN 0875362540. Also available online as the *Bibliography of Native North Americans*.

The continuing scholarly research on Native Americans is evidenced by this supplement to the *Ethnographic Bibliography of North America*. It includes approximately 26,000 citations to literature published between 1973 and 1987, and the compilers estimate that this total represents only half of what was actually published. The supplement provides a significant update of the classic bibliography, drawing together a large body of literature from diverse sources, including references to published books and articles as well as government publications (United States federal and state, and Canadian), dissertation and theses, ERIC documents, manuscripts and archival documents, and nonprint materials (films, maps, etc.) from the sixteenth century to 1987.

603. **Native American Bibliography Series.** Lanham, MD: Scarecrow, 1980-. ISBN various.

Beginning in 1980, this continuing series has published over 25 separately issued bibliographies dealing with specific Native North American peoples (Pawnee, Shawnee, Dine, etc.), or specific topics ranging from language to health care. The bibliographies are well organized, and contain descriptive annotations.

Together they represent broad and deep coverage of the literature of the twentieth century.

604. Native Canadian Anthropology and History: A Selected Bibliography.
Krech, Shepard III. Rev. ed. Norman, OK: University of Oklahoma Press, 1994. 212p. ISBN 0806126175.

This second edition updates the original 1986 publication of the same title. An excellent introduction provides a context and thorough literature review. The first section of the bibliography focuses on general reference works, as well as standard archival records relating to Canadian Aboriginal history. Regional cultures and specific ethnic groups are included in the second section, while the third covers thematic topics such as gender, health, etc. Over 3,000 references in English and French are drawn from books, chapters in books, periodical articles, conference papers and proceedings, monographic series. Popular items, most government documents, and Internet sites are excluded.

Published Library Catalogs and Guides

605. Catalogue of the Arctic Institute of North America. Arctic Institute of North America Library. Boston, MA: G. K. Hall, 1968–1980. 4v. ISBN 0816110301.

Indexing one of the three largest polar libraries in the world (preface), this catalog includes materials on the physical, biological, and social sciences of Artic peoples. Valuable not only for the books, speeches, reports, theses, and newspapers it identifies, the catalog also includes citations for journal articles (4,500 in the main set). The subject headings are similar to those of the Library of Congress, but each item is extensively indexed. According to the preface, up to 20 subject headings may be given to any one work. Holdings added to the collection of the Artic Institute after 1979 can be searched via the online catalog at the University of Calgary (http://library.ucalgary.ca).

606. Dictionary Catalog of the American Indian Collection. Huntington Free Library. Boston, MA: G. K. Hall, 1977. 4v. ISBN 0816100659.

This catalog represents the library holdings of what was originally the Heye Foundation's Museum of the American Indian (now the Smithsonian's National Museum of the American Indian). The extensive collection, now called the Huntington Free Library Native American Collection, was moved to Cornell University in 2004. Though the catalog does not include materials added since 1977 (digital finding aids will no doubt be available in the future), it is valuable for identifying unique materials including manuscripts, diaries, photographs, field notes, etc. of interest to the specialist in Native American culture and history.

607. Dictionary Catalog of the American Indian Collection. Newberry Library. Boston, MA: G.K. Hall, 1977. 4v. ISBN 0816100659.

Focusing more closely on history than on contemporary ethnology, this catalog of the prestigious Edward E. Ayer Collection at the Newberry Library is nonetheless useful for its extensive coverage of unique materials. In addition to extensive rare book and government documents holdings, the catalog identifies extensive manuscript holdings, maps, photographs, and drawings. Though Newberry's online catalog includes all items acquired since 1978, the titles in this book catalog have not yet been incorporated into the online catalog.

Internet Gateways

608. **Artic Circle.** Chance, Norman. Available online at <arcticcircle.uconn.edu>.
Anthropologist Chance has designed an extensive portal to websites relating to the Arctic. With an emphasis on natural resources, history and culture, and social equity and environmental justice, he has selected and organized links to hundreds of articles, reports, visual images, and related websites, often produced by indigenous peoples.

609. **Native American Sites.** Mitten, Lisa. Available online at <www.nativeculturelinks.com/indians.html>.
Developed and maintained by Native American librarian Lisa Mitten, in conjunction with the American Indian Library Association, the goal of this website is to facilitate access to home pages of Native American Nations and organizations and to other authoritative websites. Examples of links include Native media, languages, pow-wows and festivals, as well as topics such as the mascot issue.

Latin America and the Caribbean

The ethnographic literature on Latin America is particularly rich, with an extensive body of research in Spanish, Portuguese, and English. A similarly impressive collection of reference sources have been published that identifies and organizes this scholarship, notably ethnographic surveys and bibliographies. The titles that follow represent important but highly selected reference sources.

Latin American studies within anthropology are represented by the AAA's Society for Latin American Anthropology (entry 766).

Guides to Reference Literature

610. **Latin America and the Caribbean: A Critical Guide to Research Sources.** Covington, Paula, editor. New York: Greenwood, 1992. 924p. ISBN 0313264031.

One of several guides to research sources on Latin America, this work not only covers multidisciplinary sources, but includes separate chapters on research in specific disciplines, including anthropology. Each section is introduced by a scholarly essay followed by a bibliography of important titles.

611. **Latin American Studies: A Basic Guide to Sources.** McNell, Robert A., and Barbara G. Valk, editors. 2nd ed. Metuchen, NJ: Scarecrow Press, 1990. 458p. ISBN 0910922369.

This work serves as a guide to research on Latin America in the social sciences and humanities for researchers working on the region from Mexico to Tierra del Fuego and the Caribbean islands. Cited materials include items written in English, Spanish, Portuguese, and other Western European languages and date from early printed sources through the late 1980s. The first section focuses on the use of library classification schemes and sources such as library and manuscript catalogs: the second section covers general, subject, national, and personal bibliographies; the third section identifies additional print sources such as encyclopedias, handbooks, maps and atlases, theses and dissertations, and official publications. Nonprint sources (e.g., databases, microforms) and specialized information such as biographies and censuses are also discussed. The final section, "Research and Career Development," serves as a directory of universities and research centers, societies and associations, and language and study-abroad programs.

612. **Middle American Anthropology.** McGlynn, Eileen. Los Angeles: Latin American Center and University Library, University of California at Los Angeles, 1975. 131p. ISBN 0879033010.

Though this bibliographic guide is dated, it provides a useful historical sketch of early anthropologists who contributed significantly to the development of anthropological research on Central America, and a well organized bibliography of books in English and Spanish through the early 1970s.

Literature Surveys and Reviews

613. **"Central America since 1979, Part I."** Smith, Carol, Jefferson Boyer, and Martin Diskin. *Annual Review of Anthropology* 16 (1987): 197–221.
    (See entry 614)

614. **"Central America since 1979, Part II."** Smith, Carol, Jefferson Boyer, and Martin Diskin. *Annual Review of Anthropology* 17 (1988): 331–364.

These reviews of the literature cover major works written in the early 1980s, when modern scholarship on the region first began to be published. Part 1 covers the countries of Guatemala and Honduras, and Part 2 focuses on Costa Rica, El Salvador, Nicaragua, and the Atlantic Coast. Principle developments, issues, and problems encountered in both archaeology and cultural anthropology are discussed and areas for further anthropological research are suggested. These offer an exhaustive review of the literature with a total of 231 references.

Indexes, Abstracts, and Databases

615. **Bibliografía Mesoamericana.** Weeks, John, and Sandra Noble. Museum Library of the University of Pennsylvania and the Foundation for the Advancement of Mesoamerican Studies, Philadelphia, PA. Available online at <http://research.famsi.org/mesobib.html>.

This bibliographic database of published literature pertaining to the anthropology of Mesoamerica is based on the holdings of the Museum Library of the University of Pennsylvania and the Foundation for the Advancement of Mesoamerican Studies (FAMSI). Content includes citations to archaeology, ethnography, ethnohistory, art history, linguistics, physical anthropology, and other related disciplines.

616. **Handbook of Latin American Studies.** Washington, DC: Library of Congress. 1935. Annual. ISSN 0072-9833. Available in print and online as *HLAS Online*. <http://lcweb2.loc.gov/hlas/>.

Edited by the Hispanic Division of the Library of Congress, the *Handbook* is an index to the current periodical literature. The social science volumes of this index are essentially biennial because each annual volume alternates between the social sciences and the humanities. With over 400 journals, coverage is broader than *HAPI* (entry 617). The print index is well organized and includes sections on the disciplines of anthropology, economics, education, geography, linguistics, and physical anthropology, with over 1,400 entries annually. Each section is preceded by a bibliographic review essay that provides an overview of current issues (such as the obstruction of research in Central America) and is subdivided geographically. Subject and author indexes are available at the back. The online version of the complete is now available free via the Internet. In addition to expediting searching, the online version has advantage of currency since it is updated weekly.

617. **Hispanic American Periodical Index (HAPI).** Los Angeles: UCLA Latin American Center. 1970-. Annual. ISSN 0072-9833. Available in print and online by subscription.

HAPI is one of the premier indexes for Latin American studies. It provides bibliographic citations to the periodical literature both from and about Central and South America, the Caribbean, and Hispanics/Latinos in the United States. Over 275 key academic journals in the social science and humanities are indexed. With articles in six languages represented (Spanish, Portuguese, English, French, German, and Italian), the international coverage is a particular strength.

Dictionaries, Encyclopedias, and Handbooks

618. **Dictionary of Afro-Latin American Civilization.** Núñez, Benjamín. Westport, CT: Greenwood Press, 1980. 525p. ISBN 0313211388.

An interesting compendium of terms reflecting African cultural influence in Latin America, the dictionary bridges Afro-American, African, and Latin

American studies. The dictionary documents and illustrates the impact of African civilizations and peoples upon the New World, particularly in the Caribbean. Terms are in English, French, Portuguese, and African and Creole languages and include an eclectic collection of words and phrases for foods, gods, ceremonies, and other cultural manifestations.

619. **Dictionary of Latin American Racial and Ethnic Terminology.** Stephens, Thomas M. 2nd ed. Gainesville, FL: University of Florida Press, 1999. 863p. ISBN 081301705X.

Of interest to researchers in racial and ethnic studies and to Latin Americanists, this dictionary focuses on racial and ethnic terms in Spanish, Brazilian Portuguese, and French Creole, and reflects the extensive range of social categories within these cultures. Containing contemporary and historic words and phrases, including pejorative terms, the extensive listing of terms ranges from sexual orientation to musical ability, and reflects an exhaustive range of social categories. In addition to providing definitions, entries include dates of usage, country or region, variations in meaning, and references to source material from which definitions and examples were taken. Many of the words and phrases appear to be unique to this source, and are not found in standard foreign-language or bilingual dictionaries. Stephens' work is useful for quick definitions of words or as a source for linguistic and cultural analysis in its own right.

620. **Dictionary of Twentieth Century Culture: Hispanic Culture of Mexico, Central America, and the Caribbean.** Standish, Peter, editor. Detroit: Gale, 1996. 327p. ISBN 0810384841.

A broad introduction for the general public, this work defines culture in the very broad sense, and covers literature, politics, history, and the arts of the Spanish-speaking countries neighboring North America. The relatively brief (50 to 1,000 words) signed essays also feature biographical information. Numerous black and white photos, and a timeline from 1898 to 1995 provide additional information.

621. **Encyclopedia of Contemporary Latin American and Caribbean Cultures.** Balderston, Daniel, Mike Gonzalez, and Ana M. Lopez, editors. New York: Routledge, 1999. 3v. ISBN 041513188X.

Like other encyclopedias with similar titles, this set focuses less on ethnography than on cultural events, history and politics, notable people, and historic sites, etc., of Latin America and the Caribbean. Signed entries range from one to two paragraphs to several pages in length, some with a list of additional readings. The list of contributors is notable, and overall the work is a scholarly ready-reference source.

622. **Encyclopedia of Latin American History and Culture.** Tenenbaum, Barbara A., editor. New York: Scribner's, 1996. 5v. ISBN 0684192535.

This encyclopedia set represents the work of over 800 contributors and covers Central and South America (including Brazil), and the Caribbean. Lengthy essays are provided on individual countries, indigenous groups, and general topics (e.g., music) and events, though a large number of entries provide brief biographies of historical and contemporary figures. Many entries contain bibliographic references, and black-and-white illustrations are provided throughout. The emphasis is on contemporary Latin American history, politics, and culture.

623. Handbook of Middle American Indians. Wauchope, Robert, editor. Austin, TX: University of Texas Press, 1964–1976. 16v. ISBN 0292700148.

Each volume in this important series has a separate title and editor. These include v.1, *Natural Environment and Early Cultures*, Robert C. West, ed.; v.2–3, *Archaeology of Southern Mesoamerica*, Gordon R. Willey, ed.; v.4, *Archaeological Frontiers and External Connections*, Gordon F. Ekholm and Gordon R. Willey, eds.; v.5, *Linguistics*, Norman A. McQuown, ed.; v.6, *Social Anthropology*, Manning Nash, ed.; v.7–8, *Ethnology*, Evon Z. Vogt, ed.; v.9, *Physical Anthropology*, T. Dale Stewart, ed.; v.10–11, *Archaeology of Northern Mesoamerica*, Gordon R. Ekholm and Ignacio Bernal, eds.; v.14–15, *Guide to Ethnohistorical Sources*. Howard F. Cline, ed.; v.16, *Sources Cited and Artifacts Illustrated*, Margaret A. Harrison, ed.

This set serves as a standard reference source on the anthropology of Mesoamerica. As with other anthropological handbooks, the format consists of virtually all aspects of anthropological research on Middle America through the mid-1970s. The articles are characterized by a clearly written text, numerous maps, charts, and photographs, and bibliographic references. A subject and proper-name index to each volume is provided; bibliographic references are cumulated into a 3,500-item bibliography in Volume 16.

624. Handbook of Middle American Indians. Supplement. Bricker, Victoria B., and Jeremy A. Sabloff, editors. Austin, TX: University of Texas Press, 1981. ISBN various.

As with the original set, volumes in this set have been issued as separately edited titles. These include v.1, *Archaeology,* Jeremy Sabloff, ed.; v.2, *Linguistics,* Victoria Bricker and Munro Edmonson, eds.; v.3, *Literature,* Munro Edmonson, ed.; v.4, *Ethnohistory,* Ronald Spores, ed.; v.5, *Epigraphy,* Victoria Bricker, ed.; v.6, *Ethnology,* Victoria Bricker and John Monagham, eds. Intended to update or supplement the *Handbook of Middle American Indians*, these titles do not replace the original set. Following the format of the main set, the supplement provides contemporary scholarship on many of the topics contained in the old set as well as breaks new ground.

625. Handbook of South American Indians. Steward, Julian H., editor. Washington, DC: Government Printing Office, 1946–1959. 7v. (Bureau of American Ethnology Bulletin, 143).

A monumental work, this handbook serves as an encyclopedia, history, and bibliography of South American indigenous peoples. The first four volumes focus on the cultures of the four major geographic regions, including parts of Mesoamerica and the Caribbean. Written by distinguished scholars in the field, each chapter deals with a specific ethnic group, provides an overview of the history and archaeology of the area, then focuses on cultural characteristics (region and mythology, social life, life cycle, material culture). The handbook thus provides a concise a summary of ethnographic research conducted through the mid-twentieth century. Numerous line drawings and photographs supplement the text. Each chapter contains bibliographic references, and a cumulated bibliography (with somewhat abbreviated citations) is located at the back.

626. **Oxford Encyclopedia of Mesoamerican Cultures: The Civilizations of Mexico and Central America.** Carrasco, David, editor. New York: Oxford University Press, 2001. 3v. ISBN 0195108159.

A team of anthropologists, archaeologists, historians, and other scholars in the social sciences and humanities contributed over 600 essays that introduce the reader to ancient and contemporary Mesoamerican cultures. Skillfully incorporating historical background and current issues, the text is enhanced by numerous illustrations. Suggestions for further reading are also provided.

627. **Peoples of the Caribbean: An Encyclopedia of Archaeology and Traditional Culture.** Saunders, Nicholas J. Santa Barbara, CA: ABC-Clio, 2005. 300p. ISBN 1576077012.

Combining history, archaeology, and anthropology, *Peoples of the Caribbean* explores the population of the Caribbean Islands, from the earliest inhabitants through the time of first contact with Europeans and the slave trade to the current ethnic diversity of the region. Topics include religion and spirituality, the material culture of the Caribbean peoples, economic concerns and slavery, and social relations. Most entries include a reference list of articles and books, with an extensive bibliography in the appendix.

Bibliographies

628. **Bibliografía de Arqueología y Etnografía: Mesoamérica y Norte de México, 1514–1960.** Bernal, Ignacio. Mexico City: Instituto Nacional de Antropología e Historia, 1962. 634p. (Instituto Nacional de Antropología e Historia. Memorias, 7).

This important retrospective bibliography of books and articles in English, Spanish, and other European languages represents a massive effort at identifying and organizing the scholarly literature on the anthropology of Mesoamerica published from the early-sixteenth through the mid-twentieth centuries. Over 13,000 unannotated items are included, and citations are clear and comprehensive (no doubt to the relief of interlibrary loan personnel). Entries are organized by topic (religion, arts, social organization) within general geographic area, and the book has an index to authors.

629. **Bibliografía Indigenista de México y Centroamérica (1850–1950).** Parra, Manuel German, and Wigberto Jiménez Moreno. México City: Institution Nacional Indigenista, 1954. 342p.

Over 6,000 books, articles, reports, and other materials are included in this extensive bibliography identifying scholarship on the indigenous peoples of Mexico and Central America from the mid-nineteenth through mid-twentieth centuries. The unannotated citations are organized by topic, including ethnography, economy, technology, social and political organization, arts, and others and indexed by ethnic group.

630. **The Complete Caribbeana, 1900–1975: A Bibliographic Guide to the Scholarly Literature.** Comita, Lambros. Millwood, NY: KTO Press, 1977. 4v. ISBN 0527188204.

With a heavy emphasis on social science literature, this exhaustive bibliography provides over 17,000 references to books, proceedings, dissertations, journal articles, and reports on the Caribbean in English and other European languages. Citations are divided into major thematic sections: "People," "Institutions," and "Resources." The first section includes references in the field of archaeology and history and has a major focus on anthropology, particularly in regard to studies on the Afro-Caribbean, East Indian, Amerindian, and Black Carib peoples of the region. "Institutions" includes references to folklore, culture change, folk medicine, and related anthropological topics; "Resources" identifies political, economic, and agricultural research.

631. **Complete Haitiana.** Laguerre, Michel. Millwood, NY: Kraus, 1982. 2v. ISBN 0527540404.

Because Haiti is not included in Comita's *Complete Caribbeana* (entry 630), Laguerre's bibliography fills a void. Though this bibliography is not specifically ethnographic, a significant portion of the books and articles cited relate to the social sciences.

632. **Ethnographic Bibliography of South America.** O'Leary, Timothy. New Haven, CT: Human Relations Area Files, 1963. 387p.

This classic bibliography remains an important sources for ethnographic literature (books, articles, reports) in English, Spanish, and other European languages published on South American peoples through 1960. The scope is restricted to continental South America, with no coverage of Panama and the Caribbean and is organized by country or geographic area. More than 2,500 unannotated citations are listed under tribal groups, which follow the classification in the *Outline of World Cultures* (see entry 485). Though maps and an ethnic group index are included, no access by subject is available.

633. **The Indians of South America: A Bibliography.** Welch, Thomas L., compiler. Washington, DC: Columbus Memorial Library, Organization of American States, 1987. 594p.

This recent bibliography of over 9,000 items was developed from the collection of the Columbus Memorial Library of the Organization of American States. The selected listing of books and reports represents works in English, Spanish, and other European languages concerning the indigenous peoples of South

America. Organized by five major subject divisions, "General Works," "Topical Works," "Specific Regions," "Specific Peoples," and "Languages," each is further subdivided by topic. The titles date from the sixteenth century through the mid-1980s and represent an extensive and focused bibliography for anthropologists conducting topical or regional research.

Published Library Catalogs and Guides

634. **Bibliographic Guide to Latin American Studies.** Boston, MA: G.K. Hall. 1978-. Annual. ISSN 0162-5314.

With a truly outstanding collection of Latin American materials, particularly for Mexico and Central America, the Benson Latin American collection at the University of Texas at Austin Library (www.lib.utexas.edu/benson/) constitutes a major international resource. This bibliography identifies newly acquired and cataloged items in the Library's collection, and includes not only books, but pamphlets, dissertations, government documents, media and gray literature that go beyond items found in publisher's catalogs.

635. **Catalogos de la Biblioteca Nacional de Antropología e Historia.** Biblioteca Nacional de Antropología e Historia, Mexico. Boston: G.K. Hall, 1972. 10v. ISBN 0916109184.

This National Library of Anthropology and History in Mexico City specializes in the anthropology of Mexico (with a particular emphasis on archaeology), though other areas within Latin America are represented as well. The catalog lists books and dissertations as well as Mexican government documents. As analytical entries for journal articles are also provided, it serves likewise as a retrospective periodical index. Materials are primarily in Spanish and other European languages, with subject headings (modified Library of Congress headings) in Spanish.

636. **A Guide to Central American Collections in the United States.** Leonard, Thomas M. Westport, CT: Greenwood, 1994. 186p. ISBN 0313286892.

Arranged alphabetically by state, this directory includes 747 collections, ranging from major holdings to a few unique items. The largest collections include the notable Bancroft Library, the Newberry Library, Tulane's Latin American Library, among others. A detailed index allows the searcher to locate specific materials. Entries include the mailing address but no phone numbers. Owing to the date of the work, no websites are provided. Nonetheless, this guide identifies the significant archival and manuscript sources available to researchers on Central America.

637. **Middle American Indians: A Guide to the Manuscript Collection at Tozzer Library, Harvard University.** Weeks, John. New York: Garland, 1985. 244p. ISBN 0824085922.

In his in-depth guide to manuscript materials in the Tozzer Library relating to southern Mexico and northern Central America, Weeks describes over 800 items in the collection. The first section is devoted to the predominately linguistic items photoreproduced from European and American archives, known as the Bowditch-Gates Collection. The second section contains description of miscellaneous manuscripts with significant ethnographic content dating from as early as the sixteenth century. The final section has the Bowditch German Translation Series of items relating to Mayan calendar systems, with translations of manuscripts dating from the nineteenth and early twentieth centuries. Locations of other copies of these manuscripts in U.S. Libraries are also noted.

Internet Gateways

638. **LANIC: Latin American Network and Information Center.** University of Texas at Austin. Available online at <http://lanic.utexas.edu/>.

This extensive and well-designed portal identifies and organizes a wide variety of quality websites for the scholar of Latin Americana. Categories include specific countries, education, humanities, libraries, society ad culture, sustainable development and others. Updated daily, this site is an exemplary illustration of a starting point for finding authoritative information on the web.

Chapter 8

Supplemental Resources

As every seasoned reference librarian knows, not all information sources are bibliographic. Depending on the question, a phone call or visit to the website of an organization, publisher, or other library may prove more effective in securing information than looking it up in a publication or database.

This final chapter, therefore, provides additional sources of information of potential utility to the anthropologist: a listing of core journals; publishers; scholarly and professional organizations; departments and programs; museums; libraries and archives; employment, internships and fieldschools; and grants and funding sources. The first two of these—journals and publishers—may also serve as aids to collection development for librarians. Because a directory of anthropological journals and organizations is a reference work in its own right, the entries in this chapter are by necessity selective and focus primarily on the United States.

Journals

The importance of journal literature in social science research cannot be overstated. Studies have indicated that journals are considered to be the most heavily utilized literature in anthropology, outranking monographs, reference books, technical reports, and dissertations (see Amudsen, Diana. "Information Problems of Anthropologists." 1968. *College and Research Libraries* 29 (March): 117–132).

Although not exhaustive, the following list includes the major journals in the field of general and sociocultural anthropology as well as representative titles from area studies literature that have significant anthropological content. A number of newer titles of particular interest (*Home Cultures*, *Identities: Global Studies in Culture & Power*) are included along with established "core" journals drawn from lists compiled by Ellen Sutton and Lori Foulke ("Coverage of Anthropology by Major Electronic Indexes: A Comparison." 1999. *Reference Services Review* 27 (2): 134–157), Finnegan et. al ("Journals of the Century in Anthropology and Archaeology." 2001. *The Serials Librarian* 39 (4): 69–78), and the previous edition of this work. ISI's *Journal Citation Report* for anthropology was also consulted to ensure that no high impact journals were inadvertently overlooked.

Levinson and Ember's *Encyclopedia of Cultural Anthropology* (entry 38) includes a more exhaustive list of anthropological periodicals that provides broader coverage of Western European and Latin American titles and includes journals from other subfields.

639. **Africa: Journal of the International African Institute/Revue de l'Institute Africain International,** Vol. 1-. Edinburgh: Edinburgh University Press for the International African Institute. 1928-. Quarterly. ISSN 0001-9720.

Focusing on African society, culture, languages, and history, this interdisciplinary journal, sponsored by the International African Institute (entry 819), encourages the "application of research to practical affairs in Africa." In addition to scholarly articles, a limited number of signed book reviews appear in each issue.

640. **African and Asian Studies,** Vol. 1-. Leiden, the Netherlands: Brill Academic Publishers. 2002-. Quarterly. ISSN 1569-2094; 1569-2108e.

This journal continues, in part, the longstanding *Journal of Asian and African Studies*. Like it predecessor, *African and Asian Studies* is thoroughly interdisciplinary, publishing original research in anthropology, sociology, history, and political science with a focus on contemporary political affairs and social issues. Most issues also include a small number of book reviews.

641. **American Anthropologist,** Vol. 1-. Berkeley, CA: University of California Press for the American Anthropological Association. 1888-. Quarterly. ISSN 0002-7294.

Sponsored by the American Anthropological Association (entry 745) this title is one of the primary journals in the field. Each issue offers five to ten major articles, along with several more concise research reports, covering all areas of anthropology. Also notable are signed book and film reviews, occasional obituaries, and the "Commentaries" section that provides replies and responses to previously published articles.

642. **American Ethnologist,** Vol. 1-. Berkeley, CA: University of California Press for the American Anthropological Association. 1974-. Quarterly. ISSN 0094-0496.

In addition to research articles in ethnology and culture, broadly defined, this publication of the American Ethnological Society (entry 746) features review articles and signed book reviews. Widely read and prestigious, this journal encompasses social, cultural, legal, linguistic, economic, political, and historical anthropology.

643. **Annual Review of Anthropology,** Vol. 1-. Palo Alto, CA: Annual Reviews. 1972-. Annual (print); continuously updated (online). ISSN 0084-6570; 1545-4290e.

(See entry 71)

644. **Anthropologica,** Vol. 1-. Waterloo, ON, Canada: Wilfrid Laurier University Press. 1955-. Semiannual. ISSN 0003-5459.

Focusing specifically on social and cultural anthropology, this journal features research articles, book reviews, and a list of books received. In 1997, this title incorporated *Culture* (0229-009X), published by the Canadian Ethnological Society.

645. **Anthropological Linguistics,** Vol. 1-. Bloomington, IN: Indiana University, Anthropology Department. 1959-. Quarterly. ISSN 0003-5483.

Published jointly by the Anthropology Department and the American Indian Studies Research Institute at Indiana University, this journal provides a "forum for the full range of scholarly study of the languages and cultures of the peoples of the world" with a particular focus on the native people of the Americas. Each issue also contains substantial (2–3 page) book reviews.

646. **Anthropological Quarterly,** Vol. 26-. Washington, DC: George Washington University Institute for Ethnographic Research. 1953-. Quarterly. ISSN 0003-5491; 1534-1518e. (Continues *Primitive Man,* 1928–1952).

The scope of this journal includes all aspects of sociocultural anthropology; occasional issues are devoted to specific topics. Signed book reviews are also included. Separately issued cumulative indexes covering 10-year periods are available.

647. **Anthropology and Archeology of Eurasia,** Vol. 1-. New York: M.E. Sharpe. 1992-. Quarterly. ISSN 1061-1959. (Continues *Soviet Anthropology and Archeology,* 1962-).

This journal provides unabridged translations of journal and book articles from several primary sources of anthropological research in the post-Soviet societies. Articles are selected that "best reflect developments in anthropology and archeology in the Newly Independent States." Although local and regional studies figure prominently, the scope is not restricted to Slavic studies.

648. **Anthropology and Education Quarterly,** Vol. 1-. Berkeley, CA: University of California Press for the American Anthropological Association. 1970-. Quarterly. ISSN 0161-7761.

Of interest to anthropologists, educators, developmental psychologists, and those in related fields, this periodical sponsored by the Council on Anthropology and Education (entry 755) publishes articles on the application of anthropology to research in education. Articles have included topics such as teaching ethnographic writing or curriculum development.

649. **Anthropology and Humanism,** Vol. 18-. Berkeley, CA: University of California Press for the American Anthropological Association. 1993-. Quarterly. ISSN 1559-9167; 1548-1409e. (Continues *Anthropology and Humanism Quarterly,* 1970–1992).

Published by the Society for Humanistic Anthropology (entry 765), this journal explores the question of what it is to be human and the relationship between anthropology and the humanities. Issues are often organized around a particular theme, such as writing and ethnography. In keeping with the society's focus, poetry (and occasionally fiction) by anthropologists or relating to anthropology is frequently published. Announcements and selected book reviews are also provided.

650. **Anthropology Today,** Vol. 1. London: Blackwell on behalf of the Royal Anthropological Institute. 1985-. Bimonthly. ISSN 0268-540X.

Though *Journal of the Royal Anthropological Institute* (entry 685) is the official organ of the Royal Anthropological Institute (entry 828), its newsletter deserves special mention. Focusing on issues of current public interest and practical concerns, it provides an informal international forum for professional anthropologists and other commentators. Aside from timely articles on issues such as the fundamentalist challenge or climate change, it provides news, interviews, and lively commentary on current concerns.

651. **Anthropos: Révue Internationale d'Ethnologie et de Linguistique,** Vol. 1. Fribourg, Switzerland: Anthropos Institute. 1906-. Semiannual. ISSN 0257-9774.

With an emphasis on ethnology and linguistics, this journal features articles on all aspects of anthropology. Features include "Reports and Comments," with correspondence from readers and general announcements. Articles and reviews are in German, French, or English. The book reviews are substantial, and a list of several hundred additional new titles makes this journal an excellent source for review of current literature.

652. **Arctic Anthropology,** Vol. 1-. Madison, WI: University of Wisconsin Press. 1962-. Semiannual. ISSN 0066-6939; 1933-8139e.

This international journal is devoted to the study of northern cultures and peoples, past and present, and takes a holistic approach. Archaeology, ethnology, ethnohistory, linguistics, and human biology are represented within its pages. Articles are often well illustrated and include translations of Russian, Japanese, Chinese, Korean, and Scandinavian research on Arctic peoples.

653. **Australian Journal of Anthropology,** Vol. 1-. Sydney, Australia: Australian Anthropological Society. 1931-. ISSN 1035-8811.

Formerly entitled *Mankind*, this journal sponsored by the Australian Anthropological Society includes all areas of anthropology and related disciplines, with a focus on Australia and adjacent countries, including mainland Asia. Signed book reviews are also provided.

654. **Chinese Sociology and Anthropology,** Vol. 1-. New York: M.E. Sharpe. 1968-. Quarterly. ISSN 0009-4625; 1558-1004e.

Not a refereed journal per se, this title includes translations of articles and essays originally published in Chinese. An entire issue is frequently devoted to a particular work, such as a recently completed dissertation.

655. **City and Society,** Vol. 1-. Berkeley, CA: University of California Press for the American Anthropological Association. 1987-. Semiannual. ISSN 0893-0465.

Sponsored by the Society for Urban, National and Transnational/Global Anthropology (entry 776), this journal publishes articles concerned with urban communities and complex societies. Articles incorporate applied as well as basic research and include case studies, comparisons, and syntheses, and methodological studies.

656. **Critique of Anthropology,** Vol. 1-. London: Sage. 1974-. Quarterly. ISSN 0308-275X.

Subtitled *A Journal for the Critical Reconstruction of Anthropology*, this title publishes scholarship reflecting a critical Marxist approach to anthropological theory and practice. Articles are frequently followed by rejoinders with input and discussion from other scholars.

657. **Cultural Anthropology,** Vol. 1-. Berkeley, CA: University of California Press for the American Anthropological Association. 1986-. Quarterly. ISSN 0886-7356; 1548-1360e.

Sponsored by the Society for Cultural Anthropology (entry 763) this journal offers articles on cultural studies, broadly conceived, and encourages new approaches, both theoretical and methodological, to ethnographically grounded research. Shorter pieces include critical essays, interviews, reports, and review essays.

658. **Cultural Critique,** Vol. 1-. Minneapolis MN: University of Minnesota Press. 1985-. 3 issues/yr. ISSN 0882-4371; 1534-5203e.

The premier journal for cultural studies, *Cultural Critique* explores the area of cultural criticism from the perspective of anthropological, literary, philosophical, and sociological studies. Utilizing Marxist, feminist, psychoanalytic, and poststructural methods, theme issues focus on topics such as theories of masculinity, Edward Said, and the politics of the irrational.

659. **Cultural Survival Quarterly,** Vol. 1-. Cambridge, MA: Cultural Survival Inc. 1976-. Quarterly. ISSN 0740-3291.

Sponsored by the nonprofit organization, Cultural Survival (entry 816), this journal seeks to inform the public and to stimulate action on behalf of tribal people and ethnic minorities. Individual issues are frequently devoted to specific topics, such as fair trade and indigenous peoples, or bridging the digital divide. News items and announcements are also included.

660. **Culture, Medicine and Psychiatry,** Vol. 1-. Boston: Kluwer Academic. 1977-. Quarterly. ISSN 0165-005X.

An international and interdisciplinary journal of comparative and cross-cultural research, this publication attempts to bridge medical and anthropological perspectives and methods. It publishes original research, theoretical and review articles and provides a bibliography of new books relevant to medical anthropology.

661. **Current Anthropology,** Vol. 1-. Chicago: University of Chicago Press. 1960-. 5/year. ISSN 0011-3204; 1537-5382e. Also available online by subscription.

The scope of *Current Anthropology*, sponsored by the Wenner-Gren Foundation (entry 833), includes all fields within the discipline, both theoretical and applied. The lengthy critical commentaries that follow each article provide an interesting forum for discussion and debate. Shorter research and conference reports, news items such as prize announcements, and letters are also included. The book reviews are useful for keeping up with current publications.

662. **Dialectical Anthropology,** Vol. 1-. Boston: Springer. 1975-. Quarterly. ISSN 0304-4092.

This journal offers a vehicle for anthropological and interdisciplinary scholarship utilizing Marxist theory and the dialectical method. It includes selected book reviews and a column for comments and announcements.

663. **Eastern Anthropologist,** Vol. 1-. Lucknow, India: Ethnographic and Folk Culture Society. 1947-. Quarterly. ISSN 0012-8686.

Published on behalf of the Ethnographic and Folk Culture Society, this journal publishes research papers, both empirical and theoretical, on themes and problems of interest to anthropologists concerned with the Indian subcontinent. Selected book reviews are included.

664. **Ethnohistory,** Vol. 1-. Durham, NC: Duke University Press. 1954-. Quarterly. ISSN 0014-1801.

Sponsored by the American Society for Ethnohistory (entry 809), the journal publishes research that utilizes historiographic methods for the study of cultural and social processes. Though worldwide in scope, the focus is generally on peoples of the Americas. Numerous book reviews are included.

665. **Ethnology,** Vol. 1-. Pittsburgh, PA: Department of Anthropology, University of Pittsburgh.1962-. Quarterly. ISSN 0014-1828.

Subtitled *An International Journal of Social and Cultural Anthropology*, this periodical was established by Human Relations Area Files founder, George Peter Murdock, and features articles on all aspects of cultural anthropology using theoretical and methodological approaches grounded in "some body of substantive data."

666. **Ethnomusicology,** Vol. 1-. Champaign, IL: University of Illinois Press. 1953-. 3/year. ISSN 0014-1836.

The official journal of the Society for Ethnomusicology (entry 832), this title publishes refereed articles representing current research and theoretical approaches to the study of music and performance in a cultural context. Includes numerous reviews of books, recordings, films, and videos. Current bibliography, discography, filmography, and videography are also published on the SEM website in conjunction with each issue.

667. **Ethnos,** Vol. 1-. London: Routledge on behalf of the National Museum of Ethnography. 1936-. Quarterly. ISSN 0014-1844; 1469-588xe.

International in scope, articles cover all aspects of sociocultural anthropology with occasional thematic issues, such as "the anthropology of knowledge." Contributors, however, are mainly from Europe and North America, and the articles are in English. Signed book reviews are provided, and the "Notes and News" section provides information about ongoing research, obituaries, and news items.

668. **Ethos,** Vol. 1-. Berkeley, CA: University of California Press for the American Anthropological Association. 1973-. Quarterly. ISSN 0091-2131.

The organ of the Society for Psychological Anthropology (entry 769), this journal features scholarly articles bearing on the "interrelations between the individual and the social milieu" and attempts to bridge the psychological and social disciplines. Book reviews of relevant titles are included.

669. **History and Anthropology,** Vol. 1-. Abingdon, Oxfordshire, UK: Routledge. 1984-. Quarterly. ISSN 0275-7206.

Articles in this journal reflect the interchange between "anthropologically-informed history and historically-informed anthropology" and include (among other topics) studies of economic, religious, and linguistic change; gender in history and culture; and colonial systems. Each issue is devoted to a specific theme or concept, and the contents are substantive.

670. **Home Cultures,** Vol. 1-. Oxford: Berg Publishers. 2004-. 3/year. ISSN 1740–6315.

This new journal is "dedicated to the critical understanding of the domestic sphere across timeframes and cultures." While the topic is tightly focused, the disciplinary perspective is broad and includes art, architecture, design, anthropology, sociology, archaeology, urban planning, geography, psychology, folklore, cultural studies, literary studies, and art history. Book and exhibition reviews are also included.

671. **L'Homme: Revue Française d'Anthropologie,** Vol. 15-. Paris: Mouton. 1975-. Quarterly. ISSN 0339-543x. (Continues *L'Homme/Ecole des Hautes Etudes en Sciences Sociales*, 1961–1974).

Founded by Claude Lévi-Strauss, Émile Benveniste, and Pierre Gourou, this journal features scholarly articles on sociocultural anthropology. Articles are generally written in French, but summaries in English and German are also provided. Brief review articles, correspondence, and book reviews (in English and French) are also included.

672. **Human Ecology,** Vol. 1-. Dordrecht, The Netherlands: Kluwer/Plenum Publishers. 1972-. 6/year. ISSN 0300-7839.

This journal focuses on the "complex and varied systems of interaction between people and their environment" from a primarily anthropological perspective, though there is much here of interest to cultural geography, environmental studies, and other social sciences. Recent articles include "Aboriginal Burning Regimes and Hunting Strategies in Australia's Western Desert" and "The Catch-22 of Conservation: Indigenous Peoples, Biologists, and Cultural Change." Book reviews are also included.

673. **Human Organization,** Vol. 9-. Washington, DC: Society for Applied Anthropology. 1949-. Quarterly. ISSN 0018-7259. (Continues *Applied Anthropology*, 1941–1948).

This is the official journal of the Society for Applied Anthropology (entry 829). The primary objective of *Human Organization* is to apply the principles of anthropology to the solution of practical problems. Articles focus human behavior in its community context, whether traditional villages or urban neighborhoods.

674. **Identities: Global Studies in Culture and Power,** Vol. 1-. Abingdon, Oxfordshire, UK: Routledge. 1994-. Quarterly. ISSN 1070-289X (Continues *Ethnic Groups*, 1976–1993).

This journal "explores the relationship of racial, ethnic and national identities and power hierarchies within national and global arenas" from an ethnographic perspective. Most issues include at least one substantial review essay analyzing a group of thematically related recent publications.

675. **The Indigenous World,** Copenhagen: International Work Group for Indigenous Affairs (IWGIA). 1994-. Annual. ISSN 1024-0217.

Continuing the *IWGIA Yearbook*, this annual publication provides an update on the status of indigenous peoples worldwide. Each issue provides region and country reports focusing on the salient issues and developments of the preceding year. Contributions come from indigenous and nonindigenous scholars and activists, giving voice to indigenous peoples and their concerns.

676. **International Journal of American Linguistics,** Vol. 1-. Chicago: University of Chicago Press. 1917-. Quarterly. ISSN 0020-7071; 1545-7001e.

Founded by Franz Boas in 1917, this journal focuses on Amerindian languages. Each issue also includes substantial (2–3 page) book reviews.

677. **Journal de la Société des Américanistes,** Vol. 22-. Paris: Société de Américaniste. 1930-. Semiannual. ISSN 0037-9174. (Continues *Journal de la Société des Américanistes de Paris,* 1896–1929).

A publication of the French-based Société des Américanistes, this journal takes a holistic approach to studies of the Amerindian and includes articles dealing with archaeology, ethnology, linguistics, physical anthropology, and history. Articles are generally in French or English.

678. **Journal of American Folklore,** Vol. 1-. Champaign, IL: University of Illinois Press. 1888-. Quarterly. ISSN 0021-8715; 1535-1882e.

This long-established journal maintains its strong ties with anthropology. Sponsored by the American Folklore Society (entry 808), the journal represents the scholarly tradition within folklore. Though originally focused on the North American traditional cultures, the scope is now international and encompasses a broad definition of both folklore and "folk," including contemporary groups (e.g., flight attendants) as well as traditional cultures. Numerous signed book, record, and film reviews are also included.

679. **Journal of Anthropological Research,** Vol. 29-. Albuquerque, NM: Department of Anthropology, University of New Mexico. 1973-. Quarterly. ISSN 0091-7710. (Continues *Southwestern Journal of Anthropology*, 1945–1972*).*

Although originally entitled the *South West Journal of Anthropology* (1945–1972*)* and focused on the American Southwest, this journal is no longer restricted in scope or content to a particular region. Articles include all branches of anthropology relating to cultures both past and present. Review articles and book reviews are also provided.

680. **Journal of Asian Studies,** Vol. 16-. Ann Arbor, MI: Association for Asian Studies. 1956-. Quarterly. ISSN 0021-9118. (Continues *Far Eastern Quarterly*, 1941-).

A publication of the Association for Asian Studies (entry 812), this journal is concerned with studies of Asian cultures from both humanities and social sciences perspectives. The geographic scope is broad, and numerous book reviews are included.

681. **Journal of Latin American Anthropology,** Vol. 1-. Berkeley, CA: University of California Press for the American Anthropological Association. 1995-. Semiannual. ISSN 1085-7052; 1548-7180e. (Continues *Latin American Anthropology Review*, 1989–1994).

The official organ of the Latin American Anthropology Section of the American Anthropological Association, this peer reviewed journal publishes original research articles on Latin America, here broadly defined to include all of Central America, South America, and the Caribbean. Generally written in English, abstracts in Spanish and Portuguese are provided. Issues generally have a theme, such as "Cuba's Alternative Geographies" or "Indigenous Peoples and New Urbanisms." Book and film reviews are included.

682. **Journal of Linguistic Anthropology,** Vol. 1-. Berkeley, CA: University of California Press for the American Anthropological Association. 1991-. Semiannual. ISSN 1055-1360; 1548-1395e.

A publication of the American Anthropological Association's Society for Linguistic Anthropology (entry 767), this journal "publishes articles on the anthropological study of language, including analysis of discourse, language in society, language and cognition, and language acquisition of socialization." Critical essays, interviews, commentaries, discussions, brief translations are commonly included in addition to research articles. The SLA website also provides access to audio and video clips, full color illustrations, and other files associated with "web-enhanced articles." Most issues include eight to ten book reviews and a list of recently published titles.

683. **Journal of Material Culture,** Vol. 1-. London; Thousand Oaks, CA: Sage. 1996-. 3/year. ISSN 1359-1835.

Encompassing anthropology, archaeology, history of design and museology, this journal "explores the relationship between artefacts and social relations." Book reviews of relevant titles are also included.

684. **Journal of Ritual Studies,** Vol. 1-. Pittsburgh, PA: Department of Anthropology, University of Pittsburgh. 1987-. Semiannual. ISSN 0890-1112.

This journal encourages collaboration on the topic of ritual among scholars in he disciplines of anthropology, religion, sociology, psychology, history, and the arts. Articles reflect theoretical, comparative, quantitative, and historical approaches to ritual studies.

685. **The Journal of the Royal Anthropological Institute,** Vol. 1-. London: Blackwell for the Royal Anthropological Institute. 1995-. Quarterly. ISSN 1359-0987. (Continues *Man*, 1966–1994).

Sponsored by the Royal Anthropological Institute (entry 828), this core journal publishes articles with a theoretical emphasis in all fields of anthropology, particularly social and cultural. Major articles include abstracts in English and French. Book reviews, a list of books received, and correspondence is also included.

686. **JPS: The Journal of the Polynesian Society,** Vol. 1-. Auckland, New Zealand: Polynesian Society. 1892-. Quarterly. ISSN 0032-4000.

Published by the long-established Polynesian Society (entry 827), this journal provides a forum for the discussion of history, ethnology, physical anthropology, sociology, archaeology, and linguistics of the New Zealand Maori peoples and other Pacific Island cultures. In addition to scholarly articles, the journal includes several signed book reviews and a list of publications received. A "centennial index" for the first 100 issues (1892–1991) was published in 1993.

687. **Language in Society,** Vol. 1-. Cambridge, England: Cambridge University Press. 1972-. Quarterly. ISSN 0047-4045.

The focus of this journal is sociolinguistics, i.e., language and speech as aspects of social life. A typical issue includes 4–6 research articles, 6–12 book reviews and a list of publications received.

688. **Medical Anthropology,** Vol. 1-. Philadelphia, PA: Routledge. 1977-. Quarterly. ISSN 0145-9740; 1545-5882e.

Subtitled *Cross Cultural Studies in Health and Illness*, this journal explores the relationships between health, disease, illness, treatment, and human social life. The articles frequently reflect a sociocultural focus and an empirical orientation.

689. **Medical Anthropology Quarterly,** Vol. 1-. Washington, DC: Society for Medical Anthropology. 1983-. Quarterly. ISSN 0745-5194. (Continues *Medical Anthropology Newsletter*, 1970–1982).

The official organ of the Society for Medical Anthropology (entry 768), this journal was initiated to stimulate debate and the development of ideas and methods in medical anthropology. It provides both theoretical and theory-based research articles, along with reviews of books dealing with cultural and social analyses of health.

690. **Oceania,** Vol. 1-. Sydney, Australia: University of Sidney Oceania Publications. 1930-. Quarterly. ISSN 0029-8077.

Oceania publishes original research on the social and cultural anthropology of indigenous peoples of Australia, Melanesia, Polynesia, Micronesia, and insular Southeast Asia. A limited number of book reviews are also published.

691. **Plains Anthropologist,** Vol. 1-. Lincoln, NE: Plains Anthropological Society. 1954-. Quarterly. ISSN 0032-0447.

Sponsored by the Plains Anthropological Society (entry 826), this journal publishes original papers on the anthropology of the plains and adjacent areas of North America. Articles range from archaeology and prehistory to contemporary issues such as litigation involving Native Americans. Announcements and book reviews are also included.

692. **Practicing Anthropology,** Vol. 1-. Oklahoma City, OK: Society for Applied Anthropology. 1978-. Quarterly. ISSN 0888-4552.

Sponsored by the Society for Applied Anthropology (entry 829), this publication provides a means of communicating about nonacademic anthropological careers, explores the uses of anthropology in policy research, and encourages links between practice inside and outside educational institutions.

693. **Reviews in Anthropology,** Vol. 1-. Philadelphia, PA: Gorden & Breach. 1974-. Quarterly. ISSN 0093-8157; 1556-3014e.

This publication is comprised entirely of review essays that examine a cluster of books on a particular theme (e.g., indigenous movements in Latin America or "Africa bewitched"). The 10–20 essays included in each issue provide an analytical synthesis of the literature on a topic to date and include references. Titles included have generally been published 1–2 years prior to the review.

694. **Urban Anthropology and Studies of Cultural Systems and World Economic Development,** Vol. 14-. Brockport, NY: Institute for the Study of Man.

1985-. Quarterly. ISSN 0363-2024. (Continues *Urban Anthropology*, 1972–1984).

When the title was amended to include "*Studies of Cultural Systems and World Economic Development*," the emphasis expanded beyond a strictly urban orientation to include the study of world processes such as development, urbanization, colonialism, and globalization.

695. **Visual Anthropology,** Vol. 1-. Philadelphia, PA: Taylor and Francis. 1987-. 5/year. ISSN 0894-9468; 1545-5902e.

Published in cooperation with the Commission on Visual Anthropology (entry 806), this journal provides a forum for the world community of visual anthropologists. Areas of concern range from visual theory to practical applications and include articles, ethnographic photo essays, research reports, and film, book, and exhibition reviews.

696. **Visual Anthropology Review,** Vol. 7-. Berkeley, CA: University of California for the American Anthropological Association. 1991-. Semiannual. ISSN 1058-7187; 1548-7458e. (Continues *Society for Visual Anthropology Review*, 1970–1990).

This journal, published by the Society for Visual Anthropology (entry 777) of the American Anthropological Association, includes articles, commentary, and reviews on topics related to visual aspects of culture, including architecture and material culture. The scope of the journal also extends to kinesics, proxemics, and related forms of body motion communication.

697. **Zeitschrift für Ethnologie,** Vol. 1-. Berlin: Dietrich Reimer Verlag. 1869-. Semiannual. ISSN 0044-2666.

This journal is the flagship publication of two longstanding German anthropological associations: Deutsche Gesellschaft für Völkerkunde and Berliner Gesellschaft für Anthropologie, Ethnologie und Urgeschichte. The scope is worldwide and includes all aspects of ethnology. Articles are in Western European languages, primarily German, English, and French.

Publishers

The publishers identified here represent a selective list of presses with a significant focus on sociocultural anthropology or a related area of specialization, or those that publish major series in the field. Many university presses publish titles in anthropology—particularly as it ties into regional/area or topical interests of the press, such as Southwestern studies at the University of New Mexico Press, or women's studies at the University of Minnesota Press. Societies like the American Anthropological Association and the Royal Anthropological Institute often publish works that might not be commercially viable but contribute to scholarship in the discipline. A variety of commercial presses publish titles in anthropology ranging from popular accounts to textbooks and reference works.

For a more detailed account of publishing in anthropology, see Peacock, James. (January 2005). *Publication in Anthropology: A White Paper for the UNC-Chapel Hill Scholarly Communications Convocation* <www.unc.edu/scholcomdig/whitepapers/peacock.html>.

698. **Aldine Transaction**
Transaction Publishers
35 Berrue Circle
Piscataway, NJ 08854-8042
Phone: 732-445-2280
Toll-Free Phone: 888-999-6778
E-mail: orders@transactionpub.com
<http://www.transactionpub.com/>
Acquired from Walter de Gruyter by Transaction Publishing in 2004, Aldine remains a separate imprint with a focus on anthropology, sociology and economics. Sociobiology and physical anthropology have been recent areas of focus.

699. **AltaMira Press**
4501 Forbes Boulevard, Suite 200
Lanham, MD 20706
Phone: 301-459-3366
Fax: 301-429-5748
E-mail: custserv@rowman.com
<http://www.AltaMirapress.com/>
A division of Rowman & Littlefield Publishing Group, AltaMira offers an outstanding selection of books and journals in anthropology and related fields, including cultural studies, gender studies, race and ethnic studies, religious studies, pagan studies, and social science research methods. AltaMira also covers archaeology, cultural resource management, and museum studies. They publish monographic series for a number of anthropology-related organizations such as the Society for American Archaeology and the Society for Economic Anthropology (entry 831).

700. **Archaeopress**
Gordon House
276 Banbury Road
Oxford OX2 7ED, England
Phone/Fax: 44 (0) 1865-311914
E-mail: bar@archaeopress.com
<http://www.archaeopress.com/default.asp>
Owned by archaeologists, Archaeopress is best known for its highly esteemed "BAR" Series (*British Archaeological Reports* and *BAR International*), but they also publish an extensive catalog of titles related to Arabic studies. Archaeopress recently launched the *3rd guide* series of "new editions of classic travel accounts that have an emphasis on culture, history, and archaeology (as well as landscape and sense of place)."

701. **Berg Publishers**
1st Floor, Angel Court, 81 St Clements Street
Oxford OX4 1AW, UK.
Phone: 44 (0) 1865-245104
Fax: 44 (0) 1865-791165
E-mail: enquiry@bergpublishers.com

Ordering:
Palgrave Macmillan
c/o Holtzbrinck Publishing Services/VHPS
16365 James Madison Hwy
Gordonsville, VA 22942
<http://www.bergpublishers.com>

Owned by Oxford International Publications but independently operated, Berg focuses on the "intellectual activity ... at the edge of more traditional disciplines." Their catalog includes material and visual culture, cultural/media studies, food, sport and anthropology. Palgrave Macmillan (entry 714) is the U.S. distributor for Berg.

702. **Berghahn Books**
USA/150 Broadway, Ste 812
New York, NY 10038
Phone: 212-233-6004
Fax: 212-233-6007
Toll-Free Phone: 800-540-8663
E-mail: info@berghahnbooks.com
<http://www.berghahnbooks.com/>

Based in Oxford and New York, this relative newcomer specializes in European studies and transatlantic scholarship including a distinguished list of books and journals in anthropology, cultural and migration studies, travel and tourism, as well as history, politics and Jewish studies. In 2005, Berghahn launched the *European Anthropology in Translation* series for the Society for the Anthropology of Europe (entry 771).

703. **Blackwell Publishing**
Commerce Place
350 Main Street
Malden, MA 02148
Phone: 781-388-8200
Fax: 781-388-8210
<http://www.blackwellpublishing.com/>

Publishing theoretical works on cultural anthropology, linguistics, and history, Blackwell also issues the *Blackwell Companions to Anthropology,* a series of handbook-type syntheses of the subdisciplines, research areas, and geographic regions in the field.

704. **Brill**
   112 Water Street, Suite 601
   Boston, MA 02109
   Phone: 617-263-2323
   Fax: 617-263-2324

   Ordering:
   P.O. Box 605
   Herndon, VA 20172
   Telephone: 703-661-1585
   Fax: 703-661-1501
   Toll-Free Phone: 800-337-9255
   E-mail: cs@brillusa.com
   <http://www.brill.nl>

Based in Leiden, Brill is primarily a humanities publisher with an extensive catalog of mostly English language titles in Near East, Asian and African studies. In recent years, however, they have expanded their social science coverage and are now publishing a large number of titles in anthropology and sociology.

705. **Cambridge University Press**
   32 Avenue of the Americas
   New York, NY 10013-2473
   Phone: 212-924-3900
   Fax: 212-691-3239
   Toll-Free Phone: 800-937-9600
   E-mail: information@cambridge.org

   Ordering:
   100 Brook Hill Drive
   West Nyack, NY 10994-2133
   Phone: 845-353-7500
   Toll-Free Phone: 800-872-7423 (orders, returns, credit & accounting)
   E-mail: customer_service@cup.org
   <http://www.cambridge.org/>

A major publisher in the field, the press is particularly strong in area studies and current issues. Cambridge also distributes books in the following series: *Biosocial Society Symposium Series; Cambridge Studies in Biological and Evolutionary Anthropology; Cambridge Studies in Oral and Literate Culture; Language, Culture and Cognition; New Perspectives on Anthropological and Social Demography; Res Monographs in Anthropology and Aesthetics;* and *University of Cambridge Oriental Publications.*

706. **Duke University Press**
   Duke University Press
   PO Box 90660
   Durham, NC 27708-0660
   Phone: 919-687-3600

Fax: 919-688-4574
<http://www.dukeupress.edu>
Duke publishes an extensive catalog of ethnographies, as well as rich selection of area and cultural studies titles.

707. **Greenwood Press**
P.O. Box 6926
Portsmouth, NH 03802-6926
Phone: 800-225-5800
Fax: 603-431-2214
E-mail: customer-service@greenwood.com
<http://www.greenwood.com/greenwood_press.aspx>
With a solid list in the social sciences, Greenwood publishes a number of reference books in anthropology and related areas.

708. **Harvard University Press**
79 Garden Street
Cambridge, MA 02138
Toll-Free Phone: 800-405-1619
Toll-Free Fax: 800-406-9145
E-mail: Contact_HUP@harvard.edu
<http://www.hup.harvard.edu/>
The Harvard University Press distributes the publications of the Peabody Museum Press (http://www.hup.harvard.edu/publishing_partners/peabody/index.html) including works by scholars affiliated with the Museum and Harvard's Department of Anthropology and by specialists working with the museum's collections. In addition to a number of series (including *Papers of the Peabody Museum*), the Peabody catalog focuses Old World and New World archaeology, zooarchaeology, biological and sociocultural anthropology, indigenous arts and material culture.

709. **Human Relations Area Files (HRAF) Press**
755 Prospect Street, New Haven, CT 06511-1225
Tel: 203-764-9401 or 1-800-520-4723
FAX: 203-764-9404
E-mail: hraf@yale.edu
<http://www.yale.edu/hraf/>
HRAF (see also entry 817) is well known as the producer of the *eHRAF Collection of Ethnography* (entry 481) and associated user guides and products. Over the last decade HRAF has cooperated with other publishers and distributors to produce a number of fine encyclopedias and bibliographies, including the *Bibliography of Native North Americans* (entry 600), *Countries and Their Cultures* (entry 467), *Encyclopedia of Medical Anthropology* (entry 336) and *Encyclopedia of World Cultures* (entry 473).

710. **Indiana University Press**
Indiana University Press

601 N. Morton St.
Bloomington, IN 47404
Phone: 812-855-8817
Toll-Free Phone: 800-842-6796
E-mail: iupress@indiana.edu
Ordering e-mail: iuporder@indiana.edu
<http://www.iupress.indiana.edu/catalog/>

Among the strengths of the Indiana University Press are its publications on language, women's studies, folklore, and area studies, with an emphasis on Africa, Asia, and the Middle East.

711. **Mouton De Gruyter**
500 Executive Boulevard
Ossining, NY 10562
Phone: 914-762-5866
Fax: 914-762-0371
E-mail: info@degruyterny.com
Ordering e-mail: degruytermail@presswarehouse.com
<http://www.degruyter.com/rs/191_ENU_h.htm>

A division of Walter De Gruyter, Mouton is a well-established publisher of scholarly works in the area of linguistics and communications. They publish a number of monographic series, including *Studies in Anthropological Linguistics*.

712. **Oxbow Books/David Brown**
PO Box 511 (28 Main Street)
Oakville CT 06779
Toll-free: 800 791 9354
Tel: 860 945 9329
Fax: 860 945 9468
E-mail: david.brown.bk.co@snet.net
<http://www.oxbowbooks.com/>

Oxbow is known primarily as an archaeology publisher, but their catalog includes prehistory, near eastern studies and related environmental and cultural heritage topics.

713. **Oxford University Press**
2001 Evans Road
Cary, NC 27513
Phone: 1-800-445-9714
Fax: 1-919-677-1303
E-mail: custserv.us@oup.com
<www.oup.com/us/>

Although anthropology is not a major area of focus, Oxford does publish a few high-quality titles related to cultural anthropology, with an emphasis on large-scale modern social formations and urban societies.

714. **Palgrave Macmillan**
175 Fifth Avenue
New York, NY 10010
Phone: (888) 330-8477
Fax: (800) 672-2054
E-mail: customerservice@vhpsva.com
<http://www.palgrave.com/>

Palgrave Macmillan publishes a number of monographs and reference books in anthropology proper, and their catalog also includes related areas such as cultural, gender, and media studies. In addition, Palgrave is the North American distributor of some U.K. publishers active in the social sciences, including Berg Publishers (entry 701), I. B. Tauris, Manchester University Press, and Zed Books.

715. **Praeger**
Greenwood Publishing Group, Inc.
P.O. Box 6926
Portsmouth, NH 03802-6926
Phone: 800-225-5800
Fax: 603-431-2214
E-mail: customer-service@greenwood.com
<http://www.greenwood.com/praeger.aspx>

Now a division of Greenwood Press (entry 707), Praeger has a distinguished history of producing scholarly titles in the social sciences and humanities, with special strengths in contemporary social issues.

716. **Prentice-Hall**
One Lake St.
Upper Saddle River, NJ 07458
Phone: 800-922-0579
E-mail: csweb@pearsoned.com
<http://www.prenticehall.com/>

Prentice-Hall enjoys a long-established reputation for its introductory textbooks and surveys.

717. **Prickly Paradigm Press**
Prickly Paradigm Press, LLC
5629 South University Avenue
Chicago, IL 60637
Phone: 773-241-5459
Fax: 773-241-7016
E-mail: info@prickly-paradigm.com
<http://www.prickly-paradigm.com/>

Prickly Paradigm, an imprint of the University of Chicago Press founded by Marshall Sahlins, is "committed to the unconventional, in anthropology, critical theory, philosophy, politics, and more." The press occupies a unique niche, publishing pamphlet-length treatises written by major figures in the field reflecting on theory and practice.

718. **Princeton University Press**
    41 William Street
    Princeton, NJ 08540-5237
    Phone: 609-258-4900
    Fax: 609-258-6305
    Orders@cpfsinc.com

Princeton focuses on scholarly titles in the humanities, social sciences, and natural sciences and includes a fairly substantial listing of titles related to cultural anthropology.

719. **Routledge**
    Taylor & Francis Group Ltd
    2 Park Square
    Milton Park
    Abingdon
    Oxford OX14 4RN
    UK
    Phone: +44 (0) 20 7017 6000
    Fax: +44 (0) 20 7017 6699
    <http://www.routledge.com/>

Routledge publishes scholarly monographs and reference works in social and cultural anthropology. Areas of specialization include political and economic anthropology, globalization, gender, ethnography, medical anthropology, environmental anthropology, material culture, religion, and visual anthropology.

720. **Sage Publications**
    2455 Teller Road
    Thousand Oaks, CA 91320
    Phone: 800-818-7243 or 805-499-9774
    Fax: 805-499-0871 or 800-583-2665
    E-mail: info@sagepub.com

A major social science publisher, Sage's catalog includes extensive offerings in anthropology, material culture and area studies, including scholarly monographs, textbooks, reference works, and journals.

721. **School of American Research Press**
    P.O. Box 2188
    Santa Fe, NM 87504-2188
    Phone: 505-954-7206
    Fax: 505-954-7241

Toll-Free Phone: 888-390-6070
E-mail: press@sarsf.org
<http://www.sarpress.sarweb.org>
Since 1979, the SAR Press as produced an impressive catalog of titles focusing on indigenous arts and aesthetics, the past and present peoples of the Southwest United States, and anthropology and archaeology in general.

722. **Springer**
11 W. 42nd St., 15th Fl.
New York, NY 10036 USA
Phone: 212-431-4370
Fax: 212-941-7842
Toll-Free Phone: 877-687-7476
E-mail: Springer@springerpub.com, journals@springerpub.com, or Editorial@springerpub.com
<http://www.springerpub.com>
A major scholarly publisher best known for their science and technology books and journals, Springer acquired Kluwer in 2004. A number of significant reference titles in anthropology have been published under the Kluwer imprint, including the three volumes (*Encyclopedia of Medical Anthropology* (entry 336), *Encyclopedia of Sex and Gender* (entry 386), and *Encyclopedia of Diasporas* (entry 392) comprising the set marketed as *Cross-Cultural Anthropology: A Reference Collection* and published in conjunction with the Human Relation Area Files (entry 709). Springer also publishes some important anthropology journals (*Dialectical Anthropology* (entry 662), *Culture, Medicine and Psychiatry* (entry 660), and the *International Journal of Primatology*) and a small, but well-respected catalog of titles in archaeology and biological anthropology.

723. **University of Alabama Press**
Box 870380, 20 Research Drive
Tuscaloosa, Alabama 35487-0380
Phone: 205-348-5180
Fax: 205-348-9201
<http://www.uapress.ua.edu>
In addition to regional studies of southern history and culture, University of Alabama also features anthropology, ethnohistory, Native American Studies and African-American Studies. The Press also publishes in southeastern, Caribbean, and historical archaeology.

724. **University of Arizona Press**
355 S. Euclid Ave.
Suite 103, Tucson, AZ 85719
Phone: 520-621-1441
Toll-Free Phone: 800-426-3797 (orders only)
Fax: 520-621-8899
E-mail: uapress@uapress.arizona.edu
<http://www.uapress.arizona.edu/>

Specializing in Southwestern U.S. ethnology, the University of Arizona Press publishes in all areas of anthropology, with particular strengths in Native American Studies, human ecology, symbolic anthropology and archaeological method and theory. Series include *Anthropological Papers*, *Arizona Studies in Human Ecology*, *The Anthropology of Form and Meaning*, *The Mexican American Experience*, and *Native Peoples of the Americas*.

725. **University of California Press**
 2120 Berkeley Way
 Berkeley, CA 94704-1012
 Phone: 510-642-4247
 Fax: 510-643-7127
 E-mail: askucp@ucpress.edu
 <http://www.ucpress.edu/>

The University of California Press has long had an extensive catalog of anthropology titles, but has recently expanded their commitment to the discipline through their partnership with the American Anthropological Association (entry 745) which has involved assuming responsibility for publishing all AAA journals and hosting *AnthroSource* (entry 78). The Press also publishes a number of series, including the *California Series in Public Anthropology, California Studies in Food & Culture, Comparative Studies on Religion and Society*, and *Ethnographic Studies in Subjectivity*.

726. **University of Chicago Press**
 Editorial:
 1427 E. 60th Street
 Chicago, IL 60637

 Ordering:
 Chicago Distribution Center
 11030 South Langley
 Chicago, IL 60628
 Phone: 773-702-7700
 Toll-Free Phone: 800-621-2736 (US & Canada)
 Fax: 773-702-9756
 Toll-Free Fax: 800-621-8476 (US & Canada)
 E-mail: custserv@press.uchicago.edu
 <http://www.press.uchicago.edu/>

Building upon the University of Chicago's strong tradition in the social sciences, the Press publishes a broad range of theoretical works in anthropology, with strengths in Asian, African and Latin American Studies, along with the important journal *Current Anthropology* (entry 661).

727. **University of Hawaii Press**
 2840 Kolowalu Street
 Honolulu, HI 96822-1888
 Phone: 808-956-8255

Fax: 808-988-6052
Toll-Free Phone: 888-847-7377
Toll-Free Fax: 800-650-7811
E-mail: uhpbooks@hawaii.edu
<http://www.uhpress.hawaii.edu/cart/shopcore/?db_name=uhpress>

With a strong emphasis on Pacific and East Asian studies, the University of Hawaii Press publishes several titles in association with the Center for Pacific Islands Studies.

728. **University of Nebraska Press**
1111 Lincoln Mall
Lincoln, NE 68588-0630
Phone 800-755-1105
Fax: 402-472-6214
Toll-Free Fax: 800-526-2617
E-mail: pressmail@unl.edu
<http://unp.unl.edu/>

The focus of the anthropological program at the University of Nebraska Press is on the Native Americans of the Great Plains region, the Pacific Northwest, and other areas explored by Lewis and Clark.

729. **University of Oklahoma Press**
2800 Venture Drive
Norman, OK 73069-8216
Phone: 405-325-2000
Toll-Free Phone: 800-627-7377
Fax: 405-364-5798
E-mail: customerservice@oupress.com
<http://www.oupress.com/>

Specializing in Southwestern ethnology, the University of Oklahoma Press has an extensive catalog covering Native American art, material culture, and anthropology.

730. **University of Pennsylvania Museum of Archaeology & Anthropology Publications**
Editorial:
3260 South St.
Philadelphia, PA 19104 USA
Phone: 215-898-5723
Fax: 215-573-2497
E-mail: publications@museum.upenn.edu

Ordering:
P.O. Box 50370
Hampden Station
Baltimore, MD 21211-4370

Phone: 800-537-5487
Fax: 410-516-6998
<http://www.museum.upenn.edu/publications/>
The publishing arm of the University of Pennsylvania Museum of Archaeology and Anthropology, University Museum Publications publishes scholarly and general interest books about Museum exhibits and symposia, as well as titles dealing with anthropology and archaeology worldwide.

731. **University of Pennsylvania Press**
 3905 Spruce Street
 Philadelphia, Pennsylvania 19104-4112
 Phone: 215-898-6261
 Fax: 215-898-0404
 Toll-Free Phone: 800-537-5487 (book orders)
 E-mail: custserv@pobox.upenn.edu
 <http://www.upenn.edu/pennpress/>
Publishing in anthropology, linguistics, folklore, and cultural studies, the University of Pennsylvania Press reflects new directions in the discipline with its *Contemporary Ethnology* series and publishes the monograph series of the Association of Social Anthropology in Oceania.

732. **University of Texas Press**
 P.O. Box 7819
 Austin, TX 78713-7819
 Phone: 512- 471-7233
 Toll-Free Phone: 800-252-3206
 Fax: 512-232-7178
 E-mail: utpress@uts.cc.utexas.edu
 <http://www.utexas.edu/utpress/>
With strengths in Mesoamerican studies, languages and linguistics, folklore and religion, archaeology and ethnology, the University of Texas Press frequently collaborates with the University's Center for Middle Eastern Studies, Center for Mexican American Studies, and Institute for Latin American Studies.

733. **University of Washington Press**
 P.O. Box 50096
 Seattle, WA 98145-5096
 Phone: 206-543-4050
 Toll-Free Phone: 800-441-4115
 Fax: 206-685-3460
 Toll-Free Fax: 800-669-7993
 E-mail: uwpord@u.washington.edu
 <http://www.washington.edu/uwpress/>
The University of Washington Press offers a strong publications program in Northwest Coast ethnology and in area studies for Latin America, Africa,

Asia, and Oceania that reflect both traditional concerns and new directions in the discipline.

734. **University of Wisconsin Press**
1930 Monroe Street
3rd Floor
Madison, WI 53711-2059
Phone: 608-263-1110
Toll-Free Phone: 800-621-2736 (orders only)
Fax: 608-263-1120
Toll-Free Fax: 800-621-8476 (orders only)
E-mail: uwiscpress@uwpress.wisc.edu
<http://www.wisc.edu/wisconsinpress/>

In addition to a strong catalog in African studies and Great Lakes ethnography, the University of Wisconsin Press publishes the series *History of Anthropology* (entry 326) and a number of area studies series such as *Africa and the Diaspora: History, Politics, Culture* and *Southeast Asian Studies*.

735. **University Press of America**
4501 Forbes Blvd., Suite 200
Lanham, MD 20706
Phone: 301-459-3366
Toll-Free Phone: 800-462-6420
Fax: 717-794-3803
Toll-Free Fax: 800-338-4550
E-mail: custserv@rowman.com
<http://www.univpress.com/>

Now a division of the Rowman & Littlefield Publishing Group, the University Press of America publishes titles in anthropology, as well as in area studies, political science, and world history. Unfortunately, the Press's website does not provide a useful list of titles by subject, with titles such as "John Calvin and the Natural World" and "Matthew and the Messianic Tradition" listed under the heading "Anthropology."

736. **Waveland Press**
4180 IL Route 83
Suite 101
Long Grove, IL 60047
Phone: 847-634-0081
Fax: 847-634-9501
E-mail: info@waveland.com
<http://www.waveland.com/>

Waveland Press publishes general textbooks in cultural anthropology and numerous case studies with a contemporary focus on cultures throughout the world. Topical case studies in anthropology include cultural ecology, culture change and modernization, ethnic studies, humanistic/reflective anthropology and fieldwork and ethnography, among others.

737. **Westview Press**
Editorial:
5500 Central Ave.
Boulder, CO 80301
Phone: 303-444-3541
Fax: 720-406-7336

Ordering:
1094 Flex Drive
Jackson, TN 38301
Phone: 800-343-4499
Fax: 800-351-5073
E-mail: perseus.orders@perseusbooks.com
<http://www.westviewpress.com>

Since 1975, Westview has published textbooks and scholarly titles for use in undergraduate and graduate courses. The selection of anthropology titles is extensive. The well-known series, *Westview Case Studies in Anthropology*, endeavors to publish new ethnographies that "focus on contemporary ways of life, forces of social change, and creative responses to novel situations" and is an excellent source of ethnographies to support undergraduate programs in anthropology.

Departments and Programs

738. **Guide: A Guide to Departments, A Directory of Members.** Arlington, VA: American Anthropological Association. 1995-. Annual. ISSN not supplied. (Continues *AAA Guide*, 1989/90–1994/95 and *AAA Guide to Departments of Anthropology*,1962/63–1988/89).

More than just a listing of academic departments, this comprehensive directory provides detailed information on the degree programs, faculty, and staff, size, requirements, special programs, and facilities of anthropology departments in over 400 colleges and universities, as well as community colleges. It also identifies more than 90 museums, research institutions, and government agencies in the field, providing information regarding their staff, facilities, publications, etc. See entry 62 for a complete annotation of this source.

Organizations and Institutes

Learned societies, professional organizations, and research institutes serve a critical function in supporting research and the advancement of knowledge in a given field. They offer access to an established network of scholars as members share the results of their research at regularly scheduled meetings (see the section on "Conference Proceedings" in Chapter 2) and in newsletters and journals sponsored by the organization.

Richard Wilk has noted that "anthropological organizations may be formed around a particular goal (applied anthropology), the study of a particular area

(Oceania) or topic (work), a theoretical position (humanistic), or the identity of the members (Latino and Latina, European)." ("Associations of Anthropologists," *Theory in Anthropology*, <http://www.indiana.edu/~wanthro/assoc.htm>). The organizations listed here include all of these types. Because of the eclectic and multidisciplinary nature of sociocultural anthropology, organizations in area studies and related anthropological fields are highly relevant and have also been included. New and continuing societies were identified by combing the professional literature and Internet gateways. The information included in each entry was generated, most often by checking the group's website or consulting the directories listed in this chapter. In many instances (e.g., the IUAES Commissions), these organizations do not have a permanent home base but can be contacted thought the presiding officer.

Directories

739. **Encyclopedia of Associations.** Detroit, MI: Gale. 1956-. Annual. ISSN 0071-0202. Available in print and online by subscription.

A standard reference work, this title provides the name, address, phone number, executive officer, descriptions of an organization's aims, dates, and locations of conferences, and publications for a wide variety or organizations.

Over 100 associations are listed under the keyword "anthropology" and literally hundreds fall within the general category of "Cultural Organizations." The basis for inclusion is not always obvious, e.g., not all of the American Anthropological Association's individual units are included and coverage of international associations is poor. Nonetheless, the *Encyclopedia of Associations* provides a good starting point for identifying North American organizations.

740. **Local Practitioner Organizations (LPOs).** National Association for the Practice of Anthropology (NAPA). Available online at <http://www.practicinganthropology.org/lpos/>.

Local practitioner organizations (LPOs) are voluntary groups organized on a local or regional level to meet the needs of anthropologists working outside the university setting. This website lists LPOs with regional or metropolitan bases throughout the country, such as the High Plains Society for Applied Anthropology and the New York Association for the Practice of Anthropology (NYAPA). Entries provide a link to the website (if any), list the primary contact person, and briefly describe the organization. In addition to providing information on organizations not included in standard sources (like the *Encyclopedia of Associations*, entry 739), this directory serves the profession by increasing the visibility of these important groups.

741. **Research Centers Directory.** Detroit, MI: Gale. 1965. ISSN 0080-1518. Also available online.

With a broad definition of "research center," this directory lists over 11,700 university-related or other nonprofit research organizations in the United States and Canada. The directory is organized by broad subject categories, including social and behavioral sciences, humanities and religion (which includes anthropology and archaeology), and area studies.

The subject index identifies over 70 entries for anthropology and 60 for ethnology, with some overlap. For the most part, the research centers listed are units of anthropology department, laboratories, or museums, or in a few cases, independent institutions. The information provided includes address, phone numbers, chief officer, and a description of the organization and its activities and publications. Each edition is updated periodically by *New Research Centers*.

742. **World Directory of Social Science Institutions.** 5th ed. Paris: UNESCO, 1990. 1,211p. ISBN 923002556.

This extensive directory provides information on nearly 2,000 institutions, including scholarly and professional associations and research centers from around the world. Entries include name (and acronym), address and phone number, name of the director and senior researchers, scope and area of activity, and a list of publications. Entries are arranged alphabetically by country; the lack of a subject index limits directory's usefulness.

743. **World Guide to Scientific Associations and Learned Societies. International Verzeichnis Wissenschaftlicher Verbande und Gesellschaften.** New York: K. G. Saur. 1978-. Biennial. ISSN 0340-1332.

The associations and learned societies of over 60 countries are represented in this volume. Entries include name, founding date, address, phone number, publications, presiding officer, and number of members. The guide is arranged alphabetically by country. A subject index includes over 400 entries for ethnology and anthropology, many of which are not included in other sources. Though its coverage of the United States does not match the *Encyclopedia of Associations*, its international coverage is superior.

744. **World of Learning.** London: Europa Publications Limited. 1947-. Annual. ISSN 0084-2117. Also available online by subscription.

In addition to providing information regarding colleges and universities throughout the world, this important reference source lists the principal learned societies in each country. Under the subdivision "Religion, Sociology, Anthropology," the name, address, phone number, founding date, executive officer, number of members, and publications (including those concerning area studies) of important anthropological associations and institutes are listed. Issued annually, *World of Learning* provides extensive and timely coverage of anthropological associations worldwide.

American Anthropological Association

745. **American Anthropological Association**
 <http://www.aaanet.org/>

Founded in 1902 "to advance anthropology as the science that studies humankind in all its aspects, through archeological, biological, ethnological, and linguistic research; and to further the professional interests of American anthropologists," the AAA is now the world's largest organization of individuals involved with anthropology. Membership is open to anyone with a scholarly or professional interest in the field.

The society sponsors an active research and publication program, including publication of *American Anthropologist* (entry 641) and holds an annual meeting. Proceedings of the meeting are not published (though individual sessions may be published independently), but the association does issue abstracts (entry 88) of papers presented. The AAA also publishes an annual directory of departments of anthropology and members (entry 62).

Currently the AAA has 36 units that represent functional or topical interests within the field. A number of these sections were originally established independently and retain intellectual, if not organizational, autonomy. Most of the units meet in conjunction with the annual meeting of the AAA, but some also sponsor their own professional meetings. The units related to cultural anthropology are listed in this chapter and are all linked from the AAA website.

The AAA website <http://www.aaanet.org/> provides information on the organization and its sections, interest groups and programs, AAA publications (some with table of contents or full-text online), a list of meetings of interest to anthropologists, and current job openings. The "News/Media" section includes an online bulletin for announcements (grants, fellowships, prizes, call for papers, etc.), highlights from the current issue of *Anthropology News* (entry 98) and links to daily news articles relating to the "human sciences" and "Members in the News."

746. **American Ethnological Society**
<http://www.aaanet.org/aes/index.htm>

Founded in 1842, the American Ethnological Society (AES) is one of the oldest associations of anthropologists in the United States. Its members are concerned specifically with cultural and social anthropology from both descriptive and theoretical perspectives. The AES publishes *American Ethnologist* (entry 642) and actively sponsors scientific and scholarly exchanges.

747. **Anthropology and the Environment**
<http://www.eanth.org/>

One of the AAA's newest units, Anthropology and the Environment provides a forum for anthropologists interested in ecology, the environment and environmentalism, sponsors awards to scholars, and maintains the Eanth-L Listserv.

748. **Association for Feminist Anthropology**
<http://sscl.berkeley.edu/~afaweb/>

One of AAA newer units, the Association for Feminist Anthropology was established in 1988 to foster the development of feminist theoretical perspectives within the anthropological community.

749. **Association for Political and Legal Anthropology**
<http://www.aaanet.org/apla/index.htm>
This unit was established in 1976 to foster communication and cooperation among scholars interested in the fields of political and legal anthropology, including nationalism, citizenship, political and legal processes, the state, civil society, colonialism and post-colonial public spheres, multiculturalism, globalism, immigration, refugees and media politics. APLA publishes the *PoLAR: The Political and Legal Anthropology Review.*

750. **Association of Black Anthropologists**
<http://www.cas.usf.edu/ABA/mainpages/index2.htm>
The Association of Black Anthropologists was established in 1970 to provide a forum for African-Americans in anthropology and related disciplines. In addition to serving as a vehicle for communication, the organization promotes anthropological research on Black peoples and publishes the newsletter *Transforming Anthropology.*

751. **Association of Latino and Latina Anthropologists**
<http://www.aaalla.org/>
The Association of Latino and Latina Anthropologists provides professional support and development for Latino/a anthropologists, promotes research, and facilitates the sharing of information about Latino communities in the United States.

752. **Association of Senior Anthropologists**
<http://www.aaanet.org/asa/index.htm>
The Association of Senior Anthropologists offers senior and retired anthropologists "a continuing presence and voice in the discipline, allowing them to put their accumulated knowledge and insights to significant use."

753. **Central States Anthropological Society**
<http://www.aaanet.org/csas/index.htm>
One of two regional units of the AAA, Central States Anthropological Society was organized in 1921 to promote scholarly exchange among anthropologists in the Central States. The society publishes the *CSAS Bulletin.*

754. **Council for Museum Anthropology**
<http://www.nmnh.si.edu/anthro/cma>
Established to preserve and improve anthropological collections in museums, the Council for Museum Anthropology is involved with facilitating the use of collections for research and education, training personnel developing policies for the acquisition, exchange, loan, and exhibition of anthropological specimens. The Council sponsors the publication of *Museum Anthropology* and holds annual meetings in conjunction with the AAA and the American Association of Museums. The Council became an AAA affiliate in 1991.

755. Council on Anthropology and Education
<http://www.aaanet.org/cae/index.htm>
The purpose of the Council on Anthropology and Education (CAE), established in 1968, is to "advance and stimulate scholarship on schooling in social and cultural contexts and on human learning both inside and outside of schools." CAE publishes *Anthropology and Education Quarterly* (entry 648).

756. Culture and Agriculture Group
<http://colfa.utsa.edu/organization/culture&agriculture/>
Founded in 1976 to study agrarian systems from an anthropological perspective, Culture and Agriculture Group encourages the dissemination of scientific research, effective instruction and communication among persons and organizations engaged in agricultural research. This unit also sponsors the publication *Culture and Agriculture*.

757. General Anthropology Division
<http://www.aaanet.org/gad/index.htm>
Established in 1984 to foster scholarly exchange in issues common to all subfields of anthropology, this unit of the AAA represents the interest of those who support and promote holistic perspectives within anthropology. The unit publishes *American Anthropologist* (entry 641).

758. Middle East Section
<http://www.aaanet.org/mes/index.htm>
One of the most recently formed units of the AAA, the Middle East Section encourages the involvement of researchers for all four field of anthropology to advance understanding of this dynamic region.

759. National Association for the Practice of Anthropology
<http://www.practicinganthropology.org/>
This unit of the AAA was organized in 1983 for those who practice anthropology as a profession as well as to represent the interests of anthropologists in nonacademic positions such as social service organizations, government agencies, and business firms. The National Association for the Practice of Anthropology (NAPA) regularly sponsors training workshops and supports an active publication program that includes the *NAPA Bulletin* (entry 161) and the *Directory of Practicing Anthropologists* (entry 61).

760. National Association of Student Anthropologists
<http://www.aaanet.org/nasa/index.htm>
The purpose of this organization, established in 1986, is to address the concerns of graduate and undergraduate students in anthropology and to promote their involvement in the profession. The association publishes *NASA Bulletin*.

761. Northeastern Anthropological Association
<http://www.neaa.org/>

Organized in 1961, this regional unit of the AAA provides a forum for communication among anthropologists in the northeastern states of the United States and the eastern provinces of Canada.

762. **Society for Anthropology in Community Colleges**
<http://ccanthro.bizland.com/>
Established in 1978 to facilitate communication among teachers of anthropology in community colleges and precollegiate institutions, the society is involved with instruction and program development as well as improvement in the teaching of anthropology.

763. **Society for Cultural Anthropology**
<http://www.aaanet.org/sca/index.htm>
The Society for Cultural Anthropology was established in 1983 and represents theoretical perspectives from the field of cultural studies and culture theory broadly conceived. The society aims to connect with scholars in other relevant disciplines and publishes the journal *Cultural Anthropology* (entry 657).

764. **Society for East Asian Anthropology**
<http://www.aaanet.org/seaa/index.html>
One of the newer AAA units, the Society for East Asian Anthropology (SEAA) provides a worldwide forum for scholars interested in the anthropology of East Asia and the East Asian diaspora.

765. **Society for Humanistic Anthropology**
<http://www.smcm.edu/sha/>
The society, founded in 1974, encourages the involvement of anthropology in humanistic concerns such as literature and the arts and publishes *Anthropology and Humanism* (entry 649).

766. **Society for Latin American Anthropology**
<http://www.aaanet.org/slaa/Slaa1.htm>
This unit was established in 1969 to advance the anthropological study of Latin America. SLAA provides a forum for the discussion of current research, scholarly trends, and human rights concerns in Latin America and publishes the *Journal of Latin American Anthropology* (entry 681).

767. **Society for Linguistic Anthropology**
<http://www.aaanet.org/sla/index.htm>
Established in 1983 to encourage communication among scholars in the field, the Society for Linguistic Anthropology (SLA) seeks to advance the study of language in its social and cultural context. The SLA also publishes the *Journal of Linguistic Anthropology* (entry 682).

768. **Society for Medical Anthropology**
<http://www.medanthro.net/index.html>

The society was founded in 1971 to promote the study of anthropological aspects of health, illness, health care, and related topics and publishes *Medical Anthropology Quarterly* (entry 689).

769. Society for Psychological Anthropology
<http://www.aaanet.org/SPA/index.htm>

An interdisciplinary unit including anthropologists, cognitive and developmental psychologists, psychiatrists, and related professionals, the Society for Psychological Anthropology (SPA) was established in 1977 to support research and communication reflecting the interrelationship between culture and psychology. The SPA publishes the journal *Ethos* (entry 668).

770. Society for the Anthropology of Consciousness
<http://sacaaa.org/>

Established in 1980, the society provides a forum for the multidisciplinary study of consciousness. Areas of interest include shamanic and spiritual practices and philosophies, states of consciousness, indigenous healing practices, and anomalous phenomena. The unit publishes the journal *Anthropology of Consciousness*.

771. Society for the Anthropology of Europe
<http://www.h-net.org/~sae/sae/index.html>

Founded in 1986 to promote the anthropological study of Europe, the society facilitates communication among Europeanists in North America and Europe and publishes *Journal of the Society for the Anthropology of Europe*. In 2005, the SAE launched a new series, *European Anthropology in Translation*, in partnership with Berghahn Books (entry 702).

772. Society for the Anthropology of Food and Nutrition
<http://www.aaanet.org/cna/index.htm>

Representing a broad range of interests including biological, archaeological, social, and cultural aspects of food and nutrition, the Society for the Anthropology of Food and Nutrition (SAFN), formerly known as the Council on Nutritional Anthropology, was organized in 1974 in response to "increased interest in the interface between social sciences and human nutrition." The official publication of the Society is the peer-reviewed journal *Nutritional Anthropology*.

773. Society for the Anthropology of North America
<http://sananet.org/>

On the newest AAA units, the Society for the Anthropology of North America (SANA) is the first anthropological society to focus on the region encompassing United States, Canada, and Mexico as an "area" of study. SANA publishes the newsletter *North American Dialogue* and is developing a comprehensive bibliography and list of syllabi focusing on the region.

774. Society for the Anthropology of Religion
<http://www.aaanet.org/sar/>

This section was created in 1997 by the integration of three previously existing scholarly groups: the Anthropology of Religion Interest Group (affiliated with the AAA), the Society for the Anthropology of Religion (an independent nonprofit organization), and an informal group of anthropologists who were working separately toward the formation of a section. The section promotes teaching and research in the anthropological study of religion and provides a forum for communication among interested scholars. Though the Society does not publish a journal, it does sponsor a book series, *Contemporary Anthropology of Religion*, which is published in collaboration with Palgrave Macmillan (entry 714).

775. **Society for the Anthropology of Work**
<http://www.aaanet.org/saw/index.htm>
This organization was established to promote a cross-cultural approach to the study of theoretical and practical issues concerning the workplace and publishes the *Anthropology of Work Review*.

776. **Society for Urban, National and Transnational/Global Anthropology**
<http://www.sunta.org/>
A reformulation and expansion of the Society for Urban Anthropology, SUNTA focuses on the interrelationships of urban, national, and transnational processes in everyday life and publishes the journal *City & Society* (entry 655).

777. **Society for Visual Anthropology**
<http://www.societyforvisualanthropology.org/>
Established in 1984, the society promotes the study of visual representation and media and publishes *Visual Anthropology Review* (entry 696).

778. **Society of Lesbian and Gay Anthropologists**
<http://www.uvm.edu/~dlrh/solga/index.html>
Formerly known as the Anthropology Research Group on Homosexuality (ARGOH), this society serves as a forum for research and for the interests of lesbian and gay anthropologists.

International Union of Anthropological and Ethnological Sciences (IUAES)

779. **International Union of Anthropological and Ethnological Sciences (IUAES)**
<http://www.leidenuniv.nl/fsw/iuaes/>
The International Union of Anthropological and Ethnological Sciences (IUAES) was established in 1948 as a world organization of social and biological anthropologists and institutions dedicated to promoting international communication among scholars. Every 5 years, the IUAES sponsors the International Congress of Anthropological and Ethnological Sciences, a forum for the discussion and dissemination of research. The organization likewise sponsors seminars and symposia and issues the *IUAES Newsletter*. Nearly 30 separate commissions

within the IUAES have been established to investigate and research specific areas of anthropological interest. Most of the publishing activity of the IUAES takes place from the symposia they organize. The commissions (as of August 2006) are listed below:

780. **Commission on Aging and the Aged**
 <http://www.leidenuniv.nl/fsw/iuaes/06-01aging.htm>

781. **Commission on Anthropology in Policy and Practice**
 <http://www.leidenuniv.nl/fsw/iuaes/06-12policypractice.htm>

782. **Commission on Anthropology, Peace and Human Rights**
 <http://www.leidenuniv.nl/fsw/iuaes/06-11peace.htm>
 This group publishes the journal *Social Justice: Anthropology, Peace and Human Rights*.

783. **Commission on Bioethics**
 <http://www.leidenuniv.nl/fsw/iuaes/06-23bioethics.htm>

784. **Commission on Cultural Dimensions of Global Change**
 <http://www.leidenuniv.nl/fsw/iuaes/06-06globalchange.htm>

785. **Commission on Documentation**
 <http://www.leidenuniv.nl/fsw/iuaes/06-03documentation.htm>

786. **Commission on Ethnic Relations**
 <http://www.leidenuniv.nl/fsw/iuaes/06-20ethnicrelations.htm>

787. **Commission on Folk Law and Legal Pluralism**
 <http://www.leidenuniv.nl/fsw/iuaes/06-04law.htm>

788. **Commission on Food and Food Problems**
 <http://www.leidenuniv.nl/fsw/iuaes/06-05food.htm>

789. **Commission on Human Ecology**
 <http://www.leidenuniv.nl/fsw/iuaes/06-07humanecology.htm>

790. **Commission on Human Rights**
 <http://www.leidenuniv.nl/fsw/iuaes/06-25human%20rights.htm>

791. **Commission on Indigenous Knowledge and Sustainable Development**
 <http://www.leidenuniv.nl/fsw/iuaes/06-19indigenousknowledge.htm>

792. **Commission on Linguistic Anthropology**
 <http://www.leidenuniv.nl/fsw/iuaes/06-27linguistic%20anthropology.htm>

793. **Commission on Medical Anthropology and Epidemiology**
 <http://www.leidenuniv.nl/fsw/iuaes/06-08medical.htm>

794. **Commission on Migration**
 <http://www.leidenuniv.nl/fsw/iuaes/06-24migration.htm>

795. **Commission on Museums and Cultural Heritage**
 <http://www.leidenuniv.nl/fsw/iuaes/06-09museums.htm>

796. **Commission on Nomadic Peoples**
 <http://www.leidenuniv.nl/fsw/iuaes/06-10nomadicpeoples.htm>

797. **Commission on Primatology**
 <http://www.leidenuniv.nl/fsw/iuaes/06-26primatology.htm>

798. **Commission on the Anthropology of AIDS**
 <http://www.leidenuniv.nl/fsw/iuaes/06-02.aids.htm>

799. **Commission on the Anthropology of Children, Youth and Childhood**
 <http://www.leidenuniv.nl/fsw/iuaes/06-22children.htm>

800. **Commission on the Anthropology of Mathematics**
 <http://www.leidenuniv.nl/fsw/iuaes/06-21mathematics.htm>

801. **Commission on the Anthropology of Tourism**
 <http://www.leidenuniv.nl/fsw/iuaes/06-14tourism.htm>

802. **Commission on the Anthropology of Women**
 <http://www.leidenuniv.nl/fsw/iuaes/06-18women.htm>

803. **Commission on Theoretical Anthropology**
 <http://www.leidenuniv.nl/fsw/iuaes/06-13theory.htm>

804. **Commission on Urban Anthropology**
 <http://www.leidenuniv.nl/fsw/iuaes/06-15urban.htm>

805. **Commission on Urgent Anthropological Research**
 <http://www.leidenuniv.nl/fsw/iuaes/06-16urgent.htm>

806. **Commission on Visual Anthropology**
 <http://www.leidenuniv.nl/fsw/iuaes/06-17visual.htm>

Cultural Anthropology-Related Organizations

807. **African Studies Association**
<http://www.africanstudies.org/>
Established in 1957 to foster communication and to stimulate research among scholars on Africa, the African Studies Association (ASA) includes researchers from social science and humanities fields. The ASA Archives and Libraries Committee is of particular interest to librarians and researchers, as is the quarterly journal *African Studies Review*.

808. **American Folklore Society**
<http://www.afsnet.org/>
This distinguished society, established in 1888, boasts several prominent anthropologists among its current and former members. Promoting scholarship in folklore and folklife as well as public-sector folklore, American Folklore Society seeks to further both the profession and the discipline and publishes *Journal of American Folklore* (entry 678) as well as the *American Folklore Society Newsletter*.

809. **American Society for Ethnohistory**
<http://ethnohistory.org/>
The society was founded in 1954 and its members include anthropologists, historians, geographers, and other social scientists interested in promoting ethnohistorical research. The organization sponsors the journal *Ethnohistory* (entry 664).

810. **Anthropology and Sociology Section of the Association of College and Research Libraries (ACRL)**
<http://www.ala.org/acrl/anss/>
The Anthropology and Sociology Section (ANSS) of the American Library Association (ALA) represents the interests of library specialists in anthropology, sociology, and related fields. ANSS sponsors programs at the ALA annual meeting, publishes reviews and bibliographies of key sources, maintains active liaison programs with organizations in anthropology and sociology, and convenes committees and discussion groups that enable members to share their expertise.

811. **Association for Africanist Anthropology**
<http://www.ibiblio.org/afaa/>
The purpose of the Association for Africanist Anthropology (AFAA) is to advance anthropology by promoting the study of Africa, as well as Africanist scholarship and the professional interests of Africanist anthropologists worldwide.

812. **Association for Asian Studies**
<http://www.aasianst.org/>
Founded in 1941, this interdisciplinary society maintains several committees that may be country- or area-specific (such as Indonesian Studies or Southeast

Asia); topically oriented (Women in Asian Studies); or library related (South Asia Libraries and Documentation). ASA also supports an active publications program, including the *Journal of Asian Studies* (entry 680) and *Bibliography of Asian Studies* (entry 512).

813. **Association for the Study of Play**
 <http://www.csuchico.edu/kine/tasp/>
 Formerly titled The Association for the Anthropological Study of Play, this multidisciplinary organization was founded in 1973 to promote and encourage scholarly exchange among social and behavioral scientists and others involved in play research and theory. Publications include the annual *Play and Culture Studies* and the *TASP Newsletter*.

814. **Association of Social Anthropologists of the UK and Commonwealth**
 <http://www.theasa.org/>
 Drawing membership worldwide, the association was founded in 1946 to promote the study and teaching of social anthropology. With an active publications program, it sponsors monographic series (such as *ASA Research Methods in Social Anthropology*), conference papers, and a newsletter.

815. **Australian Institute of Aboriginal and Torres Strait Islander Studies**
 <http://www.aiatsis.gov.au/>
 Founded in 1961, the institute promotes research on all aspects of aboriginal studies, both traditional and contemporary. In addition to providing funds for research, the institute also publishes *Australian Aboriginal Studies* and an *Annual Bibliography*. The Institute's library includes substantial collection of audio tapes, prints and color slides, and film and video tapes.

816. **Cultural Survival**
 <http://209.200.101.189/>
 A private organization whose members include indigenous peoples, anthropologists, and other individuals and agencies interested in indigenous rights, Cultural Survival sponsors projects primarily in the areas of human rights, land reform and health care systems designed to help indigenous people survive both physically and culturally and gain as much control as possible over their destinies. As a center for research and documentation on the problems facing threatened societies, it has established a worldwide network of native and support organizations and distributes their reports. The society publishes *Cultural Survival Quarterly* (entry 659).

817. **Human Relations Area Files**
 <http://www.yale.edu/hraf/>
 The Human Relations Area Files (HRAF) was founded in 1949 at Yale University as a private, not-for-profit membership consortium of universities, colleges, and research institutions with a mission to encourage and facilitate the cross-cultural study of human culture, society, and behavior. HRAF also publishes

encyclopedias in conjunction with reference publishers such as Macmillan, Henry Holt, and Plenum, and helps produce the *Bibliography of Native North Americans* (entry 600).

818. **Institute for Development Anthropology**
Crestmont Rd.
Binghamton, NY 13905 USA
Phone:(607) 797-2820
Fax: (607) 773-8993
E-mail: devanth@binghamton.edu
Founded in 1976, this institute specializes in applied anthropology, particularly with regard to international development issues that enhance the ability of low-income populations to protect their human rights. Involved with development research and training, associates of the institute also develop projects to promote equitable distribution of the world's resources. Examples of programs include analysis and management of desert and tropical ecosystems as well as colonization and refugee settlements. The institute also maintains an 8,000-volume library specializing in development agency documents and sponsors seminars and workshops. As of this writing, the Institute's website was not available.

819. **International African Institute**
<http://www.iaionthe.net/>
Founded in 1926 as the International Institute of African Languages and Cultures, the International African Institute (IAI) promotes the study of African peoples, with an emphasis on languages, cultures, social life, beliefs and values, patterns of ethnic organization, and emerging social and political developments. The institute is governed by a council with balanced representation from African and non-African countries. IAI has long been involved with organizing and preserving the bibliographic record of research on Africa and has sponsored the publication of the journal *Africa* (entry 639) in addition to numerous reference publications.

820. **International Association for Cross-Cultural Psychology**
<http://www.iaccp.org/>
An interdisciplinary association of psychologists, psychiatrists, and anthropologists interesting in comparative dimensions of human behavior, this society publishes the *Journal of Cross-Cultural Psychology*.

821. **International Congress of Americanists**
Address not available
Established in 1875, this multinational association includes archaeologists, anthropologists, historians, linguists, sociologists, political scientists, and other scholars interested in the study of peoples in the Americas. The proceedings of its triennial conference are published.

822. **International Women's Anthropology Conference**
<http://homepages.nyu.edu/~crs2/index.html>
This organization of anthropologists and sociologists was established to encourage research and information exchange on topics such as gender, women's role in development, feminism, and other issues involving women in society.

823. **Latin American Studies Association**
<http://lasa.international.pitt.edu/>
Founded in 1966 to encourage research in Latin American studies, the association also seeks to provide library resource materials in the field and provide centralized information services. LASA publishes the *Latin American Research Review*.

824. **Library-Anthropology Resource Group**
<http://www.lib.uchicago.edu/e/su/anthro/larg.html>
The Library-Anthropology Resource Group (LARG) is a cooperative of anthropologists and librarians associated with research libraries in the Chicago concerned with bibliographic needs in the field and the development of useful reference works to address those needs. LARG was founded in 1971 by the late Sol Tax, Professor of Anthropology at the University of Chicago; Jan Wepsiec, Social Sciences Bibliographer at the University of Chicago Library; and Francis X. Grollig, Professor of Anthropology at Loyola University of Chicago. The group's most recent publication is *Anthropological Resources: a Guide to Archival, Library and Museum Collections* (entry 834).

825. **Middle East Studies Association**
<http://mesa.wns.ccit.arizona.edu/>
Established in 1966, the association promotes scholarship and instruction in Middle East studies, facilitates communication among scholars, and fosters cooperation among persons and organizations concerned with the scholarly study of the Middle East. Geographic focus ranges from "Morocco to Pakistan and from Turkey to Sudan." Among other titles, the Association publishes the *International Journal of Middle East Studies* and the *MESA Bulletin*, a quarterly newsletter.

826. **Plains Anthropological Society**
<www.ou.edu/cas/archsur/plainsanth/>
Focusing on the anthropology of the Plains and adjacent areas of North America, the society takes a holistic approach, including both cultural and physical anthropology, and publishes the journal *Plains Anthropologist* (entry 691).

827. **Polynesian Society**
<http://www.arts.auckland.ac.nz/departments/index.cfm?P=9144>
The Polynesian Society was formed in 1892 to promote the study of anthropology, ethnology, philology, history, and antiquities of Polynesian and related peoples. The society sponsors an active publications program that includes a

memoir series, a series on Maori texts, and *JPS: Journal of the Polynesian Society* (entry 686).

828. Royal Anthropological Institute
<http://www.therai.org.uk/>

Established in 1843 as the Ethnological Society of London, the institute was established as a "centre and depository for the collection and systemization of all observations made on human races." RAI members are scholars interested in social anthropology, physical anthropology, and pre-historic archaeology. Membership is not restricted to the United Kingdom but includes significant international representation.

The RAI sponsors an active research and publications program, including the *Journal of the Royal Anthropological Institute* (entry 685), the newsletter *Anthropology Today* (650), an occasional papers series, and the invaluable *Anthropological Index* (entry 75). Lectures, film screenings, and conferences are regularly organized. To support the research needs of fellows, the institute helps support a distinguished library collection at the Anthropology Library at the British Museum's Centre for Anthropology (entry 848) and also maintains their own archives and manuscript collection (entry 854) at the RAI office.

829. Society for Applied Anthropology
<http://www.sfaa.net/>

With membership drawn from professionals in anthropology, sociology, psychology, education, and the health professions, the society promotes the application of anthropological methods and theories to the resolution of human problems and publishes *Human Organization* (entry 673) and *Practicing Anthropology* (entry 692).

830. Society for Cross-Cultural Research
<http://www.sccr.org/>

Representing the fields of anthropology, education, political science, psychology, and sociology, the Society for Cross-Cultural Research (SCCR) supports and encourages interdisciplinary and comparative research to establish scientifically derived generalizations about human behavior across cultures. Founded by George Murdock, Ronald Rhoner, and others in 1971, SCCR publishes the quarterly journal *Cross-Cultural Research*.

831. Society for Economic Anthropology
<http://sea.org.ohio-state.edu/>

The Society for Economic Anthropology was formed in 1981 to stimulate communications among interested scholars and practitioners in economic anthropology. In addition to annual conferences, the society publishes *SEA Newsletter* and the series *Monographs in Economic Anthropology,* available from AltaMira Press (entry 699).

832. Society for Ethnomusicology
<http://webdb.iu.edu/sem/scripts/home.cfm>

Founded in 1955, the Society for Ethnomusicology includes ethnomusicologists, anthropologists, musicologists, and laypersons interested in cultural aspects of music in all historical periods and cultural contexts. Publications include a newsletter and the journal *Ethnomusicology* (entry 666).

833. **Wenner-Gren Foundation for Anthropological Research**
<http://www.wennergren.org/>
Founded in 1941, this private foundation supports basic research in all branches of anthropology and related disciplines concerned with human origins, development, and variation. For more details on its grants to support research, see entry 877. Wenner-Gren has also been instrumental in sponsoring international and regional conferences and seminars on topics and concerns within anthropology. Among its publications is the journal *Current Anthropology* (entry 661).

Museum Directories

Directories listing institutions with significant anthropological collections are included here, but we do not list individual museums.

834. **Anthropological Resources: A Guide to Archival, Library and Museum Collections.** Dutton, Lee S., editor. Compiled by Library-Anthropology Resource Group New York: Garland, 1999. 517p. ISBN 0815311885.

A nearly comprehensive overview of more than 150 collections pertaining to anthropological scholarship held in selected archives, libraries, or museums all over the world, this guide focuses on primary, nonartifactual documentation of anthropological significance, like scholars' fieldnotes, site reports, papers, manuscripts, archives, oral history collections, sound recordings, photographs, films, and videos. A personal name index and a keyword index with ethnic group names facilitate the location of particular collections.

835. **Council for Museum Anthropology**
<http://www.nmnh.si.edu/anthro/cma>
The Council for Museum Anthropology's (entry 754) website includes a listing of "Anthropology Museums on the Web."

836. **"Museums."** *Guide: A Guide to Departments, a Directory of Members.* Washington, DC: American Anthropological Association, 1962-.

The "Museum" section of the annual AAA *Guide* (entry 62) provides a handy and up-to-date directory of nearly 50 anthropological and archaeological museums within the United States and Canada. The entry for each museum includes a complete list of all professional staff and research associates and information regarding the collection, facilities for visiting scholars, and any sponsored publications.

837. **Museums of the World.** Schulze, Marco, and Boris Eggers. 13th ed. München: K. G. Saur, 2006. 2v. ISBN 3598206933.

This directory provides brief information (name, address, museum type, and scope of the collection) for nearly 18,000 museums in 163 countries. Arrangement is alphabetical by country and city. The subject index at the back provides general headings (nearly 600 listings for anthropology) as well as more specific terms (masks, tools) for collections of interest to anthropologists.

838. **The Official Museum Directory.** New York: American Association of Museums. 1971-. Annual. ISSN 0090-6700.

Listing nearly 7,000 museums in the United States, this reference tool is enhanced by its detailed annotations and comprehensive indexing. Arranged alphabetically by state and city, the annotations include the name, address and phone; type of museum; scope of the collection; facilities; activities; personnel and hours of operation. A particularly useful feature is the listing of museum publications. The subject index identifies museums by category, with nearly 300 represented in the area of anthropology, ethnology and Native American museums. They range in size from local history collections to the American Museum of Natural History. A classified buyers' guide is appended, listing products and services such as consultants, museum-shop merchandise, and security systems.

Libraries, Archives, and Special Collections

This section highlights just a few of the most prominent North American and Western European anthropological libraries and archives. Institutions with a particular regional focus are listed in the appropriate section of Chapter 7 (e.g., the Bernice Pauahi Bishop Museum Library is listed in the section on Australia and Pacific). Similarly, libraries and archives with a particular topical specialty are listed in the corresponding section (e.g., Archive of Folk Culture can be found in the "Folklore and Mythology" section of Chapter 6). Published catalogs are listed separately, with those of major anthropology libraries appearing in the "Bibliographic Tools" section of Chapter 2 and those focusing on a particular topic or region listed in the relevant chapter and section.

Much to the frustration of researchers, anthropological collections are scattered across institutions; the directories listed below are useful for identifying library and archival collections dealing with a particular geographical or topical area. Council for the Preservation of Anthropological Records (entry 839) is working to encourage researchers to deposit their papers and fieldnotes into an appropriate repository to facilitate access to these unique resources.

For a concise history of the development of the major anthropology libraries in North America and elsewhere, see Janet L. Steins (2006) "Anthropology Libraries" (entry 841).

839. **Council for the Preservation of Anthropological Records**
<http://www.nmnh.si.edu/naa/copar/bulletins>
The Council for the Preservation of Anthropological Records (CoPAR) was formed 1995 to "identify, encourage the preservation, and foster the use of the

records of anthropological research." CoPAR is sponsored by the major U.S. anthropological organizations in cooperation with other relevant professional organizations, such as the Society for American Archivists and the American Library Association, and government agencies, such as the National Park Service. As of this writing, the old CoPAR website at Arizona State University was no longer functional and a new one was under development at the National Anthropological Archives. The status of CoPAR's ongoing project to compile a *National Guide to Anthropological Records* listing all major anthropological collections in a handy online database is unclear at this time. The CoPAR handbook *Preserving the Anthropological Rec*ord (entry 123) is an invaluable guide to those working with anthropological records, as well as for researchers interested in preserving their own collections for the future.

Directories

840. **Anthropological Resources: A Guide to Archival, Library and Museum Collections.** Dutton, Lee S., editor. Compiled by Library-Anthropology Resource Group. New York: Garland, 1999. 517p. ISBN 0815311885.
    (See entry 834)

841. **"Anthropology Libraries."** Steins, Janet. *Encyclopedia of Library and Information Science*. 2nd ed. New York: Marcel Dekker, pp. 53–63.
    In this substantial encyclopedia entry, Steins (Associate Librarian for Technical Services and Collections at Harvard's Tozzer Library) traces the historical development of anthropology libraries worldwide and reflects on current trends that are shaping their future. A handful of the most noteworthy libraries in North America and Europe that were created during the formative period between 1830s–1920s are described individually.

842. **Directory of Anthropological Resources in New York City Libraries.** New York: Wenner-Gren, 1979. 64p. ISBN not assigned.
    This directory serves as an inventory of the wide range of information resources in the New York City area that are of interest to anthropologists. Over 50 academic, public, and special libraries are profiled from the American Museum of Natural History to the Zionist Archives and Library. Each entry includes information regarding access, services, collection, subject strengths, and special collections. Although some of the specifics may be dated (e.g., size of the collection), much of the information is still useful. A subject and geographic-area index aids in the identification of relevant collections for topical and area-studies research.

843. **Directory of Archives and Manuscript Repositories in the United States.** National Historical Publications and Records Commission. 2nd ed. Phoenix: Oryx Press, 1988. 853p. ISBN 0897744756.
    Seeking to assist researchers interested in historical topics, the National Historical Publications and Records Commission sponsored the publication of

this directory of over 4,500 archive repositories in the United States. Arranged by state and city, information includes name, address, and phone number; hours and access; materials solicited; and holdings of each archive. The institutions at which the archives are located include colleges and universities, libraries, museums and societies, and professional associations.

The subject index lists over 25 archives specifically relating to anthropology and ethnology as well as others in folklore, medicine, and specific area studies and ethnic groups, among others. Since the individual holding of many archives are too extensive to list (university archives for instance, frequently house the papers of faculty from their institutions), the directory is not exhaustive. It does, however, identify the major U.S. repositories for archival materials.

844. **Directory of Special Libraries and Information Centers.** Detroit, Mich.: Gale Research Co., 1963-. Irregular. ISSN 0731-633X.

The directory is arranged alphabetically by institution. Information includes the name, address, phone number, and a description of the holdings and policies for libraries of specific agencies (museums, historical societies, professional societies) as well as special collections within public, academic, or special libraries. A subset of this directory is also published as *Subject Directory of Special Libraries and Information Centers* (1971-).

There are nearly 300 entries in anthropology and ethnology. The criteria for inclusion are unfortunately too broad, and libraries with relatively limited holdings are undifferentiated from more important collections. In many cases, no indication as to the strength or uniqueness to the collection is given. The subject index does include specific headings, such as "Pomo Indians," when an entry includes more detail.

845. **Subject Collections.** New York: Bowker. 1958-. Irregular. ISSN 0000-0140.

Entries are arranged alphabetically by broad subject, such as anthropology. Libraries are then listed by state. Information provided includes the institution's name and address and a brief description of the scope and holdings of the collection.

Over 70 libraries are listed for anthropology and ethnology, with others listed under specific area studies or peoples (e.g., Seneca Indians). The relative importance of the collections listed varies considerably, as does the detail provided in the annotations. For example, some entries merely note "holdings in ethnology;" others provide details such as "includes Brinton collection on aboriginal American linguistics." Though no subject access is available, the listing provides a useful starting point for the identification of notable anthropological collections.

Major Libraries and Archives

846. **American Museum of Natural History Library**
Central Park West at 79th Street
New York, NY 10024

Phone: 212-769-5400
Fax: 212-769-5009
<http://library.amnh.org/>

The American Museum of Natural History was established as a private institution in 1869 to provide a museum and a library of natural history and to "advance the general knowledge of kindred subjects." One of ten other units, the Department of Anthropology was established both to develop the museum's exhibitions (the museum's collection includes over 8 million anthropological artifacts) and to carry on research. Its publications include *Anthropological Papers, Bulletin of the American Museum of Natural History*, and the *American Museum Novitiates*.

The library of the American Museum of Natural History includes an extensive collection in general anthropology, ethnology, and museology. Its archives include a photographic collection of nearly 500,000 cataloged black and white photographs and more than 60,000 color transparencies of the museum's habitat groups, exhibitions, specimens and other subjects, as well as the Natural History Film Archives and rare books and manuscripts. Services include reference and interlibrary loan, and the museum is open to the public.

847. **American Philosophical Society Library**
American Philosophical Society Library
105 South Fifth Street
Philadelphia, PA 19106-3386
(215) 440-3400
<http://www.amphilsoc.org/library/>

For historians of anthropology and specialists in American Indian linguistics, the archives of this library provide a wealth of resources. From Darwin and evolution to the fieldnotes of Franz Boas, the library includes the papers of numerous eminent anthropologists. A guide to the collection has been published under the title *The Proper Study of Mankind* (entry 115).

848. **Anthropology Library at the British Museum's Centre for Anthropology**
Anthropology Library
Centre for Anthropology, British Museum
Great Russell Street, London WC1B 3DG, United Kingdom
Telephone: +44 (0)20 7323 8031
E-mail: anthropologylibrary@thebritishmuseum.ac.uk
<http://www.therai.org.uk/MoM/MoM.html>

The Anthropology Library at the British Museum's Centre for Anthropology houses the library collections of the Royal Anthropological Institute (entry 828) and the British Museum's Department of Africa, Oceania and the Americas (formerly the Department of Ethnography). It should be noted that while the RAI library has been merged into the British Museum collections, the RAI still maintains its own manuscript, archive, photographic, and film holdings (entry 854).

The scope of the collections is worldwide, with particular emphasis on Commonwealth countries and former British colonies, Eastern Europe, and Mesoamerica. The holdings are impressive, with more than 120,000 books and 4,000 journals (1,500 of which are current). The library is noted for its full runs of nineteenth- and twentieth-century periodicals, built largely on a robust exchange program with scholarly institutions across the globe. The journal collection is indexed by the RAI's *Anthropological Index Online* (entry 75).

849. **ArchivesUSA.** 1997-. Available online at <http://archives.chadwyck.com/>.

Available online by subscription.

A unified catalog like *WorldCat*, but for archives and manuscript collections, *Archives USA* is a gateway to almost 6,000 repositories and over 150,000 collections of primary source material across the United States. Researchers can search across the database, read collections descriptions, and find contact information, access policies and hours of service for the library or archives that holds a given collection. Collection descriptions are submitted directly by repositories and are more and more likely to include online finding aids. The database also incorporates all listings from the *National Union Catalog of Manuscript Collections* (NUCMC) and ProQuest UMI's *National Inventory of Documentary Sources in the United States (NIDS)* and makes these invaluable resources searchable in an electronic format.

850. **Field Museum of Natural History**
1400 S. Lake Shore Dr
Chicago, IL 60605-2496
(312) 922-9410
<http://www.fieldmuseum.org/research_collections/library/default.htm>

Established in 1893 as an outgrowth of the World's Columbian Exposition held in Chicago, the Field Museum is dedicated to the collection, preservation, exhibition, and research in anthropology, botany, geology, and zoology. Prior to WWII the museum sponsored extensive expeditions to collect artifacts (the collection includes over 800,000 archaeological and ethnological specimens collected worldwide), but the emphasis has now shifted to problem-oriented fieldwork and the collection of data. The scientific contributions of the research staff are considerable, having taken their lead from the first curator of anthropology, the eminent Franz Boas.

The Field Museum's library houses extensive collections in all fields of natural history, with an emphasis on evolutionary biology and the archaeology and ethnology of the Americas, Africa, East Asia, and Oceana. The collection is particularly strong in museum publications, reports, and "fugitive" materials, as the library maintains a publications exchange program with museums throughout the world. A serials exchange program provides similar extensive coverage of the publications of learned societies, academies, and other research institutions worldwide. Through its Reading Room, the library operates as a noncirculating collection for all who have need of its materials.

For additional information, see "Field Museum of Natural History Library," by Benjamin W. Williams and W. Peyton Fawcett in *Sci/Tech Libraries*, 1985: 27–33.

851. **George and Mary Foster Anthropology Library**
   230 Kroeber Hall
   Berkeley, CA 94720
   Phone: 510-642-2400
   Fax: 510-643-9293
   <http://www.lib.berkeley.edu/ANTH/>

The library maintains general research collections covering all aspects of social and physical anthropology, anthropological linguistics, folklore, and archaeology. Collections focus on historical areas of faculty interest (e.g., Andean Prehistory, Mesoamerica, California Indian culture, social behavior of primates, and fossil man) along with current research interests (e.g., medical anthropology, anthropology of gender, anthropology of law, California archaeology). A particular strength lies in its extensive serials holdings; the library has subscriptions to over 700 current periodicals. The library is open to the public.

852. **The John Wesley Powell Library of Anthropology at the Smithsonian Institution**
   Location:
   National Museum of Natural History,
   10th Street and Constitution Ave., N.W.
   Washington, D.C. 20560-0112
   Telephone: (202) 633-1640
   Fax: (202) 357-1896
   E-mail:libmail@si.edu

   Mailing Address:
   Smithsonian Institution Libraries
   Smithsonian Institution
   PO Box 37012
   Anthropology Library
   Washington, DC 20013-7012
   <http://www.sil.si.edu/libraries/anth-hp.htm>

Founded in 1846, the Smithsonian is an independent federal institution supported by both private and government funds. Established for the "increase and diffusion of knowledge," its involvement extends to the arts, sciences, and social sciences. Interest in anthropology has been manifested through the programs and collections of the National Museum of Natural History, the National Museum of the American Indian, and the closely associated Bureau of American Ethnology.

The John Wesley Powell Library of Anthropology was formed in 1965 by the merger of the Bureau of American Ethnology library with collections held by various divisions within the Department of Anthropology. The Anthropology

Library, as it is known, is one of 20 branch libraries in the Smithsonian Institution Libraries' system and holds 80,000 volumes, including 400 serial titles. Geographic interests include North, Central, and South America; Africa; Asia (particularly Southeast Asia); Oceania; and the Arctic, but its greatest strength continues to be in the area of Native American studies. The rare book collection includes travel accounts as well as reproduction of paintings and drawings of early European explorers on the American continent. The Department of Anthropology also maintains the National Anthropological Archives (entry 853) and engages in an active publications program. Among other titles, it publishes the *Handbook of North American Indians* and *Smithsonian Contributions to Anthropology*.

The Anthropology Library is primarily intended to support the research needs of the Anthropology Department and other Smithsonian museums and units in the areas of physical and cultural anthropology, archaeology, and linguistics, but is open to the public (appointment recommended). Smithsonian Libraries' collection can be accessed through SIRIS, the Smithsonian Institution Research Information System, <http://www.siris.si.edu/>.

853. **National Anthropological Archives**
Smithsonian Institution Museum Support Center
4210 Silver Hill Road
Suitland, MD 20746
Phone: 301-238-1300
Fax: 301-238-2883
<http://www.nmnh.si.edu/naa/index.htm>

Organized in 1965 as part of the Anthropology Department of the Smithsonian Institution's National Museum of Natural History Library, the National Anthropological Archives (NAA) is the successor to the former Bureau of American Ethnology Archives. Its purpose is to serve as a depository for the records of the Department of Anthropology and to collect private papers relating to all cultures of the world and to history of anthropology. The NAA collects and preserves historical and contemporary anthropological materials that document the world's cultures and the history of the discipline. Its collections represent the four fields of anthropology—ethnology, linguistics, archaeology, and physical anthropology—and include manuscripts, fieldnotes, correspondence, photographs, maps, sound recordings, film and video created by Smithsonian anthropologists and other preeminent scholars.

The archives' holdings include nearly 635,000 ethnological and archaeological photographs (including some of the earliest images of indigenous people worldwide); 20,000 works of native art (mainly North American, Asian, and Oceanic); 11,400 sound recordings; and more than 8 million feet of original film and video materials. The strength of the collection lies in general anthropology, linguistics, archaeology, history of anthropology, and history of American Indians. Special collections dating from 1847 include the Bureau of American Ethnology manuscript collection, over 60,000 photographs of American Indians, records from the Institute for Social Anthropology and the Center for the Study of Man, as well as professional papers of anthropologists and records of anthropological organizations.

For detailed descriptions of the collections, see the *Guide to the National Anthropological Archives* (entry 113). Many of the fieldnotes, journals, manuscripts, photographs, moving images, artwork, maps, and more than 40,000 digital images (from both the National Anthropological Archives and related collections at the Smithsonian) are described in the Archival, Manuscript and Photographic Collections portion of *SIRIS*, the Smithsonian online catalog <http://www.nmnh.si.edu/naa/guides.htm>. To browse new collections that may not yet appear in SIRIS, see "What's New at the National Anthropological Archives" <http://www.nmnh.si.edu/naa/whatsnew.htm>.

854. **Royal Anthropological Institute Collection**
50 Fitzroy Street
London W1T 5BT
United Kingdom
Phone: +44 (0)20 7387 0455
Fax: +44 (0)20 7388 8817
E-mail: archives@therai.org.uk.
<http://www.therai.org.uk/rainews/raiCollection.html>

The Royal Anthropological Institute (entry 828) Collection comprises the RAI's manuscript, archive, photographic, and film holdings. The collection includes the extensive archives and manuscript collections of the RAI, documenting 150 years of anthropological research through association records, the papers of its fellows (including Evans-Pritchard, Malinowski and Radcliffe-Brown) and other manuscript collections donated to the RAI. The Institution's rich holdings also include an impressive collection of photographic material and ethnographic videos that may be previewed on site. Note, however, that the RAI library materials (books and journals) are now integrated into the Anthropology Library at the British Museum's Centre for Anthropology (entry 848).

Fellows and members of the RAI, as well as undergraduate students, can access the collection free of charge; others are charged a modest daily fee and can visit by appointment only.

855. **Tozzer Library**
21 Divinity Avenue
Harvard University
Cambridge, MA 02138
617-495-2253
<http://hcl.harvard.edu/tozzer>

Formerly the Library of the Peabody Museum of Archaeology and Ethnography at Harvard University, the Tozzer Library is one of the premier anthropological libraries in the world. The collection includes all subfields of anthropology, with particular strength in Latin American archaeology and ethnography. The serials collection is especially impressive, with current subscriptions to over 2,000 periodicals, all of which are indexed in *Anthropological Literature* (entry

76). An extensive microform collection includes the John Harrington Papers, the University of Chicago American Indian Cultural Anthropology Manuscripts, Middle American Cultural Anthropology, and the Professional Papers of Franz Boas. The library also includes a Rare Book Room with significant manuscript holdings including the Adolph F. Bandelier Collection (Indian of the Southwest), the Henry O. Beyer Collection (Philippine Islands ethnography), the fieldnotes of Alfred M. Tozzer, and the personal papers of Cora Du Bois. Both the Peabody Museum and the Harvard University Archives also house unpublished papers and manuscripts in anthropology. Tozzer's holdings can be searched via HOLLIS, the catalog of the Harvard University Libraries <http://hollis.harvard.edu/>.

For more detailed information on the Library's history and collections, see John Weeks, "Tozzer Library: A 'National' Library for Anthropology in the United States," *Current Anthropology* 28(1) (Feb. 1987): 133–137.

Career Development Resources

Anthropology News (entry 98) includes a substantial listing of job openings in its "Career Development" section.

Career Handbooks

856. **Anthropology in Practice: Building a Career Outside the Academy.** Nolan, Riall W. Boulder, CO: Lynne Rienner Publishers, 2003. 213p. ISBN 1555879578; 1555879853pa.

Drawing on his experience working for international development agencies, Nolan (Director, Institute of Global Studies and Affairs, U. of Cincinnati) provides an eminently practical guide for anthropologists (and anthropologists-in-training) interested in pursuing careers outside the academy. He offers advice to those still in school on academic training and graduate study, as well as more general advice on the job search, career development, and tips for successfully advancing the anthropological perspective in policy and planning. Sample resumes, cover letters and an appendix of resources that includes websites of potential employers are among the tools Nolan provides to make the job search easier.

857. **Federal Job Opportunities for Anthropologists.** Givens, David B. Washington, DC: American Anthropological Association, 1986. 28p. (Special Publication of the American Anthropological Association, No.14). ISBN not assigned.

Though some of the specifics are out of date, this brief guide may still be helpful to those who are considering federal government employment and are uncertain about employment opportunities for anthropologists and about the official and unofficial procedures for obtaining such positions. Beginning with a description of Civil Service levels and tips for completing the appropriate paperwork, Givens then lists a sample of potential federal jobs for all subfields of anthropology. The final section addresses applying for a GS (Government Service) rating and identifying appropriate jobs. Although not extensive, the booklet identifies a smorgasbord of potential positions and illustrates the diversity of job opportunities for the anthropologist.

858. **Great Jobs for Anthropology Majors.** Camenson, Blythe. 2nd ed. New York: VGM Career Books, 2005. 180p. ISBN 0071437339.

This guide for students preparing for the transition to a career in anthropology covers every aspect of identifying and getting started in a career, from exploring options to conducting an effective job search. It shows students how to write a resume, network, interview, and evaluate job offers. The book includes sample resumes and job descriptions, statistics, salary ranges and sources for more information.

859. **A Guide to Careers in Physical Anthropology.** Ryan, Alan S., editor. Westport, CT: Bergin & Garvey, 2002. 308p. ISBN 0897896939.

Chapters written by anthropologists working in diverse settings explore the range of career options open to people with training in physical anthropology, from journalism to university teaching.

860. **Introduction to Museum Work.** Burcaw, George Ellis. 3rd ed. Lanham, MA: AltaMira, 1997. 237p. ISBN 0761989250; 0761989269pa.

Endorsed by the Documentation Center of the International Conference of Museums as exemplary of museum training, this has long been a standard reference book for practicing museum professionals as well as a standard classroom textbook. The basics of museum building and design, finances, and day-to-day operation are covered.

861. **State Job Opportunities for Anthropologists.** Givens, David B. Washington, DC: American Anthropological Association, 1986. 29p. ISBN not assigned.

Focusing on the employment opportunities for anthropologists at the state level, Givens provides an overview of anthropology-related jobs such as urban planner, criminologist, and museum administrator, followed by a discussion of state hiring procedures and personnel departments. Like Given's pamphlet on federal jobs (entry 857), this continues to be a useful introduction to the process of pursuing government employment despite its age.

862. **Training Manual in Applied Medical Anthropology.** Hill, Carole E. Washington, DC: American Anthropological Association, 1991. 237p. ISBN 0913167460.

(See entry 339)

Employment, Field Schools, and Internships

863. **Anthropology Field Schools.** American Anthropological Association. Available online at <http://www.aaanet.org/ar/fs/fschool.htm>.

Hosted by American Anthropological Association (entry 745), this website includes links to information about field schools and internship opportunities. As of this writing, a new section on "Current Field School Opportunities" was under development that will provide a place to post current field school opportunities, as well as a "searchable announcements system."

864. **Archaeological Fieldwork Opportunities Bulletin.** New York: Archaeological Institute of America. 1981-. Annual. ISSN 1061-8961.

This comprehensive resource provides students, volunteer fieldworkers, and archaeological tourists with hundreds of fieldwork opportunities from around the world. Travel tips and resources, excavation guidelines, and the Archaeological Institute of America's codes of Ethics and Professional Standards are also provided. A handy index of archaeological offices within governmental agencies is included.

865. **Archaeologyfieldwork.com.** Available online at <http://archaeologyfieldwork.com>.

Established in 1996, this frequently updated site provides a clearinghouse for job postings, volunteer opportunities, announcements, discussion forums, and career development resources for archaeologists-in-training.

866. **Careers in Anthropology.** American Anthropological Association. Available online at <http://www.aaanet.org/careers.htm>.

This listing on the American Anthropological Association (entry 745) website includes a database of recent job postings and a place for job seekers to post their resumes, as well as an extensive listing of sites advertising positions for anthropologists, fellowship and internship opportunities, and career resources information.

867. **Chronicle of Higher Education: Chronicle Careers: Anthropology.** Available online at <http://chronicle.com/jobs/100/800/1000>.

The openings posted at *The Chronicle* come from a wide range of academic and research institutions. New jobs are posted daily.

868. **NAPA Job Center.** National Association for the Practice of Anthropology. Available online at <http://www.practicinganthropology.org/employment/>.

NAPA provides a place for employers to post job openings, job seekers to post resumes, and a collection of resources to help aspiring applied anthropologists find employment. The positions posted here are current and varied, and include academic positions in related areas (such as global studies or applied linguistics), as well as business, community development, cultural resources management, government, IT, not-for-profit, and social services opportunities.

Grants and Funding

The listing below primarily includes directories and guides that compile multiple sources of funding. We have, however, included a highly selective listing of a few of the most notable individual funding sources, such as the National Science Foundation (entry 874), the Social Science Research Council (entry 876), and Wenner-Gren (entry 877).

869. **Financial Aid for Research and Creative Activities Abroad.** San Carlos, CA: Reference Service Press. 1992–1994. Biennial. ISSN 1072-530X.

Updated every 2 years, *Financial Aid for Research and Creative Activities Abroad* is a well-organized and easy-to-use directory of scholarships and grants for students, postdocs, and professionals inside and outside of the academy doing research outside the United States.

870. **Funding for Anthropological Research.** Cantrell, Karen, and Denise Wallen, editors. Phoenix, AZ: Oryx Press, 1986. 308p. ISBN 0897741544pa.

Although dated, this remains the only printed directory of research support specifically geared toward professional anthropologists and graduate students in anthropology. The editors (themselves anthropologists) compiled the directory because of frustration with not being able to utilize standard reference works efficiently in a field as diverse as anthropology. As a result of their labors, more than 700 sponsored research programs were identified from private and corporate foundations, government agencies, associations and organizations, institutes and centers, museums and libraries, and professional societies in the United States.

Entries are listed alphabetically, and the information provided includes address and phone number, type of program, description, eligibility/limitations, fiscal information, deadline, application information, and subject scope. A detailed subject index identifies programs by topic (from abortion rights to zoology) and type of support (doctoral dissertation support, faculty development). Sponsoring agencies are also indexed by type (federal, corporate).

871. **FundSource: A Search Tool for Research Funding in the Behavioral and Social Sciences.** Available online at <http://www.decadeofbehavior.org/fundsource/>.

Designed especially for social and behavioral scientists, *FundSource* is a freely available web-based database that includes short descriptions, contact information, and web links to programs in federal agencies, international organizations, and private foundations that fund social science research. Disciplines covered include anthropology and archaeology.

872. **Grants for Individuals: Anthropology.** Harrison, Jon, editor. Michigan State University Libraries. Available online at <http://www.lib.msu.edu/harris23/grants/3anthrop.htm>.

This site includes websites, databases, and books that point to funding sources for anthropology research. It is maintained by the Michigan State University Library system. While the site appears to be frequently updated, not all links were current and some were not particularly useful.

873. **Money for Graduate Students in the Social & Behavioral Sciences.** Schlachter, Gail A., and R. David Weber. El Dorado Hills, CA: Reference Service Press, 2005. 326p. ISBN 1588411419.

Updated every 2 years, *Money for Graduate Students in the Social & Behavioral Sciences* is an extremely useful directory of sources of funding to support research and study for graduate students in the social sciences. It is also useful for identifying funding opportunities to support the research of established scholars. Over 1,000 grants, fellowships, and awards are listed in the two main sections: "Study and Training" or "Research and Creative Activities." Each entry includes complete contact information, as well as purpose, eligibility, financial data, duration, special features, limitations, number awarded, and application date. The indexes are particularly helpful and provide access by calendar (i.e., due date), residency, tenability, subject, and sponsoring organization.

874. **National Science Foundation: Behavioral and Cognitive Sciences Division.** Available online at <http://www.nsf.gov/div/index.jsp?org=BCS>.

The National Science Foundation (NSF) supports a wide range of anthropological research, with programs in cultural anthropology, archaeology, linguistics, and physical anthropology. In addition to these program areas, NSF also has periodic funding opportunities targeting specific areas, such as "methodological training for cultural anthropology scholars." Undergraduate, K-12, and dissertation research support is also available.

875. **Scholarships, Fellowships, and Postdoctoral Awards: Anthropology, Economics, Geography, Law, Political Science, Psychology, Sociology.** Tomei Torres, Francisco Alberto, compiler. Available online at <http://scholarships.fatomei.com/social.html>.

This website provides a compilation of scholarship, fellowship, postdoctoral resources for social scientists maintained by Francisco Alberto Tomei Torres, Ph.D. The database is regularly updated.

876. **Social Science Research Council.** Available online at <http://www.ssrc.org/fellowships/>.

The Social Science Research Council (SSRC) is a nongovernmental, not-for-profit, international association dedicated to interdisciplinary research in the social sciences. SSRC funds interdisciplinary workshops and conferences, fellowships and grants, and working groups. Research activities focus on four major program areas: global security and cooperation, migration, knowledge institutions, and the public sphere. The support programs provide student funding opportunities, including dissertation fellowships, as well as postdoctoral fellowships, and advanced research grants in the social sciences and humanities.

877. **Wenner-Gren Foundation for Anthropological Research: Individual Research Grants Program.** Available online at <http://www.wennergren.org/programs>.

Wenner-Gren's mission is to encourage innovative research on the human species and to foster the development of an international community of anthropological scholars. The Foundation (entry 833) funds dissertation fieldwork, postdoctoral fellowships, and research grants. Grants awarded are up to $25,000 for research in all branches of anthropology and may additionally be used to fund particular project expenses or to attract aid from other funding agencies. The Foundation expressly invites projects with comparative perspectives or that integrate several subfields of anthropology. Though the foundation is based in the United States, financial aid is not restricted to U.S. scholars and institutions. Some awards are set aside for projects designed to develop resources for anthropological research and scholarly exchange.

AUTHOR INDEX

For names of publishers and organizations listed in Chapter 8, see the Title Index. Numbers refer to entry numbers.

Aarrne, Antii, 441
Abrahams, Roger D., 456
Abu-Lughod, Lila, 561
ACRL. *See* Association of College and Research Libraries (ACRL)
Afonso, Ana Isabel, 186
Alvarez Roldán, Arturo, 319
American Anthropological Association, 44, 66, 152, 863, 866
  AIDS and Anthropology Working Group, 340
American Folklore Society, 173
American Museum of Natural History, 116
Amit, Vered, 53
Angrosino, Micheal V., 138
Anthro TECH, 69
ANSS. *See* Association of College and Research Libraries (ACRL)
Appiah, Anthony, 574
Archaeological Objects Thesaurus Working Party, 215
Archaeological Research Institute. *See* Arizona State University
Arctic Institute of North America Library, 605
Aretxaga, Begoña, 346
Arizona State University, Archaeological Research Institute, 231
Aronson, Amy, 387
Asher, R. E., 257
Ashliman, D. L., 444
Aston, Mick, 209
Association of College and Research Libraries (ACRL), Anthropology and Sociology Section (ANSS), 82
Atkinson, Paul, 136, 143
Australian Institute of Aboriginal and Torres Strait Islander Studies, 543
Aversa, Elizabeth Smith, 419
Azzolina, David, 440

Babcock, Barbara A., 54
Bahn, Paul G., 211, 227

Bailey, Carol A., 141
Baker, Philip, 504
Balderston, Daniel, 621
Baltes, Paul B., 13, 357
Bankoti, T. S., 523
Barfield, Thomas, 32
Barkan, Elliott Robert, 583
Barker, Graeme, 216
Barnard, Alan, 39
Barnes, R. H., 510
Barrett, Christopher B., 146
Barrett, Stanley R., 119
Bartis, Peter, 450
Bäuml, Betty J., 256
Bäuml, Franz H., 256
Baxter, Pam M., 353
Becker, Howard S., 23
Belk, Russell W., 308
Bell, Daphne, 533
Bellenir, Karen, 370
Bennett, Gillian, 451
Bennett, Tony, 15
Bernal, Ignacio, 628
Bernard, H. Russell, 121, 124
Berry, John W., 359
Bial, Henry, 464
Biblioteca Nacional de Antropología e Historia, Mexico, 635
Biebuyck, Daniel P., 498
Biella, Peter, 196
Birx, H. James, 37
Bisht, Narendra S., 523
Blackhurst, Hector, 494
Blazek, Ron, 419
Bolaffi, Guido, 471
Bolton, Ralph, 341
Bonte, Pierre, 36
Borgerhoff Mulder, Monique, 318
Borneman, John, 546
Borofsky, Robert, 170
Bosco, Joseph, 511
Boyer, Jefferson, 613, 614
Bragdon, Kathleen J., 587
Breitborde, Lawrence B., 396

Breman, Jan van, 509
Bricker, Victoria B., 624
British Museum, Anthropology Library, 75
Brooks, Alison S., 242
Brothwell, Don R., 224
Brubaker, Dale L., 22
Bryant, Carol A., 273
Bryman, Alan, 21, 135
Buckland, Theresa, 462
Bullwinkle, Davis, 495
Burcaw, George Ellis, 176, 860
Bureau of American Ethnology. *See* Smithsonian Institution
Burg, Barbara A., 505
Burgess, Robert G., 144
Burling, Robbins, 145
Burt, Eugene C., 293–294

Calhoun, Craig, 11
Camenson, Blythe, 858
Campbell, George L., 262
Cantrell, Karen, 870
Carneiro, Robert L., 317
Carrasco, David, 626
Carrier, James G., 305
Cason, Jeffrey W., 146
Cassanelli, Lee V., 316
Cassell, Joan, 155
Centre d'Edition Numérique Scientifique du CNRS, 281
Champagne, Duane, 599
Chance, Norman, 608
Childs, S. Terry, 175
Chippindale, Christopher, 223
Christen, Kimberly A., 442
Christensen, Karen, 513
Ciolek, T. Matthew, 100
Claus, Peter J., 459
Clements, William, 446
Clist, Bernard Oliver, 67
CNRS. *See* Centre d'Edition Numérique Scientifique du CNRS
Cohen, Selma Jean, 465
Columbia University Libraries, 568–569
Comita, Lambros, 630
Comrie, Bernard, 253, 265
Conference of Directors of National Libraries of Asia and Oceania, 541
Conklin, Harold C., 300

Cooper, A. M., 412
Cordell, Karl, 552
Courtney, Anita, 273
Covington, Paula, 610
Crane, Julia G., 138
Crystal, David, 254–255
Curran, Sara R, 142

Daly, Richard, 30
Damien, Yvonne M., 101
Darnell, Regna, 325
Darvill, Timothy, 217
Das, Veena, 517
De Laet, S. J., 40
Delamont, Sara, 545
Delson, Eric, 242
DeMiller, Anna L., 249, 274, 374
DeWalt, Kathleen M, 273
Diamond, Sarah, 459
Dicks, Bella, 147
Dietler, Michael, 411
Dirks, Robert, 280
Diskin, Martin, 613–614
Dotson, Lillian Ota, 527
Doty, William G., 434
Dryer, Matthew S., 253
Du Bois, Christine M., 268
Duranti, Alessandro, 250
Dutton, Lee S., 834, 840

Eades, J. S., 511
Economic and Social Research Council. *See* Oxford University
Edelman, Marc, 388
Eggers, Boris, 837
Eickelman, Dale F., 560
El-Shamy, Hasan, 438
Ellen, R. F., 134, 296
Ellis, Linda, 214
Ember, Carol R., 336, 386, 392–393, 407, 467, 471, 479–480
Ember, Melvin, 38, 221, 336, 386, 392–393, 407, 467, 471, 479–480, 575
Embree, John Fee, 527
Emerson, Robert M., 149
Erickson, Ken C., 130
Erickson, Paul A., 320, 324
Eriksen, Thomas Hylland, 321
Erixon, Sigurd, 447

Ethnodoc, 197
Etkin, Nina L, 274

Fagan, Brian, 226
Faheem, Ahmed D., 363
Fairclough, Norman, 118
Farragher, Leslie E., 352
Favazza, Armando R., 362–363
Feener, R. Michael, 559
Feinman, Gary M., 199
Ferguson, R. Brian, 352
Fernández-Armesto, Felipe, 553
Ferris, William, 581
Fetterman, David M., 137
Fife, Wayne, 129
Finnegan, Gregory A., 103
Foley, John Miles, 453
Folsom, Franklin, 228
Forde, Daryll, 502
Fowler, Nick, 546
Francoeur, Robert T., 384
Frawley, William J. 260
Freedman, Robert L., 277–278
Fretz, Rachel I., 149
Fridman, Eva Jane Neumann, 371
Fung, Karen, 507
Furby, Lita, 308
Fürer-Haimendorf, Elizabeth von, 519

Gacs, Ute, 60
Gaillard, Gérald, 55
Galens, Judy, 580
Gall, Timothy L., 477
Garry, Jane, 438
Gates, Henry Louis, Jr., 574
Geller, Pamela L., 401
George and Mary Foster Anthropology Library. *See* University of California at Berkeley
Gil, David, 253
Gill, Sam K., 442
Givens, David B., 857, 861
Glasser, Irene, 396–397
Glazier, Stephen D., 365
Gleach, Frederic W., 325
Glenn, James R., 113
Goddard, Victoria A., 544
Gonzalez, Mike, 621
Gordon, Raymond G., Jr., 263

Gravel, Pierre, 150
Graves, Carol, 229
Green, Michael D., 588
Green, Rayna, 590
Gregg, Robert, 579
Grenier, Louise, 167
Grills, Scott, 128
Grollig, Francis X., 104
Grossberg, Lawrence, 15
Gudeman, Stephen, 304
Gutmann, Matthew, 378

Haggerty, George, 385
Hall, Lena E., 355
Hammersley, Martyn, 136
Hampton, William, 276
Handler, Richard, 326
Hansen, Karen Tranberg, 288
Harris, P.M.G., 394
Harrison, Jon, 872
Harvard University
    Library of the Peabody Museum of Archaeology and Ethnology (now the Tozzer Library), 114
    Tozzer Library, 107
Haspelmath, Martin, 253
Hatcher, Evelyn Payne, 285
Haugerud, Angelique, 388
Heath, Dwight B., 412
Heider, Karl G., 190
Heizer, Robert F., 229
Henrich, Joe, 318
Herdt, Gilbert, 377
Hermer, Carol, 190
Herron, Nancy L., 2, 25
Hester, Thomas R., 229
Hickey, Gerald C., 525
Hill, Carole E., 339, 862
Hirst, K. Kris, 232
Hobbs, Dick, 148
Hockings, Paul, 185
Hodge, Frederick W., 594
Holloway, Ralph L., 245
Hollowell-Zimmer, Julie, 153
Homiak, John P., 188
Howarth, Glennys, 414
Hoxie, Frederick E., 591
Hultkrantz, Ake, 447
Huntington Free Library, 606
Husmann, Rolf, 187

Inda, Jonathan Xavier, 389
Ingold, Cindy, 398
Ingold, Tim, 31
Inhaber, Herbert, 295
International Committee for Social Science Information and Documentation, 81
International Council of Museums, 179
Izard, Michel, 36

Jaarsma, Sjoerd R., 156
Jackson, M., 528
Jacobs, Sue-Ellen, 155
Jameson, Robert, 218
Janzing, Gereon, 41
Jarvis, Hugh W., 63, 90, 189
Jiménez Moreno, Wigberto, 629
Johns, Alan, 458
Johnson, Michael G., 596
Johnson, Thomas M., 332
Jones, Alison, 448
Jones, Steve, 239
Jorgensen, Peter F., 356
Joseph, Suad, 565

Kagan, Alfred, 493
Kanitar, Helen A., 520
Kastenbaum, Robert, 415
Katz, Solomon H., 275
Katzner, Kenneth, 264
Kearney, M., 390
Kedia, Satish, 165
Kelliher, Susan, 498
Kennedy, Raymond, 526
Kidd, Kenneth K. 248
Kimmel, Michael, 387
King, Victor T., 521
Kipfer, Barbara Ann, 222
Klass, Morton, 366
Klepinger, Linda L., 244
Kohn, George Childs, 337
Krech, Shepard, III, 604
Krikos, Linda A., 398
Kuper, Adam, 17, 51
Kuper, Jessica, 17
Kurti, Laszlo, 186
Kurtz, Donald V., 348

Laguerre, Michel, 631
Lassiter, Luke E., 126

Lawless, Robert, 299
Lawson, Edwin D., 417
Layton, Robert, 283
Leach, Maria, 445
Leaman, Oliver, 414
LeBar, Frank M., 524–525
LeCompte, Margaret D., 132
Lee, Richard B., 30
Lemming, David Adams, 449
Leonard, Thomas M., 636
Leopold, Robert, 111
Levinson, David, 38, 356, 473, 475–476, 513, 575
Lewellen, Ted C., 347
Lewin, Ellen, 400
Lewis-Beck, Michael S., 21
Lewis, Isabelle, 406
Li, Tze-chung, 1
Liao, Tim Futing, 21
Library of Congress, 489
    American Folklife Center, 460
    Peabody Library. *See* Harvard University
Lichtenberg, Kara Ellynn, 376
Little, Paul E., 313
Liu, Alan, 422
Loeb, Catherine, 398
Lopez, Ana M., 621
Lutins, Allen, 67
Lye, Keith, 500

Macintyre, Martha, 538
Madison, D. Soyini, 127
Magocsi, Paul Robert, 578
Malarney, Shaun, 508
Malaro, Marie C., 177
Malinowski, Sharon, 593
Malmkjćr, Kirsten, 261
Manley, John, 210
Mann, Thomas L., 46
Marstine, Janet, 178
Martin, M. Marlene, 600, 602
Martin, Robert, 239
Maschner, Herbert D. G., 223
Matsumoto, David, 360
Matthews, Holly F., 361
Maurer, Bill, 303
McDonald, David R., 85
McDonogh, Gary W., 322, 579
McFarlane, Alan, 50

McGlynn, Eileen, 612
McKinney, Carol Virginia, 140
McNell, Robert A., 611
McRose, Linda, 498
Measure DHS, 343
Mercatante, Anthony S., 443
Merry, Sally Engle, 344
Michie, Jonathan, 16
Middleton, John, 499
Mignon, Molly Raymond, 219
Mikaere, Buddy, 535
Miller, Wayne Charles, 585
Mills, Margaret Ann, 459
Milner, Richard, 241
Minahan, James, 472
Minnesota State University, Mankato, 52
Mintz, Sidney W., 268
Mirzoeff, Nicholas, 182
Missionary Research Library, 109
Mitten, Lisa, 609
Moerman, Dan, 272
Monger, George P., 329
Mood, Terry Ann, 457
Moore, Carmella C., 361
Moore, Henrietta L., 399
Moore, Sally Falk, 345
Moran, Emilio, 314
Morphy, Howard, 284
Morris, Brian, 367
Morris, Meaghan, 15
Morton, Leslie T., 330
Munro, David, 20
Murdock, George Peter, 484–485, 600–601
Murphy, Liam Donat, 320
Murphy, Timothy F., 375
Murray, Jocelyn, 497
Murray, Tim, 208, 220
Musgrave, John K., 525

Nagengast, Carole, 349
NAPA. *See* National Association for the Practice of Anthropology
National Association for the Practice of Anthropology (NAPA), 61, 740, 868
National Historical Publications and Records Commission, 843
National Library of Canada, 87
National Park Service, Archeology and Ethnography Program, 206

National Museum of Ethnology, Osaka, Japan, 483
Nelson, Bonnie, 112
Nettl, Bruno, 424
Newberry Library, 607
Newman, Jacqueline M., 279
Newman, Richard, 505
Ng, Franklin, 576
Nielsen, Finn Sivert, 65, 321
Noble, Sandra, 615
Nolan, Riall W, 159, 163, 856
Noonan, Raymond J., 384
Northey, Margot, 19
Núñez, Benjamín, 618
Nuttall, Mark, 592

O'Brien, Nancy P., 309
O'Leary, Timothy J., 554, 602, 632
O'Neil, Dennis, 338
O'Reilly, Karen, 133
Ogburn, Joyce L., 25, 28, 103
Oliver, Douglas L., 534
Oliver-Smith, Anthony, 416
Olson, James S., 503, 551
Oman, Mary, 362
Opiyo-Omolo, Beldina, 384
Organization for the European Minorities, 557
Orozco, Gail, 341
Overing, Joanna, 42
Oxford University, Economic and Social Research Council, 191

Pandey, Janak, 359
Parezo, Nancy J., 54, 123
Parker, Philip M., 468
Parra, Manuel German, 629
Partapuoli, Kari Helene, 65
Partridge, William, 165
Paterek, Josephine, 589
Pearson, Roger, 29
Peek, Philip M., 455
Pennbridge, Julia N., 395
Perdue, Theda, 588
Perecman, Ellen, 142
Peregrine, Peter N., 207, 221
Perkins, Morgan, 284
Peterson, Leighton C., 418
Phillips, Lynne, 269
Pilbeam, David, 239

Pink, Sarah, 183–184, 186
Pitt, David C., 125
Plattner, Stuart, 157, 306
Pole, Christopher J., 139
Pollard, A. Mark, 224
Ponzetti, Jr., James J., 328, 356
Poortinga, Ype H., 359
Post, Jennifer C, 423
Price, David H., 478
Price, T. Douglas, 199
Pritzker, Barry M., 597–598
Prucha, Francis Paul, 315
Pyatt, Sherman E., 458

Quinlan, Mary Kay, 122
Quinn, Naomi, 120

Rapport, Nigel, 42
Reed, A. W., 535
Regal, Brian, 234
Reynolds, Michael, 84
Ridinger, Robert B. Marks, 150
Ripley, William Zebina, 556
Rodgers, Bradley A., 174
Rogers, Susan Carol, 322
Rosaldo, Renato, 389
Ross, Norbert, 297
Roy, Christian, 372
Rudmin, Floyd W., 308
Rust, Ezra Gardner, 466
Ryan, Alan S., 859

Sabloff, Jeremy A., 624
Sadie, Stanley, 427
Salamone, Frank A., 369
Sandager, Elizabeth E., 505
Sargent, Carolyn Fishel, 332
Saunders, Nicholas J., 627
Scarre, Christopher, 154
Scarre, Geoffrey, 154
Schechner, Richard, 463
Schemberg, Annegret, 409
Schensul, Jean J., 132
Schlachter, Gail A., 873
Schulze, Marco, 837
Schuursma, Ann Briegleb, 429
Schwartz, Jeffrey H., 245, 273
Seager, Joni, 406
Sebeok, Thomas Albert, 259
Seligman, Edwin R. A., 12, 56

Selin, Helaine, 298, 301–302
Seymour-Smith, Charlotte, 33
Shapiro, Michael Steve, 172
Shaw, Ian, 218
Shaw, Linda L., 149
Sheets, Anna, 580
Sherrow, Victoria, 286
Sills, David L., 14, 59
Silverman, Eric K., 331
Silverman, Sydel, 123
Simon, Reeva S., 558
Singer, Peter, 342
Singh, K. S., 518
Skoggard, Ian, 392, 471
Skreslet, Paula Youngman, 492
Smart, Alan, 391
Smart, Josephine, 391
Smelzer, Neil, 13, 357
Smith, Carol, 613–614
Smith, J. Christina, 103
Smith, Margo L., 101
Smith, Paul, 451
Smith, Raymond A., 335
Smithsonian Institution, 80, 192, 432
   Department of Anthropology, 108
Sommer, Barbara W., 122
Spencer, Frank, 243, 246, 323
Spencer, Jonathan, 39
Standish, Peter, 620
Stansfield, Geoffrey, 171
Stazny, Phillip, 258
Steinfirst, Susan, 433
Steins, Janet, 841
Stephens, Thomas M., 619
Stevenson, Joan C., 240
Steward, Julian H., 625
Stewart, Alex, 131
Stockett, Miranda K., 401
Strange, Heather, 410
Strijp, Ruud, 567
Stull, Donald D., 130
Sturtevant, William C., 595
Sullivan, Lynne P., 175
Sweet, Louise Elizabeth, 554, 564
Szwed, John F., 456

Tattersall, Ian, 242, 245
Tax, Sol, 104
Taylor, Clyde Romer Hughes, 537, 539
Taylor, Richard P., 413

Taylor, Tim, 209
Teitelbaum, Michele, 410
Telban, Borut, 151
Tenenbaum, Barbara A., 622
Texas A&M University, Department of Anthropology, 97, 102
Thawley, John, 536
Theodoratus, Robert J., 555
Thernstrom, Stephan, 582
Thomas, Helen, 461
Thomas, R. Murray, 22
Thompson, Stith, 439, 441
Tilley, Chris, 287
Tindale, Norman B., 532
Titus, Elizabeth McKenney, 342
Tomei Torres, Francisco Alberto, 875
Tozzer Library. *See* Harvard University
Tseng, Wen-Shing, 358
Turner, Harold W., 373
Turner, Jane, 292
Tyrrell, John, 427

University of California at Berkeley, George and Mary Foster Anthropology Library, 45
University of Texas at Austin, 638
University of Wisconsin, 514
Urciuoli, Bonnie, 266

Valk, Barbara G., 611
Van Couvering, John A., 242
Van der Pas, H.T., 307
Van Keuren, David K., 115
Van Willigen, John, 158, 164–165, 168
Vermeulen, Han F., 319
Visweswaran, Kamala, 402
Vitelli, Karen D., 153
Vogel, Jean, 501
Vogel, Joseph O., 501

Vogt, W. Paul, 18

Wallace, Anthony, 316
Wallace, Tim, 160
Wallen, Denise, 870
Walter, Mariko Namba, 371
Wauchope, Robert, 623
Weber, R. David, 873
Weeks, John M., 27, 615, 637
Weeks, Richard V., 566
Weinberger, Steven H., 267
Welch, Thomas L., 633
Westerman, R.C., 26
White, Eric J., 64
White, Philip M., 586
Wilder, William D., 521
Wilson, John D., 576
Wilson, Samuel M., 418
Wilson, Thomas M., 322
Winick, Charles, 34
Winters, Christopher, 57
Winthrop, Robert H., 35
Wintle, Pamela, 188
Wodehouse, L., 282
Wolfe, Linda D., 247
Wolff, Stefan, 552
Wong, Cindy H., 579
Woodhead, Peter, 171, 198
Worell, Judith, 408
Wright, Richard, 148

Yamashita, Shinji, 511
Yankah, Kwesi, 455
Yon, Daniel A, 310
Young, Robin V., 580

Zell, Hans M., 491
Zimmerman, Bonnie, 385
Zimmerman, Larry J., 153

TITLE INDEX

Numbers refer to entry numbers.
Includes publishers and organizations listed in Chapter 8.

AAA Ethics Homepage, 152
AAA Guide. See *Guide: A Guide to Departments, A Directory of Members*
AAA Style Guide, 44
AATA Online: Abstracts of International Conservation Literature, 200
Aboriginal Tribes of Australia, 532
Abstracts in Anthropology, 73
Abstracts in German Anthropology, 74
Abstracts of the Annual Meeting, 88
Africa Bibliography, 494
Africa: Journal of the International African Institute/Revue de l'Institute Africain International, 639
Africa South of the Sahara: Selected Internet Resources, 507
African and Asian Studies, 640
African Ethnonyms: Index to Art-Producing Peoples of Africa, 498
African Folklore: An Encyclopedia, 455
African Studies Association, 807
African Studies Companion: A Resource Guide & Directory, 491
Africana: The Encyclopedia of the African and African American Experience, 574
Afro-American Folk Culture: An Annotated Bibliography of Materials from North, Central and South America and the West Indies, 456
Aging and Cultural Diversity: New Directions and Annotated Bibliography, 410
Agricola, 270
AIDS and Anthropology Bibliography, 340
The AIDS Bibliography: Studies in Anthropology and Related Fields, 341
"Alcohol: Anthropological/ Archaeological Perspectives," 411

Alcohol Use and World Cultures: A Comprehensive Bibliography of Anthropological Sources, 412
Aldine Transaction, 698
ALFRED: The ALlele FREquency Database, 248
AltaMira Press, 699
America, History and Life, 570
America's Ancient Treasures: A Guide to Archaeological Sites and Museums in the United States and Canada, 228
American Anthropological Association, 745
American Anthropologist, 641
American Bibliography of Slavic and East European Studies, 547
American Ethnological Society, 746
American Ethnologist, 642
American Folklife Center, 454
American Folklore Society, 808
American Immigrant Cultures: Builders of a Nation, 575
American Indian Studies: A Bibliographic Guide, 586
American Museum of Natural History Library, 846
American Philosophical Society Library, 847
American Regional Folklore: A Sourcebook and Research Guide, 457
American Society for Ethnohistory, 809
Analyzing Discourse: Textual Analysis for Social Research, 118
Annual Review of Anthropology, 71, 643
  Articles in, 268–269, 288, 303, 310, 313, 331, 344, 346, 349, 378, 390–391, 402, 411, 416, 418, 546, 561, 613–614
ANSS Reviews, 82
Anthro.Net, 64
AnthroBase, 65
AnthroGlobe Bibliographies, 100

261

Anthropologica, 644
Anthropological Abstracts, 74
Anthropological Ancestors, 50
Anthropological and Cross-Cultural Themes in Mental Health: An Annotated Bibliography, 1925–1974, 362
Anthropological Bibliographies: A Selected Guide, 101
Anthropological Bibliography of South Asia, 519–520
Anthropological Fieldwork: An Annotated Bibliography, 150
Anthropological Glossary, 29
Anthropological Index, 75
Anthropological Index to Current Periodicals in the British Museum Library. See *Anthropological Index*
Anthropological Linguistics, 645
Anthropological Literature, 76
Anthropological Quarterly, 646
"Anthropological Research on Hazards and Disasters," 416
Anthropological Resources: A Guide to Archival, Library and Museum Collections, 834, 840
Anthropologists and Anthropology: The Modern British School, 1922–1972, 51
Anthropology, 25
Anthropology: A Student's Guide to Theory and Method, 119
Anthropology and Archeology of Eurasia, 647
"Anthropology and Circumcision," 331
Anthropology and Education Quarterly, 648
Anthropology and Humanism, 649
"Anthropology and International Law," 344
Anthropology and Sociology Section (ANSS) of the Association of College and Research Libraries (ACRL), 810
Anthropology and the Environment, 747
Anthropology Bibliographies, 102
Anthropology Biography Web, 52
Anthropology Field Schools, 863

Anthropology in Practice: Building a Career outside the Academy, 163, 856
Anthropology in the News, 97
Anthropology in Use: A Bibliographic Chronology of the Development of Applied Anthropology, 168
Anthropology in Use: A Source Book of Anthropological Practice, 164
"Anthropology Libraries," 841
Anthropology Library at the British Museum's Centre for Anthropology, 848
Anthropology News, 98
The Anthropology of Art, 283
The Anthropology of Art: A Reader, 284
Anthropology of Asia (series), 508
The Anthropology of Development and Globalization: From Classical Political Economy to Contemporary Neoliberalism, 388
The Anthropology of Europe: Identity and Boundaries in Conflict, 544
Anthropology of Food, 281
"The Anthropology of Food and Eating," 268
Anthropology of Globalization: A Reader, 389
"The Anthropology of Money," 303
"The Anthropology of Online Communities," 418
Anthropology of Religion: A Handbook, 365
The Anthropology of War: A Bibliography, 352
Anthropology Plus, 77
Anthropology Resources on the Internet, 66
Anthropology Resources on the Internet: WWW Virtual Library of Archaeology and Prehistory, 67
Anthropology Review Database, 90, 189
Anthropology Today, 650
Anthropos: Révue Internationale d'Ethnologie et de Linguistique, 651
AnthroSource, 78, 91
Appetites and Identities: An Introduction to the Social Anthropology of Western Europe, 545

Applied Anthropology: An Introduction, 158
Applied Anthropology Documentation Project, 169
Applied Anthropology: Domains of Application, 165
Archaeological Fieldwork Opportunities Bulletin, 864
Archaeological Method and Theory: An Encyclopedia, 214
Archaeological Objects Thesaurus, 215
The Archaeologist's Manual for Conservation: A Guide to Non-toxic, Minimal Intervention Artifact Stabilization, 174
Archaeologist's Toolkit, 175
Archaeology: A Bibliographical Guide to the Basic Literature, 229
Archaeology at the Millennium: A Sourcebook, 199
Archaeologyfieldwork.com, 865
Archaeopress, 700
Archetypes and Motifs in Folklore and Literature: A Handbook, 438
Archive of Folk Culture, 430
Archives of Traditional Music, 431
ArchivesUSA, 849
ArchNet, 231
Arctic Anthropology, 652
Art as Culture: An Introduction to the Anthropology of Art, 285
Art Index, 289
Artic Circle, 608
Arts and Humanities Citation Index, 420
ARTstor, 193
Asian American Encyclopedia, 576
Asian Anthropology, 509
Association for Africanist Anthropology, 811
Association for Asian Studies, 812
Association for Feminist Anthropology, 748
Association for Political and Legal Anthropology, 749
Association for the Study of Play, 813
Association of Black Anthropologists, 750
Association of Latino and Latina Anthropologists, 751

Association of Senior Anthropologists, 752
Association of Social Anthropologists of the UK and Commonwealth, 814
Atlas of Archaeology, 209
The Atlas of Past Worlds: A Comparative Chronology of Human History 2000BC–AD 1500, 210
The Atlas of World Archaeology, 211
Atlas of World Cultures: A Geographical Guide to Ethnographic Literature, 478
Australasia and South Pacific Islands Bibliography, 536
Australian Institute of Aboriginal and Torres Strait Islander Studies, 543, 815
Australian Institute of Aboriginal and Torres Strait Islander Studies. Annual Bibliography, 529
Australian Journal of Anthropology, 653
Author and Subject Catalogues of the Tozzer Library, 107

A Basic Guide to Cross-Cultural Research Using the HRAF Collections, 479
Berg Publishers, 701
Berghahn Books, 702
Bernice Pauahi Bishop Museum Library, 540
Bibliografía de Arqueología y Etnografía: Mesoamérica y Norte de México, 1514–1960, 628
Bibliografía Indigenista de México y Centroamérica (1850–1950), 629
Bibliografía Mesoamericana, 615
Bibliographic Guide to Anthropology and Archaeology. See *G.K. Hall Bibliographic Guide to Anthropology and Archaeology*
Bibliographic Guide to Latin American Studies, 634
Bibliographie Internationale d'Anthropologie. See *International Bibliography of Anthropology*
Bibliographies (International Council of Museums website), 179

Bibliography of Africana Periodical Literature, 495
Bibliography of Anthropology of Quantification, 299
Bibliography of Asian Studies, 512
A Bibliography of Ethnographic Films, 187
Bibliography of Fieldwork, Research Methods and Ethnography in Sociocultural Anthropology, 151
A Bibliography of Foodways, Zooarchaeology, and Faunal Identification on Historical Sites, 276
Bibliography of Indonesian Peoples and Cultures, 526
Bibliography of Native North Americans, 600
Bibliography of New Religious Movements in Primal Societies, 373
Bibliography of Publications on the New Zealand Maori and the Moriori of the Chatham Islands, 537
Bibliography of the History of Art, 290
Bibliography of the Peoples and Cultures of Mainland Southeast Asia, 527
Biographical Dictionary of Social and Cultural Anthropology, 53
Biographical Directory of Anthropologists Born Before 1920, 46
Biography and Genealogy Master Index, 47
Biography Reference Bank, 48
Biography Resource Center, 49
Biological Abstracts, 236
Blackwell Companions to Anthropology, 250
Blackwell Publishing, 703
The Body, Dance, and Cultural Theory, 461
Book Review Digest, 92
Book Review Index, 93
Brill, 704
Bulletin Signalétique. See *FRANCIS*
Bulletin/Smithsonian Institution, Bureau of American Ethnology, 80
Bureau of American Ethnology Bulletin, 625

CAB Abstracts, 271
The Cambridge Encyclopedia of Human Evolution, 239
The Cambridge Encyclopedia of Hunters and Gatherers, 30
The Cambridge Encyclopedia of Language, 254
Cambridge History of the Native Peoples of the Americas, 577
Cambridge University Press, 705
"Careers in Anthropology," 866
A Catalog of the C.F. and F.M. Voegelin Archives of the Languages of the World, 266
A Catalog to Manuscripts at the National Anthropological Archives, 108
Catalogos de la Biblioteca Nacional de Antropología e Historia, 635
Catalogue of the Arctic Institute of North America, 605
Catalogue of the Library of the Peabody Museum of Archaeology and Ethnology. See *Author and Subject Catalogues of the Tozzer Library*
Categorical Impulse: Essays on the Anthropology of Classifying Behaviour, 296
CEAL: Council on East Asian Libraries, 515
"Central America since 1979, Part I," 613
"Central America since 1979, Part II," 614
The Central Middle East: A Handbook of Anthropology and Published Research on the Nile Valley, the Arab Levant, Southern Mesopotamia, the Arabian Peninsula, and Israel, 564
Central States Anthropological Society, 753
The Chicago Guide to Collaborative Ethnography, 126
Chicano Database, 571
Chinese Sociology and Anthropology, 654
Chronicle of Higher Education—"Chronicle Careers: Anthropology," 867

CIAO: Columbia International Affairs Online, 350
Circum-Mediterranean Peasantry: Introductory Bibliographies, 554
City and Society, 655
Clinician's Guide to Cultural Psychiatry, 358
Clowns & Tricksters: An Encyclopedia of Tradition and Culture, 442
Collins Dictionary of Archaeology. See *Penguin Archaeology Guide*
The Columbia Guide to American Indians of the Northeast, 587
The Columbia Guide to American Indians of the Southeast, 588
Combined Retrospective Index to Book Reviews in Scholarly Journals, 1886–1974, 94
Commission on Aging and the Aged, 780
Commission on Anthropology in Policy and Practice, 781
Commission on Anthropology, Peace and Human Rights, 782
Commission on Bioethics, 783
Commission on Cultural Dimensions of Global Change, 784
Commission on Documentation, 785
Commission on Ethnic Relations, 786
Commission on Folk Law and Legal Pluralism, 787
Commission on Food and Food Problems, 788
Commission on Human Ecology, 789
Commission on Human Rights, 790
Commission on Indigenous Knowledge and Sustainable Development, 791
Commission on Linguistic Anthropology, 792
Commission on Medical Anthropology and Epidemiology, 793
Commission on Migration, 794
Commission on Museums and Cultural Heritage, 795
Commission on Nomadic Peoples, 796
Commission on Primatology, 797
Commission on the Anthropology of AIDS, 798
Commission on the Anthropology of Children, Youth and Childhood, 799
Commission on the Anthropology of Mathematics, 800
Commission on the Anthropology of Tourism, 801
Commission on the Anthropology of Women, 802
Commission on Theoretical Anthropology, 803
Commission on Urban Anthropology, 804
Commission on Urgent Anthropological Research, 805
Commission on Visual Anthropology, 806
Companion Encyclopedia of Anthropology: Humanity, Culture and Social Life, 31
Companion Encyclopedia of Archaeology, 216
A Companion to Linguistic Anthropology, 250
Compendium of the World's Languages, 262
The Complete Caribbeana, 1900–1975: A Bibliographic Guide to the Scholarly Literature, 630
Complete Haitiana, 631
A Comprehensive Bibliography for the Study of American Minorities, 585
The Concise Oxford Dictionary of Archaeology, 217
Contemporary Legend: A Folklore Bibliography, 451
Contemporary Women's Issues, 403
The Continuum Complete International Encyclopedia of Sexuality, 384
CoPAR. See Council for the Preservation of Anthropological Records
Council for Museum Anthropology, 180, 754, 835
Council for the Preservation of Anthropological Records (CoPAR), 839
Council on Anthropology and Education, 755

Countries and their Cultures, 467
Critical Ethnography: Method, Ethics, and Performance, 127
Critique of Anthropology, 656
Cross-Cultural Research Methods, 480
Cross-Cultural Statistical Encyclopedia of the World, 468
Cultural Anthropology, 657
Cultural Anthropology of the Middle East: A Bibliography, 567
Cultural Atlas of Africa, 497
Cultural Critique, 658
The Cultural Feast: An Introduction to Food and Society, 273
Cultural Survival, 816
Cultural Survival Quarterly, 659
Culture and Agriculture Group, 756
Culture and Customs (series), 469
Culture & Cognition: Implications for Theory and Method, 297
Culture, Medicine and Psychiatry, 660
Culture, Mind, and Society (series), 364
Curating Archaeological Collections: From the Field to the Repository, 175
Current Anthropology, 661

Dance in the Field: Theory, Methods, and Issues in Dance Ethnography, 462
Daughters of the Desert: Women Anthropologists and the Native American Southwest, 1880–1980, 54
Death and the Afterlife: A Cultural Encyclopedia, 413
Demographic and Health Surveys, 343
Development Anthropology: Encounters in the Real World, 159
Dialectical Anthropology, 662
Dictionary and Catalog of African American Folklife of the South, 458
Dictionary Catalog of the American Indian Collection, 606–607
Dictionary Catalog of the Missionary Research Library, New York, 109

Dictionary of Afro-Latin American Civilization, 618
Dictionary of Anthropology, 32–34
A Dictionary of Archaeology, 218
Dictionary of Art, 292
Dictionary of Concepts in Archaeology, 219
Dictionary of Concepts in Cultural Anthropology, 35
Dictionary of Concepts in Physical Anthropology, 240
Dictionary of Latin American Racial and Ethnic Terminology, 619
A Dictionary of Linguistics & Phonetics, 255
Dictionary of Multicultural Psychology: Issues, Terms, and Concepts, 355
Dictionary of Race, Ethnicity and Culture, 470
Dictionary of Statistics and Methodology: A Nontechnical Guide for the Social Sciences, 18
Dictionary of the Social Sciences, 11
Dictionary of Twentieth Century Culture: Hispanic Culture of Mexico, Central America, and the Caribbean, 620
Dictionary of Worldwide Gestures, 256
Dictionnaire de l'Ethnologie et de l'Anthropologie, 36
Dictionnaire des Ethnologues et des Anthropologues, 55
Directory of Anthropological Resources in New York City Libraries, 842
Directory of Archives and Manuscript Repositories in the United States, 843
Directory of Practicing Anthropologists, 61
Directory of Special Libraries and Information Centers, 844
Dissertation Abstracts International. See *Proquest Dissertations and Theses*
Doing Ethnographic Research: Fieldwork Settings, 128
Doing Fieldwork: Ethnographic Methods for Research in Developing Countries and Beyond, 129
Doing Team Ethnography: Warnings and Advice, 130

Doing Visual Ethnography: Images, Media, and Representation in Research, 183
Duke University Press, 706

Eastern Anthropologist, 663
Ecce Homo: An Annotated Bibliographic History of Physical Anthropology, 246, 323
Economic Anthropology, 304, 306
Economic Anthropology 1940–1972: An Annotated Bibliography, 307
Edible Medicines: An Ethnopharmacology of Food, 274
Education: A Guide to Reference and Information Sources, 309
Education Index, 311
Educational Resources Information Center. See ERIC
eHRAF Collection of Archaeology, 201
eHRAF Collection of Ethnography, 481
Encyclopaedia of the History of Science, Technology, and Medicine in Non-Western Cultures, 298
Encyclopaedia of the Social Sciences, 12, 56
Encyclopaedia of the South-East Asian Ethnography: Communities and Tribes, 523
Encyclopedia of Africa South of the Sahara, 499
Encyclopedia of African Peoples, 500
Encyclopedia of AIDS: A Social, Political, Cultural, and Scientific Record of the HIV Epidemic, 335
Encyclopedia of American Indian Costume, 589
Encyclopedia of Anthropology, 37
Encyclopedia of Archaeology: History and Discoveries, 220
Encyclopedia of Archaeology: The Great Archaeologists, 208
Encyclopedia of Associations, 739
Encyclopedia of Canada's Peoples, 578
Encyclopedia of Contemporary American Culture, 579
Encyclopedia of Contemporary Latin American and Caribbean Cultures, 621
Encyclopedia of Cultural Anthropology, 38
Encyclopedia of Death and Dying, 414
Encyclopedia of Diasporas: Immigrant and Refugee Cultures around the World, 392, 471
The Encyclopedia of Evolution: Humanity's Search for Its Origins, 241
Encyclopedia of Food and Culture, 275
Encyclopedia of Hair: A Cultural History, 286
Encyclopedia of Human Emotions, 356
Encyclopedia of Human Evolution and Prehistory, 242
The Encyclopedia of Language and Linguistics, 257
Encyclopedia of Latin American History and Culture, 622
Encyclopedia of Lesbian and Gay Histories and Cultures, 385
Encyclopedia of Library and Information Science, 841
Encyclopedia of Linguistics, 258
Encyclopedia of Medical Anthropology: Health and Illness in the World's Cultures, 336
Encyclopedia of Modern Asia, 513
Encyclopedia of Native North America, 590
Encyclopedia of North American Indians, 591
Encyclopedia of Plague and Pestilence: From Ancient Times to the Present, 337
Encyclopedia of Precolonial Africa: Archaeology, History, Languages, Cultures, and Environments, 501
Encyclopedia of Prehistory, 221
Encyclopedia of Religious Rites, Rituals, and Festivals, 369
Encyclopedia of Sex and Gender: Men and Women in the World's Cultures, 386, 407
Encyclopedia of Social and Cultural Anthropology, 39
Encyclopedia of the Arctic, 592
Encyclopedia of the Stateless Nations: Ethnic and National Groups around the World, 472

Encyclopedia of Urban Cultures: Cities and Cultures around the World, 393
Encyclopedia of Women and Gender: Sex Similarities and Differences and the Impact of Society on Gender, 408
Encyclopedia of Women and Islamic Cultures, 565
Encyclopedia of World Cultures, 473
Encyclopedic Dictionary of Archaeology, 222
Encyclopedic Dictionary of Semiotics, 259
"Environments and Environmentalisms in Anthropological Research: Facing a New Millennium," 313
ERIC (Educational Resources Information Center), 312
Ethical Issues in Archaeology, 153
The Ethics of Archaeology: Philosophical Perspectives on Archaeological Practice, 154
Ethnic Diversity within Nations (series), 474
Ethnic Groups of Insular Southeast Asia, 524
Ethnic Groups of Mainland Southeast Asia, 525
Ethnic Groups Worldwide: A Ready Reference Handbook, 475
Ethnic NewsWatch, 572
Ethnic Relations: A Cross-Cultural Encyclopedia, 476
Ethnoart: Africa, Oceania, and the Americas: A Bibliography of Theses and Dissertations, 294
Ethnoarts Index, 291
The Ethnographer's Method, 131
Ethnographer's Toolkit, 132
Ethnographic Bibliography of North America, 601
Ethnographic Bibliography of North America, Supplement, 602
Ethnographic Bibliography of South America, 632
Ethnographic Methods, 133
Ethnographic Research: A Guide to General Conduct, 134
Ethnographic Resources Related to Folklore, Anthropology, Ethnomusicology, and the Humanities, 460
Ethnographic Survey of Africa (series), 502
Ethnographic Thesaurus (ET), 173
Ethnography, 135
Ethnography: Principles in Practice, 136
Ethnography Step By Step, 137
Ethnohistorical Dictionary of the Russian and Soviet Empires, 551
Ethnohistory, 664
The Ethnohistory Series, 316
Ethnologue: Languages of the World, 263
Ethnology, 665
Ethnomusicology, 428, 666
Ethnomusicology: A Guide to Research, 423
Ethnomusicology Research: A Select Annotated Bibliography, 429
Ethnopolitical Encyclopaedia of Europe, 552
Ethnos, 667
Ethos, 668
Eurominority: Portal of European Stateless Nations and Minorities, 557
Europe: A Selected Ethnographic Bibliography, 555
European Anthropologies: A Guide to the Profession, 322
"Europeanization," 546
Evolutionism in Cultural Anthropology: A Critical History, 317
Excerpta Indonesica, 522

Facts on File Encyclopedia of World Mythology and Legend, 443
Family and Society Studies Worldwide: An International Perspective on the Family & Society, 327
Federal Job Opportunities for Anthropologists, 857
Feminism and Anthropology, 399
Feminist Anthropology: A Reader, 400
Feminist Anthropology: Past, Present, and Future, 401
Field Museum of Natural History, 850
Field Primatology: A Guide to Research, 247

Field Projects in Anthropology: A Student Handbook, 138
Fieldwork, 139
Fieldwork and Footnotes: Studies in the History of European Anthropology, 319
Fieldwork in the Library: A Guide to Research in Anthropology and Related Area Studies, 26
Films for Anthropological Teaching, 190
Financial Aid for Research and Creative Activities Abroad, 869
Finding Culture in Talk: A Collection of Methods, 120
Folk and Fairy Tales: A Handbook, 444
Folk Classification: A Topically Arranged Bibliography of Contemporary and Background References through 1971, 300
Folklife Sourcebook: A Directory of Folklife Resources in the United States, 450
Folklore and Folklife: A Guide to English-Language Reference Sources, 433
"Food and Globalization," 269
FRANCIS, 3, 202, 548
Fundamentals of Forensic Anthropology, 244
Funding for Anthropological Research, 870
FundSource: A Search Tool for Research Funding in the Behavioral and Social Sciences, 871
Funk and Wagnalls Standard Dictionary of Folklore, Mythology, and Legend, 445
The Future of Visual Anthropology: Engaging the Senses, 184

G.K. Hall Bibliographic Guide to Anthropology and Archaeology, 110
Gale Encyclopedia of Multicultural America, 580
Gale Encyclopedia of Native American Tribes, 593
Gender Studies Database, 379
Gender Watch, 380
General Anthropology Division, 757

Geobase, 203
GeoRef, 204
George and Mary Foster Anthropology Library, 851
GLBT Life, 381
Global Gateway: World Culture & Resources, 489
Globe Trotting in Sandals: A Field Guide to Cultural Research, 140
Göttinger Kulturwissenschaftliche Schriften, 187
Grants for Individuals: Anthropology, 872
Great Jobs for Anthropology Majors, 858
Greenwood Encyclopedia of American Regional Cultures, 581
Greenwood Encyclopedia of World Folklore and Folklife, 446
Greenwood Press, 707
Grove Music Online, 427
Guide: A Guide to Departments, A Directory of Members, 62, 83, 738, 836
Guide to African American and African Primary Sources at Harvard University, 505
Guide to Anthropological Fieldnotes and Manuscripts in Archival Repositories, 111
A Guide to Careers in Physical Anthropology, 859
A Guide to Central American Collections in the United States, 636
A Guide to Published Library Catalogs, 112
A Guide to Qualitative Field Research, 141
Guide to the Collections of the Human Studies Film Archives, 188
Guide to the National Anthropological Archives, Smithsonian Institution, 113
A Guide to Theses and Dissertations: An International Bibliography of Bibliographies, 84

Haddon: The Online Catalogue of Ethnographic Footage 1895–1945, 191

Handbook for Research in American History: A Guide to Bibliographies and Other Reference Works, 315
A Handbook for Social Science Field Research: Essays & Bibliographic Sources on Research Design and Methods, 142
Handbook of American Indians North of Mexico, 594
Handbook of Archaeological Methods, 223
Handbook of Archaeological Sciences, 224
Handbook of Cross-Cultural Psychology, 359
The Handbook of Culture & Psychology, 360
A Handbook of Economic Anthropology, 305
Handbook of Ethnography, 143
Handbook of Latin American Studies, 616
Handbook of Material Culture, 287
Handbook of Methods in Cultural Anthropology, 121
Handbook of Middle American Indians, 623
Handbook of Middle American Indians. Supplement, 624
Handbook of North American Indians, 595
Handbook of South American Indians, 625
Handbook of World Mythology (series), 452
Handbook on Ethical Issues in Anthropology, 155
Handle with Care: Ownership and Control of Ethnographic Records, 156
HAPI. See *Hispanic American Periodical Index*
Harvard Encyclopedia of American Ethnic Groups, 582
Harvard University Press, 708. See also Tozzer Library
Hawai'i Pacific Journal Index, 530
"Highlights and Overview of the History of Educational Ethnography," 310
Hispanic American Periodical Index (HAPI), 617
Historical Abstracts, 205, 549
Histories of Anthropology Annual, 325
"Histories of Feminist Ethnography," 402
History and Anthropology, 669
A History of Anthropological Theory, 320
A History of Anthropology, 321, 326
History of Anthropology Bibliography, 324
The History of Human Populations, Volume II: Migration, Urbanization, and Structural Change, 394
The History of Humanity, 40
History of Physical Anthropology: An Encyclopedia, 243
Home Cultures, 670
L'Homme: Revue Française d'Anthropologie, 671
HRAF. See *Human Relations Area Files*. See also *eHRAF Collection of Ethnography*
HRAF Source Bibliography: Cumulative, 482
Human Adaptability: An Introduction to Ecological Anthropology, 314
Human Ecology, 672
Human Evolution: A Guide to the Debates, 234
Human Food Uses: A Cross-Cultural, Comprehensive Annotated Bibliography, 277
Human Food Uses: Supplement, 278
The Human Fossil Record, 245
Human Organization, 673
Human Relations Area Files, 481, 817
Human Relations Area Files (as a publisher), 709
Human Subjects Protections and Anthropology, 157
Human Studies Film Archives. See National Anthropological Archives
The Humanities: A Selective Guide to Information Sources, 419
Humanities Index, 421

ICSSR Journal of Abstracts and Reviews: Sociology and Social Anthropology, 516
Identities: Global Studies in Culture and Power, 674
In the Field: An Introduction to Field Research, 144
Index Islamicus, 562
Index Medicus. See *MEDLINE*
Index to Subject Headings, 114
Index to the Human Relations Area Files, 483
Indiana University Press, 710
The Indians of South America: A Bibliography, 633
Indigenous Architecture Worldwide: A Guide to Information Sources, 282
Indigenous Peoples of Asia, 510
The Indigenous World, 675
Industrial Anthropology: A Selected Annotated Bibliography, 395
Information Sources in the Medical Sciences, 330
Institute for Development Anthropology, 818
International African Institute, 819
International Association for Cross-Cultural Psychology, 820
International Bibliography of Anthropology = Bibliographie Internationale d'Anthropologie, 79
International Bibliography of the Social Sciences (IBSS), 4, 79
International Congress of Americanists, 821
International Development Abstracts, 5
International Dictionary of Anthropologists, 57
International Dictionary of Regional European Ethnology and Folklore, 447
International Directory of African Studies Research, 504
International Directory of Anthropologists, 58
International Encyclopedia of Dance, 465
International Encyclopedia of Linguistics, 260

International Encyclopedia of Marriage and Family, 328
International Encyclopedia of the Social and Behavioral Sciences, 13, 357
International Encyclopedia of the Social Sciences, 14, 59
International Index to Black Periodicals, 573
International Journal of American Linguistics, 676
International Union of Anthropological and Ethnological Sciences (IUAES), 779
International Women's Anthropology Conference, 822
Internationale Bibliographie der Zeitschriftenliteratur, 550
Internationale Volkskundliche Bibliographie. International Folklore Bibliography. Bibliographie Internationale des Arts et Traditions Populaires., 435
Introduction to Library Research in Anthropology, 27
Introduction to Museum Work, 176, 860
Intute: Anthropology, 68
Intute: Social Sciences, 24
Islam in World Cultures: Comparative Perspectives, 559

The John Wesley Powell Library of Anthropology at the Smithsonian Institution, 852
Journal de la Société des Américanistes, 677
Journal of American Folklore, 678
Journal of Anthropological Research, 679
Journal of Asian Studies, 680
Journal of Latin American Anthropology, 681
Journal of Linguistic Anthropology, 682
Journal of Material Culture, 683
Journal of Ritual Studies, 684
The Journal of the Royal Anthropological Institute, 685
"Journals of the Century in Anthropology and Archaeology," 103

JPS: The Journal of the Polynesian Society, 686

Keyguide to Information Sources in Archaeology, 198
Keyguide to Information Sources in Museum Studies, 171
The Kula: A Bibliography, 538

Language and Language Behavior Abstracts. See *Linguistics and Language Behavior Abstracts*
Language in Society, 687
The Languages of the World, 264
LANIC: Latin American Network and Information Center, 638
Larousse Dictionary of World Folklore, 448
Latin America and the Caribbean: A Critical Guide to Research Sources, 610
Latin American Studies: A Basic Guide to Sources, 611
Latin American Studies Association, 823
Law and Anthropology: A Reader, 345
Learning a Field Language, 145
Legal Primer on Managing Museum Collections, 177
Libraries of Asia Pacific Directory, 541
Libraries with Major Middle East Collections, 568
Library-Anthropology Resource Group, 824
Linguistics: A Guide to the Reference Literature, 249
Linguistics and Language Behavior Abstracts (LLBA), 251
Linguistics Encyclopedia, 261
List of Publications of the Bureau of American Ethnology, With Index to Authors and Titles, 80
"The Local and the Global: The Anthropology of Globalization and Transnationalism," 390
Local Practitioner Organizations (LPOs), 740
London Bibliography of the Social Sciences, 6

Macmillan Encyclopedia of Death and Dying, 415
Macmillan Encyclopedia of Native American Tribes, 596
"Madening States," 346
The Making of Anthropology in East and Southeast Asia, 511
Making Sense: A Student's Guide to Research and Writing: Social Sciences, 19
Manuals in Archaeological Method, Theory, and Technique, 225
Marriage Customs of the World: From Henna to Honeymoons, 329
Masks from Antiquity to the Modern Era: An Annotated Bibliography, 295
Masters' Theses in Anthropology: A Bibliography of Theses from United States Colleges and Universities, 85
Medical Anthropology, 688
Medical Anthropology: Contemporary Theory and Method, 332
Medical Anthropology Glossary, 338
Medical Anthropology Quarterly, 689
MEDLINE, 333
Mehrsprachiges Wörterbuch für die Ethnologie: Deutsch, Englisch, Französisch, Spanisch, Portugiesisch, Russisch, Esperanto, 41
Melting Pot: An Annotated Bibliography and Guide to Food and Nutrition Information for Ethnic Groups in America, 279
Melville J. Herskovits Library of African Studies, 506
Men and Masculinities: A Social, Cultural, and Historical Encyclopedia, 387
Men's Studies Database, 382
Middle American Anthropology, 612
Middle American Indians: A Guide to the Manuscript Collection at Tozzer Library, Harvard University, 637
Middle East: Abstracts and Index, 563
The Middle East and Central Asia: An Anthropological Approach, 560

Middle East Section, 758
Middle East Studies Association, 825
Middle East Studies Internet Resources, 569
MLA International Bibliography, 252, 436
The Modern Anthropology of South-East Asia: An Introduction, 521
The Modern Middle East: A Guide to Research Tools in the Social Sciences, 558
Money for Graduate Students in the Social & Behavioral Sciences, 873
Motherhood and Reproduction: An International Bibliography, 409
Motif-Index of Folk-Literature: A Classification of Narrative Elements in Folktales, Ballads, Myths, Fables, Mediaeval Romances, Exempla, Fabliaux, Jest-Books and Local Legends, 439
Mouton De Gruyter, 711
Multilingual Dictionary for Ethnology: German, English, French, Spanish, Portuguese, Russian, Esperanto, 41
The Museum: A Reference Guide, 172
Museum Anthropology, 754
"Museums," In *AAA Guide*, 836
Museums of the World, 837
The Music and Dance of the World's Religions: A Comprehensive, Annotated Bibliography of Materials in the English Language, 466
Music Index, 425
Muslim Peoples: A World Ethnographic Survey, 566
Mythography: The Study of Myths and Rituals, 434

NAPA Bulletin, 161
NAPA Job Center, 868
Nation of Peoples: A Sourcebook on America's Multicultural Heritage, 583
National Anthropological Archives, 853
The National Archeological Database (NADB), 206
National Association for the Practice of Anthropology, 759

National Association of Student Anthropologists, 760
National Library of Australia, 542
National Science Foundation: Behavioral and Cognitive Sciences Division, 874
Native America Today: A Guide to Community Politics and Culture, 597
Native American Bibliography Series, 603
Native American Encyclopedia: History, Culture, and Peoples, 598
Native American Ethnobotany Database, 272
Native American Sites, 609
Native Canadian Anthropology and History: A Selected Bibliography, 604
Native North American Almanac: A Reference Work on Native North Americans in the United States and Canada, 599
Native Web: Resources for Indigenous Cultures around the World, 490
New Americans (series), 584
New Grove Dictionary of Music and Musicians, 427
New Keywords: A Revised Vocabulary of Culture and Society, 15
New Museum Theory and Practice: An Introduction, 178
New to New Zealand: A Guide to Ethnic Groups in New Zealand, 533
New Penguin Dictionary of Archaeology. See *Penguin Archaeology Guide*
Northeastern Anthropological Association, 761
Northern Africa: A Guide to Reference and Information Sources, 492

OAIster, 194
Oceania, 690
Oceania: The Native Cultures of Australia and the Pacific Islands, 534
The Official Museum Directory, 838
Oral-Formulaic Theory and Research: An Introduction and Annotated Bibliography, 453

The Oral History Manual, 122
Ordered Universes: Approaches to the Anthropology of Religion, 366
Origins of Human Behavior and Culture (series), 318
Outline of Archaeological Traditions, 207
Outline of Cultural Materials, 484
Outline of World Cultures, 485
Overseas Research: A Practical Guide, 146
Oxbow Books/David Brown, 712
The Oxford Companion to Archaeology, 226
Oxford Dictionary of the World, 20
Oxford Encyclopedia of Mesoamerican Cultures: The Civilizations of Mexico and Central America, 626
Oxford India Companion to Sociology and Social Anthropology, 517
Oxford University Press, 713

Pacific Bibliography: Printed Matter Relating to the Native Peoples of Polynesia, Melanesia and Micronesia, 539
Pacific Islands Studies: A Survey of the Literature, 528
PAIR: Portal to Asian Internet Resources, 514
PAIS Bulletin. See *PAIS International*
PAIS Foreign Language Index. See *PAIS International*
PAIS International, 162, 351
Palgrave Macmillan, 714
Past Worlds: The Times Atlas of Archaeology, 212
PCI Periodicals Contents Index, 95
Penguin Archaeology Guide, 227
The Penguin Atlas of Women in the World, 406
Peabody Museum of Archaeology and Ethnology Library Catalogue. See *Author and Subject Catalogues of the Tozzer Library*
People of India Project, 518
The Peoples of Africa: An Ethnohistorical Dictionary, 503

Peoples of the Caribbean: An Encyclopedia of Archaeology and Traditional Culture, 627
Performance Studies: An Introduction, 463
Performance Studies Reader, 464
Personal Names and Naming: An Annotated Bibliography, 417
Pictures of Record (UM Image Source), 195
Plains Anthropological Society, 826
Plains Anthropologist, 691
Political Anthropology: An Introduction, 347
Political Anthropology: Power and Paradigms, 348
Polynesian Society, 827
Population Index, 334
Practicing Anthropology, 692
Praeger, 715
Prentice-Hall, 716
Preserving the Anthropological Record, 123
Prickly Paradigm Press, 717
PrimateLit, 237
Princeton University Press, 718
Principles of Visual Anthropology, 185
Proceedings First, 89
The Proper Study of Mankind: An Annotated Bibliography of Manuscript Sources on Anthropology & Archeology in the Library of the American Philosophical Society, 115
Proquest Dissertations and Theses, 86
Psychological Abstracts. See *PsycINFO*
Psychology: A Guide to Reference and Information Sources, 353
Psychology of Cultural Experience, 361
PsycINFO, 354
Public Anthropology, 170
Publications of the American Folklore Society, Bibliographical and Special Series, 456
PubMed. See *MEDLINE*

Qualitative Research and Hypermedia: Ethnography for the Digital Age, 147

Qualitative Research Methods Series, 131
Quarterly Index of African Periodical Literature, 496

Reader's Guide to the Social Sciences, 16
Reader's Guide to Lesbian and Gay Studies, 375
Reference Guide to Africa: A Bibliography of Sources, 493
Religion and Anthropology: A Critical Introduction, 367
Religion Index, 368
Religious Holidays and Calendars: An Encyclopedic Handbook, 370
Research Catalog of the Library of the American Museum of Natural History, 116
Research Centers Directory, 741
A Research Guide to Human Sexuality, 376
Research Methods in Anthropology: Qualitative and Quantitative Methods, 124
Resources for Anthropology & Sociology Librarians & Information Specialists, 28
Resources for Third World Health Planners, 342
Reviews in Anthropology, 72, 693
RILM Abstracts, 426
Routledge, 719
The Routledge Dictionary of Anthropologists, 55
Royal Anthropological Institute, 828
Royal Anthropological Institute Collection, 854
Répertoire International des Etudes Africaines, 504
The Sage Encyclopedia of Social Science Research Methods, 21
The SAGE Handbook of Fieldwork, 148

Sage Publications, 720
Same Sex, Different Cultures: Exploring Gay and Lesbian Lives, 377
Scarecrow Area Bibliographies (series), 486

Scholarships, Fellowships, and Postdoctoral Awards: Anthropology, Economics, Geography, Law, Political Science, Psychology, Sociology, 875
School of American Research Press, 721
School of Oriental and African Studies Library, 488
Science Across Cultures: An Annotated Bibliography of Books on Non-Western Science, Technology, and Medicine, 301
Science Across Cultures: the History of Non-Western Science (series), 302
Selected Bibliography of the Anthropology and Ethnology of Europe, 556
Serial Publications in Anthropology, 104
Serials Guide to Ethnoart, 293
Sexual Diversity Studies: Gay, Lesbian, Bisexual & Transgender Abstracts, 383
Shamanism: A Selected Annotated Bibliography, 374
Shamanism: An Encyclopedia of World Beliefs, Practices, and Cultures, 371
SIRIS Image Gallery, 192
Smithsonian Global Sound, 432
Smithsonian Institution, Bureau of American Ethnology, Bulletin, 594
See also The John Wesley Powell Library of Anthropology. See also National Anthropological Archives
Social and Cultural Anthropology: The Key Concepts, 42
Social Science Abstracts. See *Social Sciences Index*
Social Science Bibliography on Property, Ownership, and Possession: 1580 Citations from Psychology, Anthropology, Sociology, and Related Disciplines, 308
Social Science Encyclopedia, 17
Social Science Full Text. See *Social Sciences Index*
Social Science Reference Sources: A Practical Guide, 1
Social Science Research Council, 876

The Social Sciences: A Cross-Disciplinary Guide to Selected Sources, 2, 25
Social Sciences Citation Index, 7
Social Sciences Index, 8, 96
Society for Anthropology in Community Colleges, 762
Society for Applied Anthropology, 829
Society for Cross-Cultural Research, 830
Society for Cultural Anthropology, 763
Society for East Asian Anthropology, 764
Society for Economic Anthropology, 831
Society for Ethnomusicology, 832
Society for Humanistic Anthropology, 765
Society for Latin American Anthropology, 766
Society for Linguistic Anthropology, 767
Society for Medical Anthropology, 768
Society for Psychological Anthropology, 769
Society for the Anthropology of Consciousness, 770
Society for the Anthropology of Europe, 771
Society for the Anthropology of Food and Nutrition, 772
Society for the Anthropology of North America, 773
Society for the Anthropology of Religion, 774
Society for the Anthropology of Work, 775
Society for Urban, National and Transnational/Global Anthropology, 776
Society for Visual Anthropology, 777
Society of Lesbian and Gay Anthropologists, 778
SocINDEX, 9
Sociological Abstracts, 10
South Asian Folklore: An Encyclopedia: Afghanistan, Bangladesh, India, Nepal, Pakistan, Sri Lanka, 459
South Pacific Periodicals Index, 531
Speech Accent Archive, 267
Springer, 722
State Job Opportunities for Anthropologists, 861

Storytelling Encyclopedia: Historical, Cultural, and Multiethnic Approaches to Oral Traditions around the World, 449
Studies on Women and Gender Abstracts, 404
The Study of Ethnomusicology: Thirty-one Issues and Concepts, 424
Style Guides for Authors, 45
Subject Collections, 845

Tale-Type and Motif-Indexes: An Annotated Bibliography, 440
Taonga Tuku Iho: Illustrated Encyclopedia of Traditional Maori Life, 535
Thematic List of Descriptors: Liste Thematique des Descripteurs: Anthropologie, 81
Themes in Cultural Psychiatry: An Annotated Bibliography, 1975–1980, 363
Theses and Dissertations: A Guide to Planning, Research and Writing, 22
Theses Canada Portal, 87
The Times Guide to the Peoples of Europe, 553
Tourism and Applied Anthropologists: Linking Theory and Practice, 160
Tozzer Library, 855
  Publications of, 76, 114, 117
Tozzer Library Index to Anthropological Subject Headings, 117
Traditional Festivals: A Multicultural Encyclopedia, 372
"Trafficking in Men: The Anthropology of Masculinity," 378
Training Manual in Applied Medical Anthropology, 339, 862
Training Manual in Development Anthropology, 166
Tricks of the Trade: How to Think about Your Research While You're Doing It, 23
Types of the Folktale: A Classification and Bibliography, 441

Ulrich's Periodicals Directory, 105
Understanding Ancient Civilizations (series), 230

UNESCO Culture Sector, 181
University of Alabama Press, 723
University of Arizona Press, 724
University of California at Berkeley Anthropology Library. *See* George and Mary Foster Anthropology Library
University of California Press, 725
University of Chicago Press, 726
University of Hawaii Press, 727
University of Nebraska Press, 728
University of Oklahoma Press, 729
University of Pennsylvania Museum of Archaeology & Anthropology Publications, 730
University of Pennsylvania Press, 731
University of Texas Press, 732
University of Washington Press, 733
University of Wisconsin Press, 734
University Press of America, 735
Ur-List: Web Resources for Visual Anthropology, 196
Urban Anthropology and Studies of Cultural Systems and World Economic Development, 694
Urban Anthropology in the 1990s: A Collection of Syllabi and an Extensive Bibliography, 396
Urban Life on Film and Video: A Collection of Reviews for the Teaching of Urban Anthropology, 397
"Urbanization and the Global Perspective," 391
Using Historical Sources in Anthropology and Sociology, 125

"Violence, Terror, and the Crisis of the State," 349
Visual Anthropology, 695
Visual Anthropology.net, 197
Visual Anthropology Review, 696
The Visual Culture Reader, 182
Voice of the Shuttle UCSB, 422

Waveland Press, 736
WebRef: Anthropology, 43
Wenner-Gren Foundation for Anthropological Research, 833

Individual Research Grants Program, 877
Westview Press, 737
Wilson Social Science Abstracts. *See Social Sciences Index*
Wilson Social Science Full Text. *See Social Sciences Index*
Women Anthropologists: Selected Biographies, 60
Women, Race and Ethnicity: A Bibliography, 1970–1990. *See Women's Studies International*
Women's Studies Abstract. *See Women's Studies International*
Women's Studies: A Recommended Bibliography, 398
Women's Studies International, 405
Working Images: Visual Research and Representation in Ethnography, 186
Working with Indigenous Knowledge: A Guide for Researchers, 167
The World Atlas of Archaeology, 213
World Atlas of Archaeology on the Web, 232
The World Atlas of Language Structures, 253
World Bibliographical Series, 487
World Cultures Today, 469
World Directory of Social Science Institutions, 742
World Folklore Online, 437
World Folklore and Folklife, 437
World Food Habits: English-Language Resources for the Anthropology of Food and Nutrition, 280
World Guide to Scientific Associations and Learned Societies = International Verzeichnis Wissenschaftlicher Verbande und Gesellschaften, 743
"The World in Dress: Anthropological Perspectives on Clothing, Fashion, and Culture," 288
World List of Social Science Periodicals: Liste Mondial des Periodiques Specialises dans les Sciences Sociales, 106
World of Learning, 744
The World's Major Languages, 265

Worldmark Encyclopedia of Cultures and Daily Life, 477
Worldwide Email Directory of Anthropologists (WEDA), 63
Writing Ethnographic Fieldnotes, 149
WWW Virtual Library: Anthropology, 69
WWW Virtual Library: Archaeology, 233

Yahoo Directory: Social Science: Anthropology and Archaeology, 70
Yahoo! News: Anthropology and Archaeology, 99
Yearbook of Physical Anthropology, 235

Zeitschrift für Ethnologie, 697
"Zones of Theory in the Anthropology of the Arab World," 561
Zoological Record, 238

SUBJECT INDEX

Numbers refer to entry numbers.

Africa and African studies
   atlases, 497
   bibliographies, 491–493, 554
   dictionaries and encyclopedias, 499–500, 503, 574
   directories, 504
   ethnographic surveys, 502
   ethnonyms, 498
   history, 501
   indexes, 494–496
   Internet resources, 507
   libraries, 488, 505–506
   organizations, 807, 811, 819
African-Americans
   dictionaries and encyclopedias, 574
   folklore, 456, 458
   indexes, 573
   organizations (anthropological), 750
Aging, 410
   organizations (anthropological), 780
Agriculture
   indexes, 270–271
   organizations (anthropological), 756
AIDS/HIV, 335, 340–341, 343, 798
Alcohol use, 411, 412
American Anthropological Association. *See* Organizations
Anthropologists
   biography, 33–34, 37, 39, 46, 51–61
   directories, 58, 61–63
   oral history, 50
Anthropology. *See also* specific topics
   as a career, 24, 163, 165, 339, 856–862, 866–868
   as a discipline, 31, 35, 42
   bibliographies, 26–28, 71, 100–102, 110
   current events and news, 97–99
   dictionaries and encyclopedias, 29, 32–34, 36–39, 43
   directories, 322
   indexes, 73–80
   Internet resources, 64–70
   librarianship, 28
   literature surveys and reviews, 71–72, 643
   multilingual dictionaries, 41. *See also* Thesauri
   journal directories, 103–104. *See also* Journals
   programs and departments, 62, 83, 738, 863
Applied anthropology, 164–165, 169
   bibliographies, 168
   development projects, 159, 166–167. *See also* International development
   handbooks, 158
   indexes, 162
   Internet resources, 170
   journals, 673, 692
   organizations, 759, 781, 829
Archaeologists, biography, 208
Archaeology, 230
   atlases, 209, 210–213
   bibliographies, 198, 229
   classification, 207
   databases, 206
   dictionaries and encyclopedias, 40, 217–222, 226–227
   directories, 228
   handbooks, 214, 216, 219, 224
   indexes, 200–204
   Internet resources, 231–233
   methods, 223, 225
   North America, 199
Archetypes and motifs, 438–441
Architecture, 282
Archives, 108, 111, 113, 115, 123, 169, 188, 834, 839, 853–854
   directories, 843, 849
Arctic circle, 592, 605, 608, 652
Area and ethnic studies, 478–479
   bibliographies, 486–487
   dictionaries and encyclopedias, 467, 469–470, 473, 475, 477
   Internet resources, 489–490
   statistics, 468

279

280 Subject Index

Art and material culture, 282–285, 287
  bibliographies, 294
  conservation and curation, 156, 174–175
  dictionaries and encyclopedias, 292
  indexes, 289–291
  journals, 683, 696
Asia and Asian studies, 509
  Central, 560
  dictionaries and encyclopedias, 513
  East, 508, 511, 515, 764
  ethnic groups, 510
  folklore, 459
  indexes, 512
  Internet resources, 514
  journals, 653–654, 680
  organizations, 812
  South, 511, 516–520, 663
  Southeast, 521–527
Asian-Americans, 576
Associations. *See* Organizations
Australia and the Pacific Islands
  bibliographies, 528, 536, 538–539
  dictionaries and encyclopedias, 532–534
  indexes, 529–531
  Internet resources, 543
  journals, 653, 686, 690
  libraries, 540–542
  organizations, 815, 827

Behavioral ecology, 318
Biography, indexes, 47–49. *See also* Anthropologists, biography
Biological anthropology, 235, 323. *See also* Human evolution; Human variation; and Primatology
  bibliographies, 246
  dictionaries and encyclopedias, 240, 243
  indexes, 236, 238
Body movement and nonverbal communication, 256, 696
Book reviews, 72, 82, 90–91
  indexes, 92–96
Bureau of American Ethnology, 108
  publications, 80

Calendars, 298, 301, 370

Caribbean, 618, 620–621, 625, 627, 630–631
Central America, 613–614, 620, 623. *See also* Mesoamerica
  bibliographies, 612, 629
  libraries, 636
Circumcision, 331
Citation indexes, 7, 420
Classification (anthropology of), 296, 300
Clothing, 288, 589
Cognitive anthropology, 253, 297
Conference proceedings, 88–89
Consciousness, 770
Conservation techniques, 174
Cultural artifacts, 175
Cultural resource management, 153–154
Cyber-communities. *See* Online communities

Dance, 461, 462, 465, 466
Death, 413–415
Development. *See* International development. *See also* Applied anthropology, development projects
Diasporas. *See* Immigrants and immigration
Disasters, 416
Disease, 337, 342
Dissertations
  bibliography, 62, 84–85
  indexes, 86–87
  style and writing guides, 22

Ecology. *See* Environmental anthropology
Economic anthropology, 303–308, 388
  indexes, 162
  organizations, 831
Education, 309–310
  indexes, 311–312
  organizations (anthropological), 755
Employment. *See* Anthropology as a career
Environmental anthropology, 313–314
  journals, 672
  organizations, 747, 789
Ethics, 152–158, 175
Ethnic conflicts, 474, 476

Subject Index 281

Ethnic identity, 544–546
Ethnic studies. *See* Area and ethnic studies
Ethnobotany, 272, 274
Ethnographic films, 187–188, 190–191
　reviews, 189
Ethnography. *See* Research methods, ethnography
Ethnohistory, 316
　journals, 664, 669
　organizations, 809
Ethnology
　regional, 447
　organizations, 746, 779
Ethnomusicology, 423–424, 428–429
　archives, 431
　dictionaries and encyclopedias, 427
　discographies, 432
　indexes, 425–426
　journals, 666
　organizations, 832
Ethnopharmacology, 274
Europe, 544–546
　anthropology in, 319, 322
　bibliographies, 555–556
　dictionaries and encyclopedias, 36, 552–553
　Eastern, 547, 551
　indexes, 548, 550
　Internet resources, 557
　organizations (anthropological), 771
　Southern, 554
Eurasia, 551
　journals, 647
Evolution. *See* Human evolution
Evolutionary anthropology, 317–318

Fairy tales, 444
Family. *See* Marriage and family
Feminist anthropology, 399–402. *See also* Women's studies
　organizations, 748
Field language learning, 145
Fieldnotes, 123, 169
　ethnographic records, 156
Fieldwork, 128–129, 134, 136–142, 144, 148–149. *See also* Ethics
　archaeological, 214, 223, 225
　bibliography, 150–151
　language learning, 145

training and schools, 863–865
Films. *See* Ethnographic films
Folklore, 433, 445
　African–American, 456, 458
　American, 455, 457
　archives, 430, 454
　Asia, 459
　databases, 437
　dictionaries and encyclopedias, 446, 448
　directories, 450
　indexes, 435–436
　Internet resources, 460
　journals, 678
　organizations, 808
Folktales, 444
Food and foodways, 268–269, 273, 275–278, 280–281. *See also* Nutrition
　indexes, 270–271
　North America, 279
　organizations (anthropological), 772, 788
Forensic anthropology, 244, 245

Gay and lesbian studies, 375, 377, 381, 383, 385
　organizations (anthropological), 778
Gazeteers, 20
Gender studies, 378–380, 382, 386–387, 404, 407–408
Gesture. *See* Body movement and nonverbal communication
Globalization, 344, 349, 388–391, 674, 694
　organizations (anthropological), 776
Grants and funding, 131, 869–877

Hair, 286, 589
Health. *See* Medical anthropology
Hispanic-Americans. *See* Latino Americans
History. *See also* Ethnohistory
　American, 315
　indexes, 205, 549, 570
History of anthropology, 50, 55, 58, 317, 320–321, 325–326
　bibliographies, 246, 323–324
　Europe, 319, 322
History of science, 298

Human evolution, 37, 234, 239, 241–242, 245
Human geography, 203
Human Relations Area Files (HRAF), 201, 207, 478–485
Human rights, 659, 782, 816, 818
Human subjects research, 157
Human variation, 248
Humanities, 419–421
  Internet resources, 422
  journals, 649
  organizations (anthropological), 765
Humor, 442
Hunters and gatherers, 30

Images. *See* Visual anthropology
Immigrants and immigration, 390, 392, 394, 472, 557
  organizations (anthropological), 794
Impact factor. *See* Citation indexes
India. *See* Asia, South
Indexes and abstracts, general anthropology, 73–79. *See also* specific subjects
Indigenous knowledge, 167, 342
  organizations (anthropological), 791
Indigenous rights
  journals, 659, 675
  organizations, 816
International development, 5, 203, 388, 694
Islamic cultures, 559
  ethnographic surveys, 566
  indexes, 562
  women, 565

Journals, 161, 293, 639–697
  directories, 105–106

Kula, 538

Latin America. *See also* South America
  bibliographies, 610–611, 634–635
  dictionaries and encyclopedias, 577, 618–622, 625
  indexes, 616–617
  Internet resources, 638
  journals, 681
  libraries, 635
  organizations, 766, 823

Latino-Americans, 571
  organizations (anthropological), 751
Legal anthropology, 344–345
  organizations, 749, 787
Legend, 443, 445
Libraries, 834, 841–842, 846–848, 850–852, 854–855
  directories, 844–845
Library catalogs, 107, 108–110, 114–117
  directories, 112
  Latin America and the Caribbean, 107
Linguistics and language, 145
  archives, 266–267
  atlases, 253
  bibliographies, 249
  dictionaries and encyclopedias, 250, 254–255, 257–258, 260
  handbooks, 261, 262–265
  indexes, 251–252
  journals, 676, 682, 687
  organizations (anthropological), 767, 792
Lithics, 204

Maori, 535, 537
Marriage and family, 327–329, 409
Masks, 295
Material culture. *See* Art and material culture
Medical anthropology, 332, 336, 862
  bibliographies, 342
  glossaries, 338
  handbooks, 339
  Internet resources, 343
  journals, 689
  organizations, 768, 793
Medicine, indexes, 330, 333
Men and masculinities, 378, 382, 387
Mesoamerica, 615, 623–624, 626. *See also* Central America
  bibliographies, 628–629
  dictionaries and encyclopedias, 577
  libraries, 635, 637
Middle East, 560, 561. *See also* Islamic cultures
  bibliographies, 558, 567
  ethnographic surveys, 564
  indexes, 563
  Internet resources, 569
  libraries, 568
  organizations, 758, 825

Migrations. *See* Immigrants and Immigration
Missionaries, 109
Multimedia, reviews of, 189
Multilingual dictionaries. *See* Anthropology, multilingual dictionaries
Museum studies, 172, 175, 178
  bibliography, 171, 179
  directories, 180
  organizations (anthropological), 754, 795
Museums, 834
  directories, 836–838, 840
  Internet resources, 181
  management, 176–177, 860
Mythology, 434, 443, 445, 452

Names and naming, 417
Native North Americans, 578, 586–589
  bibliographies, 600–604
  dictionaries and encyclopedias, 577, 590–591, 593–599
  Internet resources, 609
  libraries, 606–607
  journals, 676, 691
  organizations (anthropological), 826
News and current events. *See* Anthropology, current events and news
North America. *See also* Native North Americans, African-Americans, Asian-Americans, Latino-Americans
  dictionaries and encyclopedias, 579
  ethnic groups, 575, 578, 580, 582–585
  indexes, 572
  journals, 677
  organizations (anthropological), 773
  regional cultures, 581
Nutrition, 270–271, 273–275, 279–281, 343
  organizations (anthropological), 772, 788, 821

Oceania. *See* Australia and the Pacific Islands
Online communities, 147, 418
Oral-formulaic theory, 453
Organizations, 807–833, 835, 839, 877. *See* "Title Index" for names of specific organizations. *See also* specific topics
  American Anthropological Association, 745
    abstracts of the annual meeting, 88
    AnthroSource, 78
    directory of members, 62
    newsletter, 98
    specific units, 745–778
    directories, 739–740, 743–744
  IUAES units, 779–806

Pacific islands. *See* Australia and the Pacific Islands
Performance studies, 461–464
Periodicals. *See* Journals
Physical anthropology. *See* Biological anthropology
Play, 813
Political anthropology, 346–349, 388
  databases, 350
  indexes, 162, 351
  organizations, 749
Political science, indexes, 4
Population studies, 334
Prehistory, 40
Primatology, 237–238, 242, 247
Professional societies. *See* Organizations
Psychiatry, 358, 363
Psychological anthropology, 353, 355, 359–362, 364
  journals, 660, 668
Psychology, 356, 357
  indexes, 354
  organizations (anthropological), 769, 820
  women and gender, 408
Publishers, 698–737

Quantification, 299

Race, 470, 619
Refugees, 392, 472, 557
Religion, 365–367, 369–373
  indexes, 368
  mythology, 40
  new age, 367, 269
  organizations (anthropological), 774

Research centers and institutes, 818–819, 828
  directories, 741–742, 744
Research methods, 18, 21, 23, 119, 121, 124
  collaborative approaches, 126, 130
  cross-cultural, 480
  discourse analysis, 118, 120
  ethnography, 127–129, 131–137, 143, 402
  fieldwork, 138–142, 144, 146, 148–149
  historical sources, 125
  multimedia, 183–186
  online and multimedia, 147
  oral history, 122
Ritual, 365–366, 369, 370, 372, 434, 466
  journals, 684

Scholarly societies. *See* Organizations
Science and technology, 301–302
Semiotics, 256, 259. *See also* Body movement and nonverbal communication
Sexuality, 376, 384, 386, 407
Shamanism, 365–367, 371, 374
Social sciences
  bibliographies, 1, 2, 16, 25
  dictionaries and encyclopedias, 11–17
  indexes, 3–10
  Internet gateways, 24
Sociology, 9, 10
South America, 625, 632–633. *See also* Latin America
Statistics, 18, 21
Storytelling, 449
Style and writing guides, 19, 22, 44–45, 121, 129, 131, 149

Terrorism, 349
Thesauri, 81, 173, 215
  multilingual, 81, 322
Theses. *See* Dissertations
Tourism, 160
Transnational studies, 694. *See also* Globalization
Tricksters, 442

Urban anthropology, 391, 393–394, 396, 694
  films, 397
  journals, 655, 694
  organizations, 776, 804
Urban legends, 451

Violence, 349, 352
  of states and governments, 346, 349
Visual anthropology, 182–183, 186, 695–696
  handbooks, 184–185
  images, 192–195
  Internet resources, 196–197
  journals, 695–696
  organizations, 777, 806

War and warfare, 352
Women
  Anthropologists, 54, 60. *See also* Anthropologists, biography
  anthropology of, 399–401, 406, 409
  atlas of, 406
  in Islamic cultures, 565
  organizations (anthropological), 802, 822
Women's studies, 398, 403–405, 408
Work and workers, 395
  organizations (anthropological), 775

Z5111
.J33
2007

12-13-07 ML

5236446

DISCARDED
MILLSTEIN LIBRARY

LIBRARY
UNIVERSITY OF PITTSBURGH
AT GREENSBURG

About the Authors

JOANN JACOBY is the anthropology and sociology subject specialist at the University of Illinois at Urbana-Champaign Library, and holds both an M.A. in anthropology and an M.L.S. She is an active member of the Anthropology and Sociology Section of the Association of College and Research Libraries and publishes on topics related to both libraries and anthropology.

JOSEPHINE Z. KIBBEE is the former head of reference at the University of Illinois at Urbana-Champaign Library, and holds an M.A. in Folklore and Intercultural Studies and an M.L.S. She is the author of the first edition of this book, which was named a *Choice Notable Book*, and publishes on reference and international librarianship. Prior to her position in Central Reference Services, she was a subject specialist in anthropology.